PRACTICAL SUPPLY CHAIN AND LOGISTICS ANALYTICS

An Introduction

Tan Miller

Routledge
Taylor & Francis Group
LONDON AND NEW YORK

Designed cover image: Shutterstock

First edition published 2026
by Routledge
4 Park Square, Milton Park, Abingdon, Oxon, OX14 4RN

and by Routledge
605 Third Avenue, New York, NY 10158

Routledge is an imprint of the Taylor & Francis Group, an informa business

British Library Cataloguing-in-Publication Data
A catalogue record for this book is available from the British Library

ISBN: 978-1-032-95554-4 (hbk)
ISBN: 978-1-032-95553-7 (pbk)
ISBN: 978-1-003-58544-2 (ebk)

DOI: 10.4324/9781003585442

Typeset in Times New Roman
by Newgen Publishing UK

PRACTICAL SUPPLY CHAIN AND LOGISTICS ANALYTICS

Practical Supply Chain and Logistics Analytics provides essential analytical techniques for managing distribution, transportation, inventory, manufacturing, network design, customer logistics, and procurement across the supply chain.

This book delivers practical decision-analysis methodologies that supply chain professionals can immediately implement in their daily operations. Readers will gain a working knowledge of fundamental logistics analytical methods that offer critical quantitative perspectives for better decision-making. The text presents a comprehensive range of techniques with step-by-step guidance, real-world examples, and actionable insights that bridge theory and practice. Each chapter builds analytical competency through accessible explanations and implementable frameworks, enabling professionals to address specific logistics management challenges efficiently while developing their quantitative skill set for long-term career advancement.

University lecturers will find it complements traditional supply chain textbooks and can also serve as the primary text for a first supply chain analytics class, while logistics professionals at all levels can use it as a reference guide for developing analyses to address specific management decisions.

Tan Miller is a supply chain Professor in the Norm Brodsky College of Business at Rider University and currently serves as an advisor to the university's supply chain program. He joined Rider in 2008 to lead the development of a then-new supply chain major and served as the first Director of the Rider Global Supply Chain Management Program until 2022. Before coming to Rider, he worked in private industry for over 25 years where most recently he was responsible for the operations of Johnson & Johnson's U.S. Consumer Distribution Network. Prior to that, he held a similar role leading the operations of the U.S. Consumer Healthcare Logistics Network of Pfizer Inc., and he has also previously held production and distribution management, as well as consulting positions with Mercer Management Consulting, Unisys, Warner-Lambert, American Olean Tile Company, and Chase Econometrics. Tan has published 8 books and over 80 articles and has made over 100 industry and academic conference presentations on supply chain and logistics operations, planning, and analytics. His previous books include *Supply Chain Planning: Practical Frameworks for Superior Performance* (Second Edition), *Logistics Management: An Analytics-Based Approach*, and *Hierarchical Operations and Supply Chain Management*. He has also served on the editorial and advisory boards of several trade and educational journals and councils, and he received an M.A., M.B.A., and Ph.D. from the University of Pennsylvania.

Mastering Business Analytics

Marketing Analytics
Statistical Tools for Marketing and Consumer Behaviour using SPSS
José Marcos Carvalho de Mesquita and Erik Kostelijk

Digital Analytics for Marketing
A. Karim Feroz, Gohar F. Khan, and Marshall Sponder

Consumer Behaviour and Analytics
Andrew Smith

Creating Value with Data Analytics in Marketing
Mastering Data Science
Peter C. Verhoef, Edwin Kooge, Natasha Walk, and Jaap E. Wieringa

Supply Chain Analytics
Using Data to Optimise Supply Chain Processes
Peter W. Robertson

Essentials of Pricing Analytics, 2nd Edition
Tools and Implementation with Excel
Erik Haugom and Per Kristian Alnes

Practical Supply Chain and Logistics Analytics
An Introduction
Tan Miller

For more information about this series, please visit: www.routledge.com/Mastering-Business-Analytics/book-series/BUSAN

This book is dedicated to my wife Jeanne and sons Lucas and Nate, who have been so supportive and put up with me for all these years.

CONTENTS

PREFACE

What Is the Role of Supply Chain and Logistics Analytics, and Why Study It?

Data-based analysis facilitates sound supply chain and logistics management. It provides the quantitative dimension that managers require to complement their qualitative assessments and judgments. Together these two perspectives (i.e., the quantitative and qualitative) enable supply chain professionals to make good, well-informed decisions.

In order to evaluate an analytic result, we have to understand the basic process that generated the solution. If we do not understand how a solution was developed, we will not have the ability to evaluate whether an answer is valid, or if something is incorrect and we need to revise our approach and solution.

For Whom Is the Book Written?

This book has been written with two primary groups in mind: (1) supply chain students and (2) supply chain professionals.

Supply chain students can use this book as an introduction to the basic concepts and methods that comprise supply chain and logistics analytics. I employ the same approach in writing this book that I have used for over 15 years in the classroom, and prior to that in private industry. Namely, utilizing Excel-based analyses and straightforward illustrative cases, this book describes and teaches analytic concepts and methods used to support a broad array of operations all across a firm's supply chain ranging from the procurement of raw materials to the delivery of finished goods to customers.

This book presents supply chain analytic concepts and methods in an easy-to-understand format. Specifically, the book offers numerous analytic examples and detailed case studies, accompanied by easy-to-follow, step-by-step equations and explanations for the student.

Supply chain professionals can employ this book for several purposes as described below:

1 to be a reference resource for ideas on how to analyze different real-world problems
2 to understand potential analytic approaches to specific problems that may arise in practice

   - For example, we explain and illustrate an original methodology to integrate inventory costs into a firm's transportation mode choice strategy.

3 to provide training for a supply chain department's newly hired professionals who have only limited experience in logistics analytics

What Professional Experiences Is the Book Based Upon?

Many of the methods published in this book are based upon my personal experiences using analytics as a supply chain analyst, manager, and consultant in private industry for many years. Additionally, 15+ years teaching students in supply chain classes ranging from introductory freshmen classes to graduate business classes has provided me an invaluable education on what approaches work (and do not work) in communicating to students and professionals alike the "how" and "what for" of analytic methods. This book has been written based upon the knowledge obtained from these many years of learning, teaching, developing, and implementing supply chain analytics. Finally, this book draws upon many of the materials and methodologies that I have previously developed and published on supply chain analytics in numerous articles and books, and that I have presented at professional and academic conferences.

1

INTRODUCTION

What is supply chain and logistics analytics, why is it so important, and where and how is it used in supply chain management? In this book, we address these questions and provide a broad overview of concepts, techniques, and methodologies utilized in real-world supply chain planning and analysis. Using easy-to-understand examples, and step-by-step instructions and formulas, we explain and illustrate a diverse set of practical methods used to support all operations across a supply chain ranging from the procurement of raw materials to the delivery of finished goods to customers. We discuss why a strong supply chain and logistics analytics organizational capability has become essential for a firm to operate a successful supply chain and business. Additionally, we describe the need for, and present examples of, supply chain and logistics analytics decision support at all planning and operations levels from the long-run strategic, to the medium-term tactical, to the short-run operational.

1.1 What Is Supply Chain and Logistics Analytics?

Supply chain and logistics analytics[1] provides decision support for all facets of operations, planning, and scheduling across the supply chain. The Association for Supply Chain Management (ASCM) offers the following simple definition of analytics:

> The review of typically large sets of business data using mathematics, statistics, and computer software to identify meaningful patterns in the data to help in decision-making.[2]

As the ASCM definition suggests, firms utilize combinations of databases and analytic tools to monitor and improve the efficiency and effectiveness of their supply chain operations and logistics networks. We characterize the many different data sources, databases, computer software systems, and analytic tools that a firm uses as the set of decision support systems (DSSs) that help to guide all supply chain planning and operations activities.

Analytics decision support methods and systems for supply chain planning span a broad array of methodologies and techniques. These include spreadsheet-based analyses, statistical

DOI: 10.4324/9781003585442-1

- ❑ **Optimization Models**
- ❑ **Simulation Models**
- ❑ **Forecasting Models**
- ❑ **Statistical Models**
- ❑ **Visualization Tools**
- ❑ **Spreadsheet Models**
- ❑ **Database Tools**
- ❑ **Social Media Monitoring Tools**
- ❑ **Smart Phone Apps (Applications)**
- ❑ **Artificial Intelligence-Based Tools**

FIGURE 1.1 Sample Supply Chain Analytics Decision Support Tools.

analyses, data mining and database analyses, sophisticated mathematical optimization and simulation models, and artificial intelligence-based applications. Figure 1.1 presents a small sample of selected models and tools frequently found in a firm's supply chain analytics DSS.

The role of analytics in guiding both supply chain planning and operational activities has dramatically spiked in the 21st century. Examples of this abound as in recent years, many firms both large and small have launched new *Data Science* or similarly titled groups. As the phenomenon of "Big Data" took hold in the early 2000s, more and more firms began to devote increasingly significant resources to large-scale data mining and supply chain analytics. The fear of competitive disadvantage and the promise of gaining competitive advantage through data analytics has stimulated enormous investments in labor (i.e., data scientists), hardware, and software across industry. Most recently, the advances in commercial applications of artificial intelligence-based tools have further propelled enhanced investment in, and emphasis on, supply chain analytics.

1.2 What Planning Levels and Time Horizons Do Supply Chain Analytics Span?

The planning activities and decisions that management must make for the supply chain and logistics functions range from the extremely long run to the short run day to day.[3] Further, the characteristics of these activities and decisions range from those requiring vast resources and managerial time (as measured by cost, required planning inputs, level of risk, and other attributes) to those requiring relatively minimal time and resources. For example, consider the vast differences in the required inputs for, and implications of, a plant location and sizing decision versus a 1-week production line scheduling decision. To effectively address this broad spectrum of management and operational control activities and decisions required in any major logistics function (e.g., manufacturing), it is necessary to separate the future planning horizon into three buckets:

1 Strategic Planning,
2 Tactical Planning, and
3 Operational Planning

These three planning horizons must be closely and hierarchically linked to ensure aligned decision-making.[4]

Figure 1.2 displays a generic logistics planning framework. We describe this framework as *generic* because it illustrates that the planning activities of any individual logistics function can (and should) be linked into the overall business and logistics strategic planning process of an organization. Examples of significant individual logistics functions include, but are not limited to:

- Manufacturing,
- Distribution,
- Customer service,
- Inventory, and
- Transportation

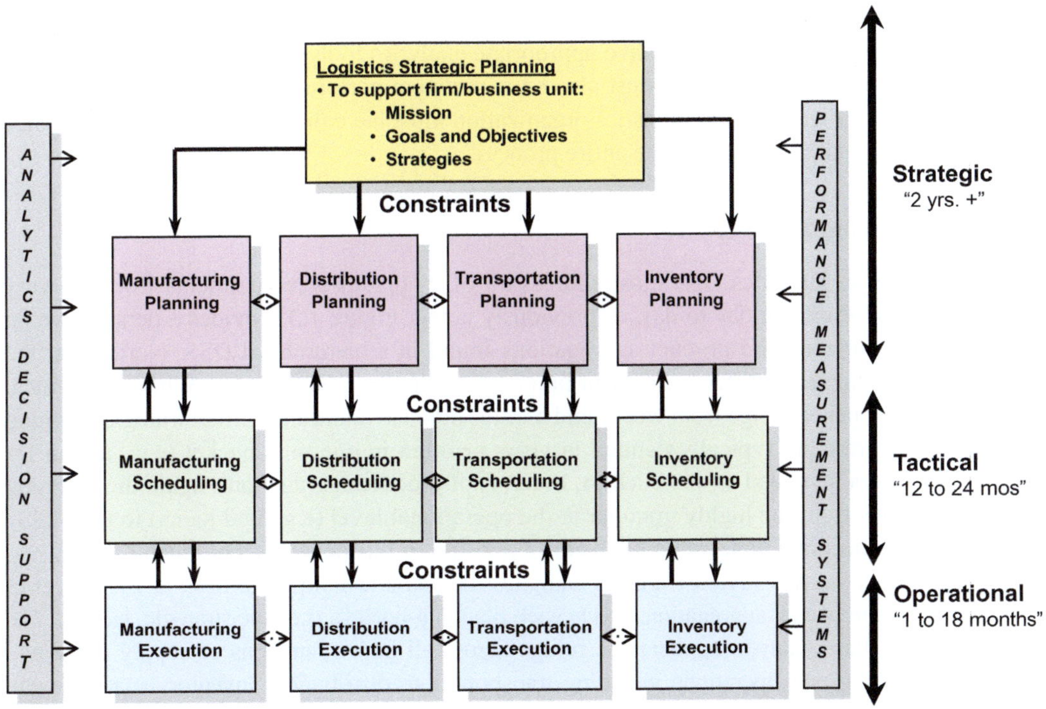

FIGURE 1.2 A Logistics Planning Framework.

The definition of what constitutes a major individual logistics function will vary by firm. For example, some firms may consider manufacturing as separate from logistics. Some firms consider customer service as a component of their logistics organization, while other firms do not. Regardless of how many functions within a supply chain or logistics organization a firm chooses to define as major individual units, the framework in Figure 1.2 provides a well-defined, holistic organizational approach.

Note that in this framework, each individual function delineates the future planning horizon into strategic, tactical, and operational planning buckets. Thus, each logistics function has its own strategic, tactical, and operational planning processes. To illustrate the different types of decisions and management controls exercised at each planning level, note in Figure 1.2 that at the tactical level we use "scheduling" as a function descriptor, while at the operational level "execution" is the function descriptor. In practice, at the tactical level, one observes both planning and scheduling activities, while at the operational level, planning, scheduling, and execution activities all occur.

Analytics Decision Support Performance Metrics

Analytics decision support methods and systems for logistics planning span a broad array of methodologies and techniques, as previously highlighted in Figure 1.1. Performance measurement systems provide managers with indicators of how efficiently and effectively their logistics network is operating. Additionally, good performance measurement systems (PMSs) also offer advance warnings or indications of potential future problems. Figure 1.2 depicts the integral role that analytics-based decision support and performance measurement systems play in logistics planning and operations across the entire planning horizon. As illustrated, each individual logistics function must have appropriate analytics tools at each level of its planning process. Similarly, each function must also have pertinent performance metrics to monitor its activities. And collectively, the logistics organization must have the analytics and performance metrics tools required to manage the entire process.

Logistics Planning Time Horizons

A firm's logistics analytics DSS must address all of its planning requirements from the very long run to the short run day to day, as previously noted. Figure 1.3 provides a perspective on the planning horizons and product aggregations found in a hierarchical DSS. Notice that the three planning horizons differ not only in timeframe, but also in granularity. While operational planning time buckets range from weeks and months down to hours and shifts, strategic planning time buckets are more typically defined in years or often in one time bucket (e.g., a plan for the next 3–5 years viewed as one bucket). In terms of product aggregations, again the planning hierarchy flows from the highly granular at the operational level (e.g., end items) to the highly aggregated at the strategic level (e.g., an entire division or business unit's products).

In this book, we will review logistics analytics tools and techniques utilized at each level of product and time bucket aggregation, and at each planning horizon (i.e., the strategic, tactical, and operational). These analytic applications bridge across all major functions of supply chain and logistics planning and operations including transportation, distribution, inventory management, manufacturing, logistics, and procurement. Figure 1.4 displays a sample of the supply chain analytics techniques and methodologies, as well as other concepts explained and illustrated in this book.

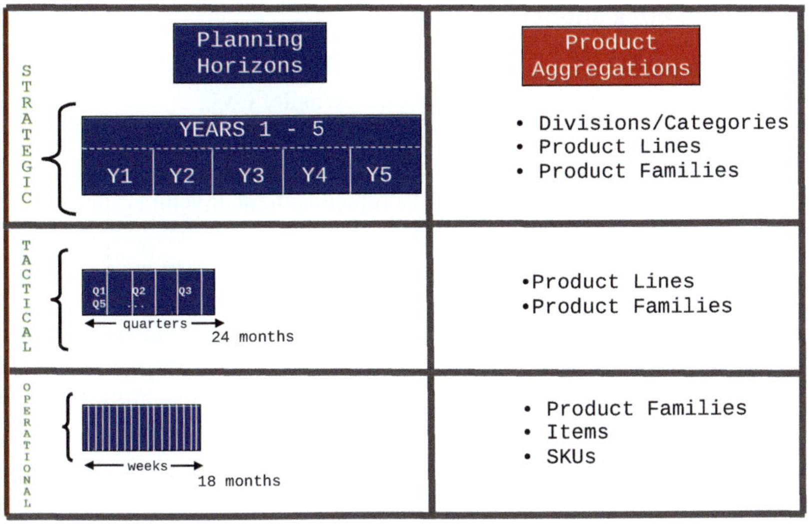

FIGURE 1.3 Planning Horizons and Product Aggregations for Logistics Planning.

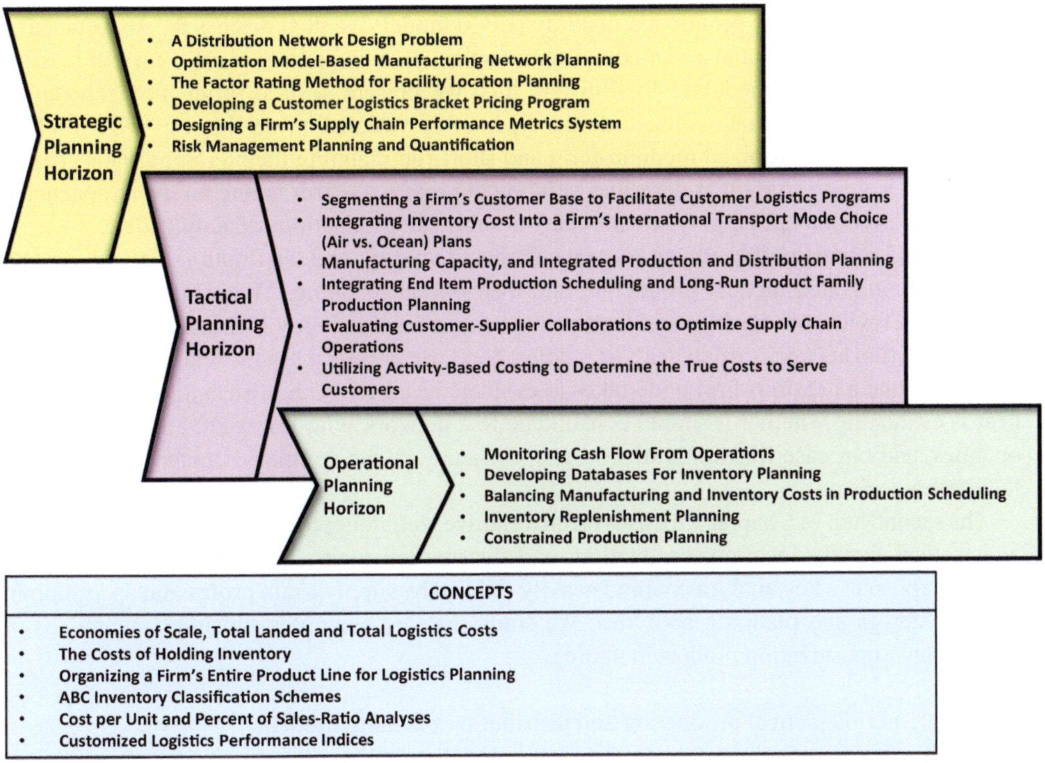

FIGURE 1.4 A Sample of the Supply Chain Analyses, Methods, and Concepts Reviewed in This Book.

1.3 Organization of the Book and Its Contents

The remainder of this book explores logistics analytics applications for all major functions and planning time horizons of the supply chain, and is organized as follows.

In Chapter 2, we illustrate analytic methods and concepts used to provide decision support for transportation and distribution management. We begin with a case study where a firm must choose between using air or ocean transport to ship replenishment inventory internationally from its plants to its distribution centers (DCs) across the ocean. The analytic methodology presented in this case integrates inventory investment and inventory carrying costs into this transportation network strategy decision. Chapter 2 also reviews the subject of distribution network design strategy. The discussion includes an analysis of key cost and service variables that require evaluation when designing a network.

Chapter 3 presents a broad range of methodologies and concepts on inventory planning and management. Topics and analyses covered include the costs of holding inventory, a framework for organizing a firm's product line, a methodology to classify all the individual items (i.e., products) in a company's inventory, the development of databases to facilitate inventory planning, and other related inventory topics.

In Chapter 4, we turn to the subject of manufacturing. The chapter starts with a general review of manufacturing metrics and production planning concepts. Next, we explore the need to evaluate inventory carrying cost trade-offs when developing production plans. This includes a review of the economic production quantity (EPQ) model. We then discuss the importance of linking short-run operational and medium-term tactical planning to assure efficient and feasible short-run production schedules. To illustrate this, we present several production scheduling scenarios and analyses that demonstrate the types of operational issues that can arise if a firm does not have a synchronized medium-term and short-run planning methodology. This chapter also includes a case study that describes solution approaches a firm facing an over-capacitated production environment employs to alleviate its short-run production capacity deficit.

Chapter 5 returns to the subject of strategic manufacturing and distribution network design, as well as integrated tactical production and distribution planning. The chapter starts with a background review of variables and factors that companies frequently include in manufacturing and distribution network design analytic studies. Next, we present a highly detailed, Excel-based case study that a fictitious firm undertakes to evaluate its current U.S. distribution network. The firm is evaluating whether it should consolidate to a network with fewer DCs than it currently operates, and our case illustrates step-by-step the analyses the company's planners develop to facilitate a decision.

The second half of Chapter 5 focuses on quantitative techniques used to generate both strategic and tactical facility location, production, and distribution plans. Mathematical optimization models represent a key analytic method heavily utilized by supply chain professionals to support network design and planning activities. We study detailed examples and implementations of supply chain optimization models including:

- a single-period tactical production and distribution planning model,
- a multi-period tactical production, inventory, and distribution planning model, and
- a strategic plant location model

We first describe these models in words without any mathematical notation; focusing on how these models work, the data they require, and the planning outputs that they generate. However, for users interested in actual mathematical formulations, an appendix to this chapter presents two additional optimization models based on real-world, industry implementations:

- a tactical production and distribution planning model and
- a strategic network design facility location model

Chapter 5 concludes with a short analytic case study of a firm making a facility location decision using another analytic tool called the *factor rating method*, a straightforward methodology for quantifying different decision factors. The factor rating method has many different applications, and this case illustrates how to use it for supply chain location decision-making.

Chapter 6 offers a broad overview of illustrative methodologies employed by companies to develop their *customer logistics* programs. The chapter begins with a review of the typical objectives of a supplier's customer logistics program, including its financial goals. The discussion then considers the analytic techniques suppliers employ in preparation for developing their customer logistics initiatives. Next, we detail step-by-step the analyses that planners utilize to evaluate the potential benefits for a supplier of creating and implementing customer bracket pricing and logistics service programs. Finally, the chapter concludes with a short case study where a supplier must respond to a logistics program proposal by one of its customers.

In Chapter 7, we present a diverse set of analytic techniques and business logistics constructs that companies employ end-to-end across the supply chain. The chapter commences by introducing a framework that a firm can implement to organize all of its supply chain and logistics metrics. Next, we offer an analytics illustration of how supply chain operations can impact a firm's cash flow. This leads to a review of activity-based costing, an important technique that facilitates a clearer, more accurate understanding for a company of its true costs to serve individual customers and to produce individual products. Later in the chapter we illustrate how planners must also use both cost per unit and ratio analyses in order to facilitate accurate assessments of costs.

As noted, Chapter 7 also addresses several business logistics constructs that strongly influence supply chain decision-making. The desire to enhance the efficiency of operations by achieving economies of scale and by minimizing total logistics costs represent two very strong influences on supply chain and logistics decision-making. Chapter 7 presents analytic illustrations of both of these concepts. Risk management represents another business tenet that has gained increasing weight in supply chain decision-making, and we also introduce and illustrate this subject in Chapter 7.

Finally, Chapter 8 concludes this book with some final observations and summary thoughts on supply chain and logistics analytics.

1.4 Objectives of the Book

1 Provide a text that introduces, explains, and illustrates a broad array of practical analytics techniques used to facilitate sound logistics and supply chain decision-making. In particular, offer tools and methodologies that can be applied across all major functions of the supply chain.
2 Present supply chain analytic methods through illustrative examples that supply chain professionals can easily implement for themselves in practice, and which students can readily understand and utilize in the future as supply chain professionals. To facilitate this objective, many methodologies are explained step-by-step, and the illustrative analytic tables display the key underlying equations to assure clarity of understanding.

3 Describe and explain key concepts and drivers that influence supply chain plans such as customer logistics efficiency programs, economies of scale, total landed costs, weeks of supply of inventory, and so on.
4 Explain and demystify how advanced analytics tools such as mathematical optimization and simulation models work and are used for decision support.
5 Offer a text that can serve as:

   A an introductory logistics and supply chain analytics textbook for university students, and
   B a resource and reference document of analytic tools and ideas for supply chain professionals.

6 Illustrate the value of investing in analytics to support improved decision-making that facilitates more efficient and effective supply chain planning and operations.

Notes

1 For purposes of brevity, the phrases "supply chain analytics" and "logistics analytics" will be used interchangeably and will both refer to the overall field of supply chain and logistics analytics.
2 ASCM 17th Dictionary (2022).
3 Portions of this section are adapted from Miller and Liberatore (2020).
4 The interested reader is referred to Liberatore and Miller (2021) to learn more about the theory and process of hierarchical planning, the types of decisions made at each level of the planning process, and techniques to facilitate the critical linkages required between the logistics management function and a firm's business, mission, objectives, and strategies.

2

TRANSPORTATION, DISTRIBUTION, AND WAREHOUSE PLANNING

Integrated with Inventory Management

The activities of transportation, warehousing, and inventory management represent three fundamental functions of logistics and supply chain operations. Firms often describe these activities collectively as their distribution function.[1] In more general terms, one can think of distribution as the management system by which a firm stores and delivers its products to its customers. Thus, distribution is a critical, high-visibility function that ultimately has responsibility for customer deliveries.

In this chapter, we review selected analytical techniques and measures that supply chain professionals employ to monitor and manage transportation, warehousing, and inventory (i.e., distribution). By studying these analytical methods, we will enhance our understanding of these three functions, and the types of quantitative analyses used to provide management decision support for these critical logistics activities. Importantly, we will also illustrate the highly dependent, linked relationships that exist between transportation, inventory management, and warehouse operations.

The choice of what transportation modes and which carriers a firm employs to move materials and products across its network is extremely important. There are many dimensions to consider, and while some transportation decisions can be made in isolation, many decisions require an integrated, multi-function perspective. Factors that determine whether a stand-alone or integrated transportation decision should be made include:

- What is the planning time horizon (e.g., short-run one-off decisions vs. long-run strategies)?
- Will the transportation mode choice for shipments from the origin to the destination significantly affect inventory requirements at the receiving location?
- What transportation options are available between an origin and a destination?

To offer insights into the interdependent relationship that exists between a firm's long-run transportation mode choice strategy on a major transportation lane (e.g., air vs. ocean, or rail vs. truck), and the firm's inventory investment requirements, in the next section, we consider an illustrative transportation mode choice scenario.

DOI: 10.4324/9781003585442-2

2.1 Transportation Case Scenario: By Air or by Ocean[2]

As companies deploy their inventories across multiple countries and continents to serve growing markets, the costs of transportation itself, and just as importantly, the direct impact of transportation modal decisions on a firm's inventory investment requirements and annual carrying costs, require closer scrutiny than ever before.

To avoid the trap of focusing strictly on freight costs, firms must employ a rigorous transportation mode choice decision-making methodology that recognizes all the costs associated with their transportation decisions. In this section, we describe a methodology which combines both annual cost and long-run investment perspectives to identify the best transport mode choice.

Background

To illustrate our methodology, we pose a hypothetical scenario in which a firm must evaluate whether to ship product by air or by ocean between two of its facilities located on different continents (e.g., the Far East and the U.S.). Before proceeding, we should also emphasize that the techniques presented here are generic in that one can apply them to evaluate the inventory investment and total cost implications for shipping product or materials by any modes between two locations (e.g., truck vs. rail, or even two truck alternatives with different transit times and costs per unit).

Our hypothetical example assumes that a firm manufactures finished goods inventory (FGI) in a plant in the Far East and distributes these products to customers in Europe from its logistics center[3] located somewhere in Europe. We further assume that the firm supplies make-to-stock products on demand to its customers from this logistics center. Thus, it must maintain inventory at the logistics center to fill orders immediately as customers place them, and it must maintain a safety stock or buffer inventory to cover the variability in demand over inventory replenishment lead time and the variability of replenishment lead time. The question the firm must now answer is whether to ship FGI from its plant to its logistics center by air or by ocean.

Key Costs to Evaluate

To evaluate whether to establish air or ocean inventory pipelines to transport the firm's products between its plant and logistics center, we must consider five major cost factors which will differ depending upon which transportation mode the firm selects. These are:

1 freight costs,
2 the inventory carrying costs of inventory in the transportation pipeline,
3 the inventory carrying costs of cycle stock at the receiving logistics center,
4 the inventory carrying costs of the required safety stock at the receiving logistics center, and
5 the investment cost required to produce the inventory to fill the transportation pipeline (i.e., the average total inventory required in transit and at the logistics center)

The first four cost factors are annual recurring costs which will continue as long as the transportation inventory pipeline exists, while the fifth cost represents a one-time cost required to initiate the pipeline.

Integrating Inventory Investment Analysis and Annual Costing

The annual costs can be analyzed using traditional spreadsheet calculations once the proper supporting data have been developed, as we will illustrate shortly. However, calculating the initial inventory investment and determining the return on investment associated with an inventory pipeline modal choice is not as straightforward. Investment decisions typically involve weighing an expected return against the investment necessary to generate that return. In other words, to evaluate the pipeline modal choice from a long-term investment perspective, a company must quantify both the investment and the expected return associated with each mode.

The best approach is to perform an "incremental" analysis. Specifically, the firm must determine whether the annual savings in transport costs from an ocean pipeline justify the incremental investment in inventory needed to build it, where the incremental investment is calculated as the ocean pipeline inventory investment less the air pipeline inventory investment. This approach views the annual incremental savings or cost avoidance associated with ocean transport as the incremental stream of income resulting from the incremental investment in an ocean pipeline. An ocean pipeline will, of course, always require a larger initial inventory investment than an air pipeline because the transit time – and hence days of inventory – is longer.

With the incremental annual stream of income and the incremental pipeline investment defined, one can now calculate standard measures for evaluating the alternatives, such as return on investment and the investment payback period.

The Data and Analytic Methodology

Table 2.1 illustrates both the annual cost and the investment analysis of our hypothetical scenario. Note that Table 2.1 has three sub-sections. The *Decision Data and Support Analysis* section displays the data required to perform this analysis. Next, the *Annual Analysis* and *Investment Analysis* sections evaluate the mode choice decision from annual cost and investment perspectives, respectively. The data requirements and the formulas to perform these analyses will be reviewed shortly.

The *Annual Analysis* section indicates that utilizing an ocean pipeline to transport the firm's product from its Far East plant to its European logistics center will save $352,000 per year. The higher annual inventory carrying costs ($168,000) resulting from the longer transit time of ocean passage are outweighed by the substantially higher freight savings ($520,000) yielded by ocean.

The *Investment Analysis* section of Table 2.1 evaluates the ocean vs. air decision from two perspectives: (1) return on investment and (2) the payback period of the investment. Dividing the annual savings ($352,000) generated from using ocean by the incremental inventory investment ($672,000) required to support ocean produces a 52.4% return on the incremental inventory investment. To project the number of years it will take for the additional inventory investment required by ocean to "pay for itself," we divide the incremental inventory investment ($672,000) by the annual "ocean" savings ($352,000). This calculation shows that in just under 2 years (1.9), the savings generated from utilizing ocean transport will pay for the incremental inventory investment. This provides an important perspective for the decision-maker.

To illustrate this further, consider Table 2.2, which summarizes an annual cost and investment analysis for two products. Product A (which has a unit cost of $210) is the same product evaluated

TABLE 2.1 Choosing between Two Transportation Modes: An Air vs. Ocean Example

Decision Data and Support Analysis	*Air*	*Ocean*	*Air – Ocean*
Annual forecast for, or shipments of, a product between facilities (units)	13,000	13,000	
The dollar value per unit at cost of the product	$ 210	$ 210	
The freight cost per unit to ship the product (door-to-door)	$ 50	$ 10	
The average total inventory in transit and at the receiving location (units)	600	3,800	
The average total inventory in transit and at the receiving location (dollars) = ***(avg total inventory in units × cost per unit)***	$ 126,000	$ 798,000	$ (672,000)
The assumed annual inventory carrying cost interest rate (r%)	25%	25%	
Annual Analysis	*Air*	*Ocean*	*Air – Ocean*
Annual freight cost = (annual units shipped × frt cost per unit)	$ 650,000	$ 130,000	$ 520,000
Annual inventory carrying cost = (r% × avg total inventory $)	$ 31,500	$ 199,500	$ (168,000)
Total annual freight plus inventory carrying cost	$ 681,500	$ 329,500	$ 352,000
Investment Analysis			*Air – Ocean*
Total annual savings (freight + inventory carrying cost) from using ocean transport			$ 352,000
Incremental inventory investment required to support ocean transport			$ 672,000
Incremental return on investment in an ocean pipeline = ***(annual savings / inventory investment)*** =	**$352,000/$672,000**		**52.4%**
Payback period on incremental investment in ocean pipeline (years) = ***(inventory investment / annual savings)*** =	**$672,000/$352,000**		**1.9**

in Table 2.1, while B ($570 unit cost) is a second, more expensive product our fictitious firm produces in the Far East and ships to its logistics center to serve European demand.

Table 2.2 shows that the ocean option represents the cost-minimizing alternative for both products B ($64,000 annual savings) and A ($352,000). Importantly, however, from an incremental inventory investment perspective, the savings for product B from an ocean pipeline generates only a 3.5% annual return, and, further, would require over 28 years to pay for itself. The additional perspective offered by the investment analysis strongly suggests that the annual savings generated by an ocean pipeline for product B would not justify the required extra inventory investment.

A firm that only considers the annual costs of transport mode alternatives, and which neglects the investment component of this decision, is far more vulnerable to making poor transport mode choices (e.g., selecting ocean transport for product B).

Notes on the Data and Formulas in Table 2.1

This section reviews the data and calculations displayed in Table 2.1. The data inputs include the annual forecast for shipments in units, the dollar value at cost of the product, the freight cost per unit for each transport mode, and the firm's annual inventory carrying cost interest rate. Company functions such as Marketing, Transportation, Finance, Demand Management, and Inventory Management typically provide this data. Note that in some cases, Logistics may have

TABLE 2.2 Investment Costs for Two Different Products

Decision Data and Support Analysis	*Product A*			*Product B*		
	Air	*Ocean*	*Air – Ocean*	*Air*	*Ocean*	*Air – Ocean*
Average inventory in transit and at logistics center (units)	600	3,800		600	3,800	
Average cost per unit inventory in transit and at logistics center	$ 210	$ 210		$ 570	$ 570	
Pipeline investment: avg cost of inventory in pipeline and at logistics center	$ 126,000	$ 798,000	$ (672,000)	$ 342,000	$ 2,166,000	$ (1,824,000)
Annual freight and inventory carrying costs of pipeline	$ 681,500	$ 329,500	$ 352,000	$ 735,500	$ 671,500	$ 64,000
Investment Analysis						
Incremental return on investment in an ocean pipeline			**52.4%**			**3.5%**
Payback period on incremental investment in ocean pipeline (years)			**1.9**			**28.5**

to develop more disaggregated, detailed data from higher-level data. For example, Logistics will need to break out individual plant to logistics center unit shipment forecasts from higher-level (e.g., country level) forecasts generated by Marketing. Historical data on origin–destination shipment flows also represent excellent sources of data.

In the *Annual Analysis* and *Investment Analysis* sections, observe that there are formulas that describe some of the calculations. We encourage the reader to review each formula carefully. This will confirm for the reader that he/she understands each calculation in this analysis, and will also enable the reader to utilize this methodology for their own purposes. Additionally, Exhibit 2.1 provides the formulas for all the rows in Table 2.1 where the formula is not already displayed in the table itself.

EXHIBIT 2.1 NOTES ON CALCULATIONS IN TABLE 2.1

- Average total inventory in transit and at the receiving location in units = (in transit units + cycle stock units at logistics center + safety stock units at logistics center), where:
  - *In transit units* = (average daily demand) × (average transit days of the transport mode)
  - Average daily demand = (annual forecast) / (365 days)
  - Average transit days is the average number of days a shipment takes to move from the origin location (e.g., the plant) to the destination location (e.g., the logistics center).
  - *Cycle stock units*[4] = (average shipment quantity in units) / 2

- Average shipment quantity = (annual forecast total units shipped) / (the number of shipments per year)
- Number of shipments per year is based on the planned shipping frequency. For example, if a plant generally makes one shipment per week to a logistics center, there would be 52 shipments per year.
- *Safety stock units*[5] is generally provided by Inventory Management for each transport mode. The actual calculation of safety stock is generally based on either a statistical formula or is based on a planned, average weeks of supply targeted to be maintained in inventory at the logistics center. Safety stock requirements at the logistics center are based on the order cycle lead time from the plant to the logistics center and the variability of that lead time, and the demand on the logistics center and the variability of demand over lead time.

Critical Points to Consider

Although the actual calculations required to evaluate alternative transport pipelines are straightforward, developing and analyzing all the necessary data presents difficult challenges requiring a rigorous methodology. Critical guidelines to facilitate successful results include the following. Firms must:

- evaluate the total logistics network costs of a pipeline transport mode decision, incorporating, for example, the impact of modal choice on a logistic center's safety stock requirements,
- evaluate pipeline transport mode decisions from both an annual cost and an inventory investment perspective rather than focusing on just annual costs or, even worse, focusing on just freight costs,
- evaluate other costs where pertinent such as the potential salvage value[6] of an inventory pipeline as discussed in Miller and Liberatore (2020), and
- conduct sensitivity analysis on the initial quantitative results to determine how results (and decisions) may change under different scenarios such as variations in assumed inventory carrying cost interest rates, fluctuations in freight rates, and so on

In conclusion, we note again that the methodology presented here for performing an air vs. ocean pipeline is generic and should be applied to any long-run transport mode choice decision for shipping products or materials between two locations. Further, one can easily enhance this methodology to incorporate any special cost factors (e.g., pipeline salvage value) which may vary by mode, and which are relevant to a specific mode choice decision or case. Finally, one can enhance the investment analysis illustrated in this section to include other measures such as net present value, if appropriate.[7]

2.2 Distribution Network Design and Analysis

The design of a firm's supply chain network of sources, manufacturing facilities, distribution centers (DCs), and retail locations ranks among the most important strategies a company must develop and implement. Further, a firm's network must evolve and adapt over time to accommodate market forces such as changing demand levels and product preferences, increasing customer service expectations and competitive threats. Additionally, a firm almost never owns all the physical locations (assets) that comprise its end-to-end manufacturing and distribution network (i.e., most companies are not fully vertically integrated). Reflecting on this point and the evolution of distribution networks, Bowersox et al. (2024) pointed out that "no firm could be totally self-sufficient ... (and this) acknowledged dependence between business firms created the study of what (has become) known as distribution or marketing channels." Thus, for an individual firm, an important component of distribution network design strategy consists of analyzing how its network will seamlessly work with the company's upstream suppliers and downstream customers and consumers.

In this section, we illustrate the type of analysis that firms typically perform to formulate their distribution network design strategy. Specifically, we consider the case of a firm evaluating alternative networks of DCs to service its market. For illustrative purposes, we limit this example to a fictitious firm deciding whether to serve its U.S. market with two DCs or four DCs. A critical first step in a logistics analysis consists of evaluating what variables and trade-offs are pertinent to consider. Once a firm conducts this qualitative assessment, then it can perform a quantitative analysis utilizing appropriate data and variables. For this reason, in the following case, we perform a qualitative analysis. Later, in Chapter 5, we will illustrate a quantitative analysis of a distribution network design problem.

Distribution Network Design Case Background[8]

Firm XYZ is a domestic consumer products manufacturer with one manufacturing plant located in Lebanon, Kansas, approximately the geographic center of the U.S. XYZ is currently deciding whether its future U.S. distribution network should have two DCs or four DCs.

XYZ distributes its products to a large customer base of major, mid-size, and small retailers. These retailers stock XYZ's products in their own stores and sell these products to their own local customers (i.e., consumers). Having inventory on their shelves readily available for their customers is critical to the success of XYZ's retail customers. Thus, XYZ must provide consistent, reliable delivery service so that its retail customers can maintain high in-stock levels of XYZ's products. XYZ offers delivered pricing to its retail customers.[9] This means that the firm pays the freight costs both from its plant to its DCs, and from its DCs to its retail customers. Additionally, this firm exclusively utilizes truck transportation (a mix of truckload and LTL[10] services) for all plant to DC, and DC to retailer shipments.

XYZ has identified that its analysis of the two alternative networks should address several key questions. Specifically, XYZ wants to determine if the following costs and customer service levels will be higher, lower, or about the same on a two-DC network compared to a four-DC network:

1 plant to DC freight costs,
2 DC to retail customer freight costs,
3 total finished goods inventory investment,
4 total warehousing costs, and
5 customer order cycle time (i.e., the order cycle time to serve XYZ's retailers from XYZ's DCs)

Good quantitative and qualitative analysis also requires well-founded, realistic assumptions. XYZ has made the following assumptions to facilitate its qualitative comparison of the two-DC vs. four-DC alternatives:

- Both networks will serve the same total national demand.
- The individual retail customer locations will order the identical quantities and product mix regardless of the distribution network used by XYZ.
- Each network will provide the same line-item fill rate service to XYZ's customers.[11]
- The delivery frequency from XYZ's plant to its DCs will be the same (e.g., the plant will make shipments once per week to each DC) – whether there are four DCs or two DCs.
- The two DCs or the four DCs will each be located 500 miles from the plant.
- All plant to DC shipments will use regular truck transportation (i.e., next-day air and other expedited, more expensive transport modes will not be used).
- The order cycle time between the plant and the DCs will be identical on each network (because all DCs will be 500 miles from the plant, and truck transportation is used for all shipments).
- A fully-loaded truckload shipment from the plant to a DC will contain 40,000 lbs. of product.

Figure 2.1 depicts the two alternative networks under consideration. For discussion purposes, as noted, we assume each DC on either network would be located 500 miles from the plant. We now consider the five cost and service questions that XYZ wants to explore.

Qualitative Analysis

We begin with this analysis of the five individual questions because understanding the trade-offs, one variable at a time, between a two-DC network and a four-DC network facilitates an improved understanding of the final analytic solution – where all the variables and trade-offs are

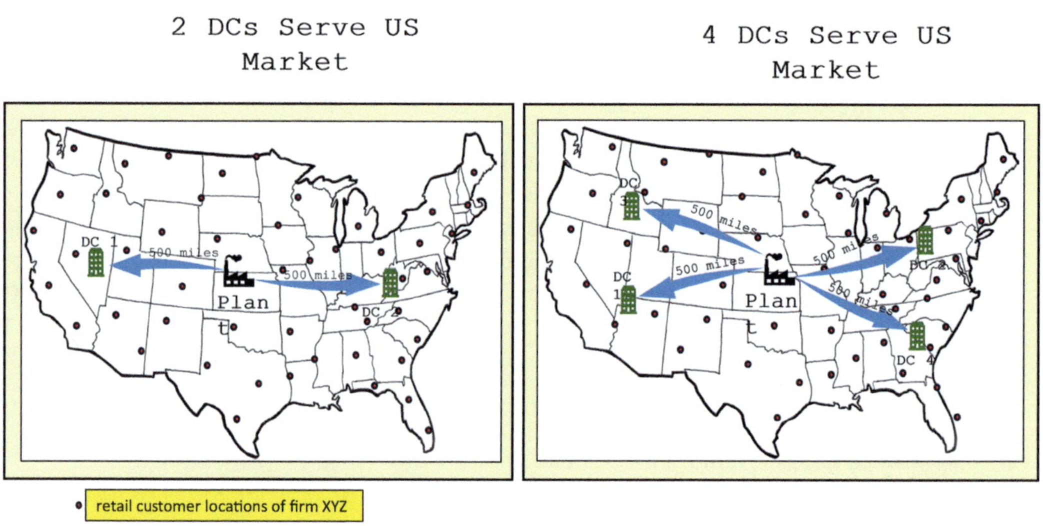

FIGURE 2.1 A Two-DC and a Four-DC Network.

simultaneously evaluated. Thus, this individual variable analysis allows us to better understand how our final overall optimal solution is determined, and what are the underlying factors that will drive our eventual solution.

Plant to DC Freight Costs

The annual total freight costs of all shipments from the plant to the DCs should either be lower on the two-DC network than on the four-DC network, or they should be equal. The following points illustrate how we make this assessment:

1 Recall that the frequency of shipments from the plant to the DCs is assumed to be the same (e.g., once per week or once per day), and the distance traveled by truck between the plant and each DC is identical (e.g., 500 miles).
2 For illustration, assume the plant will make a shipment to each DC once per week (e.g., every Monday). Now consider two different scenarios.

   Scenario A: assume the plant will ship 160,000 lbs. of product in total every Monday to the DCs, with each DC receiving an equal quantity. This would mean that:

   ✓ On a four-DC network, one 40,000 lb. truck is shipped from the plant to each DC every Monday – (4 × 40,000 lbs. = 160,000 lbs. per week).
   ✓ On a two-DC network, two 40,000 lb. trucks are shipped to each DC every Monday – (2 × 2 × 40,000 lbs. = 160,000 lbs. per week).[12]
   ✓ The total freight costs on a two-DC or a four-DC network are the same because on each network there are four 40,000 lb. equidistant shipments per week.

   Scenario B: assume the plant will ship 80,000 lbs. of product in total every Monday to the DCs, with each DC receiving an equal quantity. This would mean that:

   ✓ On a four-DC network, one (half-full) 20,000 lb. truck is shipped from the plant to each DC every Monday – (4 × 20,000 lbs. = 80,000 lbs. per week).
   ✓ On a two-DC network, one (full) 40,000 lb. truck is shipped to each DC every Monday – (2 × 40,000 lbs. = 80,000 lbs. per week).
   ✓ The total freight costs on a two-DC network would be less than those on a four-DC network because only two truck shipments, rather than four, are required per week.[13]

Scenarios A and B illustrate that given our assumptions, total annual plant to DC freight costs will either be lower or the same on a two-DC network compared to a four-DC network. The total tonnage shipped by the plant drives this relationship. Briefly, the more DCs the plant must ship to, the higher must be the total tonnage produced and shipped by the plant to ensure efficient, full truckload shipments. Further, the planned regular frequency of re-supply shipments from the plant to the DCs also affects this relationship. For example, if the plant is expected to ship daily to each DC (rather than weekly), this means that a higher daily shipment tonnage (e.g., in the previous scenarios 160,000 lbs. a day) is required to facilitate full 40,000 lb. truckload shipments to four DCs. A two-DC network would require only half that tonnage (80,000 lbs. per day) to facilitate full 40,000 lb. truckload shipments. The impact of the assumed frequency of plant to DC replenishment shipments (e.g., once per week vs. once per day) illustrates the importance of assumptions. We will return to the importance of good assumptions throughout the text.

DC to Retail Customer Freight Costs

The annual total freight costs of all shipments from the DCs to the stores of XYZ's retail customer locations should be lower on the four-DC network than on the two-DC network. Briefly, the logic underpinning this assessment is as follows:

1 XYZ serves the entire U.S. mainland market.
2 The average distance (i.e., miles) between an XYZ DC and an XYZ customer location should be less on a four-DC network than on a two-DC network. Figure 2.1 provides a visual illustration of this concept.
3 Truck freight costs are determined in large part by the distance traveled and by the weight (and/or cubic volume) of the shipment.
4 The units and weight shipped from a DC to a customer location will be identical whether XYZ employs a two-DC or a four-DC network. (i.e., Individual customer demand will be identical regardless of the DC network configuration.)
5 Therefore, because the average distance between an XYZ DC and a customer location will be less on a four-DC network, outbound freight costs from the DCs to the customers will be lower on a four-DC network

Total Finished Goods Inventory Investment

XYZ's total finished goods inventory (FGI) investment requirements;[14] *and therefore, its annual inventory carrying costs,*[15] *should be lower on a two-DC network than on a four-DC network.* We first present simple graphical and mathematical illustrations to describe intuitively why the two-DC network would require a lower total inventory investment. Then, we briefly discuss the well-researched principle that serving any defined market area, such as the mainland of the U.S., from fewer rather than more FGI stocking locations reduces (or smooths) the variability of demand on each individual stocking location (e.g., on a DC). This facilitates a lower required inventory investment, as we now explain.

The variability of demand impacts forecast error, which is a major determinant of the level of safety stock inventory that a firm must maintain for each item stocked at a DC. Specifically, the higher the forecast error for a stockkeeping unit (SKU)[16] at any stocking location (e.g., a DC or a store), the higher the safety stock quantity required to:

- protect against demand exceeding supply and
- facilitate achieving a desired customer item fill rate (e.g., 98%)[17]

Intuitively, it stands to reason that the higher the variability of demand for an SKU (e.g., the higher the variability of daily or weekly demand), the more difficult it becomes to forecast accurately the demand for that item – leading to higher forecast errors. And as noted, the greater the forecast error for an item, the greater the safety stock required for that item.

Figure 2.2 further assists us to understand why we should expect a higher level of demand variability as the number of DCs that serve a market area increases.[18] This figure displays another alternative pair of two-DC and four-DC networks, each serving the entire U.S.

In practice, different firms' actual locations will vary; however, a typical two-DC U.S. network divides the customer service areas of the warehouses into one large eastern and one large western

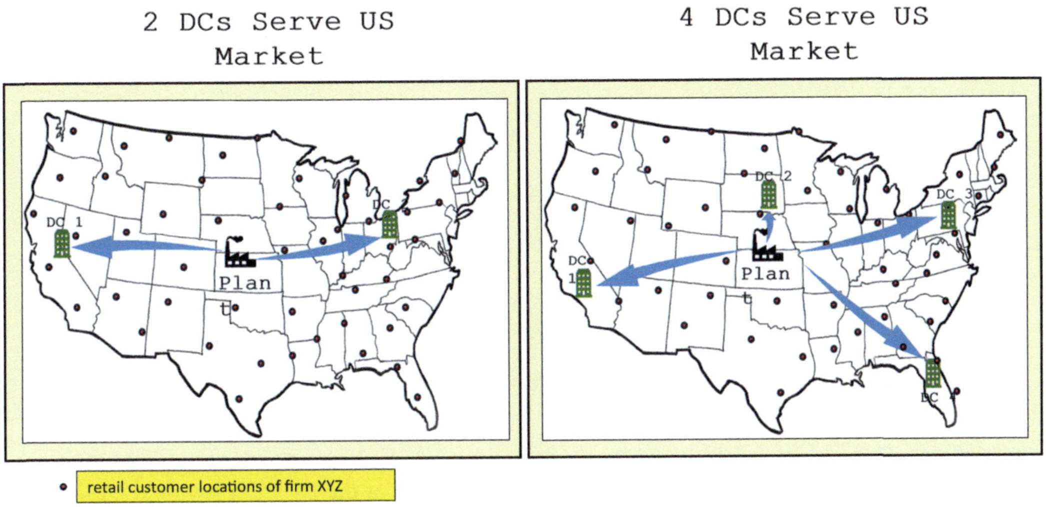

FIGURE 2.2 Another Two-DC and Four-DC Network.

region. On a four-DC network, each location will serve a smaller market area than on a two-DC network, and it is not uncommon on a four-DC network to locate one of the four DCs in Florida to serve exclusively the large geographic area and growing population of this state. Similarly, the far western location on a four-DC network, often located in California or Nevada, will cover a smaller market area than the western DC on a two-DC network.

What are the implications for demand variability and forecast error on a network with many DCs (e.g., four or more) rather than a few DCs (e.g., two) – given the comparatively smaller market area and total demand served by each DC on a larger network?

Assume that the customer service region of the Florida DC pictured on the four-DC network in Figure 2.2 covers only the state itself. Now consider what happens almost every year in Florida in the late summer and fall time-period. There are hurricane warnings and actual hurricanes. How does this affect the daily demand for many consumer goods such as food, medical care items, and items used to protect homes from water and wind damage? The answer is that clearly hurricanes can create major spikes as well as ebbs in the demand for certain items before, during, and after the storm. Consider the difference this would make on the variability of demand at a DC on both a two- and four-warehouse network. In Figure 2.2, the eastern DC located in the mid-Atlantic states on the two-DC network serves Florida and many other states, while on the four-DC network, the Florida location serves only that single state. A hurricane hitting Florida will increase the daily variability of demand on the eastern DC of the two-warehouse network; however, the magnitude of this variability will be smoothed (i.e., reduced) by the regular, unaffected demand placed on the eastern DC by its customers in all the other states in its service region. Conversely, a much greater relative impact on the demand variability created by the hurricane will be experienced by the Florida DC on the four-DC network. This occurs because while customers in Florida may represent just 5% of the eastern DC's total daily demand on the two-DC network, these same customers account for 100% of the dedicated Florida DC's demand.

The preceding example illustrates this principle that the fewer the number of stocking locations that serve a fixed market area (e.g., the U.S.), the lower will be the variability of

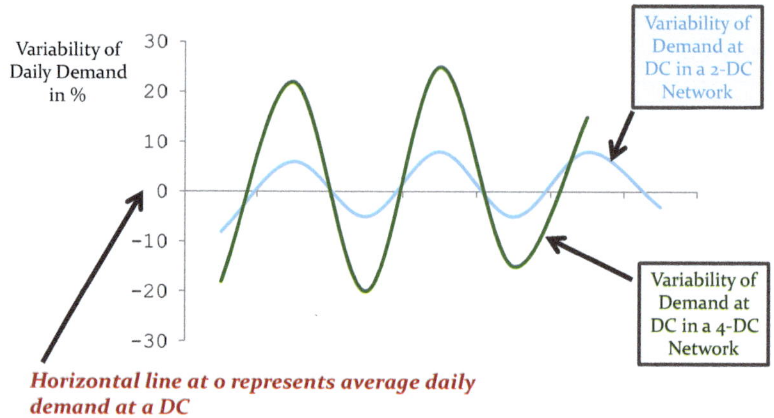

FIGURE 2.3 Smoothing Variability of Demand: Illustration (the Fewer DCs Serving a Market – the Lower the Total Inventory Investment Required at the DCs to Provide a Desired Fill Rate to the Customers in That Market).

demand on these stocking locations. This results because aggregating total demand into a few locations "smooths" or lessens the variability of demand. The larger service areas and more dispersed customer base of individual DCs on a network with fewer locations facilitates this smoothing or balancing impact. Figure 2.3 graphically illustrates this basic principle of inventory management.

To reinforce this tenet of inventory management, Figure 2.4 offers a mathematical example of the smoothing impact of demand aggregation on forecast error. For illustrative simplicity, we consider the forecast error for an item on two different network alternatives, a one-DC and a two-DC network, each serving the same market.

Network A stocks this item at two DCs, and therefore, it has two SKUs. Network B, however, serves this same market and the demand for this item from one DC.[19]

Figure 2.4 shows that for a recent historical period (e.g., last week), total actual demand was 310. We also observe that prior to this time-period the forecasts for it were:

- 100 and 200, respectively, at Network A's two DCs (A1 and A2), and
- 300 at Network B's single DC (B1)

Looking back on this prior period, it turned out that the actual demand was 310. So, in aggregate, total demand for this item exceeded the forecast for this time-period by a small amount, 10, or 3.3%. However, consider the difference in forecast error, which is defined as "forecast – actual," on Networks A and B:

- On A, there were forecast errors of -50 (at A1) and +40 (at A2), respectively.
- On B, the forecast error was −10 (at B1).

The amount of safety stock inventory required at a DC to protect against forecast error is determined at the SKU level. Therefore, on Network A, the significant forecast errors at A1

Network	DCs	Forecast (F)	Actual (A)	(F-A) Forecast Error	Absolute Value of |Forecast Error|
A	A1	100	150	-50	50
	A2	200	160	40	40
					90
B	B1	300	310	-10	10

FIGURE 2.4 Two DCs vs. One DC: Example of Smoothing the Variability of Demand.

(33%)[20] and A2 (25%) will contribute to relatively higher safety stock requirements on Network A.[21] In contrast, the lower forecast error (on Network B) will facilitate a lower total safety stock requirement on this network compared to Network A. By supplying total market demand for this item from one location rather than two locations, B aggregates and smooths the variability of demand. This facilitates more accurate demand forecasts.[22]

We have presented simple graphical and mathematical examples to illustrate the important inventory management principle that:

- *The fewer the number of stocking locations serving customer demand in a market, the lower the total inventory investment required to deliver a planned target item fill rate.*

We now close this section by restating this principle and offering several references for the reader interested in exploring this topic further.

The tenet that the centralization of stocking locations reduces the required inventory investment in safety stock needed to maintain a target fill rate rests on the principle that centralization diminishes the overall variability of demand, which in practice facilitates lower overall levels of forecast error.[23] Consolidation of stocking locations decreases demand variability[24] by "pooling" the "non-forecasted demand variability" that would otherwise occur at individual locations. This "pooling" effect acts to "smooth" the variability of demand, as illustrated in Figure 2.4, and reduce the forecast error.

The original research on this topic emanates from two related inventory models; namely, the "square root of n" model (Maister, 1976) and the "portfolio effect" model (Zinn, Levy, and Bowersox, 1989). A key contribution of these models is that they require minimal inputs, and although they each have major limitations, they provide "ballpark" guesstimates of the impact on inventory investment requirements of consolidating the number of stocking locations.[25]

Total Warehousing Costs

In general, XYZ's total annual warehousing costs should be lower on a two-DC network than on a four-DC network. We state "in general" because one can always find exceptions to the rule, and every situation requires an individual evaluation. However, the expectation is that the two-DC network would have lower annual warehouse operations costs for several reasons.

The principle of economies of scale holds that there will be "a decrease in the cost per unit of output as the volume of output increases."[26] In other words, the higher the total level of output of an activity, the lower will be the average cost per unit of that activity. Economies of scale apply in a broad array of processes ranging from manufacturing, warehousing, and transportation, to numerous activities outside the domain of supply chain operations. For example, the merger of two similar companies (e.g., two pharmaceutical firms or two consumer products firms) is often predicated on the expectation that synergies or economies of scale will facilitate greater efficiencies for the larger, merged single firm than are possible for the two smaller companies operating independently.

The following represent several examples, but by no means a complete list, of potential warehouse operating efficiencies that a firm would generate operating two larger DCs rather than four smaller DCs to serve the U.S. market.

1 *Greater use of automation and technology* – Purchasing and implementing material handling systems such as conveyors, robotics, and ASRSs (automatic storage and retrieval systems) requires a major financial investment. There are substantial one-time initial purchase costs, significant and often lengthy systems integration costs (with a firm's existing IT systems infrastructure), and ongoing annual operating and maintenance costs. To justify economically expensive investments in major automation and technology systems, a DC must have a high average daily output volume (e.g., large quantities of cases and pallets flowing through the various activities in the warehouse). If a DC does not have high throughput volume, a more manual, labor-intensive, and less automated operation is generally the more efficient approach. Serving the U.S. market from just two DCs facilitates much higher daily volume and annual throughput at each DC compared to handling that same volume through four DCs. Thus, it is more likely that on a two-DC network, a firm can economically invest in higher levels of automation and technology, thereby facilitating a lower average warehouse operating cost per unit than could be achieved on a less automated four-DC network.
2 *Higher facility utilization rates* – Consolidating all throughput into two DCs increases the probability that the warehouses may operate multi-shift operations because each DC will have to process more volume per day than if four DCs processed that same throughput level. Multi-shift operations often provide more overall flexibility,[27] and facilitate utilizing a facility and its material-handling equipment for double the number of hours per day compared to a one-shift operation.
3 *A reduction in the total network-wide warehouse floor space and cubic space required to store inventory* – We previously observed that a two-DC network requires a lower total inventory dollar investment and quantity than does a four-DC network. This would translate into less total floor square footage and/or cubic footage needed network-wide on a two-DC network compared to a four-DC network.
4 *A reduction in total indirect labor costs across the warehouse network* – It is possible that indirect labor costs across the entire network may be lower on a two-DC than on a four-DC

network because the smaller network may require fewer managers and supervisors in total. For example, each DC will need a warehouse director to lead its operations. Thus, on a two-DC network there would be only two lead warehouse directors, while a four-DC network will have four lead warehouse directors.

The previous four examples, while not an exhaustive list of advantages, illustrate why our expectations are that a two-DC network would compare favorably to a four-DC network from a cost perspective.

Customer Order Cycle Time

The order cycle time from the DCs to the retail customer locations should be shorter on the four-DC network. Briefly, we previously observed that the average distance between a DC and a customer location should be less on a four-DC network than on a two-DC network. Additionally, we assumed that all shipments would move via truck. Therefore, the average time between when a customer places an order at a DC and the time when that order arrives at the customer location (i.e., the order cycle time) should be shorter on a four-DC network since a truck will have to travel fewer miles on average to reach the customer location.

Qualitative Analysis Summary

This completes our qualitative analysis, evaluated one variable at a time, of the expected trade-offs we should anticipate in choosing between a two-DC and a four-DC network. Importantly, this analysis does not lead us to a conclusion on which network to choose. Rather, it facilitates an enhanced understanding of these alternatives, and provides a qualitative perspective that we can combine with a quantitative analysis of the two alternatives. Complex supply chain management decisions require both rigorous quantitative and qualitative assessments.

Finally, a strong qualitative understanding of the variables and their trade-offs helps analysts and decision-makers to confirm the validity of their quantitative answers. For example, suppose that a firm conducted a quantitative analysis of the two-DC vs. four-DC scenarios, and the results indicated that the DC to customer freight costs would be lower on the two-DC network. This would serve as a clue that the quantitative modeling analysis may have some incorrect assumptions or data built into it. At the very minimum, this or any other counter-intuitive quantitative results would (appropriately) inform analysts and decision-makers to review the quantitative analysis to confirm that the assumptions and data underlying the analytic model are correct. The importance of these qualitative "validity checks" on quantitative results cannot be overstated.

2.3 Summary

In this chapter, we reviewed transportation and distribution scenarios that illustrate analytic techniques and approaches to addressing two significant supply chain strategic questions:

1. what transportation mode a firm should utilize to supply a DC from its manufacturing plant[28], and

2 how many DCs should a firm operate to inventory its products and to ship its finished goods to customers in a market area such as the U.S.

In these scenarios, we analyzed the impact that transportation and distribution network design strategies have on a firm's inventory investment requirements. Both scenarios highlighted a key principle of logistics and supply chain analytics. Namely, it is imperative that in arriving at a conclusion, a company base its supply chain analyses and decisions on an integrated perspective which evaluates all pertinent variables, costs, and service factors. Analyses which omit key variables and customer service considerations will yield suboptimal results, and can lead to poor management decisions.

Notes

1 The Association for Supply Chain Management (ASCM) provides a detailed definition of distribution stating that it includes activities that "… encompass the functions of transportation, warehousing (and) inventory …" (see ASCM Dictionary, 17th edition, 2022)
2 Portions of this section are excerpted and adapted from a previous article that appeared in *Material Handling & Logistics* magazine, Miller (2016), and are used with the kind permission of *MH&L* magazine.
3 We will use the terms logistics center, warehouse, and distribution center as synonyms throughout this text.
4 This formula is explained further in Chapter 3.
5 Safety stock calculations are reviewed in Chapter 3.
6 Salvage value is the revenue that a firm can generate by selling any remaining, unused inventory at the end of a product's life cycle.
7 See Miller and Liberatore (2020) for a discussion of how to incorporate salvage value into a transportation mode choice analysis, and how to perform sensitivity analysis on initial solutions.
8 For illustrative purposes, we consider a fictitious firm XYZ. The distribution characteristics and requirements discussed are patterned after actual companies the author has worked for, consulted to, and informally advised and observed.
9 Delivered pricing means that the seller's price to its customer includes the seller's freight delivery costs. A customer paying a delivered price per unit does not know the actual freight costs incurred by the seller – because the seller's price per unit includes, but does not show, the delivery freight cost.
10 LTL is an abbreviation for "less than truckload" transportation.
11 Line-item fill rate is the percent of lines on an order filled completely by the supplier over a defined time-period. A line item is an individual item on an order, and one order can contain one to many individual line items on it. For example, it is not unusual for an order from a large consumer products retailer to a major manufacturer to have hundreds of individual line items on one order.
12 In practice, a firm may choose to ship one 40,000 lb. replenishment truck on Monday, and a second 40,000 lb. truck later in the week (e.g., Wednesday). This would reduce the overall order cycle time for the receiving DC – which is an advantage from an inventory safety stock investment requirement perspective. We will address this issue in Chapter 3.
13 The cost to a shipper to hire a truck to make a 500-mile shipment is the same whether there are 20,000 lbs. or 40,000 lbs. on the truck.
14 The total inventory investment required for its DCs to provide a planned target level item fill rate (e.g., 98%) to its retail customers.
15 Inventory carrying costs are also often called inventory holding costs.
16 A stockkeeping unit is an item inventoried at a particular location (see ASCM Dictionary, 17th edition, 2022). For example, one item stocked at four different DCs would represent four SKUs.
17 ASCM defines fill rate as "a measure of delivery performance of finished goods (or other materials) usually expressed as a percentage … (It) usually represents the number of items or dollars that were shipped on schedule for a specific time period compared with the total that were supposed to be shipped." (ASCM Dictionary, 17th edition, 2022).
18 This impact on demand variability will occur at the item level, and at the cumulative, aggregate demand level also.

19 So, Network A has two SKUs of this one item, while Network B has just one SKU.
20 33% = 50/150, 25% = 40/160, 3.3% = 10/300.
21 Note that to measure forecast error, the absolute value of the actual forecast error is often used. For example, standard measures of forecast error such as the "mean absolute" (MAD) are developed by calculating the average forecast error over a time-series of forecasts. This requires that the individual forecast errors over a defined historical period be summed up and then divided by the number of historical periods. To avoid having negative and positive individual forecast error values offset each other when they are summed up, the absolute values of the individual forecast errors are totaled and then divided by the number of historical forecast periods being evaluated to obtain an average forecast measure such as MAD. For this reason, Figure 2.4 has both "Forecast Error" and "Absolute Value of [Forecast Error]" columns.
22 Actual safety stock calculations are based on a series of forecast errors (e.g., a time series of perhaps 52 weeks or more), as well as other variables. This single-period calculation is presented to provide a simple illustration of the demand smoothing concept.
23 Stable demand with lower levels of variability is easier to forecast accurately than highly variable demand.
24 More properly, we should say "non-forecast" variability in demand. If there is variability in demand, but the demand variability can be forecast with 100% accuracy, then there is no need for safety stock even though there is variability of demand.
25 Following this initial research by Maister, and the extension that followed later to Maister's model by Zinn et al., numerous researchers have developed enhancements to these original models. Readers are referred to Miller, De Matta, and Zu (2016) and Acumen (2024) for additional references and explanation of the square root on n law of inventory management, and how it can be used in practice.
26 Venkataraman and Pinto (2020).
27 For example, customer orders received during the day can be picked and shipped on the second shift. In a one-shift operation, these orders may not be processed until the following day.
28 As noted, one can apply the transportation mode choice methodology presented in this chapter to any origin–destination pair where the origin supplies goods to a destination location that maintains an inventory of those goods.

3

INVENTORY PLANNING AND MANAGEMENT

Inventory investment requirements, costs, and plans play a central role, either directly or indirectly, in most major logistics decisions and strategies. For example, in Chapter 2, we illustrated the importance of integrating inventory considerations into long-run transportation mode choice strategies. We also reviewed that the number of DCs serving a market impacts a firm's total inventory investment requirements, and this directly affects the total warehouse square footage and/or cubic footage required network-wide for inventory storage.[1] In this chapter, we now focus directly on inventory planning and management.

We begin with a review of basic concepts and measures that underlie inventory analytics, planning, and strategy. Next, we discuss a series of analytic planning techniques frequently utilized by supply chain professionals to monitor and manage their firms' inventories both day-to-day and long-term. The topics studied include product line structures that facilitate inventory planning, ABC inventory classification schemes, approaches to create visibility internally within a company to its inventory levels, trade-offs to consider between investment levels in finished and non-finished good inventory, and inventory replenishment systems.

3.1 Inventory Types and the Cost to Hold Inventory

The Association for Supply Chain Management (ASCM) defines inventory as "those stocks or items used to support production (raw materials and work-in-process items), supporting activities (maintenance, repair, and operating supplies), and customer service (finished goods and spare parts)."[2] Thus, as this definition describes, inventory exists in three basic states:

1 finished goods inventory (FGI),
2 work-in-process (WIP), and
3 raw materials / components

The ASCM then further defines the use of inventory as follows: "Inventory functions are anticipation, hedge, cycle (lot size), fluctuation (safety, buffer, or reserve), transportation (pipeline), and service parts." As this definition conveys, inventory plays many critical roles in

DOI: 10.4324/9781003585442-3

TYPE	DESCRIPTION**
1. CYCLE	The inventory a company carries to satisfy its normal cycle of sales orders or production requirements.
2. SAFETY	The minimal level of inventory a company seeks to have on hand at all times to act as a buffer against the mismatch between forecasted and actual demand, and to protect against unexpected disruptions to regular supply replenishments.
3. IN-TRANSIT	Material moving between two or more locations, usually separated geographically (e.g., finished goods being shipped from a plant to a distribution center).
4. SEASONAL	Inventory built up to prepare for peak seasonal demand.
5. PROMOTIONAL	Inventory built up to support the expected increase in demand caused by a promotion.
6. ANTICIPATORY	Inventory built up to support the expected increase in demand caused by a specific event (e.g., increasing the inventory of goods positioned in a geographic area because a hurricane is forecast to hit the region. For example, deploying extra inventory of goods such as water pumps as well as products like bandages needed to treat injuries resulting from the event.)

FIGURE 3.1 Types of Inventory.

- Some firms also use the classification of "maintenance, repair, and operations" (MRO) to categorize inventory that supports the production of a product (e.g., nuts and bolts, machine grease, and clamps)

** These definitions are adapted and/or sourced from Venkataraman and Pinto (2020), and the ASCM Dictionary 17th edition (2022)

a supply chain from the inception of a product (in its raw material state) to its final consumption by a consumer (in its finished good form). We will focus on finished goods planning techniques; however, it is important to note that one can also frequently apply the inventory analytics illustrated in this chapter to raw materials and WIP inventory.

Finally, we note that there are several "types" of FGI, WIP, and raw material inventories. Figure 3.1 offers brief descriptions of the major types of FGI.[3]

What Are the Costs of Carrying Inventory?[4]

In this section, we address two questions:

1 What is the cost to a firm of holding inventory?
2 How should a firm determine its internal inventory carrying cost interest rate?

There are four major categories of costs that collectively constitute a firm's total annual inventory carrying costs, and form the basis for determining the firm's internal carrying cost interest rate. These four categories consist of:

1 the firm's opportunity cost of capital,
2 inventory service costs,
3 inventory taxes and storage space costs, and
4 inventory risk costs

The firm's *opportunity cost of capital* is included in the annual inventory carrying cost interest rate because to build and hold inventory requires an outlay of funds just as any other investment would require. Thus, a firm incurs an opportunity cost in holding inventory because it could alternatively realize a financial return by using the money it has tied up in inventory in some other investment. Consider the following simple example of this concept.

Suppose a company has $300 million invested in FGI. If the firm decided to lower its FGI investment to $250 million, assume the $50 million freed up by the lower inventory investment level could be used to build a new manufacturing plant. Now suppose this plant, once finished, could generate $7 million per year in net income (i.e., profit). This $50 million one-time investment in a plant would generate an ongoing annual return on investment (ROI) of 14% (i.e., $7 million / $50 million). Thus, there is what economists call an opportunity cost for the firm in choosing to invest in inventory. Namely, in this example, the extra $50 million investment in inventory represents funding that could alternatively be utilized to build a new profit-generating plant.

Given that firms must view their investment in inventory as having an opportunity cost, the question becomes how to quantify this cost. The standard approach to this question is to identify an internal annual carrying cost interest rate (r%) – which the firm can multiply by the cost of its average investment in inventory. The result of this calculation (i.e., r% multiplied by the annual average cost of the firm's inventory over a year[5]) represents the firm's annual dollar cost of holding inventory. In our previous example, where a firm has an average inventory investment of $300 million, assume this firm's internal inventory carrying cost interest rate is 20%. The annual inventory carrying cost of this firm would be $60 million (i.e., .20 × $300 million). Now we consider how a firm calculates its annual inventory carrying cost interest rate (r%).

Firms typically use their internal cost of capital interest rate or their cost of money interest rate (e.g., for a long-term loan) as the starting point to derive their firm's internal inventory carrying cost interest rate.[6] Thus, this internal interest rate represents the building block component to which a firm adds other factors to determine their annual inventory carrying cost interest rate.

Inventory service costs consist of personal property taxes as well as insurance fees on inventory. To convert each of these costs into a percentage rate, we develop a ratio of the cost of each component for a year to that year's average total inventory value.[7] For example, if a firm paid $5,000 in inventory taxes in a year, and the average total value of its inventory in that year was $500,000, then inventory taxes would represent 1% of the average total value of inventory ($5,000/$500,000). This 1% then would represent the factor which we include for taxes in developing the firm's overall annual inventory carrying cost interest rate. The same method would be used to determine what percentage for insurance costs to include in the annual inventory carrying cost interest rate.

The definition of what constitutes an *inventory storage cost* and what represents a "warehousing" cost varies slightly depending upon whether the facility housing inventory is a plant, a company-owned warehouse, or a contract warehouse (see Stock and Lambert, 2001). However, a general rule for distinguishing inventory storage costs is that only costs which vary with the level of inventory held should be included as inventory storage costs. The costs associated with taking physical inventories and the costs for warehouse storage at public warehouses are two examples of "storage" costs that will vary with the level of inventory held at a facility. Once we have quantified annual inventory storage costs, we then convert these costs to a percentage factor to be added to the opportunity cost of the capital interest rate, the percentage rate for taxes, etc.

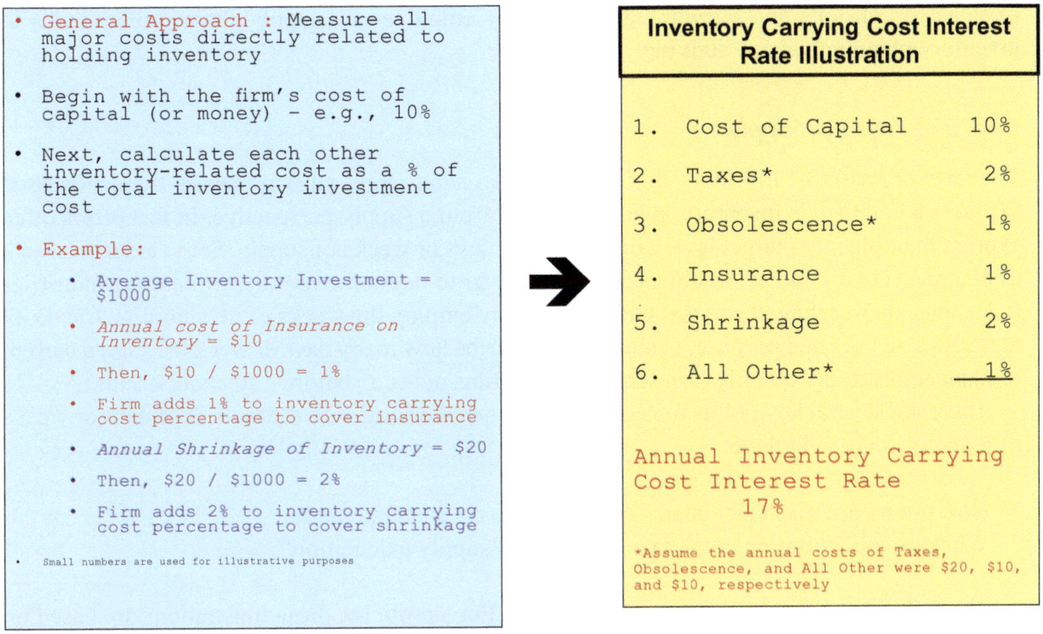

FIGURE 3.2 Example: How a Firm Develops Its Own Internal Corporate Annual Inventory Carrying Cost Interest Rate.

Inventory risk costs include such costs as obsolescence, damage, and shrinkage.[8] The exact definition of what constitutes an inventory risk cost will again vary by company. Nevertheless, the general rule remains that the portion of these costs which varies as the level of inventory held varies should be defined as inventory risk cost. Once annual inventory risk costs are quantified, we then convert them into percentage rates using the same method employed to convert inventory taxes into percentage rates.

Figure 3.2 illustrates the general approach employed to determine a firm's annual inventory carrying cost interest rate, and it presents a numerical example. The internal interest rates that individual firms employ may differ significantly because the respective costs for individual firms of the components of inventory carrying costs can vary widely (e.g., different firms have different costs of capital, shrinkage rates, etc.)

In summary, the annual inventory carrying cost interest rate represents the sum of many cost components. Determining the proper interest rate is a complex task subject to considerable interpretation. Definitions of the appropriate components to include in inventory carrying costs will vary from firm to firm. Even within a firm there may be considerable debate regarding the appropriate interest rate to use. Therefore, it is important that corporate functions such as Logistics, Finance, Manufacturing, and others align on one agreed upon, corporate-wide interest rate percentage to employ for all inventory carrying cost analyses.

3.2 Inventory Measures and Metrics

In this section, we review and illustrate several measures and metrics heavily utilized in inventory planning and management. The discussion also includes descriptions and definitions of selected concepts and terminology commonly employed by supply chain professionals in inventory planning-related activities.

Days and Weeks of Supply

The days or weeks of inventory that a firm has on hand represent two metrics frequently used to assess a company's inventory investment level from a supply perspective. In fact, firms often express their planning target level of inventory in days or weeks of supply. Some industries such as pharmaceuticals and automobiles commonly refer to days of inventory, while other industries (e.g., consumer packaged goods – CPG) frequently employ the weeks of inventory metric. Both metrics serve the same purpose; namely, they describe how many days or weeks of sales a current or planned inventory quantity can serve before it runs out (i.e., before a stockout occurs).[9]

There are several key points to keep in mind when working with the metrics of days or weeks of inventory. These include:

1 How are the metrics calculated? There are two alternate methods.
2 What are the limitations of a days or weeks of supply calculation?

The following examples address these points. For simplicity, these illustrations are based on the total FGI of a fictitious company that plans its inventory in weeks of supply.

Table 3.1 presents two alternative inventory weeks of supply calculations for a fictitious firm that has a total inventory of 1,000 units.[10] In the first method, the firm's total inventory (1,000 units) is divided by the average sales per week (100 units), indicating the firm currently has a 10-week supply of inventory. When basing this calculation on average sales (or shipments[11]) per week, it is important to use a representative historical sample of sales data (e.g., 52 weeks of sales history). It is also critical to recognize that for a product or group of products that experience significant variation in their weekly sales level because of seasonality or other

TABLE 3.1 Two Methods to Calculate Weeks Supply of Inventory

Calculation Method	*Variable*	*(units)*	
1. Based on Average Sales (or Shipments) per Week	Total Inventory	1,000	
	Average Sales per Week	100	
	Weeks of Supply	10	
2. Based on the Firm's Current Weekly Forecast as of the Current Week (t)	Total Inventory	1,000	**Cumulative Forecast**
	Forecast by Week, Beginning Next Week		
	Week (t + 1)	90	90
	Week (t + 2)	120	210
	Week (t + 3)	130	340
	Week (t + 4)	140	480
	Week (t + 5)	150	630
	Week (t + 6)	150	780
	Week (t + 7)	90	870
	Week (t + 8)	130	1,000
	Weeks of Supply	8	

factors, a calculation based on a historical average may not accurately predict how many weeks an inventory quantity at a particular time may last.

Method 2 in Table 3.1 projects the weeks of supply that an inventory quantity represents based on a weekly forward-looking forecast. Note in this example that the cumulative week-by-week forecast totals to 1,000 units after 8 weeks. Thus, while based on sales history, our fictitious company would believe it has a 10-week supply of inventory, its current weekly forecast suggests the firm has only 8 weeks' supply (or what is also called "forward coverage").

Each method of determining weeks (or days) of inventory serves a purpose, and it is not unusual for inventory planners to utilize both methods. Factors such as whether one is evaluating a single item at one location in the near term, the entire product line in total of a company over the course of a year, etc., will dictate the appropriate method. Further, it never hurts to have two perspectives, regardless of which method one deems more appropriate for a particular situation.

Limitations of Weeks (or Days) Supply Calculations

While weeks and days of supply metrics are heavily utilized, and provide a valuable supply perspective on a firm's inventory, planners must also recognize the limitations of these metrics. To illustrate these limitations, we review two alternative inventory scenarios for a firm evaluating the potential change in its total inventory investment requirements that would occur if the firm either increased or decreased its total number of DCs.

Assumptions for the Two Illustrative Inventory Requirements Scenarios

1 The firm currently determines its inventory requirements at its DCs based on an inventory management planning system that calculates safety stock requirements statistically based on historical demand and supply data.
2 The firm currently serves it retail customers in the U.S. market from three regional DCs, each of which has responsibility for approximately 1/3 of the firm's total annual demand.
3 For the current three-DC network, the inventory management planning system has determined that the firm's entire safety stock inventory requirements for all SKUs at its three DCs total to 100,000 units.[12] Based on up-to-the-minute historical data, the inventory system shows that this level of inventory investment (100,000 units) provides an overall 98% fill rate to the firm's retail customers.
4 The firm has annual sales of 520,000 units, so 100,000 units of total safety stock inventory represents 10 weeks of supply.[13]
5 The firm is considering either reducing or expanding the number of DCs it operates to serve the U.S. market.

Question: The firm wants to know if the inventory investment requirements would change from the current 100,000 safety stock units total if it increases or decreases the number of DCs on its network.

Scenario 1: Inventory planners use the weeks of supply metric to evaluate this question.

In this scenario, planners essentially say "our inventory planning system calculates that we need 10 weeks supply – so we will therefore need 10 weeks supply at each DC even if we change

TABLE 3.2 Projected Changes in Inventory Based on "Weeks Supply" Metric

Number of DCs	*Planned Target Weeks of Supply*	*Annual Sales Shipped by Each DC (units)*	*Total Company Annual Sales (units)*	*Total Inventory Requirements at Each DC (units)*	*Total Inventory Requirements on Network (units)*
1	10	520,000	520,000	100,000	100,000
2	10	260,000	520,000	50,000	100,000
3	10	173,333	520,000	33,333	100,000
4	10	130,000	520,000	25,000	100,000
5	10	104,000	520,000	20,000	100,000

Inventory Required at Each DC = (Annual Sales Shipped by DC) / (weeks in a year) × (Target Weeks Supply)
Inventory Required on Network = (Annual Sales) / (weeks in a year) × (Target Weeks Supply) = (520,000/52) × 10 = 100,000

the number of DCs on our network." Table 3.2 displays the results that this approach would lead to in the evaluation of the inventory requirements for networks with different numbers of DCs.

Table 3.2 reveals that assuming a "fixed weeks supply of inventory" (e.g., 10 weeks) at all DCs keeps total company inventory requirements constant, regardless of the number of stocking locations on the network. The sales shipped by each DC varies with the number of DCs on the network, as do their individual inventory levels. However, total network-wide safety stock inventory levels remain unchanged – using "weeks of supply" to determine inventory requirements.

This result ignores (or violates) the demand smoothing inventory management principle reviewed in Section 2.2 of Chapter 2 which holds that inventory requirements increase or decrease as the number of stocking locations serving a market increases or decreases.[14] Thus, while the weeks of inventory metric is a valuable tool for measuring how much supply of inventory a firm holds, it has limitations as an "inventory planning" tool. This does not mean that planners should not utilize the weeks of supply concept, but, rather, that when employing this metric, planners must recognize its limitations, and use it appropriately.

Scenario 2: Inventory planners use the square root of n rule to project total safety stock inventory requirements on networks with different numbers of DCs.

Table 3.3 offers a revised illustration depicting how the network-wide inventory requirements would change from those presented in Table 3.2 for a firm considering alternative distribution configurations. In this table, we use a mathematical approach, the square root of n rule, to estimate the safety stock inventory requirements of the total network (and the individual DCs) depending upon the number of locations on the network. The square root of n rule accounts for the difference in the variability of demand experienced at individual locations as the number of stocking locations (e.g., DCs) increases or decreases.[15] (See Exhibit 3.1 at the end of this section for an illustration of the square root of n rule.)

In Table 3.3, note that column 4 shows 100,000 units as the total inventory requirements for the current three-DC network. We then use the square root of n rule to calculate the projected total inventory requirements on alternative networks of one, two, four, and five DCs, respectively. The inventory requirements range from 57,735 units on a one-DC network to 129,099 units on a five-DC network. Further, the targeted weeks of supply required drops to 5.8 weeks on a one-DC network from the 10.0 weeks necessary to deliver the same customer fill rate on a three-DC network. This differential in units and weeks reflects the impact of the diminished variability of demand (i.e., the smoothing of demand) that results from consolidating all customer demands on one facility. Conversely, the heightened variability of demand that results from dispersing total demand over 5 DCs rather than 3 DCs raises the required weeks of supply to 12.9 weeks from 10.0 weeks.

Tables 3.1, 3.2, and 3.3, and the discussion in this section have highlighted the definitions, importance, and limitations of the inventory weeks (and days) supply metrics. These inventory metrics are invaluable tools for monitoring and planning a firm's inventory supply strategy. Further, planners must understand both their value and limitations to utilize them effectively. We now close this section with Exhibit 3.1, which explains the square root of n formula and offers three examples illustrating the calculations that generate the results shown in Table 3.3.

EXHIBIT 3.1 ILLUSTRATION OF THE SQUARE ROOT OF N RULE

- *Definition*: A technique that assists planners with calculating the change in total safety stock needed to maintain customer service levels within a distribution network when the number of stocking locations is changed. The square root rule states that total safety stock inventories in a specified number of facilities can be approximated by multiplying the total amount of inventory in existing facilities by the square root of the ratio of the number of future facilities divided by the number of existing facilities.[16]
- *Notation*:
    - SS^{cur} = the current total level of safety stock required at all the DCs on an existing network.
    - SS^{new} = the estimated total level of safety stock that will be required on a new network with either more or fewer DCs than the current network.
    - N^{cur} = the number of DCs on the current network.
    - N^{new} = the number of DCs on the new network.
- *Formula*:
    - $SS^{new} = [\text{sqrt}(N^{new}) / \text{sqrt}(N^{cur})] \times SS^{cur}$
- Examples**:
    1. Data → $SS^{cur} = 100{,}000$; $N^{cur} = 3$; $N^{new} = 2$
       $SS^{new} = [\text{sqrt}(2) / \text{sqrt}(3)] \times 100{,}000 = 81{,}650$
    2. Data → $SS^{cur} = 100{,}000$; $N^{cur} = 3$; $N^{new} = 4$
       $SS^{new} = [\text{sqrt}(4) / \text{sqrt}(3)] \times 100{,}000 = 115{,}470$
    3. Data → $SS^{cur} = 57{,}735$; $N^{cur} = 1$; $N^{new} = 2$
       $SS^{new} = [\text{sqrt}(2) / \text{sqrt}(1)] \times 57{,}735 = 81{,}650$

** Examples 1 and 2 illustrate the calculations for the potential change from the three-DC network to the two-DC and four-DC networks, respectively, in Table 3.3. Example 3 represents the case of the potential change from a one-DC network with an existing total safety stock inventory of 57,735 to a two-DC network.

TABLE 3.3 Projected Changes in Inventory Taking Into Account Demand Smoothing*

Number of DCs	*Annual Sales Shipped by Each DC (units)*	*Total Company Annual Sales (units)*	*Total Inventory Requirements on Network** (units)*	*Planned Target Weeks of Supply*** (units)*
1	520,000	520,000	57,735	5.8
2	260,000	520,000	81,650	8.2
3	173,333	520,000	100,000	10.0
4	130,000	520,000	115,470	11.5
5	104,000	520,000	129,099	12.9

* Exhibit 3.1 at the end of this section illustrates the square root of n formula and gives examples of the calculations that determine inventory requirements on the network.

** The total safety stock inventory requirement for the current existing three-DC network is 100,000 units as shown in row 3. The other calculations in this column are obtained by using the square root of n rule – given that the current network of 3 DCs requires 100,000 units of inventory.

*** Target weeks of supply = (Inventory required on network) / [(Company annual sales) / (weeks in a year)]. For example, the formula for a two-DC network is: 81,650 / (520,000 / 52) = 8.2.

Inventory Turns

Inventory turns, also called inventory turnover, is a closely watched metric that provides financial and efficiency perspectives on a firm's utilization of its inventory. The Association for Supply Chain Management defines inventory turnover as "the number of times that an inventory cycles or turns over during the year."[17] The standard formula to compute a firm's annual inventory turnover is:

Inventory Turnover = (Annual Cost of Goods Sold) / (Average Inventory Investment Cost)

Cost of goods sold (COGS) is the total cost to the firm of the goods that it sells to customers during a given period (e.g., 1 year).[18] Companies generally compute the average cost of their inventory for a year by calculating an average of the four end-of-quarter dollar investment levels (i.e., an average of four data points),[19] or by taking a similar more precise (e.g., monthly or daily) or less precise (e.g., the average of beginning and ending inventories – two data points) approach.

Inventory turns illuminate how efficiently a firm utilizes its inventory because in general, the higher a firm's annual turn rate, the lower the amount of time inventory sits in a stocking location incurring holding costs. Building and carrying inventory represents a cost for a firm, and the more rapidly a firm turns its inventory, the faster this asset generates revenues and profits for a firm; and the less holding costs the firm incurs.

A final important note on inventory turnover is that planners can calculate this metric based on both costs and units. While the cost-based metric represents the traditional, more commonly used financial measure, inventory turns based on units can play an important planning role.

Table 3.4 contrasts how the calculations of inventory turnover based on units and costs can differ. This table shows the inventory turns per year for five products based on both units (column 7) and costs (column 8). First, notice that while each of the five products have different turn rates, each individual item has the same turn rate based on both units and costs. For example, item 1 displays a turn rate of 15 per year in both columns 7 and 8, and this differs from the 4

TABLE 3.4 Inventory Turns Illustration

Item	*Cost per Unit*	*Average Inventory (units)*	*Average Inventory (at cost)*	*Annual Sales (units)*	*Annual Sales (at cost)*	*Inventory Turns Per Year Based on Units*	*Inventory Turns Per Year Based on Cost*
1	$ 8.00	200	$ 1,600	3,000	$ 24,000	15.0	15.0
2	$ 5.50	200	$ 1,100	4,000	$ 22,000	20.0	20.0
3	$ 3.00	2,000	$ 6,000	8,000	$ 24,000	4.0	4.0
4	$ 6.00	500	$ 3,000	6,000	$ 36,000	12.0	12.0
5	$ 4.00	1,200	$ 4,800	7,200	$ 28,800	6.0	6.0
Total		4,100	$ 16,500	28,200	$ 134,800	6.9	8.2

Annual Sales at Cost = (Cost per unit) × (Annual Sales in units)
Inventory Turns per year based on units = (Annual Sales in units) / (Average Inventory in units)
Inventory Turns per year based on cost = (Annual Sales at cost) / (Average Inventory at cost)

turns per year of item 3. *However, what happens when we calculate the annual turnover rate for all items as a single group?*

We observe on the total row at the bottom of Table 3.4 that the annual inventory turns calculated based on costs (8.2) exceed the turns based on units (6.9) by 1.3 turns per year, or about 19%. *What causes this, and why is it important?*

The five products individually have different costs per unit, average inventories (units and costs), and annual sales (units and costs). Therefore, when one sums the average inventories and sales to obtain totals for the overall product line, the totals reflect the "mix" or "relative weight" of these individual products. For example, items 3 and 5 constitute 78% of the overall units of inventory (3,200 of 4,100), but only 65% of the total inventory at cost ($10,800 / $16,500). This difference stems from the lower costs per unit of items 3 and 5, relative to items 1, 2, and 4. The 78% vs. 65% difference in the portion of the product line's total units and total costs that items 3 and 5 comprise results in the lower annual unit turn rate (6.9) compared to the annual cost turn rate (8.2) of the overall five-item product line. Specifically, the relatively low individual inventory turn rates of items 3 (4.0) and 5 (6.0) have a larger impact on the overall product line unit turn rate than on the overall product line cost turn rate.

The preceding illustration represents the type of nuance that supply chain planners and analysts must remain vigilant to recognize. To understand the importance of such nuances, consider the potential impact on storage space requirements in a warehouse of overestimating the expected annual "unit" inventory turn rate. For a given level of total annual sales, in general, the higher the turn rate, the lower will be the storage space requirements. In this turns illustration, suppose that planners did not recognize the difference between cost and unit turn rates; and therefore, using only the cost-based inventory turn metric, assumed annual turns of 8.2 for this product line. Warehouses do not "physically" store dollars of inventory. Rather, they store units of inventory – typically in the form of cases and pallets. Thus, planning warehouse storage space requirements assuming 8.2 unit turns per year rather than the actual 6.9 unit turns per year could lead to a significant underestimate of warehouse storage space requirements, and the operational issues that inadequate warehouse storage space can create.

Additional Inventory Definitions and Concepts

We conclude this section with Exhibit 3.2, which reviews selected additional inventory definitions and concepts frequently used in inventory planning and analysis.

EXHIBIT 3.2 FREQUENTLY UTILIZED INVENTORY DEFINITIONS AND CONCEPTS

Backorder:	An unfilled customer order or commitment. A backorder is an immediate (or past-due) demand against an item whose inventory is insufficient to satisfy the demand.
Fill Rate:	The percentage of customer demand that was successfully filled over a defined time-period. Fill rates can be measured based on total line items, orders, cases, dollars, and other measures of interest.
Inventory Cycle:	The length of time between two consecutive inventory replenishment shipments; for example, the cycle time between when a DC places an order on a plant, and when that plant delivers the inventory ordered to the DC.
Lost Sales:	A potential sale that was not completed, usually due to lack of availability of the item.
Stockout:	When the demand for a product, component, or material cannot be satisfied because of insufficient inventory.

Source: ASCM Dictionary, 17th Edition (2022) – for all or portions of the backorder, inventory cycle, and lost sales definitions.

3.3 Organizing a Firm's Product Line Structure

Supply chain management requires a hierarchical planning perspective spanning from the long-run strategic, to the medium-term tactical, to the short-run operational.[20] To facilitate effective planning activities across its entire planning horizon, a firm must have a well-defined product line structure. In other words, a firm needs a framework to organize its entire inventory of finished goods end items for all planning purposes ranging from the multi-year strategic to daily operations. In this section, we define and illustrate what a product line structure is.

Figure 3.3 displays a typical finished goods product line structure a manufacturing, distribution, or retail company would employ. As shown, the levels of product aggregation consist of:

- *End items* – which tree up into product families,
- *Product families* – which aggregate into major product lines, and
- *Product lines* – which combine to form the overall company product offering

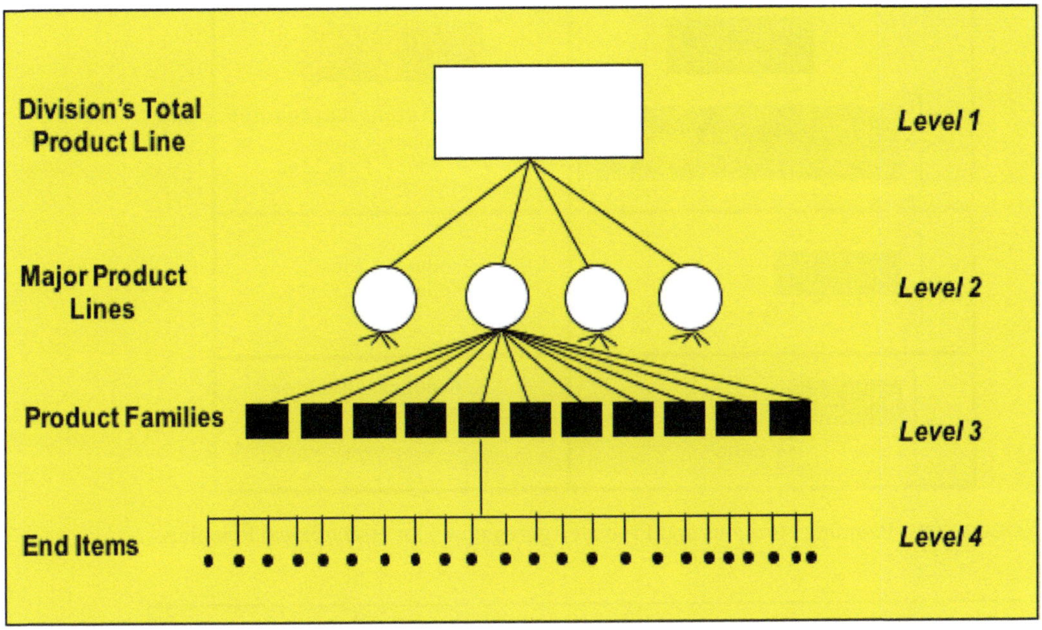

- For a single division firm, this represents the company's entire product line. For a multi-division firm (e.g., a firm with both major pharmaceutical and consumer products divisions), each division usually has its own product line structure.

FIGURE 3.3 Product Line Structure Illustration.

Why Do Firms Need a Product Line Structure?

Companies organize their finished goods into a product line structure for numerous reasons. For example, manufacturing and distribution firms with thousands of unique finished goods end items typically formulate their tactical, medium-term product plans at an aggregated product level because it is not practical to develop individual long-run plans (e.g., 12–18 months) for thousands of individual end items. Similarly, retailers that stock thousands of products cannot efficiently plan long-run, multi-year acquisition and inventory strategies at the end item level. Instead, firms develop long-run plans and strategies at an aggregated product level, and then in shorter-run operational activities, they plan and execute at the end item level. Figure 3.4 illustrates the level of product aggregation generally used for the different time horizons of a firm's overall planning process. As noted, short-run operational activities generally focus on planning and scheduling end items, while tactical activities focus on product family and/or product line planning. At the long-run strategic level, the attention turns to major product lines and a firm's entire product line.[21]

To illustrate this concept in greater detail, in Figure 3.5 we present a product line structure for a ceramic tile manufacturer and distributor. Note that end items consist of the actual products that consumers purchase, such as 4" × 4" blue wall tile. Product families are aggregations of similar end items, such as all the individual colors of 4" × 4" wall tile, and product lines represent aggregations of similar product families (e.g., all wall tile product families). Finally, the firm's total product offering to customers consists of all of its major product lines.

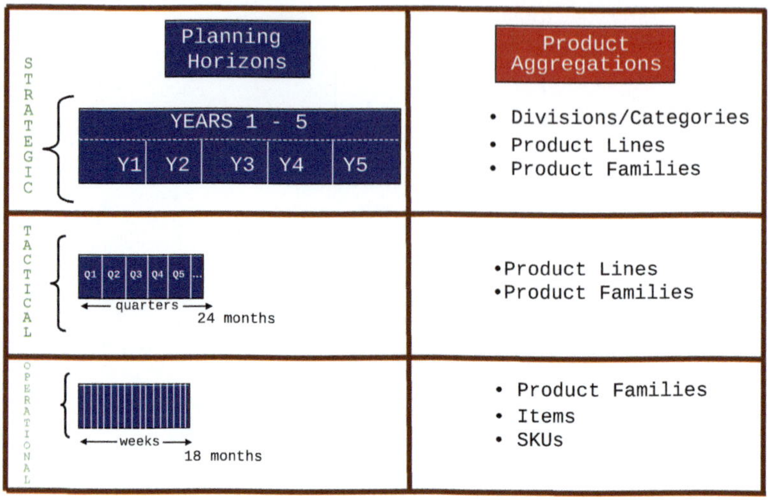

FIGURE 3.4 Planning Horizons and Product Aggregations for Hierarchical Planning.

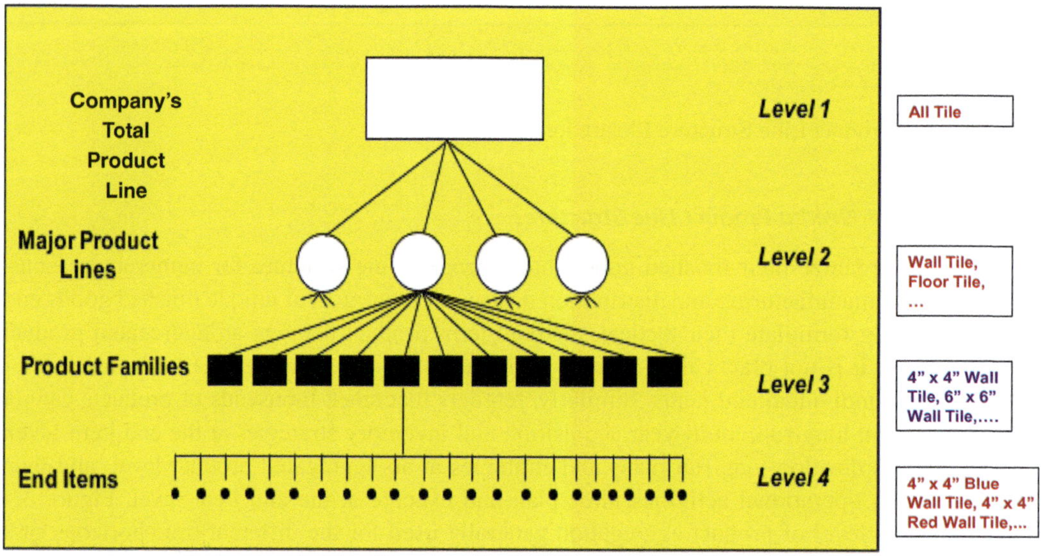

This illustrates the entire product line structure for a company that produces and sells only ceramic tile.

FIGURE 3.5 Product Line Structure for a Ceramic Tile Manufacturer.

We close this short review of product line structure by noting that product families play a particularly important role in many 12–18-month tactical supply chain planning applications. The formation of a set of product families to represent an entire product line consisting of thousands of unique end items represents a critical analytical step that requires careful planning. Further, what may be a good set of product families to represent a firm's end items for one planning application, may not work well for another application. In Chapter 4, we will review a production planning application that illustrates the importance of product families in supply chain planning.[22]

3.4 The ABC Inventory Classification Scheme

The ABC method is an analytic technique widely used to classify inventory items in terms of their relative importance to a firm. Particularly for companies that manufacture, distribute, and/or sell thousands of products, categorizing end items in an ABC system represents a critical inventory management activity. The ASCM defines the ABC classification method as follows: "The classification of a group of items in decreasing order of annual dollar volume or other criteria. This array is then split into three classes called A, B and C."[23] The percentage of items classified as As, Bs, and Cs will vary by firm; however, the basic premise is that:

- *A items* comprise only a relatively small group of a company's products, but constitute up to 80% or more of total sales.[24]
- *B items* make up the next 15% or so of sales; however, they represent up to 30% of total items.
- *C items* contribute only about 5% of total sales, yet they can account for as much as 50% or more of the total number of items in a product line.

In addition to classifying their inventory by the ABC method, companies also often utilize this approach to categorize customers, markets, and suppliers in terms of their relative value or importance. In Chapter 6, we will review a customer ABC segmentation scheme.

Finally, some firms stratify their inventory, customers, and markets into four or even five categories rather than just three. For example, consider a firm which has an inventory that includes some "discontinued products" (i.e., leftover inventory of products a firm no longer actively markets), as well as some inventory that is past its expiration date (e.g., inventory of medical products such as aspirin that was not sold by its effective date). A firm in this situation might categorize its inventory as:

- As – fast-selling, high-volume items,
- Bs – moderate-selling, medium-volume items,
- Cs – slow-moving, low-volume items,
- Ds – discontinued items, and
- Es – expired, damaged, and other non-saleable items

Tables 3.5–3.7 display an illustrative ABC inventory classification analysis. Table 3.5 shows annual sales, annual profits, and inventory cost data for a firm with a product line that contains 20 end items.[25] Column 1 indicates the firm's internal three-digit product code identifier for each item, with the items in this table listed based on their product codes in ascending order.

In addition to the criterion of annual sales revenue, many companies find it illuminating to rank their end items by other criteria such as annual unit sales, annual profit contribution, and the total inventory cost of each item. Table 3.6 shows the firm's 20 end items ranked in descending order (i.e., highest to lowest) based on annual sales revenue in columns 2–5, and based on annual unit sales[26] in columns 6–9. In these two separate analyses, notice that the items are classified as either A, B, or C in columns 5 and 9, respectively. In both rankings, we define

TABLE 3.5 Firm Data for ABC Classification Analysis

Three-Digit Product Code of Inventory Item	*Annual Sales Revenue ($)*	*Annual Sales (units)*	*Annual Profits ($)*	*Inventory at Cost ($)*
128	$ 231,000	23,100	$ 80,850	$ 28,875
292	$ 20,000	2,000	$ 8,000	$ 2,769
336	$ 67,000	6,700	$ 30,150	$ 8,504
349	$ 21,000	4,200	$ 9,450	$ 2,665
368	$ 1,400,000	280,000	$ 770,000	$ 121,154
440	$ 21,000	2,100	$ 8,400	$ 2,908
469	$ 400,000	80,000	$ 220,000	$ 34,615
480	$ 700,000	46,667	$ 315,000	$ 74,038
499	$ 18,000	1,800	$ 9,900	$ 1,869
658	$ 20,700	4,140	$ 7,245	$ 3,105
664	$ 1,000,000	100,000	$ 400,000	$ 115,385
667	$ 19,000	1,900	$ 8,550	$ 2,412
668	$ 21,000	2,100	$ 10,500	$ 2,423
669	$ 140,000	28,000	$ 56,000	$ 19,385
712	$ 141,000	14,100	$ 77,550	$ 12,202
716	$ 59,000	11,800	$ 32,450	$ 6,127
771	$ 20,800	2,080	$ 11,440	$ 2,160
803	$ 62,000	3,100	$ 21,700	$ 9,300
883	$ 20,500	4,100	$ 10,250	$ 2,365
956	$ 18,000	3,600	$ 6,300	$ 2,700
Total	**$ 4,400,000**	**621,487**	**$ 2,093,735**	**$ 454,961**

A items as those accounting for the top 80% of sales, B items comprise the next 15% of total sales (i.e., from 80% to 95%), and C items represent the last 5% of sales.

Thus, the ABC system follows the well-known 80/20 rule of the Pareto principle. In the case of inventory, the 80/20 rule posits that approximately 20% of a firm's end items contribute about 80% of total sales, while about 80% of all the remaining items account for the last 20% of sales.

Table 3.6 illustrates that depending upon the measurement criteria used, the ranking order and classification of items can vary somewhat. For example, while the same four items are designated as As, the third and fourth items (480 and 469) are in opposite order when ranked by sales revenue and sales units. Further, observe that while the "sales revenue" rankings show 6 B items (column 5), the "sales units" rankings display only five B items (column 9). Conversely, the "sales units" criterion generates one more C item than does the "sales revenue" listing. Table 3.7, which uses annual profits and inventory at cost to generate two separate additional rankings, exhibits similar variations in the items' order and classification.

While we observe only minor variations in the items' order and classifications in Tables 3.6 and 3.7, for a company with thousands or tens of thousands of end items, these variations can become more widespread. Thus, the criterion employed to perform a particular ABC inventory analysis should be carefully selected based on the purpose of its application. Exhibit 3.3 concludes this section with an illustrative list of inventory planning, management, and related activities that frequently use ABC analyses for operational guidance. The exhibit includes applications where criteria other than sales revenue represent the appropriate ranking measures.

TABLE 3.6 ABC Classifications Based on Annual Sales Revenues and Annual Unit Sales

Item Rank	*Three-Digit Product Code of Inventory Item*	*Annual Sales Revenue ($)*	*Cumulative Percent of Annual Sales Revenue*	*Inventory Classification Category*	*Three-Digit Product Code of Inventory Item*	*Annual Sales (units)*	*Cumulative Percent of Annual Sales Units*	*Inventory Classification Category*
1	368	$ 1,400,000	32%	**A**	368	280,000	45%	**A**
2	664	$ 1,000,000	55%	**A**	664	100,000	61%	**A**
3	480	$ 700,000	70%	**A**	469	80,000	74%	**A**
4	469	$ 400,000	80%	**A**	480	46,667	82%	**A**
5	128	$ 231,000	85%	**B**	669	28,000	86%	**B**
6	712	$ 141,000	88%	**B**	128	23,100	90%	**B**
7	669	$ 140,000	91%	**B**	712	14,100	92%	**B**
8	336	$ 67,000	93%	**B**	716	11,800	94%	**B**
9	803	$ 62,000	94%	**B**	336	6,700	95%	**B**
10	716	$ 59,000	95%	**B**	349	4,200	96%	**C**
11	668	$ 21,000	96%	**C**	658	4,140	96%	**C**
12	440	$ 21,000	96%	**C**	883	4,100	97%	**C**
13	349	$ 21,000	97%	**C**	956	3,600	98%	**C**
14	771	$ 20,800	97%	**C**	803	3,100	98%	**C**
15	658	$ 20,700	98%	**C**	668	2,100	98%	**C**
16	883	$ 20,500	98%	**C**	440	2,100	99%	**C**
17	292	$ 20,000	99%	**C**	771	2,080	99%	**C**
18	667	$ 19,000	99%	**C**	292	2,000	99%	**C**
19	956	$ 18,000	100%	**C**	667	1,900	100%	**C**
20	499	$ 18,000	100%	**C**	499	1,800	100%	**C**
	All	**$ 4,400,000**			**All**	**621,487**		

TABLE 3.7 ABC Classifications Based on Annual Profits and Current Inventory at Cost

Item Rank	*Three-Digit Product Code of Inventory Item*	*Annual Profits ($)*	*Cumulative Percent of Annual Profits*	*Inventory Classification Category*	*Three-Digit Product Code of Inventory Item*	*Inventory at Cost ($)*	*Cumulative Percent of Inventory at Cost*	*Inventory Classification Category*
1	368	$ 770,000	37%	**A**	368	$ 121,154	27%	**A**
2	664	$ 400,000	56%	**A**	664	$ 115,385	52%	**A**
3	480	$ 315,000	71%	**A**	480	$ 74,038	68%	**A**
4	469	$ 220,000	81%	**A**	469	$ 34,615	76%	**A**
5	128	$ 80,850	85%	**B**	128	$ 28,875	82%	**A**
6	712	$ 77,550	89%	**B**	669	$ 19,385	86%	**B**
7	669	$ 56,000	92%	**B**	712	$ 12,202	89%	**B**
8	716	$ 32,450	93%	**B**	803	$ 9,300	91%	**B**
9	336	$ 30,150	95%	**B**	336	$ 8,504	93%	**B**
10	803	$ 21,700	96%	**C**	716	$ 6,127	94%	**B**
11	771	$ 11,440	96%	**C**	658	$ 3,105	95%	**B**
12	668	$ 10,500	97%	**C**	440	$ 2,908	96%	**C**
13	883	$ 10,250	97%	**C**	292	$ 2,769	96%	**C**
14	499	$ 9,900	98%	**C**	956	$ 2,700	97%	**C**
15	349	$ 9,450	98%	**C**	349	$ 2,665	98%	**C**
16	667	$ 8,550	99%	**C**	668	$ 2,423	98%	**C**
17	440	$ 8,400	99%	**C**	667	$ 2,412	99%	**C**
18	292	$ 8,000	99%	**C**	883	$ 2,365	99%	**C**
19	658	$ 7,245	100%	**C**	771	$ 2,160	100%	**C**
20	956	$ 6,300	100%	**C**	499	$ 1,869	100%	**C**
		$ 2,093,735				**$ 454,961**		

EXHIBIT 3.3 ABC INVENTORY AND OTHER CLASSIFICATION APPLICATIONS

1 *Ranking end items to facilitate developing inventory planning strategies* for large groups of end items

- For example, establish different fill rate targets for A, B, and C items such as: As – 98%, Bs – 96%, and Cs – 92%.
- Use sales revenue or profits as criteria.

2 *Warehouse layout planning* of where to locate inventory items in a DC

- Minimize time required to pick high-volume A items by locating them closer to the warehouse pickers than the B and C items.
- Use sales units as criteria.

3 *Cycle counting in a warehouse* to maintain inventory accuracy[27]

- Count fast-selling A items more frequently than slower-selling C and B items.
- Use sales units as criteria.

4 *Inventory replenishment planning*

- In a perpetual (i.e., continuous)[28] replenishment system, check A items on a more frequent basis than B and C items to determine if a reorder is required.
- Use sales revenue or units as criteria.

5 *Production planning strategy*

- Some firms choose to produce slow-moving C items infrequently in relatively large lot sizes. This strategy aims to reduce the need for inefficient, short production runs.
- Use sales units or sales revenue as criteria.

6 *Customer segmentation strategy*

- Rank priority of customers based on their importance to the firm – e.g., revenue and/or profit contributions.[29]
- Offer higher service levels to A customers.
- Use sales revenue or profits as criteria.

3.5 Additional Inventory Planning Examples

In this section, we review two important inventory planning and management activities. First, we discuss the importance of monitoring inventory, and facilitating visibility internally within a company to the firm's inventory levels and its inventory targets. Then, we discuss the important trade-offs that companies often must make between their respective levels of inventory investment in FGI, WIP, and raw materials.

Monitoring Inventory Levels and Targets[30]

A key operational responsibility of inventory planning and management consists of monitoring a firm's adherence to inventory targets and plans.[31] There are numerous dimensions to this management component including:

1 developing appropriate FGI end item target levels by stocking location (i.e., at the SKU level),
2 executing production and purchasing plans to maintain these targeted levels,
3 monitoring customer service fill rates to ensure target rates are being met, and that these targets are competitive, and
4 monitoring and guiding overall firm FGI levels.

In this section, we will focus on one often overlooked management component of "monitoring and guiding" overall firm FGI levels; namely, creating visibility to inventory levels across a firm. Promoting visibility throughout a firm (i.e., across all departments including marketing, finance, and others) becomes extremely important when a company has prolonged periods of either excesses or shortages of inventory. In these situations, the entire firm must be aware of the inventory issue, and must collectively address the problem. For illustrative purposes, assume that a firm currently has a significant excess level of inventory at its DCs, and this situation has persisted for months with no immediate resolution in sight. This inventory excess has created major operational issues such as overcrowding and reduced productivity at the DCs, and it has also caused unplanned expenses such as using third-party outside warehousing to store excess inventories.

There are many activities required to regain control of inventory levels without damaging customer service. One important step is to ensure that appropriate organizational awareness and concern exist at all management levels. Logistics managers must take responsibility for promoting this organizational visibility. In the remainder of this section, we present an analytic and reporting methodology that this author has used successfully to generate widespread organizational awareness of serious excess inventory issues.

Pictorial Description

The figures at the close of this section illustrate an analysis of a firm's FGI reviewed at the total firm, product family, and end item levels. The reader is encouraged to consider the headline of each figure as if he or she was reviewing a monthly report that had just been issued across the firm. The headlines describe the specific data or analysis presented in a figure. Additionally, these figures serve to suggest ideas to the reader on different analytic reporting formats to utilize in communications to an organization on the status of current inventory levels at the firm.

In reviewing these figures, assume that a logistics manager wishes to convey the magnitude and cost of his/her firm's current excess inventory positions. Thus, the manager begins with several slides that communicate at an aggregate inventory, total pallet level the firm's current and recent historical positions (Figure 3.6). Then a comparison of actual inventory levels versus budget (Figure 3.7), and the total inventory housed in outside, third-party storage (Figure 3.8) are presented. After this aggregate view, the logistics manager next focuses on

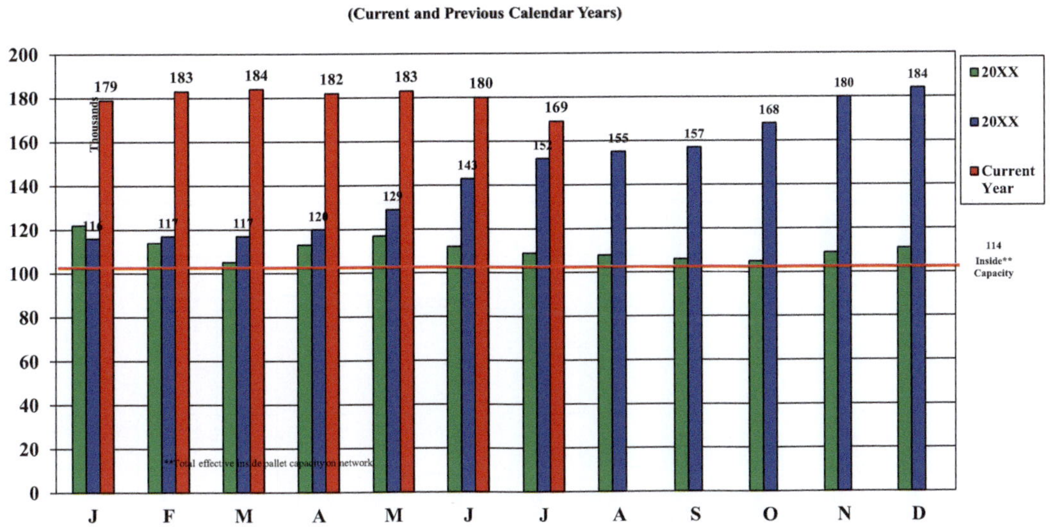

FIGURE 3.6 Historical Total FGI – All Locations' Average Pallets in Inventory per Month (Current and Previous Calendar Years).

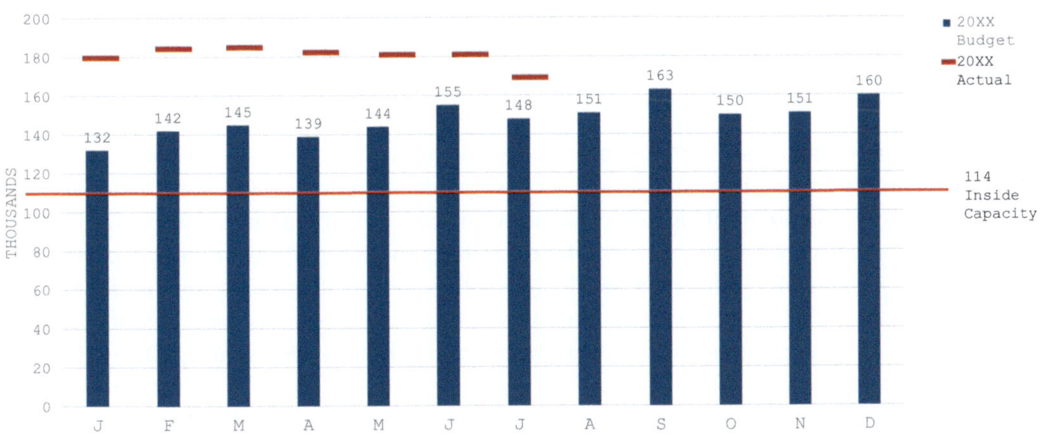

FIGURE 3.7 Total FGI: Budget vs. Actual – All Locations' Pallets in Inventory by Month.

inventory at the product family and item level. Figures 3.9 and 3.10 detail the cost to the firm of its inventories, and highlight how many thousands of pallets of inventory above safety stock plus cycle stock targets there are by product. Finally, Figures 3.11 and 3.12 communicate the quantities of inventory on hand that are: (1) not generating any revenue, (2) are literally inactive (e.g., discontinued), or (3) have been rejected for reasons such as product expiration. When disseminated effectively and regularly by logistics managers, reports such as these can rally an organization to take coordinated actions to bring its inventory down to appropriate levels.

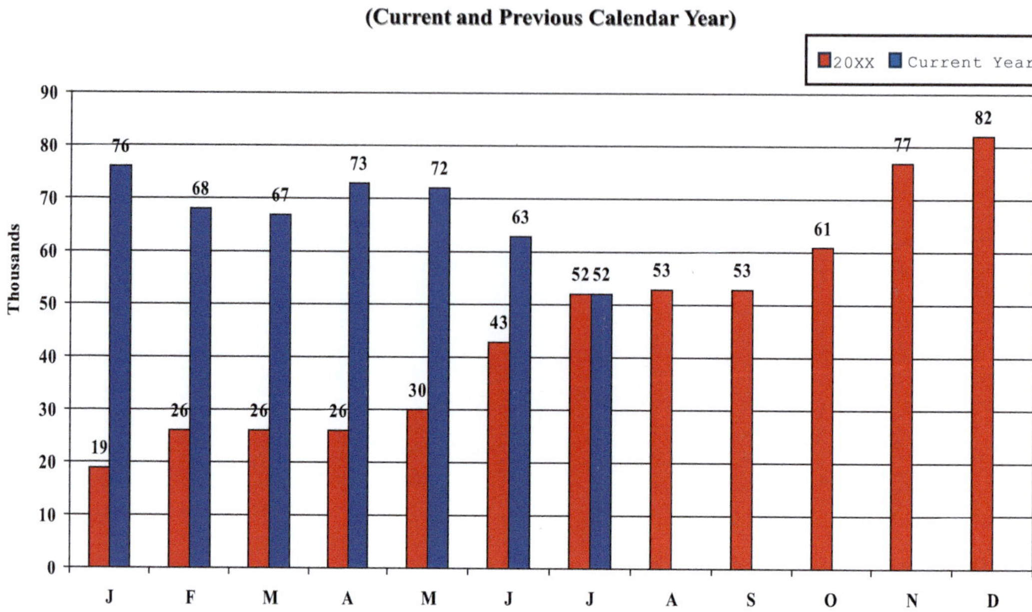

FIGURE 3.8 Total Inventory in Outside Storage Average Pallets in Outside Inventory per Month (Current and Previous Calendar Year).

FGI, WIP, and Raw Material Inventory Decisions

Manufacturers in industries such as pharmaceuticals, autos, and consumer products generally have significant inventories in finished goods, work in process, and raw materials and components. An important planning decision for companies that maintain inventories in these multiple states of completion consists of determining the optimal operational mix of these inventories. Specifically, a firm must decide the relative portion of its total inventory investment that it will hold in FGI vs. WIP vs. raw materials. A firm's decision on its own mix of inventory must also be integrated with the firm's decisions regarding how much inventory (if any) it wants its suppliers to carry, how much FGI the firm wants its retailers to hold, etc. This can be a very complex, strategic set of inventory planning decisions, and to provide a brief glimpse into this process, Figure 3.13 illustrates the supply chain network of a fictitious sneaker manufacturer and distributor, ABC Sneakers Inc.

The network of ABC Sneakers includes several material suppliers, a company-owned plant with an adjacent finished goods DC also owned by the firm, numerous company-owned retail sneaker stores, and a series of third-party retailers' stores that carry the ABC brand. In formulating its inventory strategy for this network, ABC Sneakers must address the following questions and decisions:

1 How much inventory of rubber, textiles, leather, plastics, and foam should it stock in its plant?
2 Does ABC want to use a just-in-time (JIT) approach with its suppliers, and maintain only a few days of suppliers' materials in its plant? Or does ABC want to stock larger materials and WIP inventories in its plant?

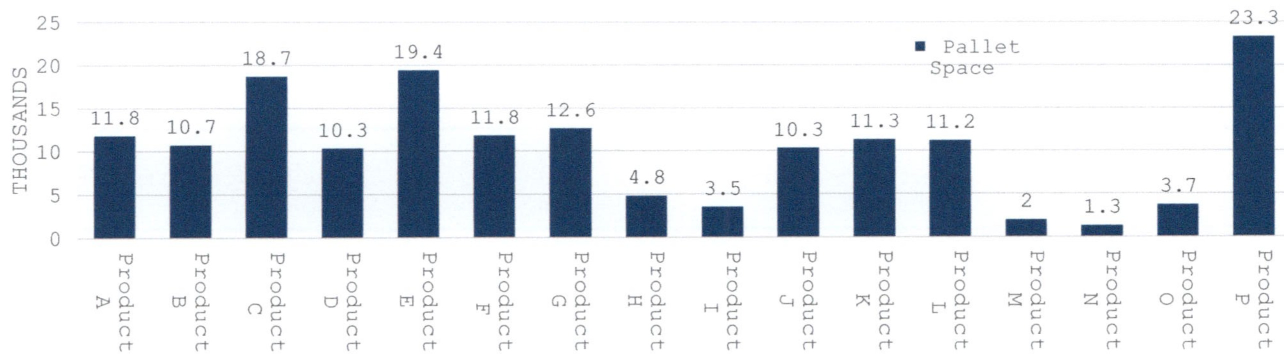

																	ALL INVENTORY
$MM at Cost	$4.9	$5.1	$8.9	$5.4	$12.5	$6.8	$6.4	$2.7	$9.3	$12.7	$38.0	$12.2	$2.9	$1.5	$2.5	$68.3	$200
Weeks Fwd Coverage	17	20	15	18	32	24	20	7	20	21	15	22	8	17	14	16	19
SS Target Inv.(Weeks)	11.2	10.2	9.7	11.7	10.7	10.0	11.2	9.8	11.2	10.2	10.5	14.0	6.6	6.9	8.0	10.0	11
Incremental Pallets Above SS Target (000)	4.5	6.1	5.8	4.3	12.5	5.8	6.4	0.0	2.0	5.9	4.9	6.3	0.4	0.9	2.1	10.3	78
Cycle Stock Lot Size in Wks	4	4	4	4	4	8	4	6	8	4	8	4	4	4	8	6	5.0
Incremental Pallets Above SS +Avg Cycle Stock (000)	3.3	5.4	3.9	3.5	11.7	4.5	5.1	0.0	1.8	4.6	3.4	5.3	0.0	0.7	0.9	7.4	62

- The Weeks Forward Coverage given is the last forecast week for which this grouping has a forecast.
- SS Target Inventory = Safety Stock weeks forward coverage target

FIGURE 3.9 Total Inventory and Forward Coverage (Total Pallets at All Locations).

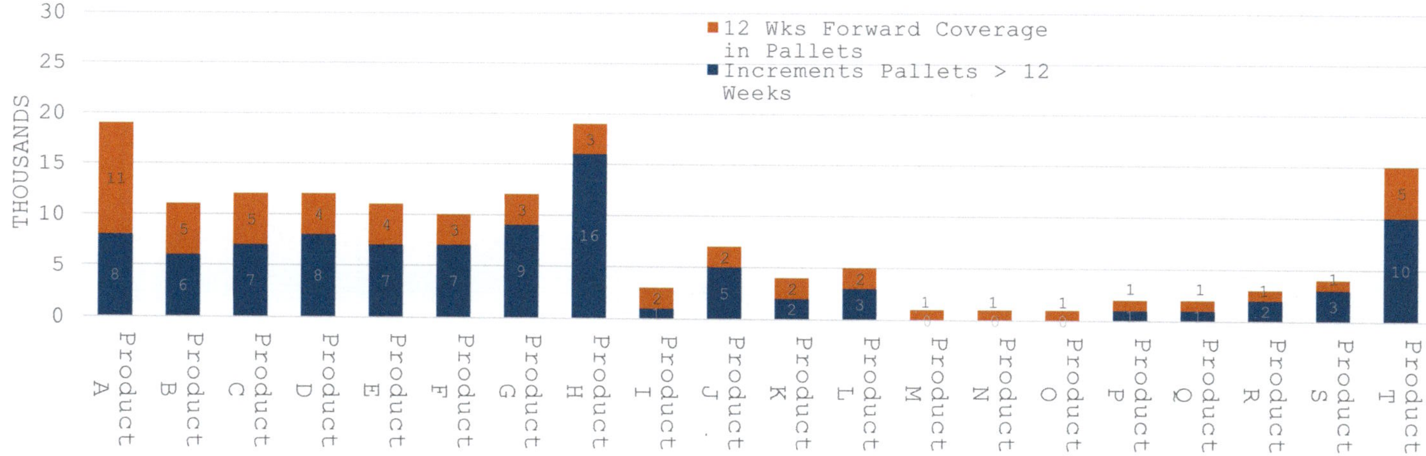

Cumulative Std Cost > 12 Wks (MM)	$7.6	$10.0	$12.6	$15.0	$19.5	$21.3	$22.6	$24.1	$27.7	$30.0	$34.3	$39.0	$41.4	$42.8	$46.5	$48.8	$50.3	$52.3	$52.7	$65.5
Cumulative Pallets > 12 Wks (000)	11.4	16.4	21.3	25.4	29.4	32.7	35.8	38.8	41.2	43.3	44.9	46.4	47.2	48.0	48.8	49.5	50.1	50.7	51.2	55.7

Based on inventory and forecast as of the beginning of the current month.

FIGURE 3.10 Products With 500 Pallets or More of Inventory in Excess of 12 Weeks' Supply.

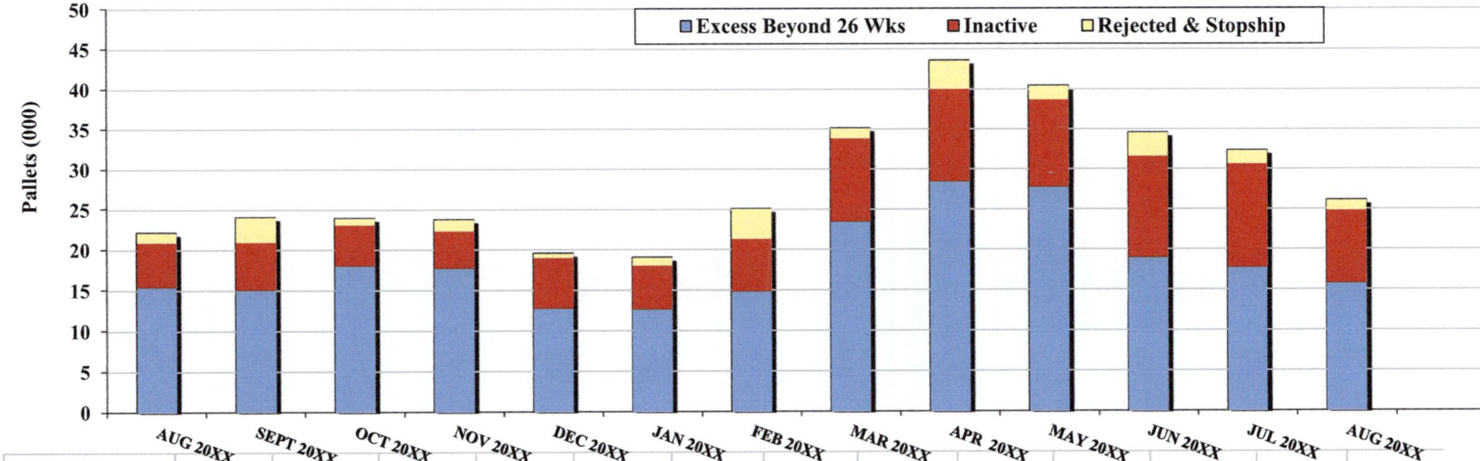

Pallets (000)	AUG 20XX	SEPT 20XX	OCT 20XX	NOV 20XX	DEC 20XX	JAN 20XX	FEB 20XX	MAR 20XX	APR 20XX	MAY 20XX	JUN 20XX	JUL 20XX	AUG 20XX
Excess Beyond 26 Wks	15.4	15.1	18.4	17.7	12.7	12.5	14.8	23.4	28.4	27.7	19.0	17.7	15.7
Inactive	5.5	5.7	5.1	4.6	6.3	5.4	6.5	10.4	11.6	11.0	13.0	12.9	9.1
Rejected & Stopship	1.2	3.1	0.8	1.4	0.5	1.0	3.7	1.3	3.5	1.7	3.0	1.7	1.2
Total	**22.1**	**23.9**	**24.3**	**23.7**	**19.5**	**18.9**	**25.0**	**35.1**	**43.5**	**40.4**	**35.0**	**32.3**	**26.0**

Based on inventory and forecast as of the beginning of the current month.

FIGURE 3.11 Non-Revenue-Generating Inventory in Pallets.

Top 10 Excess Items				*Top 10 Inactive Items*				
Items with more than 26 weeks of forward coverage.				*Items for which there is no forecasted demand.*				
Sorted by Pallets				*Sorted by Pallets*				
Item No	*Description*	*Item Type*	*Excess Pallets**	*Item No*	*Description*	*Item Type*	*Pallets*	*% Change vs Month Ago*
44335-01	Product 1	O/S	2,182	65854-00	Product 1	Promo	474	0%
00504-00	Product 2	Club	875	89919-01	Product 2	Promo	408	0%
00519-00	Product 3	O/S	600	44390-04	Product 3	Promo	330	-1%
00716-01	Product 4	Club	451	42535-04	Product 4	Promo	274	0%
44305-00	Product 5	O/S	400	42163-00	Product 5	Promo	241	0%
52122-00	Product 6	Promo	372	48839-00	Product 6	Promo	213	0%
03339-00	Product 7	Club	369	48837-00	Product 7	Promo	212	0%
65847-00	Product 8	Promo	364	70836-00	Product 8	Promo	211	-16%
60013-00	Product 9	O/S	362	00519-04	Product 9	O/S	205	0%
22890-00	Product 10	O/S	357	17215-00	Product 10	Promo	179	-46%
Sum of Top 10 Excess:			**6,332**	**Sum of Top 10 Inactive:**			**2,747**	

FIGURE 3.12 Top Ten Excess and Inactive Items.

* - Pallets beyond the first 26 weeks of forward coverage.

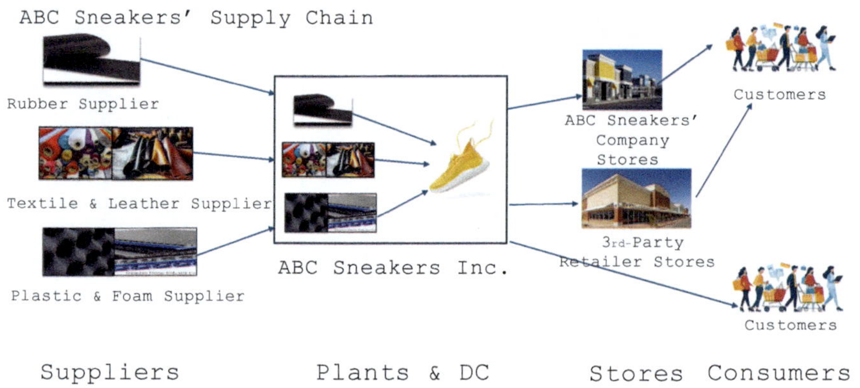

FIGURE 3.13 Inventory Decisions for Supply Chains.

3 Related to question 2, would using a JIT approach significantly increase freight costs because suppliers would deliver smaller quantities per shipment?
4 Additionally, would purchasing smaller quantities of materials at a time in a JIT approach increase ABC's purchase costs – because quantity discount pricing would not be possible on smaller purchase quantities?
5 How much FGI should ABC stock at its DC and its company-owned stores?
6 Does ABC want to use a JIT system with frequent, small deliveries to its company retail stores, or does it want to maintain larger quantities of inventory at its retail stores and make less frequent, larger shipments from its DC to its stores?

7 Similarly, what inventory and delivery strategies should ABC employ to supply its third-party retailers?
8 Should ABC serve online consumers exclusively from its DC – allowing ABC to keep its inventory for online consumers consolidated in one location? Or should ABC's retail stores also serve online consumer orders?

The preceding list of questions and decisions identifies just some of the many trade-offs and decisions that ABC Sneakers would have to evaluate. In summary, manufacturers that utilize and produce significant quantities of raw materials, WIP, and FGI must address a complex set of inventory-related decisions and strategies.

Finally, note that the cost to hold inventory increases as it progresses from raw material to WIP to FGI status. The costs that occur in transforming inventory from one state to another are incorporated into the cost per unit of inventory at its next stage (e.g., the machining, the material, and the labor costs of producing FGI from WIP inventory). Therefore, it generally costs more for a firm to hold one unit of FGI than it costs to hold however many units (one or more) of each of the components that collectively produce that one unit of FGI. When significant differences exist between the cost of a unit of FGI, and the collective cost per unit of all the quantities of the WIP and/or raw materials needed to produce that one unit of FGI; a company will often include this inventory cost differential in the complex set of trade-offs it evaluates to formulate its planned optimal investment mix of raw materials, WIP, and FGI.[32]

3.6 Inventory Replenishment Planning

The inventory replenishment planning systems that re-supply inventory from suppliers to plants, plants to DCs, and DC to stores play a critical "connecting" role within and between companies on a supply chain. Researchers and planners have developed very sophisticated replenishment decision support methodologies and tools over many decades. One of the earliest inventory management systems that enjoyed widespread usage in industry was the IBM IMPACT system, developed in the 1960s based on the pioneering work of Robert G. Brown.[33] Today, software vendors such as SAP, Oracle, Microsoft, and many others offer user-friendly platforms that allow firms to plan and execute inventory replenishments daily between supply points and stocking locations, often on a highly automated basis utilizing advanced statistical techniques. These mathematical and statistical models are beyond the scope of this text, and the interested reader is referred to Bowersox et al. (2024), Chopra and Meindl (2016), and Venkataraman and Pinto (2020) for good introductions to this subject. For our purposes, however, it is important to review briefly the basic concepts underlying the methodologies employed for inventory replenishment planning.

For situations where a supply point re-supplies inventory to a stocking location on a regular, ongoing basis (e.g., a plant that re-supplies a DC regularly), there are two primary models (i.e., methodologies) used:

1 a perpetual inventory reorder cycle model and
2 a periodic inventory reorder cycle model[34]

In a perpetual inventory reorder process, the inventory level of each SKU at a stocking location is continuously reviewed to evaluate whether that item requires inventory replenishment. Conversely, in a periodic inventory reorder process, the inventory level of each SKU at a stocking location is reviewed on a fixed time interval (e.g., once per week), to determine whether that item needs inventory replenishment.

The perpetual and periodic inventory review models each rely on two key components; namely, a reorder point (ROP) and an order quantity.[35] The ASCM defines a reorder point as

> a set inventory level where, if the total stock on hand plus on order fall to or below that point, action is taken to replenish the stock. The order point is normally calculated as forecasted usage during the replenishment lead time plus safety stock.[36]

Thus, in both a perpetual and periodic inventory system, when the inventory of an SKU drops to its ROP, this triggers a replenishment order for that item. The difference between the two methods is that when an item reaches its ROP, a perpetual inventory system generates an order immediately, while a periodic system will create an order for that item at the next scheduled review time of the system. Because a periodic system does not generate an immediate order, these fixed time interval inventory systems generally operate with a somewhat higher average inventory than do perpetual systems.[37]

As part of its overall inventory planning strategy, a firm must determine for each supply point–stocking[38] location pair on its network, whether to employ a periodic or perpetual inventory replenishment approach. Further, for any supply–stocking location pair, it is also feasible to install a mixed strategy utilizing a periodic replenishment approach for certain items and a perpetual approach for other items. In such mixed strategy situations, generally planners employ a perpetual system for higher volume, higher revenue, and profit-generating items (e.g., A items), and a periodic system for lower volume, low revenue-generating items (e.g., C items). The use of a perpetual system for A items minimizes the stockout and lost revenue risk for these key items.

3.7 Summary

In this chapter, we have explored numerous facets of inventory planning and management. We started with a review of the different inventory types, and the cost of investing in, and carrying inventory. Next, we considered a variety of commonly employed inventory metrics and concepts. An illustration and discussion of the importance of establishing a hierarchical product line structure to facilitate inventory planning over the entire planning horizon of a firm followed next. We then considered a planning approach for monitoring a firm's inventory levels, followed by a review of inventory replenishment systems. We will continue to discuss the impact and role of inventory in supply chain planning as we move on to manufacturing and other activities in later chapters.

Notes

1 Recall that the greater the number of DCs that a company utilizes to serve a market, the larger will be the firm's total inventory investment requirements, and consequently, the total warehouse storage space needed to house the inventory.
2 See ASCM Dictionary, 17th edition, 2022.
3 Note that while the descriptions of cycle, safety, in-transit, and seasonal inventories represent universally utilized terminology, there exist some minor variations in the nomenclature used by supply chain professionals to categorize the other inventory types shown in Figure 3.1. The interested reader is referred to Coyle et al. (2017), Bowersox et al. (2024), and Venkataraman and Pinto (2020) for good discussions of these minor descriptive variations.

4 The determination of a firm's inventory carrying costs represents a complex subject that we will summarize. The reader desiring a detailed explanation and illustration of how to determine the proper annual inventory carrying cost interest rate for a firm is referred to Stock and Lambert (2001) for an excellent treatment of this subject.
5 The annual average cost of a firm's inventory over a year is frequently based on the average of a firm's inventory level at the end of each of the four quarters in a year (i.e., an average of four data points), or a similar calculation. More precisely, it would be the average based on a firm's inventory level at the close of each business day in a year (e.g., about 250–365 data points, depending upon how many days a year a firm operates).
6 See Stock and Lambert (2001) for additional discussion of how a firm determines the interest rate to use internally for their inventory carrying cost interest rate.
7 Often this calculation is based on several years of data rather than just the most recent year.
8 ASCM defines inventory shrinkage as "reductions of actual quantities of items in stock, in process, or in transit. The loss may be caused by scrap, theft, deterioration, evaporation, and so forth" (17th edition, ASCM Dictionary, 2022).
9 Note that one can apply these two metrics to raw material, WIP, and finished goods inventories, although they are most commonly used to evaluate FGI.
10 Note that these calculations apply to any quantity of inventory – whether it represents the total units of inventory in a company, or an individual end item at a DC, plant, store, or other stocking location.
11 Weeks of supply are sometimes based on measures other than actual sales. For example, on a large-scale network, where some DCs act as intermediate storage locations for a firm and only ship FGI to the firm's customer-facing DCs, these intermediate DCs do not ship final sales to customers. Therefore, to measure the weeks supply of FGI that an intermediate DC stocks, one uses "total shipment quantities" to calculate weeks of supply. Similarly, days or weeks of supply of raw materials or WIP that a plant inventories to support future FGI production at its facility are calculated based on how many days or weeks of production the raw materials or WIP will facilitate.
12 In practice, the inventory management system would determine the safety stock requirements for each item at each DC (i.e., for each SKU). Each SKU would have a target fill rate in the system, and based on this target fill rate, and the historical demand and supply data in the system, a safety stock target (requirement) for each SKU would be established. The total safety stock inventory requirements would represent the total across the network for all SKUs (i.e., the sum of all the individual targets of each SKU).
13 (520,000 units / 52 weeks) × 10 weeks.
14 Recall this principle states that to serve a defined demand level on a fixed market (e.g., the U.S.), as the number of stocking locations decreases, the total network-wide inventory required to facilitate a planned target fill rate also decreases because of the "demand smoothing" effect. Specifically, consolidating demand into fewer locations has the effect of reducing the variability of demand experienced by each DC. Conversely, as the number of stocking locations increases, the total network inventory required also increases because the variability of demand at each DC rises.
15 Maister (1976) formulated the square root of n rule, and Zinn, Levy, and Bowersox (1989) later developed the portfolio effect model, a broader statistical model which extended the square root of n rule. See Bowersox et al. (2024) for an excellent, detailed discussion of the use of the square root of n model.
16 Source: ASCM Dictionary, 17th edition (2022).
17 ASCM Dictionary, 17th edition (2022).
18 COGS can be thought of as a firm's sales "stated at the firm's costs." This contrasts with "actual sales" (i.e., revenues), which are based on a firm's selling price to its customers.
19 That is, a firm's ending inventories on March 31st, June 30th, September 30th, and December 31st.
20 See Miller and Liberatore (2020), and Liberatore and Miller (2021), for extensive discussions and illustrations of frameworks and analytic techniques used in hierarchical supply chain and logistics planning.
21 Product families are most frequently used for tactical planning; however, they are sometimes also utilized at both the operational and strategic levels.
22 For examples of the development and use of product families in strategic and tactical planning applications, see Miller et al. (1996) and Miller and Liberatore (2021).
23 ASCM Dictionary, 17th edition (2022).
24 Or 80% of another criteria other than sales revenue such as inventory cost.

25 Appendix 3A presents a table (3A.1) which displays the individual data fields and formulas required to develop Table 3.5.
26 The "sales unit" is the unit by which a firm sells its product to its customers. For example, consumer products manufacturers typically measure unit sales by the number of cases sold to customers.
27 The ASCM defines cycle counting as

> An inventory accuracy audit technique in which inventory is counted on a cyclic schedule rather than once a year .... Most effective cycle counting systems require the counting of a certain number of items every workday, with each item counted at a prescribed frequency. The key purpose of cycle counting is to identify items in error, thus triggering research, identification, and elimination of the cause of the errors.

28 See Section 3.6 for a discussion of continuous replenishment systems.
29 Chapter 6 reviews customer segmentation strategies. Note that other criteria such as a customer's long-term growth prospects also play a role in the assignment of individual customers to a group.
30 Portions of this section are excerpted from Miller and Liberatore (2020).
31 A target inventory level is a predetermined inventory quantity that is high enough to provide a desired fill rate (e.g., 98%) on customer demand. Ultimately, target inventory levels must be established for all SKUs. However, firms generally set a target fill rate for a major grouping of its inventory (e.g., all "A" items), and then individually determine the actual inventory quantity required for each SKU in the grouping in order to produce the desired customer fill rate.
32 Particularly in situations where a firm believes it can deliver the same level of order cycle time and fill rate service to its customers, with alternative mixes of FGI, WIP, and raw materials; the strategy of maintaining a lower percentage of its total inventory in FGI and a higher percentage in WIP and/or raw materials may receive stronger consideration.
33 See Brown (1959, 1963, and 1967) and Rens and Kleijnon (1978).
34 We should note that there are also "single-period inventory models" which planners can use for products that are produced or ordered only once per season or per year. (That is, products that are not re-ordered and re-supplied to a stocking location on a standard, regular basis.) Products such as winter coats, Christmas trees, and other seasonal items fall into this category.
35 Whenever a perpetual or periodic inventory replenishment system generates an order for a SKU, there is usually a pre-determined, standard replenishment order quantity for each item. The well-known EOQ model (i.e., the economic order quantity model) is frequently utilized to establish this order quantity. The EOQ model determines the order quantity that minimizes the total inventory carrying costs and order placement costs associated with a SKU. The reader is referred to Bowersox et al. (2024), Chopra and Meindl (2016), and Venkataraman and Pinto (2020) for detailed reviews of the EOQ model and the mathematics underlying this model.
36 ASCM Dictionary, 17th edition (2022).
37 The higher average inventory in a periodic replenishment system is necessary because the time gap between when a SKU reaches its ROP and when that SKU is ordered requires that extra inventory be carried to cover that extra ordering lead time (i.e., the lead time between when the SKU drops to its ROP and when that SKU is ordered in a periodic replenishment system).
38 Any stocking location "receiving" inventory from a supply point.
39 For firms with several major divisions such as a company with pharmaceutical and consumer products divisions, a separate database for each major division is required.

Appendix 3A: The Development of a Database to Facilitate ABC Inventory Planning

To develop the ABC inventory classification scheme illustrated in section 3.4 requires that planners first develop a database of all the items in a firm's product line.[39] Table 3A.1 displays all the individual variables in columns 2–5, and 7, required to generate the four criteria displayed in columns 6 through 9 (of this table) that the ABC rankings were based on in section 3.4. Additionally, the formulas used to obtain the totals in columns 6, 8, and 9 are also provided.

TABLE 3A.1 Firm Data for ABC Classification Analysis – With Unit Costs and Formula

Three-Digit Product Code of Inventory Item	*Cost per Unit*	*Selling Price per Unit*	*Profit Margin per Unit*	*Current Inventory Level (units)*	*Annual Sales Revenue ($)*	*Annual Sales (units)*	*Annual Profits ($)*	*Inventory at Cost ($)*
128	$ 6.50	$ 10.00	$ 3.50	7,330	$ 231,000	23,100	$ 80,850	$ 28,875
292	$ 6.00	$ 10.00	$ 4.00	817	$ 20,000	2,000	$ 8,000	$ 2,769
336	$ 5.50	$ 10.00	$ 4.50	1,948	$ 67,000	6,700	$ 30,150	$ 8,504
349	$ 2.75	$ 5.00	$ 2.25	1,783	$ 21,000	4,200	$ 9,450	$ 2,665
368	$ 2.25	$ 5.00	$ 2.75	93,692	$ 1,400,000	280,000	$ 770,000	$ 121,154
440	$ 6.00	$ 10.00	$ 4.00	393	$ 21,000	2,100	$ 8,400	$ 2,908
469	$ 2.25	$ 5.00	$ 2.75	21,385	$ 400,000	80,000	$ 220,000	$ 34,615
480	$ 8.25	$ 15.00	$ 6.75	16,782	$ 700,000	46,667	$ 315,000	$ 74,038
499	$ 4.50	$ 10.00	$ 5.50	727	$ 18,000	1,800	$ 9,900	$ 1,869
658	$ 3.25	$ 5.00	$ 1.75	1,194	$ 20,700	4,140	$ 7,245	$ 3,105
664	$ 6.00	$ 10.00	$ 4.00	26,731	$ 1,000,000	100,000	$ 400,000	$ 115,385
667	$ 5.50	$ 10.00	$ 4.50	802	$ 19,000	1,900	$ 8,550	$ 2,412
668	$ 5.00	$ 10.00	$ 5.00	722	$ 21,000	2,100	$ 10,500	$ 2,423
669	$ 3.00	$ 5.00	$ 2.00	9,305	$ 140,000	28,000	$ 56,000	$ 19,385
712	$ 4.50	$ 10.00	$ 5.50	3,878	$ 141,000	14,100	$ 77,550	$ 12,202
716	$ 2.25	$ 5.00	$ 2.75	5,446	$ 59,000	11,800	$ 32,450	$ 6,127
771	$ 4.50	$ 10.00	$ 5.50	667	$ 20,800	2,080	$ 11,440	$ 2,160
803	$ 13.00	$ 20.00	$ 7.00	1,180	$ 62,000	3,100	$ 21,700	$ 9,300
883	$ 2.50	$ 5.00	$ 2.50	1,277	$ 20,500	4,100	$ 10,250	$ 2,365
956	$ 3.25	$ 5.00	$ 1.75	1,470	$ 18,000	3,600	$ 6,300	$ 2,700
Total				**197,530**	**$ 4,400,000**	**621,487**	**$ 2,093,735**	**$ 454,961**

Formulas:

Annual Sales Revenue ($) = (Selling Price per unit) × (Annual Sales in units)

Annual Profits ($) = (Profit Margin per unit) × (Annual Sales in units)

Inventory at Cost ($) = (Cost per unit) × (Current Inventory Level in units).

4

MANUFACTURING AND PRODUCTION PLANNING

Manufacturing and production planning encompasses a broad set of activities that span from the long-run strategic to the short-run operational. Further, firms must plan the production of materials ranging from raw materials and components, to WIP, to FGI. In this chapter, we review several planning applications which illustrate the type of analytic approaches that effective production planning requires.[1]

The chapter begins with an overview of general manufacturing capacity and production planning concepts and metrics. Next, we illustrate two applications where we explore the importance for production planning accuracy of carefully analyzing the relationship between end items and the product families that they (i.e., end items) comprise. We then turn to planning strategies that manufacturers may need to implement when their short-run production output levels cannot meet their customers' demand levels. The chapter concludes with a summary of the techniques illustrated in this chapter.

4.1 Manufacturing Capacity and Production Planning Concepts and Metrics

Manufacturers rank capacity and production planning among their most important activities. For a manufacturer to operate a successful, profitable business, first it must have the capacity to meet its customers' total demand, and then it must efficiently and effectively plan its production. In this section, we highlight several methods that firms employ to develop and execute production plans, and measures that they use to evaluate their manufacturing effectiveness and efficiency. This overview will provide general background before we explore specific production planning techniques.

Every manufacturing plant has a *design capacity*, as do each of the sub-operations and production processes within the plant. Design capacity represents the maximum output that any operation can produce, where "operation" refers to both the entire plant and each of its sub-processes. The design capacity of a plant is based on the "ideal" operating conditions where there is an assumed mix of demand for each product, a fixed maintenance schedule for each operation, the correct amount of labor always fully available, etc. Because factors such as the product mix demanded by customers, ongoing maintenance requirements, and

DOI: 10.4324/9781003585442-4

labor availability can significantly vary over time, plants frequently do not operate at design capacity.

Therefore, in recognition that plants often do not operate in ideal conditions, firms also calculate *effective capacity*. To determine a plant's maximum output capability, this measure accounts for factors such as changes in customers' product mix demands, the temporary unavailability of planned labor, and the need for unplanned maintenance and repair. For this reason, effective capacity is generally lower than design capacity.

Actual capacity or *actual output* is, as it sounds, the actual production completed by a plant. So, if a plant produced 1.2 million units (e.g., of automobiles) operating over a full year, that would be the facility's annual actual output and its average actual output per month would be 100,000 units.

The metrics of design capacity, effective capacity, and actual output facilitate the calculation of two commonly utilized manufacturing metrics: (1) *capacity efficiency* and (2) *capacity utilization*. Capacity efficiency compares a plant's actual output to its effective capacity, while capacity utilization measures actual output against design capacity.

To illustrate these measures, we consider the capacity analysis of a plant developed by a fictitious firm, XYZ Inc. Table 4.1 displays results from the firm's analysis of the plant's first 3 years of operation. The table shows the plant's design and effective annual capacities, the actual output produced, the capacity efficiency and utilization metrics, and their formulas.

While examining this table, note the following points:

- The effective capacity is lower than the design capacity, reflecting that effective capacity is based on actual conditions while design capacity is based on theoretical, ideal conditions.
- The plant had a lower effective capacity in its third year of operations than its first two years. *The following scenario illustrates just one example of why this might occur.*

<u>Illustrative Scenario Where a Plant's Annual Effective Capacity Might Change</u>

1 A firm builds a new plant which has five production lines that produce three groups of products.
2 Each production line of the plant can produce all three product groups, and the production rates per day on these lines are as follows:[2]

  - 100 units of Product Group A, or
  - 150 units of Product Group B, or
  - 200 units of Product Group C

TABLE 4.1 Capacity Analysis of XYZ Inc.'s Manufacturing Plant

Decision Data	*Year 1*	*Year 2*	*Year 3*
Annual Design Capacity (in units)	100,000	100,000	100,000
Annual Effective Capacity (in units)	94,000	94,000	92,000
Actual Output (in units)	85,000	80,000	83,000
Annual Plant Capacity Analysis	*Year 1*	*Year 2*	*Year 3*
Capacity Efficiency = (actual output / effective capacity)	90.4%	85.1%	90.2%
Capacity Utilization = (actual output / design capacity)	85.0%	80.0%	83.0%

3 When the plant was constructed, it was projected that the total demand on the plant would be split equally across the three product groups.
4 In Year 1, the total units of actual customer orders were equally divided across the three product groups as expected.
5 However, beginning in Year 2, and continuing into Year 3 and on, the product mix demanded by customers changed. The demand in units for Products A and B was about 80% of total demand, while the demand for units of Product C dropped to approximately 20% of the total.

In the scenario just described, clearly the effective capacity of the plant would decrease after Year 1. This would result because beginning in Year 2, the plant's total units produced per day would diminish as the facility would have to allocate a higher proportion of total available production hours to manufacturing Products A and B, and fewer hours to producing Product C than originally planned.[3] (Recall that each production line at the plant can produce Product C at a rate of 200 units per hour, while they can produce Products A and B at just 100 and 150 units per hour, respectively.)

In summary, capacity utilization and efficiency rates are heavily utilized and scrutinized metrics. The profitability and success of a manufacturing operation depend upon running a facility at neither too low nor too high a rate. A highly underutilized plant is costly to operate because its relatively low production output will not generate sufficient revenue to cover its costs. Conversely, a highly overutilized plant remains vulnerable to potential costly issues such as reduced productivity due to overcrowding, increased levels of machine breakdowns, higher maintenance costs, and so on. The optimal level of plant utilization varies by industry, firm, type of production technology and machinery, software systems support, etc. In general, however, many manufacturers target capacity utilization rates between 80% and 85%, plus or minus a few percent,[4] although, as noted, targets do vary.

Production and Capacity Planning Tools

Numerous well-known production and capacity planning methods abound, with many available to users via commercial software packages. While it is beyond our scope to review these tools in detail, we offer a good set of starting references below for the reader interested in exploring this subject further.[5] Additionally, Exhibit 4.1 provides brief descriptions of four key, heavily utilized manufacturing capacity and production planning methods used in industry. Figure 4.1 then describes pictorially how production planners employ these four tools together to develop synchronized finished good end item and materials production schedules.

EXHIBIT 4.1 KEY PRODUCTION AND CAPACITY PLANNING TOOLS

CRP: *Capacity Requirements Planning* – The function of establishing, measuring, and adjusting limits or levels of capacity. In this context, the term refers to the process of determining in detail the amount of labor and machine resources required to accomplish the tasks of production.

MPS: *Master Production Scheduling* – A line on the master schedule grid that reflects the anticipated build schedule for those items assigned to the master scheduler. The master scheduler maintains this schedule, and in turn, it becomes a set of planning numbers that drives material requirements planning. It represents what the company plans to produce, expressed in specific configurations, quantities, and dates.

MRP: *Material Requirements Planning* – A set of techniques that uses bill of material data, inventory data, and the master production schedule (MPS) to calculate requirements for materials.... It is time phased, and ... begins with the items listed on the MPS and determines (1) the quantity of all components and materials required to fabricate those items and (2) the date that the components and material are required.

RCCP: *Rough-Cut Capacity Planning* – The process of converting the master production schedule into requirements for key resources, often including labor; machinery; warehouse space; suppliers' capabilities; and, in some cases, money. Comparison with available or demonstrated capacity is usually done for each key resource.

Source: ASCM Dictionary, 17th edition (2022).

4.2 Balancing Manufacturing and Inventory Carrying Costs in Production Planning and Scheduling

Manufacturing scheduling decisions require planners to balance multiple costs and service levels when determining the best production schedule. The trade-off between manufacturing costs and inventory carrying costs is one of the most common of these balancing acts. In this section, we explore this trade-off first through an illustrative production planning problem for a fictitious tile company, and then by reviewing the well-known economic production quantity (EPQ) model.

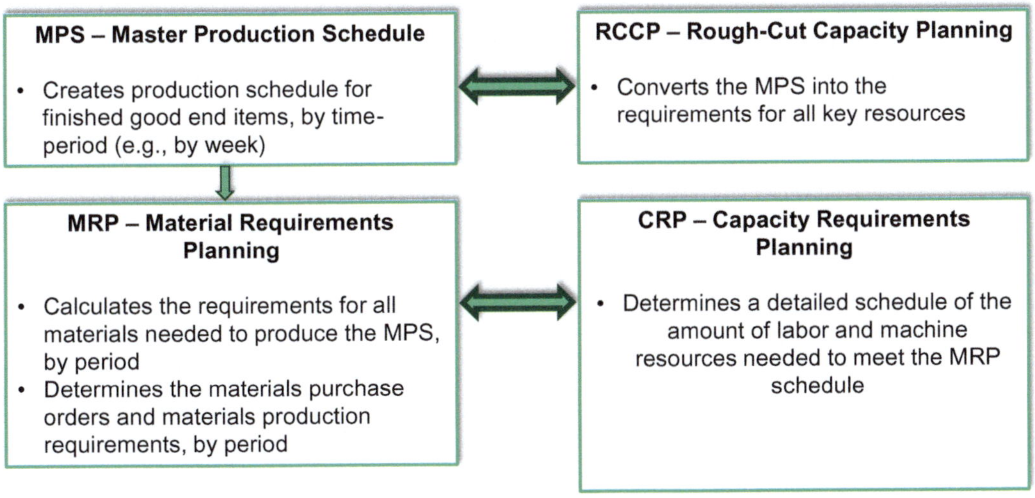

FIGURE 4.1 How Planners Create Production and Material Requirements Schedules Using MPS, RCCP, MRP, and CRP Systems.

Manufacturing Planning Problem: Production vs. Inventory Carrying Costs

PDQ Tile Company produces three major sizes of ceramic tile: 2" × 2", 6" × 6", and 12" × 12". The firm's plant has a single production line which can produce one major size at a time. PDQ offers 20 different colors of each size, and can switch over from producing one color of a size (e.g., 6 × 6 blue tile) to a second color (e.g., 6 × 6 red tile) with a simple wash-up and changeover on the production line during the workers 20-minute morning or afternoon breaks. However, the changeover to switch production from one major size to another (e.g., switching from 6 × 6 to 2 × 2) necessitates shutting down the line for an extended period, as it requires bringing in special labor to set up the machine tooling that produces the new size. Thus, a changeover and setup of a major size represents a significant fixed manufacturing cost.

PDQ's production planners must decide how many production runs of each size they will schedule next year. They have two options:

1 produce each major size twice next year or
2 produce each major size just one time next year

Option (1) would require the plant to run two 2-month production lots of each size, rotating through a schedule of 2 × 2, 6 × 6, and 12 × 12 twice. For example, the first 2 × 2 lot would run from the beginning of January until the end of February, and the second 2 × 2 lot would run during July and August. Option (2) would mean that each size would have a single 4-month production run. PDQ's production planners have developed the appropriate data, displayed in Table 4.2, to evaluate their two production options.

Table 4.2 indicates that option (2), producing each size once per year, has a higher average inventory level than does option (1) where the firm manufactures each size twice per year. *We point this out because an important aspect of supply chain analytics is evaluating whether one's data makes sense intuitively.* If the data a planner has developed does not seem directionally correct (i.e., is not intuitive), additional review of the data is required before the analysis proceeds – because this may be a clue that there was an error in the data development process.

In this example, we can intuitively explain the directional difference in the average inventory levels of the two options as follows:

TABLE 4.2 Data for Production Cost vs. Inventory Cost Trade-Off Problem

Decision Support Data	
Fixed Cost per Production Line Changeover and Setup (S)	\$ 2,000
Variable Cost per Unit Produced	\$ 40
Annual Inventory Carrying Cost per Unit (ICC)*	\$ 10
Annual Demand for Each Tile Size (units)	1,000
Number of Tile Sizes	3
Annual Average Inventory If Plant Produces Each Size Once per Year (units)	500
Annual Average Inventory If Plant Produces Each Size Twice per Year (units)	250

* The annual inventory carrying cost per unit would be determined by multiplying the firm's cost per unit to produce a piece of tile by the firm's annual inventory carrying cost interest rate.

- If the plant produces each size once per year, then whenever a production run of a size ends, there must be sufficient inventory of that size to meet customer demand for the next 8 months, or the plant will stock out.
- For example, if the plant produces 2 × 2 tile from January until the end of April, then the next 2 × 2 production run will not begin until the following January (i.e., 8 months later).
- On the other hand, if the plant produces each size twice per year, when a production run of one size ends, then another run of the same size will begin 4 months later.
- Thus, the shorter lead time between production run cycles of a size when producing each size twice per year enables the firm to maintain a lower average inventory than when it produces each size only once per year.

Table 4.3 displays the analytical results of the cost comparison of the two manufacturing options.

The table indicates that a production strategy of producing each major tile size twice per year has a lower overall cost; and, therefore, represents the better scheduling option.[6] The table shows that while producing each size twice per year results in higher annual total manufacturing costs, the savings from the lower annual inventory carrying costs of this alternative outweigh its greater production costs. Thus, by choosing the manufacture twice per year option, PDQ Tile will trade off (i.e., incur) higher production costs to realize even greater annual inventory carrying cost savings.

A review of the individual manufacturing costs in Table 4.3 reveals the following important point: the variable manufacturing costs are identical under both alternatives. In this tile production example, the variable cost components would include materials, labor, and any other input that is required to produce each unit of tile. Variable manufacturing costs are those that vary (i.e., increase) with each additional unit produced. For example, each unit of tile produced requires a certain amount of clay, as well as the other material inputs that are molded into a piece of tile and then heated in a kiln to form a finished unit of tile. In contrast, fixed manufacturing costs do not vary with the level of output. For example, the costs to changeover from one major size to another (i.e., to set up the line to produce the new size) do not vary or depend on the length of the production runs that precede and follow a changeover. For this reason, it is possible to exclude variable manufacturing costs from the decisions (i.e., from the analysis) of the quantity to produce during a production run.[7] If we eliminate variable manufacturing costs from the analysis in Table 4.3, we arrive at the same decision, namely, that producing each size twice per year represents the lower cost option by $1,500. Table 4.4 illustrates that while our analysis no longer determines total annual manufacturing costs, it does correctly identify the annual savings of the twice per year option, which also then facilitates the calculation of the production lot quantity that PDQ should run for each tile size. In the next section, we study the economic production quantity (EPQ) model, a production lot sizing tool that does not include variable manufacturing costs for the reasons just described.

The Economic Production Quantity (EPQ) Model

The EPQ model, a heavily utilized production planning decision support tool, can determine the optimal quantity of a product that should be produced regularly on a production line, in multiple production runs throughout the year. This simple mathematical optimization model determines the production quantity (i.e., lot size) that minimizes the total annual manufacturing

TABLE 4.3 Manufacturing Planning Trade-Off Problem: Production Costs vs. Inventory Carrying Costs

Annual Costs	*Production Frequency Options*	
	Produce Each Size Once per Year	*Produce Each Size Twice per Year*
Fixed Manufacturing Setup Costs – (Cost per Setup × Number of Setups × Number of Sizes)	$ 6,000	$ 12,000
Variable Manufacturing Costs – (Variable Cost per Unit × Annual Demand per Size × Number of Sizes)	$ 120,000	$ 120,000
Total Manufacturing Costs – (Variable Mfg Costs + Fixed Mfg Costs)	$ 126,000	$ 132,000
Inventory Carrying Costs – (Inventory Holding Cost per Unit × Average Units of Inventory × Number of Sizes)	$ 15,000	$ 7,500
Total Manufacturing and Inventory Carrying Costs – (Total Mfg Costs + Invcc)	$ 141,000	$ 139,500

TABLE 4.4 Manufacturing Planning Trade-Off Problem: Production Costs vs. Inventory Carrying Costs (Without Variable Manufacturing Costs)

Annual Costs	*Production Frequency Options*	
	Produce Each Size Once per Year	*Produce Each Size Twice per Year*
Fixed Manufacturing Setup Costs – (Cost per Setup × Number of Setups × Number of Sizes)	$ 6,000	$ 12,000
Inventory Carrying Costs – (Inventory Holding Cost per Unit × Average Units of Inventory × Number of Sizes)	$ 15,000	$ 7,500
Total Fixed Manufacturing and Inventory Carrying Costs – (Fixed Mfg Costs + Invcc)	$ 21,000	$ 19,500
Implied Production Lot Size Quantity for Each Size		
Annual Demand (units)	1,000	1,000
Production Lot Size Quantity for Each Size (units) – (Annual Demand / Number of Production Runs per Year)	1,000	500

setup and inventory carrying costs that will result from producing a product on the production line. The EPQ model does make a number of assumptions that must hold for the model to function correctly, and the reader is referred to Venkataraman and Pinto (2020), and Chopra and Meindl (2016), for more details on this model and its limitations. For our purposes, in this section we want to develop a basic understanding of how the EPQ model works because it is an instructive planning tool that illuminates the importance of balancing annual production setup costs and inventory carrying costs.

To understand the EPQ model, we first briefly discuss the model formula, and then offer more detailed explanations of this model in Exhibits 4.2 and 4.3. Finally, this section closes with an illustrative production lot sizing planning problem that contrasts a scheduling solution based on the EPQ model with two non-EPQ-based solutions.

For a production line that will manufacture a product on a regular basis over a year, the EPQ model calculates the optimal production quantity that will minimize:

- *Total annual fixed setup costs + annual inventory carrying costs*

The following notation and formula describe the EPQ model.

Let:

- D = the annual demand for a product in units,
- *d* = the daily demand rate for this product in units,
- *p* = the daily production rate in units when the product is being manufactured,
- S = the fixed cost to set up the production line to produce the product,
- ICC = the annual inventory carrying cost per unit,[8] and
- Q = the optimal production quantity in units (i.e., the economic production quantity)

The actual EPQ formula is:

- sqrt [(2 × D × S) / ICC] × sqrt [*p* / (*p*/*d*)]

This is not an intuitively obvious formula, and as noted, Exhibits 4.2 and 4.3 provide detailed explanations of the EPQ model. (The reader not interested in this detail can skip these exhibits and go directly to the illustrative production lot size problem that follows these exhibits). Exhibit 4.2 describes how the inventory costs are calculated in the EPQ model, while Exhibit 4.3 addresses the setup costs, and shows how the optimization formula is derived.

EXHIBIT 4.2 HOW ANNUAL INVENTORY CARRYING COSTS ARE MEASURED IN THE EPQ MODEL

- To calculate inventory carrying costs, we first must determine the average inventory quantity that is held. The following steps describe the individual components that collectively calculate the average inventory held over a production run – given a production quantity Q that is manufactured during the production run.

1. The EPQ model determines the optimal production quantity Q.
2. For illustrative purposes, assume for a minute that there was no demand for the product during the production run. So, we would start a production run with an inventory quantity of 0, and by the end of the production run, we would have Q units of inventory. Therefore, the average inventory over the days of the production run would be Q/2.

3 However, there is demand during the production run and the daily rate of demand is *d*. Therefore, Q/2 is not a good estimate of the average inventory during the production run and we must account for daily demand.
4 The production rate per day is *p*, and as noted the demand rate per day is *d*. Therefore, during the production run, inventory will increase daily at the rate of (*p*-*d*) units.[9]
5 Since inventory will increase daily during the production run at a rate of (*p*-*d*) units, and *p* is greater than *d*; the percent of daily production that is not consumed by daily demand is (*p*-*d*)/*p*. In other words, (*p*-*d*)/*d* can be thought of as the percent of daily production that goes into inventory each day of the production run.
6 In step 2, we observed that if there was no demand, then Q/2 would represent the average inventory over a production run. From step 5, we now know that (*p*-*d*)/*p* is the percent of each day's production that goes into inventory.
7 Therefore, to estimate average inventory in units during a production run, we utilize the following expression[10]:

- (Q/2) × [(*p*-*d*)/*p*].

8 Finally, annual inventory carrying costs are calculated as:

- ICC × (Q/2) × [(*p*-*d*)/*p*].

EXHIBIT 4.3 HOW ANNUAL SETUP COSTS ARE CALCULATED, AND THE EPQ OPTIMIZATION FORMULA IS DERIVED

Setup Costs

1 The number of setups per year on a production line equals the total annual demand divided by the production quantity, or D/Q.
2 Thus, annual setup costs = S × (D/Q).

Derivation of the EPQ Formula

3 The EPQ is the production quantity per lot that will minimize total annual setup costs + inventory carrying costs:

- minimize: [S × (D/Q)] + [ICC × (Q/2) × ((*p*-*d*)/*p*)].

4 It can be shown that the value of Q that will minimize total costs occurs when:[11]

- annual setup costs = annual inventory carrying costs or
- S × (D/Q) = ICC × (Q/2) × ((*p*-*d*)/*p*).

5 We rearrange the terms in the equation in step 4, and solve for Q, yielding the EPQ formula:

- Q = sqrt [(2 × D × S) / ICC] × sqrt [*p*/(*p*/*d*)].

A Lot Size Production Planning Problem

To conclude our discussion of the need to balance annual fixed setup costs and inventory carrying costs when formulating manufacturing schedules, we compare the results of production schedules based upon two different production policies and the EPQ model. Table 4.5 presents the decision data, as well as the production, inventory, and cost analyses for this problem.

In this table, a production planner considers the following three scheduling options for producing a product on a production line next year:

1 produce the product once per month (column 2),
2 produce the product twice per month (column 3), or
3 use the EPQ model to determine lot size and run frequency

In the *decision support data* section, the planner has collected the data required to evaluate these three options. The *production analysis* section displays the different production quantities of the lot sizes that the scheduling policies and the EPQ model generate. Note that while the number of production runs per year is "predetermined" for the once and twice per month policies, utilizing the EPQ model, the planner calculates (i.e., backs into) the number of runs per year after determining the optimal production quantity.

In the *cost analysis* section, we observe that the production lot size quantity recommended by the EPQ model (60,000 units) projects the lowest annual costs of the three alternatives. Exhibit 4.3 noted that to minimize the sum of total annual setup costs and inventory carrying costs, the EPQ model finds the scheduling solution (i.e., the production quantity Q) where annual production setup costs equal annual inventory carrying costs.[12] Notice in the cost analysis section that the EPQ optimization model solution results in annual costs of $400,000 each for the production setup and inventory carrying costs. In contrast, the two non-optimization model-based policies to produce once and twice a month result in non-balanced, more expensive total costs as the following recap of Table 4.5 depicts:

Production Plan or Cost	*Produce Once per Month*	*Produce Twice per Month*	*EPQ Model*
Production lot quantity in units	100,000	50,000	60,000
Number of production runs per yr	12	24	20
Annual production setup costs	$240,000	$480,000	$400,000
Annual inventory carrying costs	$666,667	$333,333	$400,000
Total production + inv carrying costs	$906,667	$813,333	$800,000

Producing the product once per month results in lower annual setup costs but creates relatively higher inventory carrying costs; while conversely, producing twice per month generates comparatively lower annual inventory carrying costs but generates higher setup costs.

As noted at the outset of this section, the EPQ model is a heavily utilized production planning decision support tool. It provides strong guidance to production planners on the appropriate production quantity lot sizes to schedule. More generally, the inherent trade-offs between production setup and inventory carrying costs that the EPQ model evaluates are representative of the constant balancing between different costs required in decision-making throughout supply chain analytics.

TABLE 4.5 Planning Production Lot Sizes

Decision Support Data	*Policy or Model Used to Determine: (1) How Frequently to Produce a Product on a Production Line, or (2) the Production Lot Size for the Product*		
	Produce the Product Once per Month (i.e., 12 times per year)	*Produce the Product Twice per Month (i.e., 24 times per year)*	*Calculate the Economic Production Quantity (EPQ)*
Annual Demand (D)	1,200,000	1,200,000	1,200,000
Business Days (i.e., Production and Selling Days) per Year[1]	300	300	300
Daily Demand (d)	4,000	4,000	4,000
Production Rate per Day (p)	12,000	12,000	12,000
Cost per Production Line Setup (S)	$ 20,000	$20,000	$20,000
Annual Inventory Carrying Cost per Unit (ICC)	$ 20	$20	$20
Production Analysis			
Production Lot Size Quantity (Q)*	100,000	50,000	60,000
Number of Times per Year to Produce the Product (i.e., number of setups needed per year) – **(D/Q)**	12	24	20
Inventory Analysis			
Average Inventory Level Carried Over the Production Run – *If There Was No Daily Demand* – **(Q/2)**	50,000	25,000	30,000
The Increase in Inventory Each Day During the Production Run – *Accounting for the Daily Demand Each Day* – **(p-d)**	8,000	8,000	8,000
The Percent of Inventory Produced Each Day That Is Not Consumed by That Day's Demand – **(p-d)/p**	66.7%	66.7%	66.7%
The Estimated Average Inventory Over the Entire Number of Days Required to Complete the Production Lot – **(Q/2) × ((p-d)/p)**	33,333	16,667	20,000
Cost Analysis			
Annual Production Setup Costs**	$ 240,000	$ 480,000	$ 400,000
Annual Inventory Carrying Costs***	$ 666,667	$ 333,333	$ 400,000
Total Annual Production and Inventory Carrying Costs	$ 906,667	$ 813,333	$ 800,000

Additional Formulas

* Production Lot Size Quantity for the EPQ Column = Sqrt[(2×D×S)/ICC] × Sqrt [p/(p/d)]

* Production Lot Size Quantity for the Produce Once and Twice per Month Columns = (D / number of production runs per year)

** Annual Production Setup Costs = (S × number of production runs per year)

*** Annual Inventory Carrying Costs = ICC × Estimated Average Inventory over the Production Run Cycle

1 In the EPQ model, p and q must be defined in the same unit of time (see Venkatamaran and Pinto, 2020). We assume the example firm's plant and selling locations (e.g., its stores and/or DCs) both operate 300 days per year (6 days per week for most weeks except for the Thanksgiving and Christmas weeks, and several other weeks with national holidays).

4.3 Integrating End Item Production Scheduling and Long-Run Product Family Production Planning

Effective and efficient manufacturing operations require close integration between long-run planning and short-run production scheduling. There are large bodies of research and literature on hierarchical supply chain and production planning, which is a field of study devoted to the development of planning frameworks and techniques to integrate long-run planning and short-run scheduling.

Before reviewing several examples of techniques used in practice to link short-run end item scheduling with long-run production planning, we offer a brief overview of hierarchical production planning (HPP). This provides the context and background for the detailed discussion of several short-run/long-run "linking" methodologies that will follow afterwards.[13]

Hierarchical Production Planning (HPP)[14]

HPP spans a firm's entire planning horizon from the strategic, to the tactical, to the operational planning and scheduling levels. Figure 4.2 presents a hierarchical manufacturing and distribution planning framework.[15] At this point in the planning process, business strategic

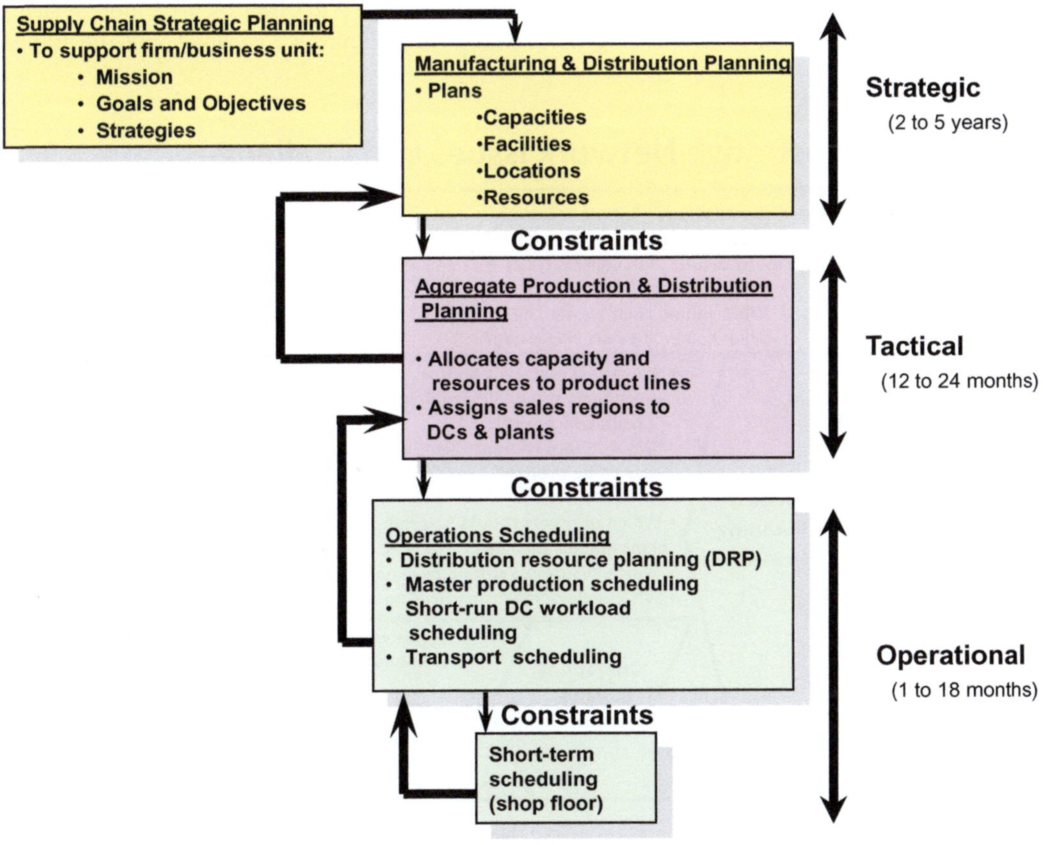

FIGURE 4.2 A Hierarchical Manufacturing and Distribution Planning Framework.

plans have been developed and approved, as have the high-level strategic plans of the overall supply chain organization. Now the manufacturing and distribution functions commence their own strategic planning processes to support the overall supply chain and business unit strategies.

At the strategic planning level, manufacturing must address such issues as planned production capacity levels for the next two years and beyond, the number of facilities it plans to operate, their locations, the resources it will assign to its manufacturing operations, and numerous other important long-term decisions. Similar decisions must be made for distribution facilities and resources. Decisions made at the strategic level place constraints on the tactical planning level. At the tactical level, typical planning activities include the allocation of capacity and resources to product lines for the next 12–24 months, aggregate planning of workforce levels, the development or fine-tuning of distribution plans, and numerous other activities. Within the constraints of the firm's manufacturing and distribution infrastructure (an infrastructure determined by previous strategic decisions) managers make tactical planning decisions designed to optimize the use of the existing infrastructure. Planning decisions carried out at the tactical level impose constraints upon operational planning and scheduling decisions. At this level, activities such as distribution resource planning (DRP), rough-cut capacity planning, master production scheduling, shop floor control scheduling, and many other decisions occur.

The hierarchical manufacturing and distribution planning (HMD) framework presented in Figure 4.2 is generic in that although individual HMD systems will differ by firm, most systems are designed within this or a similar general framework. Figure 4.3 recaps some illustrative

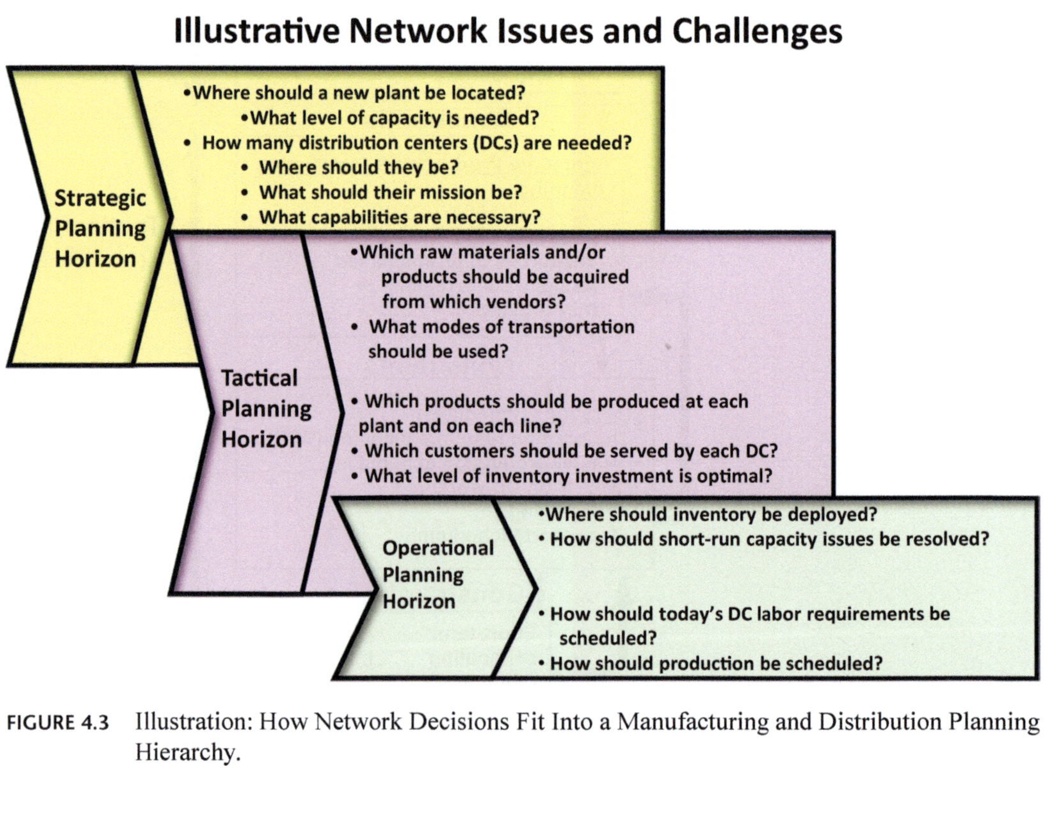

FIGURE 4.3 Illustration: How Network Decisions Fit Into a Manufacturing and Distribution Planning Hierarchy.

generic decisions that an HMD system constructed within this framework will generally address and it displays how these decisions fit into a planning hierarchy. As several of the illustrative decisions in Figure 4.3 imply, HMD systems typically extend beyond a firm's internal operations to include decisions about suppliers and customers.

This completes our brief background review of HPP, and we now turn to several illustrative HPP techniques for linking short-run and longer-run planning, as well as issues that can arise – if planners do not employ appropriate "linking" analytic tools.

Product Family Production Planning Background

Manufacturing and distribution firms with thousands of unique finished good end items typically develop their annual or tactical production and distribution plans at an aggregated product level. As discussed in Chapter 2, numerous reasons exist for this planning approach, not the least of which is that it is often simply not practical or productive to develop long-run plans (e.g., 12–18 months) for thousands of individual end items. By aggregating end items into product families, a planner can avoid creating models of unmanageable or mathematically intractable size. Figure 4.4 illustrates the levels of product aggregation which we assume. One can observe that end items tree up into product families, and product families then tree up into product lines. The examples presented later in this section will assume that the firm's annual production planning model defines products at the product family level (level 3 in Figure 4.4).

Product families are created based upon the similarity of one or more key commonly shared characteristics of each end item within a family. In a production planning industry application for which the author developed a detailed mathematical algorithm that incorporates the logic shown in the example that will follow, all end items within each family had virtually identical production rates and production costs. Additionally, to group a set of end items into one product family, the following requirement was also applied: any production line at any plant in the

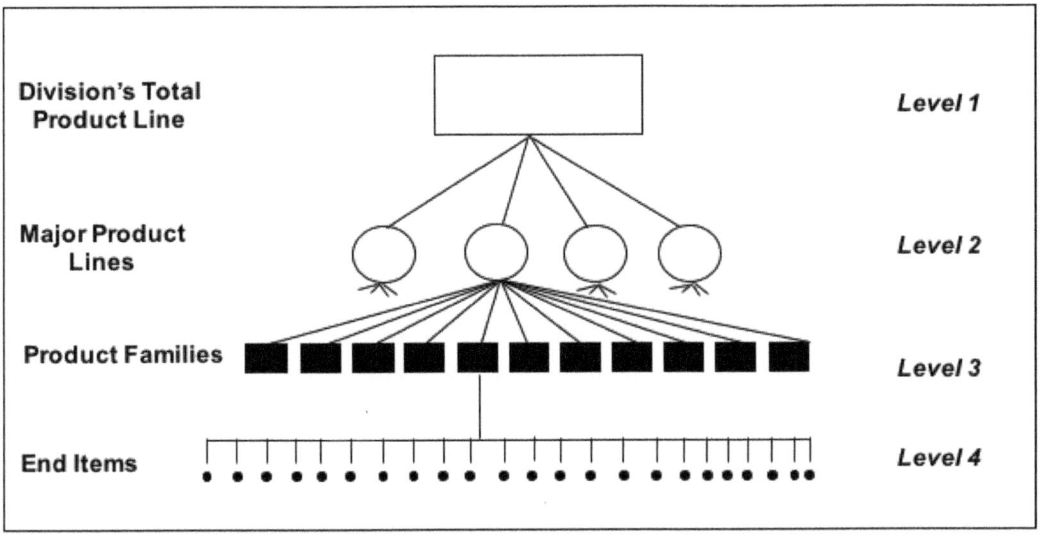

FIGURE 4.4 Product Line Structure.

firm's network that was defined as capable of producing a particular product family had to be able to produce every end item in that product family. This restriction assured that if a long-term production plan (e.g., a 12-month annual plan) assigned a product family to a production line, that production line had the capability to manufacture whatever end items in the product family customers might demand from it. Depending upon the planning application, there exist many other characteristics and constraints that one may have to consider when formulating product families for production planning. However, the preceding example depicts the types of considerations that the process of formulating product families must address.

Potential Product Family – End Item Disconnect That Planning Process Must Address: Example 1

For illustrative purposes, assume that a firm is developing a 12-month product family production plan for its entire network of manufacturing plants. This plan will specify family production assignments (i.e., production quantities and weeks of production) by plant, by production line, and by product family. Inputs that the firm's planners require include a forecast of demand by product family for the next year, and the current inventory level of each product family.

To determine *net production requirements* for the next 12 months, planners must subtract the current inventory of each product family from the projected annual demand for that product family. This will yield the actual net production requirements for each product family. The firm bases its annual production plan on these product family net requirements, rather than total demand. If the firm did not plan production based on net requirements, the inventory of a product family that currently has excessive levels well above target would remain in this costly, overstocked inventory position over the next 12-month planning horizon.[16]

To develop the beginning inventory data for each product family in the planning model, planners sum the current inventory of each item in a product family. This aggregation process generates the beginning inventory for each product family in the production planning model.

The following section will illustrate the need for a manufacturer to evaluate its inventory at the end item level across its entire network, in order to determine the correct product family beginning inventory level inputs to its annual production planning process. We will observe that determining the net production requirements of end items first (i.e., before developing product family beginning inventories) yields the correct product family beginning inventory planning data. The section includes an example of a mathematical algorithm required to ensure synchronization between current manufacturing/distribution network operating conditions and annual/tactical production planning.

Why Is It Critical to Incorporate End Item Inventory Positions into Annual Product Family Level Production Plans?

It is necessary to evaluate current end item inventory positions over the entire manufacturing/distribution network in order to assure that the firm's annual manufacturing plans do not underestimate total production requirements. Inventory data, when developed at the product family level (rather than at the end item level), can provide misleading information leading to this underestimation of capacity requirements in long-run planning models.

To illustrate this, assume we are planning the annual production requirements of a product family that has five individual end items. Let us now consider the production requirements over a planning horizon for this product family when evaluated at two different levels of inventory aggregation: the end item level and the product family level. To measure the utility of a product family's current inventory, we require two definitions:

"Useable" inventory over the planning horizon is the minimum of:[17]

1 (forecast annual sales over the planning horizon) + (the end-of-period inventory target) or
2 The current (i.e., beginning-of-period) inventory

"Excess" inventory over the planning horizon is the maximum of:[18]

1 (current or beginning-of-period inventory) – (useable inventory over the planning horizon) or
2 0

A comparison of Figures 4.5 and 4.6 reveals that the projected total production requirements over the planning horizon can vary substantially depending upon whether one evaluates requirements at the end item level (column 5, Figure 4.5 – 11,000), or at the product family level (column 4, Figure 4.6 – 8,000). Further, the firm will underestimate its true production capacity requirements if it evaluates inventory at the product family level. In this example, the underestimate of capacity needs will occur because end item 5 has an extreme surplus of inventory which masks the current inventory deficits in items 1 through 4 of this family. Because item 5's current inventory exceeds the sum of its annual selling rate plus inventory target by 3,000 units, the firm will still have an inventory excess of 3,000 units in this item at the end of its 12-month planning horizon. To plan production requirements accurately, the firm must recognize that it has 3,000 units of inventory in item 5 (and therefore in item 5's product family) which it cannot utilize over the planning horizon. For production planning purposes, including these 3,000 units in the product family's current inventory figure will overstate the true level of inventory "useable over the planning horizon" for this product family. Thus, the number displayed in column 6 of Figure 4.5 (8,000), rather

Total Production Requirements Over Planning Horizon (When Evaluated at End-Item Level)

(1)	*(2)*	*(3)*	*(4)*	*(5)*	*(6)*	*(7)*
End Item	*Beginning Inventory Position*	*Annual Selling Rate*	*End of Planning Horizon Inventory Target*	*Total Production Required Over Next 12 Months*[a]	*Useable Inventory Over Planning Horizon*[b]	*Excess Inventory Over Planning Horizon*[c]
1	400	2,000	400	2,000	400	0
2	200	3,000	600	3,400	200	0
3	100	1,000	200	1,100	100	0
4	300	4,000	800	4,500	300	0
5	10,000	6,000	1,000	0	7,000	3,000
Total	**11,000**	**16,000**	**3,000**	**11,000**	**8,000**	**3,000**

FIGURE 4.5 Evaluating Beginning Inventory at Item Level.

a) Calculation for column (5) = maximum of: [column (3)+column (4)–column (2), or 0]
b) Calculation for column (6) = minimum of: [column (2),or column (3)+column (4)]
c) Calculation for column (7) = maximum of: [column (2)–column (6),or 0]

* The planning horizon in this example is the next twelve months.
* Numbers in the "Total" row are the sum of the 5 individual item numbers above them.

Total Production Requirements Over Planning Horizon (When Evaluated at Product Family Level)					
(1)	*(2)*	*(3)*	*(4)*	*(5)*	*(6)*
Beginning Inventory Position	*Annual Selling Rate*	*End of Planning Horizon Inventory Target*	*Total Production Required Over Next 12 Months*[a]	*Useable Inventory Over Planning Horizon*[b]	*Excess Inventory Over Planning Horizon*[c]
11,000	16,000	3,000	8,000	11,000	0

FIGURE 4.6 Evaluating Beginning Inventory at Product Family Level.

a) calculation for column (4) = maximum of: [column (2) + column (3) − column (1), or 0]
b) calculation for column (5) = minimum of: [column (1), or column (2) + column (3)]
c) calculation for column (6) = maximum of: [column (1) − column (5), or 0]
* The planning horizon in this example is the next twelve months.

than the number in column 5 of Figure 4.6 (11,000), represents the proper quantity to use as this family's "beginning-of-period inventory" in an annual production planning model. Obviously for other reasons (e.g., financial, special marketing programs, etc.), one must account for this product family's excess inventory (over the planning horizon) in other planning areas.

The example in Figure 4.6 illustrates that evaluating inventory positions (and production requirements) at the product family level makes it impossible to recognize if there is any excess or unusable inventory (over the planning horizon) in any of the end items within the product family. By using the approach shown in Figure 4.5, namely, evaluating inventory positions and production requirements at the end item level, and then summing the end item results to obtain product family requirements, one can accurately evaluate a product family's current level of "useable" inventory over the planning horizon.

Algorithm to Determine Useable and Excess Inventory Over a Planning Horizon

The example in Figure 4.5 demonstrates the calculation of useable and excess inventory over the planning horizon for a stand-alone, one-location manufacturing/distribution network. In the real world of multi-location networks, the determination of proper useable and excess inventory data for product families becomes more complex. However, the same basic logic used for the one-location network can be extended to a multi-location, multi-echelon network.[19]

This section has presented a simplistic, yet effective algorithm for developing beginning-of-period inventory data at the product family level for use in production/distribution planning models. Developing beginning-of-period product family inventory data using the approach described here creates the necessary link between long-run production planning and short-run, current inventory conditions.

Potential Product Family – End Item Disconnect That Planning Process Must Address: Example 2

Our second example of the need for linkages between long-run product family production planning and end item production scheduling again involves a firm creating a 12-month

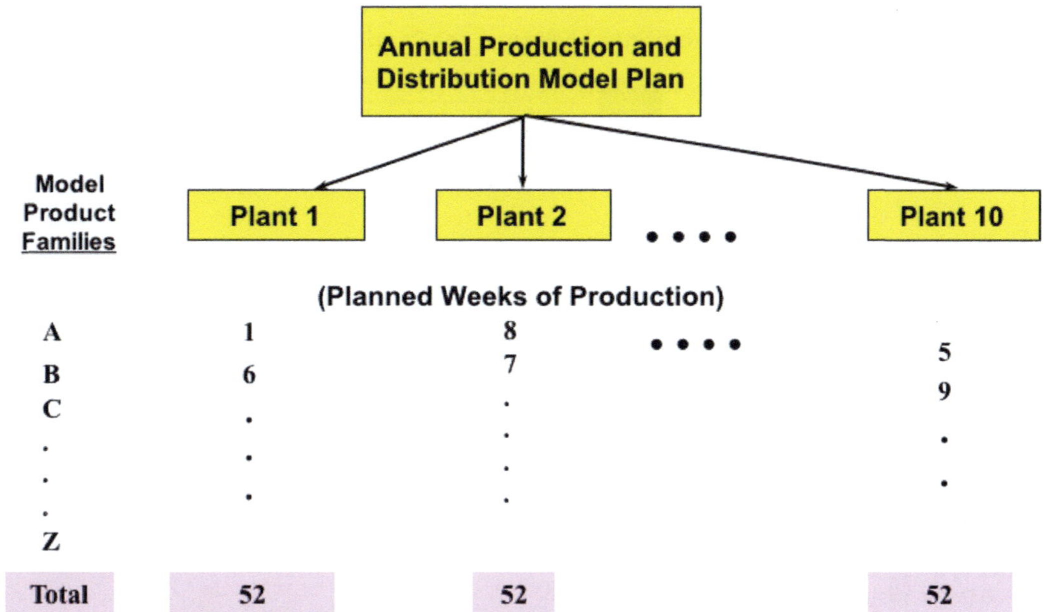

FIGURE 4.7 Illustrative Annual Production Plan Created by the Plant/DC/Family Optimization Model.

production plan at the product family level for each plant in a network. Figure 4.7 displays a network-wide annual production plan that for illustrative purposes we will assume the firm's planners have created. This plan displays the weeks of production of each product family that each plant will manufacture over a 12-month planning horizon.

For illustration we now focus on the plan that Plant 1 should produce one week of product family A. We will also assume that product family A has the following attributes:

1 It contains 20 finished good end items.
2 Each of the 20 end items has a minimum production run length of a ½ day (i.e., if the plant has to produce an item, it must produce the item for a minimum of ½ of a day).

As previously reviewed, end items are aggregated into product families for tactical (annual) planning based upon their respective similar characteristics. For example, assume that this is a ceramic tile manufacturing network of plants such as the one discussed in section 4.2, and that the 20 end items in product family A are different-colored 2" × 2" wall tile end items (e.g., blue, green, yellow, etc.). Each end item can be produced on the same production lines at the same plants, and at very similar costs per unit and at similar output rates. These similar end items would be planned as one product family in the firm's production planning model.

Now let's consider Figure 4.8, which depicts two very different scenarios (Case 1 and Case 2) under which the firm's annual production planning model could generate an initial assignment of one week of production for product family A at plant 1. The total demand for product family A consists of the sum of the demand for the 20 end items that comprise this product family.

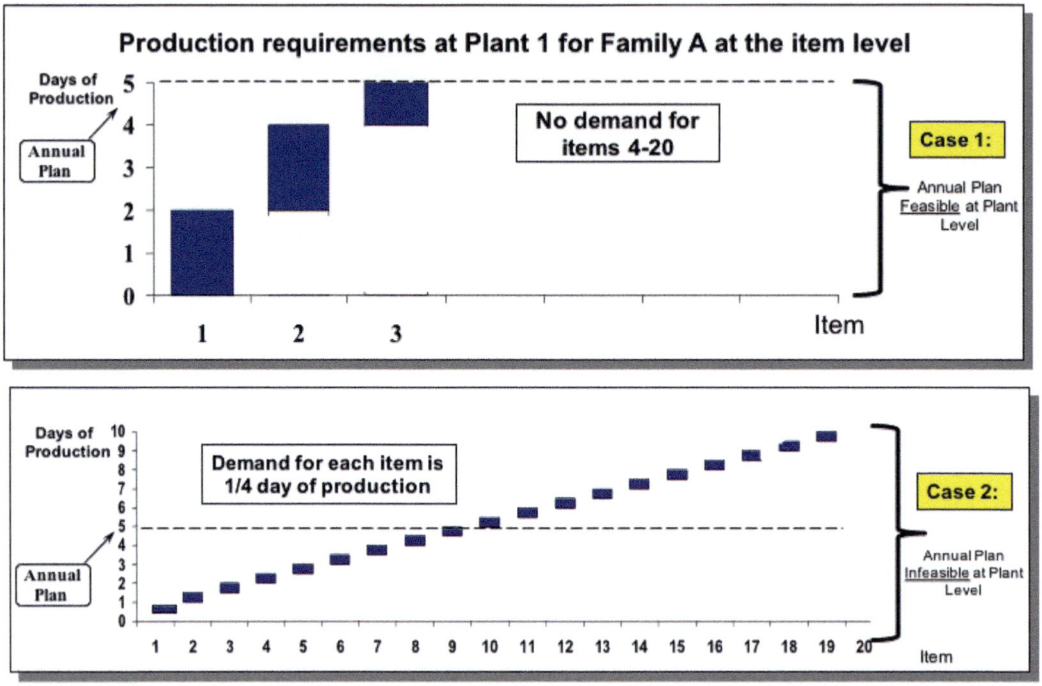

FIGURE 4.8 Two Scenarios for Product Family A at Plant 1.

(For simplicity we will also define production requirements as equal to total demand in this example.) Now consider Case 1 and Case 2 in Figure 4.8.

- *Case 1:* The total demand (and production requirements) for product family A at plant 1 is in three end items (1, 2, and 3).
  - There is no demand for end items 4 through 20 (i.e., demand = 0).
  - Thus, as Figure 4.8 depicts, to satisfy the demand for product family A at plant 1 will require two days' production of item 1, two days of item 2, and one day of item 3.
  - Therefore, plant 1 can feasibly produce the production assignment of one week of family A. (Note that we define five business days as one week in this example.)
- *Case 2:* The total demand for product family A at plant 1 consists of ¼ of a day's production for each of its 20 end items.
  - $20 \times 1/4 = 5$ business days' total demand; or one week of demand (and production) – the assignment to plant 1 for family A.
  - Recall however that plant 1 has a minimum production run length of a 1/2 day for any item.
  - Therefore, for plant 1 to produce all 20 items in family A will require $20 \times 1/2 = 10$ business days of production.
  - Thus, the production assignment to plant 1 for product family A is not feasible.

How Infeasible Production Assignments Can Occur

At the network-wide tactical (annual) planning level, production models and planners generally do not evaluate very detailed issues such as the minimum run length of individual end items at individual plants. The purpose and objectives of 12–18 months' planning exercises at the tactical level necessitate that planning/modeling be conducted at more aggregated levels (e.g., product families rather than end items). This allows the possibility that plans developed at the tactical level may in some cases be infeasible to implement at the operational level. Case 2 illustrates how these infeasibilities may arise.

In practice, operations personnel from lower planning and scheduling levels must regularly provide feedback to planning personnel at higher tactical levels to avoid the type of situation illustrated in Case 2. As plans cascade down from one planning level to the next lower level (e.g., network-wide to individual plant), managers at the lower level must evaluate these plans and communicate back any infeasibilities. This becomes an iterative process whereby tactical plans should be revised based on feedback loop communications, and then revised tactical plans are re-evaluated at the operational level. This process continues until a feasible plan, at all levels, is developed.

Finally, note that feedback loops take many forms and can range from (1) informal communications between two supply chain functions, to (2) formal, standardized data input and output exchanges between functions, to (3) detailed mathematical algorithms that coordinate modeling assumptions and inputs between different planning and operating levels.[20]

Summary

In this section, we introduced the concept of HPP. HPP is an extremely valuable framework and approach that firms employ to integrate and synchronize their manufacturing activities across their entire planning horizon, from the long-run strategic to the short-run operational. We then considered two production examples that illustrated the importance of linking long-run product family-based production planning with short-run end item scheduling.

4.4 Constrained Production Planning

An important component of real-world manufacturing planning is the management of situations where demand exceeds a firm's production capacity. Scenarios where this comes into play range from short-run instances where current demand temporarily exceeds current production capacity, to medium-term tactical and long-run strategic cases where a firm must make major investments to expand production capacity to meet projected future demand. The discussion in Chapter 5, which focuses on network design and facility location, will address longer-run supply chain planning, including manufacturing capacity planning. In this section, we focus on short-run production capacity issues and strategies in a case study.

There exist innumerable reasons why a manufacturer may find itself facing a short-run period where its production output cannot satisfy current demand. Supplier issues, internal labor shortages, machine breakdowns, unanticipated spikes in demand, and sudden changes in customers' product mix demand preferences represent just a few of the myriad factors that can cause short-term production capacity shortages. Given the almost endless reasons that short-run capacity issues can arise, understandably, there are not an easily defined set of standard strategies that a manufacturer can call upon when it suddenly finds itself unable to meet current demand. Typically, a firm must quickly develop and execute a case-specific strategy to address its insufficient short-term production capacity. The following case study is based upon an actual firm and reveals the strategy this company formulated in response to a surprise surge in customer demand that overwhelmed the firm's production capacity. Rather than use the manufacturer's actual name, we will call this firm XYZ Tile Company.

Case Study: XYZ Tile's Production Capacity Shortage Problem

XYZ Tile produces and sells a wide variety of floor and wall tile sizes and colors. The manufacturer operates a "make-to-order" business where its customer base of ceramic tile distributors and retailers place their orders, and then XYZ produces and delivers the order to its customer 4 weeks later. A make-to-order manufacturer such as XYZ produces a customer order only after receiving the order from the customer. This contrasts with "make-to-stock" manufacturers who produce stock in advance, and fill customer orders immediately from existing inventory once the customer places the order. Exhibit 4.4 provides definitions of the make-to-order and make-to-stock manufacturing environments.

EXHIBIT 4.4 MAKE-TO-ORDER AND MAKE-TO-STOCK DEFINITIONS

Make-to-Order:	A production environment where a good or service can be made after receipt of a customer's order. The final product is usually a combination of standard items and items custom-designed to meet the special needs of the customer. (Synonym: build-to-order.)
Make-to-Stock:	A production environment where products can be and usually are finished before receipt of a customer order. Customer orders are typically filled from existing stocks, and production orders are used to replenish those stocks. (Synonym: produce-to-stock.)

Source: ASCM Dictionary 17th edition (2022)

Background

Recently XYZ has experienced a dramatic increase in customer orders, and as a result, the firm's lead time on delivering customer orders has reached well over its normal lead time of 4 weeks. Further, XYZ believes that this spike in customer orders does not reflect the true market demand. Through the tile industry grapevine,[21] XYZ has heard that about 5 weeks ago rumors began circulating among their customers and competitors that XYZ had manufacturing capacity issues and that XYZ's order lead times would soon become longer than the normal 4 weeks. As these rumors quickly became more widespread, XYZ observed many of its key customers placing orders that were up to 100% greater than historical norms. XYZ did not know what precipitated the start of those rumors; however, the firm felt certain that the rumors represented the primary reason for the recent dramatic upsurge in demand. XYZ realized that it needed to develop and then execute a new strategy rapidly, or it risked losing control of the situation with lead times continuing to elongate and customers diverting orders to competitors. Exhibit 4.5 summarizes the production capacity and customer service problem that XYZ Tile faced.

EXHIBIT 4.5 SUMMARY OF XYZ'S PRODUCTION CAPACITY PROBLEM

- *Problem*: XYZ Tile produces and distributes ceramic tile to distributors and retailers on a "make-to-order" basis.

    1 Customers place orders; and then XYZ schedules a production run for the items on the order (i.e., make-to-order manufacturing).
    2 The average normal lead time quoted to customers as the delivery date is 4 weeks.
    3. The promised delivery date to customers is based upon the lead time of the longest "lead time" item on the order (see explanation below).
    4. XYZ offers 200 different sizes and colors (i.e., end items).
    5. The top 20% of items account for 80% of total sales.
    6. In the last 5 weeks, the lead time on orders has increased from 4 to 12 weeks.
    7. Customers are now entering orders that sometimes exceed their historical average order size by up to 100% (i.e., double their normal average order) – to try to "beat the system." Specifically, customers try to reserve extra capacity by entering inflated orders, and then later (e.g., 2 weeks after entering the original order) change the actual items and colors on the original order.
    8. XYZ thinks "true demand" has not significantly increased. Market rumors of production capacity shortages 5 weeks ago triggered this order crisis.

- *Delivery Date Explanation*: How is the "promised delivery date to customers" determined based upon the longest lead time item on the order?

    - Assume that a customer places an order for four end items: Blue Tile, Red Tile, Green Tile, and Yellow Tile.
    - Assume the current lead time (i.e., the time from the placement of the order until the time when the tile has been produced, packaged, and is ready to ship) is:

        - Red Tile – 4 weeks,
        - Blue Tile – 1 week,
        - Green Tile – 6 weeks, and
        - Yellow Tile – 5 weeks.

    - The order will be delivered in 6 weeks because the item with the longest lead time of the four items is green, with a lead time of 6 weeks.
    - Thus, the promised delivery date on a customer order will be equal to the lead time of the item on the order with the longest lead time.

Strategy Development Process

Before XYZ could consider strategies to address its production crisis and lengthy customer delivery dates, the firm had to understand the root causes that had created the predicament. As noted, XYZ's management had heard the industry rumors about its supposed production problems, and suspected this had led to customers deciding to inflate their normal orders. To validate their suspicions, XYZ's planners performed the following analysis:

1 They calculated each customer's average order quantity (and the product mix) for the previous 5 weeks.
2 They calculated each customer's average order quantity and mix for:

   a the previous 12-month period before the last 5 weeks, and
   b an identical period to the last 5 weeks, but 12 months ago.

   The results of this analysis clearly showed that:

a Individual customer orders for the last 5 weeks greatly exceeded their previous 12-month averages.
b A comparison of each customer's average order size for the last 5 weeks to that customer's average order size for the same 5-week period 1 year ago showed that almost all customers' average order size for the current 5 weeks were much greater than 1 year ago.

These analyses confirmed XYZ's theory that the sharp rise in orders did not reflect actual true demand. With this assurance, XYZ commenced development of a strategy to reverse its current escalating customer delivery lead times.

Fair Share Allocation

The first strategy that XYZ's planners considered was a well-known distribution strategy called *fair-share allocation* that they believed the firm could adapt to their production process. The Association for Supply Chain Management (ASCM) defines this distribution strategy as:

> The process of equitably allocating available stock among field distribution centers. Fair-share quantity logic is normally used when stock available from a central inventory location is less than the cumulative requirements of the field stocking locations. The use of fairshare quantity logic involves procedures that "push" stock out to the field, instead of allowing the field to "pull" in what is needed. The objective is to maximize customer service from the limited available inventory.[22]

Figure 4.9 displays an illustrative distribution network, and the basic data required to implement a fair share allocation process on a network.

Briefly, a fair share allocation process on this two-DC network would work as follows:

1 Determine the inventory quantities, and the days' supply of inventory that each DC currently has available.

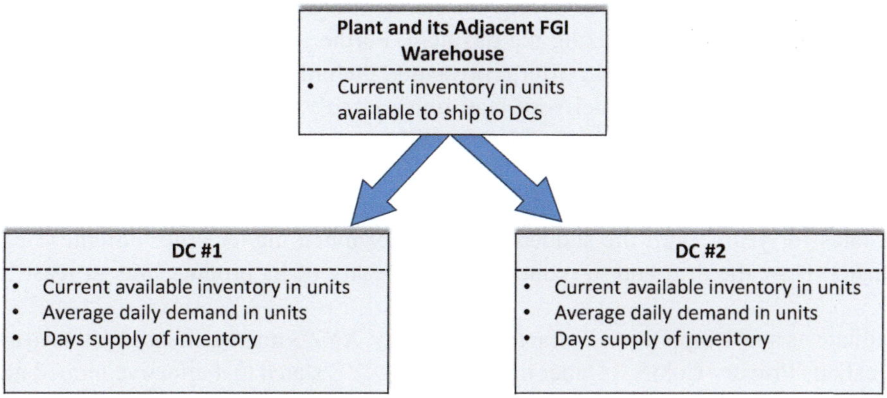

FIGURE 4.9 Fair Share Allocation on a Distribution Network.

2 Add the total inventory available at the DCs to the inventory at the plant warehouse that is available to ship to the DCs. This sum is the total inventory available on the network, and the objective is that this total inventory be allocated to, and positioned at the DCs so that each DC has the same days of inventory supply (i.e., the same forward coverage).
3 Based on the analyses performed in steps 1 and 2, determine the portion of the available inventory at the plant warehouse to ship to each DC – so that each DC would have the identical days' supply of inventory – once they receive the shipments of the currently available inventory at the plant warehouse.

A straightforward algebraic formula can be used to determine the portion of the available inventory at the plant warehouse to ship to each DC in order to equalize each DC's days of supply.[23]

XYZ's planners thought that they could devise a process whereby each of their customers would receive a "fair share" of the manufacturer's production capacity. Planners discussed implementing a system that would use their customers' historical average order quantities to allocate all available production capacity. The basic concept was, for example, that if a customer's historical orders for a defined previous period amounted to 2% of XYZ's overall customer demand, then XYZ would assign 2% of whatever production capacity it had to serve that customer. Based on this historical analysis, each of XYZ's current customers would receive a pre-determined portion of the manufacturer's total production capacity for a set time interval (e.g., a 4-week period). However, after some initial analytic work on how to implement this potential approach, XYZ's management decided the strategy would not resolve the fundamental current problem, and importantly it would not allay their customers' ongoing concerns. Additionally, management concluded this fair share production strategy would be difficult to administer.

A Second Strategy

XYZ realized that it required a short-run strategy which would address two primary issues:

1 Its customer base expected and relied upon 4-week delivery dates on their orders.
2 XYZ did not have even close to sufficient production capacity to provide 4-week delivery dates on its current weekly order volume.

XYZ's planners concluded that restoring 4-week delivery dates immediately, or as soon as possible, was paramount to stabilizing the business. Further, reducing the number of unique colors and sizes that the firm would offer represented the only short-term strategy that had a chance of successfully lowering delivery lead times rapidly. The breadth of XYZ's current product line represented a key element of its marketing strategy; however, it also necessitated numerous production line changeover and setups per week. Despite this production inefficiency, and to support its marketing strategy, the plant had maintained 4-week average delivery dates for years, until the sudden onslaught of much higher order volumes began 5 weeks earlier. Now the firm had to reduce the complexity of its product line, at least in the short run.

To facilitate its new temporary manufacturing strategy, XYZ's management announced a sales program called "Primary Colors." Under this program, XYZ stated that effective immediately,[24] it would provide 4-week delivery dates on customer orders; however, this guarantee applied only to a limited number of the firm's most popular colors and sizes. XYZ also announced that it would still accept orders for all of its other items (i.e., those not in the Primary Colors program); but the delivery dates would be much longer.

In developing this plan, XYZ correctly strategized that guaranteeing 4-week delivery dates on its key items would quickly alleviate the flow of its customers' bogus and inflated orders. Customers would receive 4-week delivery dates on normal-sized orders of popular items, and customers would also know that there was nothing they could do to expedite delivery times on non-Primary Colors items.[25]

XYZ's short-run production and customer service strategy, Primary Colors, successfully reduced delivery times rapidly. As customers placed orders for Primary Colors items and began to receive deliveries in the promised 4 weeks, they (the customers) quickly halted their practice of submitting inflated order quantities. Gradually, over a period of several months, XYZ expanded the number of items in Primary Colors until eventually 4-week delivery dates became available again on all items. To conclude this section, Exhibit 4.6 summarizes the analytic steps and logic that XYZ's planners employed to develop the Primary Colors program.

EXHIBIT 4.6 SUMMARY OF PRIMARY COLORS ANALYTIC STEPS

1. Planners ranked XYZ's 200 end items (i.e., unique tile colors and sizes) from top to bottom based on total order demand. Separate analyses of the last 5 weeks and the previous 12 months were completed to check for any recent anomalies.
2. Based on the total order demand analysis end item ranking, XYZ's planners determined how many end items they could include in Primary Colors – so that production of these items would utilize 75% to 80% of the current weekly total production capacity. Thus, XYZ started with the top-ranked end items based on unit volume, and continued down its ranked list until it reached 75% to 80% of weekly unit production capacity.
3. *Note on this strategy's logic*: by leaving a 20% to 25% extra weekly capacity margin, XYZ felt confident that it could meet its 4-week delivery promise on Primary Colors items. Failure to uphold this guarantee would unquestionably doom the effort, hence XYZ's decision to maintain a large extra capacity margin.

4 Once it developed the initial list of Primary Colors end items, XYZ reviewed historical order patterns to identify any "low volume" items that always accompanied orders of Primary Colors items. XYZ wanted to make sure that it did not inadvertently exclude any low-volume end items that were required complementary items on purchases of popular items. Overlooking this component of the ordering process would also have jeopardized the success of Primary Colors.
5 XYZ then added any critical complementary low-volume items (identified in step 4) to its Primary Colors list.
6 Next, XYZ re-calculated its original capacity analysis (step 2) to include any low-volume complementary items added to Primary Colors in step 5.
7 If the addition of these complementary items pushed the projected capacity utilization to over the 75% to 80% maximum target, then XYZ would start removing the lowest-volume "popular" Primary Colors items from its original list developed in step 2. This removal process continued until projected weekly product requirements were within the 75% to 80% of capacity range.
8 Based on the analysis completed in step 7, XYZ now had its final list of Primary Colors items to include in its announcement of the program.
9 After launching Primary Colors, XYZ then monitored and updated its analytic process weekly. This work continued throughout the several months after the program's launch until 4-week delivery dates on all items were in place.

Addendum: XYZ also initiated a long-run strategic review to assess the need for manufacturing capacity expansion – once the firm resolved its short-term capacity crisis.

4.5 Summary

This chapter began with a discussion of key manufacturing and production planning concepts. This included a review of important metrics such as capacity utilization and effective capacity. Next, we considered how firms must balance manufacturing costs and inventory carrying costs as they develop production plans and schedules. We discussed the EPQ model, a simple optimization model that determines production quantities which minimize total production setup and inventory carrying costs on a manufacturing line.

We then introduced hierarchical planning, a framework for supply chain and production planning that spans a firm's entire planning horizon from daily and short-run scheduling operations, to medium-term tactical and long-run strategic planning. To illustrate how these planning frameworks are used in practice, we reviewed two examples where effective production planning required analytic methods to link tactical (annual) product family plans with end item inventory levels and production constraints.

Section 4.4 next presented a real-world case study of a firm that had to resolve a major short-term production capacity shortage. Now that we have considered an illustrative example of a short-run capacity problem, in Chapter 5, we focus on long-run strategic planning issues such as network design, and manufacturing and distribution facility location.

Notes

1 Although the analytic planning techniques presented beginning in section 4.2 apply to finished goods, in some cases these techniques or variations on these techniques can be used for non-finished goods production planning.
2 Each production line can produce only one product per day.
3 In this example, the plant did not lower its "effective capacity" until Year 3 – even though the change in demand product mix occurred beginning in Year 2. The example illustrates that plants and firms do not immediately modify their effective capacities as demand mix, or other factors, change. However, pronounced, long-lasting changes to effective capacity should be adjusted for over time.
4 Source: Corporatefinanceinstitute.com/resources/economics/capacity-utilization, accessed 9/5/24. https://corporatefinanceinstitute.com/resources/
5 See Bowersox et al. (2024), Chopra and Meindl (2016), and Venkataraman and Pinto (2020).
6 Keep in mind that the implicit assumption in this analysis and similar analyses is that either manufacturing option will facilitate the identical service level fill rate on customer orders that the plant must fulfill. That is to say, the different inventory levels of the two options each should support providing the same fill rate. Thus, in performing an analysis such as this, it is necessary to determine for a targeted customer service fill rate the average inventory level that each production option would require to deliver the targeted fill rate. This portion of the analysis is not discussed here but it represents a critical preliminary component that must be completed before the analysis shown here can be completed.
7 Observe that the analysis in Table 4.3 implicitly is determining the production lot size quantity of each major tile size. Table 4.4 illustrates this point.
8 The annual inventory carrying cost per unit is obtained by multiplying the firm's annual inventory carrying cost interest rate by the firm's cost to produce one finished good unit of the product. The term "standard cost" is often used to describe a firm's cost to manufacture one unit of a product. Frequently firms will use a product's standard cost, or some firm-specific variation of the standard cost per unit, for purposes of calculating inventory carrying costs.
9 Note that one of the assumptions or restrictions of the EPQ model is that daily production is greater than daily demand. There is an important "nuance" about this assumption (i.e., $p > d$) that requires a clarification. To understand this nuance, we use the following definitions. A *production run* is the period between when a production line starts producing a product and when the line stops producing that product. A *production cycle* is the period between when a production line starts producing a product, and the next time (after it stops producing the product) when the production line starts producing that same product again. So, for example, assume a production line begins production of a particular product once every 10 days. Also, assume that once the line starts producing this product, it runs for 5 days and then stops (and produces a different product for the next 5 days). In this example, the production run is 5 days; however, the production run cycle is 10 days. Therefore, the EPQ model assumption of $p > d$ applies only to the 5 days of the production run (i.e., the days when the product is actually being produced). In days 6–10 of the production run cycle, there is no production of the product in question, and therefore, $p > d$ does not apply. In fact, during days 6–10 of the production run cycle, inventory would decrease at a rate of d per day because $p = 0$ in days 6–10.
10 Observe that if d is very small compared to p, the expression (p-d)/p will have a value of close to 1 (i.e., 100%), and the average inventory over the production run will then be just slightly less than Q/2.
11 See Venkataraman and Pinto (2020).
12 This can be proven mathematically – see Meindl and Chopra (2016), and Venkataraman and Pinto (2020).
13 The reader interested in exploring hierarchical supply chain and production planning in depth is referred to Liberatore and Miller (2021), and Miller and Liberatore (2020). These two books examine the many dimensions of hierarchical supply chain and logistics planning, and offer numerous real-world case studies of hierarchical planning systems implemented by firms in different industries. Additionally, the seminal articles of Hax and Meal (1975), Ackoff (1970), and Anthony (1965) provide perspective on the early origins of hierarchical planning.
14 Portions of this section are excerpted from Miller and Liberatore (2020).
15 Note that some firms have separate planning frameworks for manufacturing and distribution.
16 Note that to determine net requirements, planners must also explicitly factor safety stock targets into their calculations. Similarly, if there are any product families where there are major inventory backorders, this also must be factored in.

17 In words, "useable" inventory is the amount of beginning inventory that can be used to meet forecast sales and the end of planning horizon inventory target.
18 In words, "excess" inventory is the amount of beginning inventory (if any) that is not needed to meet the forecast sales and end of planning horizon inventory target.
19 See Miller (1991).
20 See Miller and Liberatore (2020) for further discussion about feedback loops.
21 By "grapevine" we mean the "intelligence" that individual firms and customers in an industry obtain about each other through informal contacts at industry-wide conferences, through informal discussions between manufacturers' sales personnel and individual customers, etc.
22 ASCM Dictionary, 17th edition (2022).
23 See Bowersox et al. (2024).
24 When the firm announced this program, it gave specific details such as a start date 1 week after the announcement (i.e., essentially immediately), etc.
25 When launching a strategy such as Primary Colors, in order to succeed, a firm must give its customers very specific ordering parameters, etc. One example is that XYZ as part of its announcement also stated that once they submitted orders for Primary Colors items, customers could not change the order. This was a change from XYZ's previous, more flexible policy.

5

NETWORK DESIGN AND FACILITY LOCATION

The design of its network, and the location of its plants and distribution centers represent critical strategic decisions for a firm. Whether a company is a large multinational entity or a small domestic firm, the location of its facilities and their functional capabilities have a pivotal impact on a firm's cost efficiency and customer service. In this chapter, we explore several network design and facility location strategic planning methods and concepts.

We begin this chapter with a brief review of supply chain strategic planning, which will serve to provide a general perspective on the topics of *network design* and *facility location.* This discussion includes an overview of the major factors that firms consider in their network design strategic planning process. Next, we review a case study of a distribution network design problem where a firm evaluates whether it should reduce the number of distribution centers on its current network. This case study illustrates the type of costs that a firm must analyze in a DC network design problem, and how planners calculate these costs.

We then discuss how companies employ advanced techniques such as mathematical optimization in their strategic network design and location planning processes. In this section, we describe in straightforward terms what optimization models are, and the types of strategic network design problems that they can solve.[1] Additionally, to enhance our understanding of these models and the breadth of planning applications they can support, we also review how optimization models can facilitate tactical manufacturing and distribution planning. Next, we illustrate a technique called the factor rating method. Planners often employ this simple mathematical tool to determine which potential site among a set of candidate locations in a specific geographic area best meets a firm's needs. The chapter concludes with a brief summary.

5.1 Strategic Planning Background and Network Location Factors

As introduced in Section 4.3, strategic planning represents the highest level of the hierarchy of decision-making activities which occur within a firm or a major function such as supply chain management. Ultimately, strategic planning decisions are all concerned with defining the long-term objectives of a firm and its supply chain, charting the long-term course that will allow the achievement of defined objectives, and ensuring that the proper resources and assets necessary

DOI: 10.4324/9781003585442-5

to support long-term objectives are allocated. For illustrative purposes, Exhibit 5.1 displays a sample of typical strategic logistics and supply chain issues and problems which firms must address.

EXHIBIT 5.1 SELECTED STRATEGIC SUPPLY CHAIN DECISIONS

- plant and warehouse locations and missions (i.e., network infrastructure and design),
- new plant locations and sizes, and plant closings,
- new warehouse locations and sizes, and warehouse closings,
- plant and warehouse capacity, and technology design,
- mix of owned assets vs. third-party resources utilized (i.e., outsourcing decisions),
- transportation network design, and
- global vs. regional vs. local procurement and sourcing

While the list in Exhibit 5.1 is not comprehensive, it illustrates that planning a firm's manufacturing and distribution infrastructure comprises a key component of supply chain strategic planning. In addition to decisions on the locations, capacities, and technologies of a company's plants and DCs, other key questions related to the facility design process include:

1 Which supply sources should provide raw materials and components to each plant?
2 What manufacturing processes should be performed at each plant?
3 What and how much of a material, component, or finished product are to be produced at each plant?
4 What is the amount of inventory to be held at each plant and DC?
5 What order fulfillment approach should the firm use (e.g., make-to-order vs. make-to-stock)?
6 What DCs should each plant serve?
7 What markets and customers should each DC serve?

Figure 5.1 depicts a portion of the manufacturing and distribution network of a well-known consumer products firm.[2] Clearly, on a network of this magnitude, planners must carefully formulate strategies to address the aforementioned questions such as how much inventory to hold at different facilities and echelons. Additionally, a sample of other logistics factors that affect network design and facility location decisions include:

1 *Proximity to Customers* – facilitates fast and frequent deliveries and competitive order cycle times,
2 *Good Local Suppliers* – a high-quality and competitive supplier base makes a location attractive.
3 *Good Local Infrastructure* – a strong road, rail, air, and/or sea transportation network enhances the competitiveness of a local area.
4 *Good Local Labor* – the educational and skill levels of the local labor pool must match the company's needs.

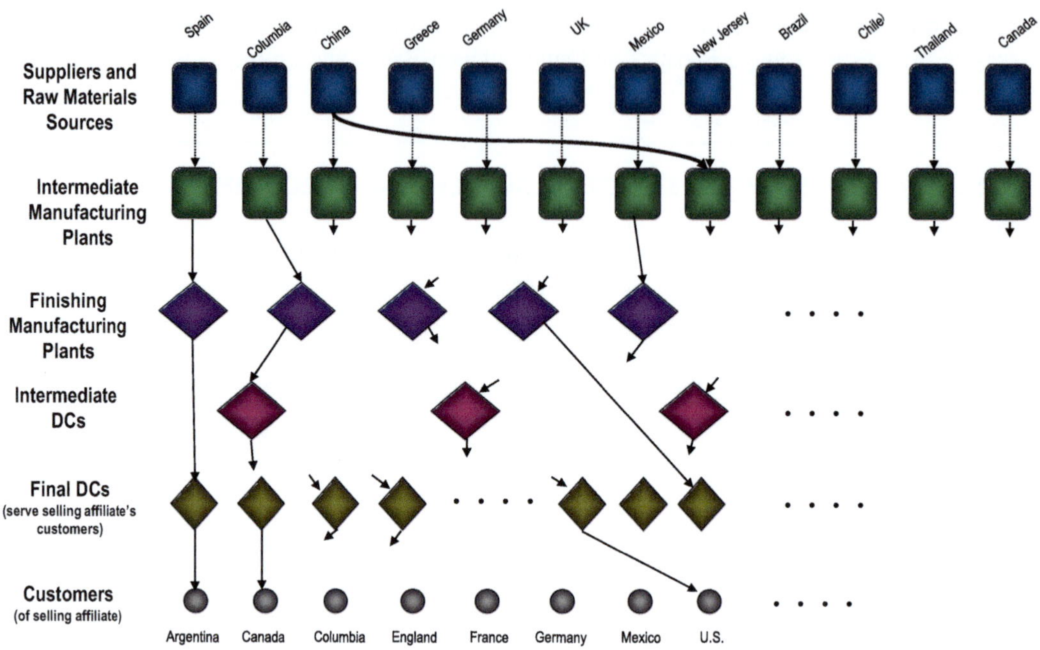

FIGURE 5.1 Illustrative Global Manufacturing and Distribution Network.

In summary, there exist a myriad of factors that a firm must evaluate in developing its network design strategy, and then continually updating it on an ongoing basis. This section has briefly introduced many of the main inputs to a firm's network design strategic planning process. We next examine several analytics techniques that companies utilize to facilitate quantitative decision support for their strategic planning.

5.2 Distribution Network Design

Firms that operate large-scale distribution systems must regularly undertake a strategic review of their network to evaluate its efficiency and effectiveness, and to determine if the current structure requires modification. While there is no standard time interval when these strategic reviews should occur, once a year to once every 2 or 3 years represent good guidelines. Additionally, specific strategic events such as a firm making a significant acquisition or divestiture of another company always warrant a review of the current network. Finally, when we say that an analysis must evaluate the "efficiency and effectiveness" of the current network, we mean the following.

1 *Effectiveness* – does the current distribution network provide the customer service levels that the firm must offer to compete successfully? Specifically, is the cycle time on customers' orders fast enough, and is the item and order fill rate high enough?
2 *Efficiency* – does the current distribution network allow the firm to minimize its costs, subject to providing the defined customer service levels required for the firm to compete successfully in its industry? Importantly, note that operating efficiently does not mean the

firm and its network's goal is to "minimize costs." Rather, once a firm first determines the customer service levels it must provide, then the firm must determine the most efficient (i.e., the cost minimizing) distribution network design that can deliver these target service levels.

A Distribution Network Design Case Study

The case study in this section follows the analytic steps that a fictitious company performs as the firm conducts a strategic review of its current distribution network. For illustrative purposes, we limit this review to selected analytic portions of the overall strategic project, and we make certain simplifying assumptions.

Background

ABC Distributors, a domestic company, currently operates a distribution network consisting of three DCs which serve ABC's hundreds of retail stores located throughout the U.S. ABC sells a wide variety of consumer products through its stores which stock and sell the firm's products. ABC has observed that most of its competitors serve retail stores in the U.S. market from just two DCs. This has prompted ABC to launch a strategic analysis of whether it should maintain its current three-DC network, or, alternatively, consolidate to a two-DC U.S. operation, similar to its chief competitors.

Figure 5.2 displays ABC's distribution network and summarizes the strategic question the firm plans to analyze. Notice that ABC has a single plant located in the center of the U.S. This plant produces consumer products and then immediately ships this FGI to the firm's three DCs. Each DC serves the ABC stores in its defined service region. These retail stores place orders on their serving DC regularly (e.g., once a week), and the DC picks and ships a retail store's orders from its inventory immediately upon receipt of the store's orders.[3]

As Figure 5.2 describes, ABC plans to evaluate the following four scenarios in its strategic review:

1 *The Base Case* – continue to utilize its current three-DC distribution network to supply the company's retail stores,
2 *Close DC A*, and serve the entire U.S. from DCs B and C.
3 *Close DC B*, and serve the U.S. from DCs A and C.
4 *Close DC C*, and serve the U.S. from DCs A and B.

ABC plans to conduct a cost analysis of each of these four options based upon the following three major costs associated with its DC operations:

- *annual freight costs* – both inbound from the plant and outbound to its retail stores,
- *annual DC operating costs* – both fixed and variable, and
- *annual inventory carrying costs* – both at the DCs and at the firm's retail stores

In addition to these three annual operating costs, ABC also will factor into the analysis the one-time costs to close a DC in scenarios 2, 3, and 4.[4]

- It is now evaluating the option of using a Two-DC Network rather than the current Three-DC Network
- Its first step will be to conduct a cost analysis of the Two-DC vs Three-DC approach
- Each of the three current DCs are candidates to be closed
- The four scenarios to evaluate are the current case (base case) and three alternative scenarios where one of the current 3 DCs is closed (i.e., A or B or C)

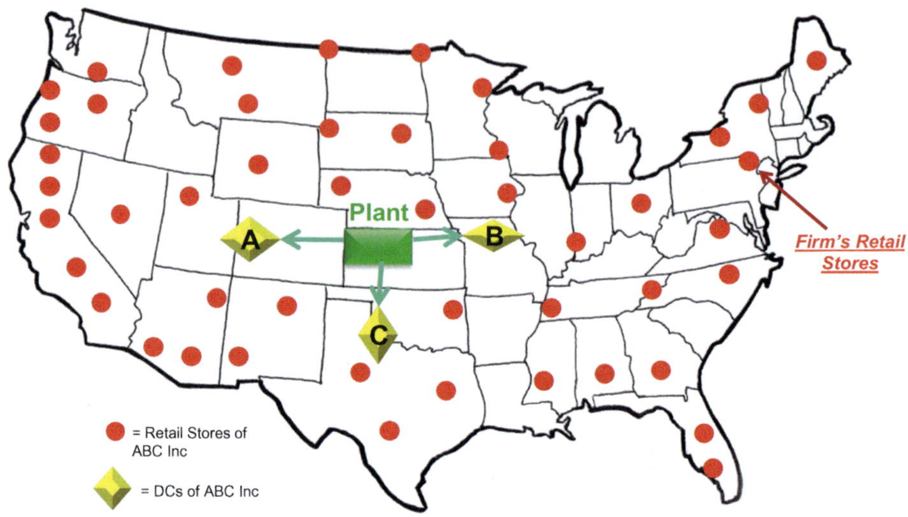

- *Three ongoing annual costs will be analyzed: Freight, DC Operations, and Inventory Carrying Costs*
- *Additionally, the one-time costs to close a DC will be considered*

FIGURE 5.2 ABC Operates a Three-DC Network to Serve Its Retail Stores in the U.S.

Setting Up the Cost Analysis

In the initial stages of a major analytic project such as a distribution network study, it is important to envision and outline the key output(s) that the project must generate. This can guide the analytic steps that an analyst must undertake. Table 5.1 displays a blank output template that ABC's distribution study seeks to populate.

Annual Costs

Before starting the data development and analysis necessary to complete the output template (i.e., Table 5.1), we briefly review DC variable handling costs and DC annual fixed costs to enhance our understanding of these factors. Figure 5.3 will assist our understanding of variable handling costs in particular. ABC's DCs pick the products that their retail stores order from them using two different methods. Orders for large quantities of single items are picked as full pallets – if the quantity of the item ordered equals or exceeds the quantity of that item held on one warehouse pallet. Orders for less than pallet quantities of a single item are picked as individual loose cases.

Figure 5.3 shows a pallet with individual cases stacked on the pallet in rows. From a cost perspective, generally it is significantly less expensive per case for warehouse personnel to pick a full pallet than to pick an individual loose case. For example, suppose that a warehouse picker has to travel 200 feet to pick a product on an order. If that worker can pick a full pallet and bring

TABLE 5.1 Output Template for Firm ABC's Distribution Network Study

ANNUAL COSTS		*ALTERNATIVE SCENARIOS*				*ANNUAL SAVINGS OF ALTERNATIVE SCENARIOS THAT CLOSE ONE OF THREE DCs: (Base Case Costs – Scenario Costs)*			*One-Time DC Shutdown Costs*	
Category	*Component*	*1. Base Case*	*2. Close DC A*	*3. Close DC B*	*4. Close DC C*	*Close DC A*	*Close DC B*	*Close DC C*	*Cost Category*	*Cost*
FREIGHT	Plant to DCs								Costs to Shutdown DC	
	DCs to Stores								Costs to Transfer Inventory	
	TOTAL FREIGHT								Total One-Time Shutdown Costs	
DC OPERATIONS	Variable									
	Fixed									
	TOTAL DC OPS									
INVENTORY	Inv CC at DCs									
	Inv CC at Retail Stores									
	TOTAL INV CC									
TOTAL ANNUAL FRT, DC, & INV CC COSTS										

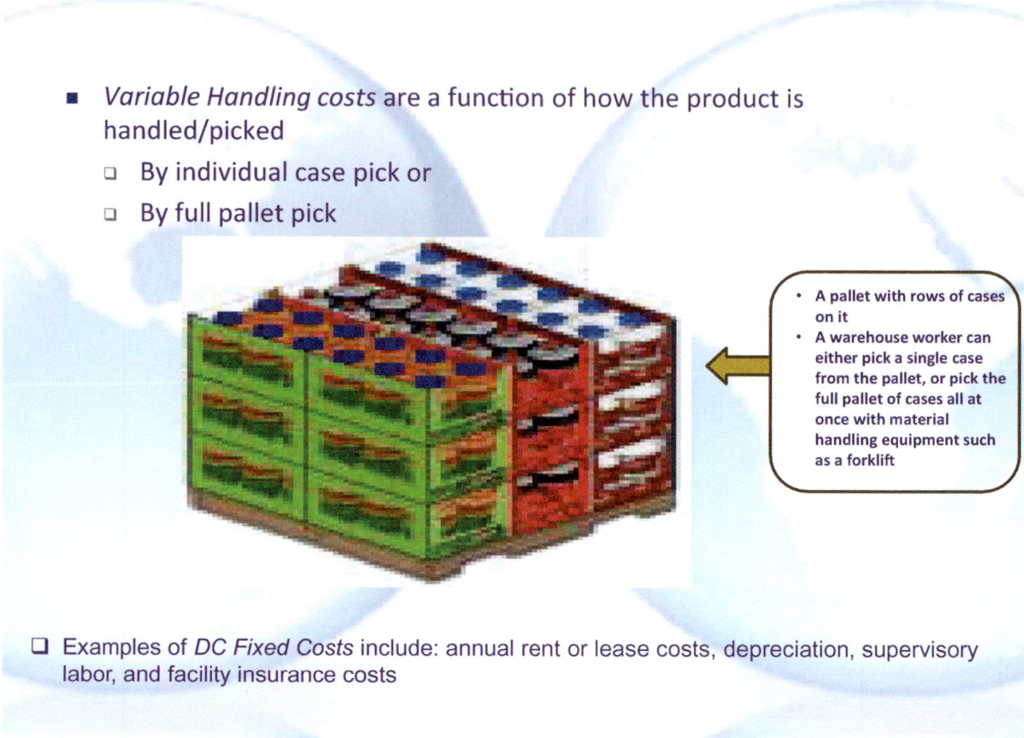

FIGURE 5.3 DC Fixed and Variable Handling Costs.

it back to the loading dock with a forklift, the cost per case will clearly be lower compared to if that same worker has to travel 200 feet and return to the loading dock with just one individual case.[5] Thus, we expect full pallet picks to have a lower handling cost per case than individual loose case picks.

Figure 5.3 also lists several of the components of the total annual fixed costs of a DC. Fixed costs represent costs that do not vary with the output level of a facility (e.g., a DC or a plant). As long as a firm owns a DC, the company will pay fixed costs such as annual rent or lease costs, depreciation on the facility itself (if the company owns the facility), depreciation on the DC's equipment that the firm owns such as forklifts and conveyors, annual insurance costs, etc.; in other words, fixed costs that ABC will pay each year, and which will not vary, regardless of how many cases of product a DC handles each year.[6]

The Data for the Distribution Network Study

In this section, we discuss the data that ABC's distribution planners organized and developed to facilitate their analytic study. Collectively, Tables 5.2 through 5.9 provide the required information on freight, DC operations, and inventory necessary to complete the analysis outlined in the template of Table 5.1.

TABLE 5.2 Item Data – Shipments (Sales), Inventory, and Unit Cost Data of ABC's DC Network

Count	*Item #*	*Cost per Unit*	*Selling Price per Unit*	*Profit Margin per Unit*	*Current Inventory Level in Units*	*Current Inventory Level in $ at Cost*	*Target Inventory Level in Units*	*Target Inventory Level in $ at Cost*	*Total Sales of Firm in Last 12 Months in Units*	*Total Sales of Firm in Last 12 Months in $ at Cost*	*Total Sales Revenue of Firm in Last 12 Months in $*	*Cumulative % of Total Sls Rev $*
1	128	$ 2.25	$ 5.00	$ 2.75	669,231	$ 1,505,769	384,615	$ 865,385	2,000,000	$ 4,500,000	$ 10,000,000	**20%**
2	133	$ 6.00	$ 10.00	$ 4.00	240,577	$ 1,443,462	173,077	$ 1,038,462	900,000	$ 5,400,000	$ 9,000,000	**38%**
3	139	$ 8.25	$ 15.00	$ 6.75	179,808	$ 1,483,413	96,154	$ 793,269	500,000	$ 4,125,000	$ 7,500,000	**53%**
4	292	$ 2.25	$ 5.00	$ 2.75	267,308	$ 601,442	192,308	$ 432,692	1,000,000	$ 2,250,000	$ 5,000,000	**63%**
5	323	$ 6.50	$ 10.00	$ 3.50	142,788	$ 928,125	86,538	$ 562,500	450,000	$ 2,925,000	$ 4,500,000	**72%**
6	336	$ 4.50	$ 10.00	$ 5.50	110,000	$ 495,000	76,923	$ 346,154	400,000	$ 1,800,000	$ 4,000,000	**80%**
7	349	$ 3.00	$ 5.00	$ 2.00	39,545	$ 118,634	27,462	$ 82,385	119,000	$ 357,000	$ 595,000	**81%**
8	368	$ 5.50	$ 10.00	$ 4.50	17,010	$ 93,555	13,500	$ 74,250	58,500	$ 321,750	$ 585,000	**82%**
9	381	$ 13.00	$ 20.00	$ 7.00	10,947	$ 142,313	6,635	$ 86,250	28,750	$ 373,750	$ 575,000	**84%**
10	440	$ 2.25	$ 5.00	$ 2.75	52,154	$ 117,346	26,077	$ 58,673	113,000	$ 254,250	$ 565,000	**85%**
11	442	$ 5.00	$ 10.00	$ 5.00	19,083	$ 95,417	12,808	$ 64,038	55,500	$ 277,500	$ 555,000	**86%**
12	469	$ 6.00	$ 10.00	$ 4.00	10,187	$ 61,124	12,577	$ 75,462	54,500	$ 327,000	$ 545,000	**87%**
13	480	$ 2.75	$ 5.00	$ 2.25	45,434	$ 124,943	24,692	$ 67,904	107,000	$ 294,250	$ 535,000	**88%**
14	499	$ 4.50	$ 10.00	$ 5.50	16,840	$ 75,782	12,115	$ 54,519	52,500	$ 236,250	$ 525,000	**89%**
15	571	$ 3.25	$ 5.00	$ 1.75	29,712	$ 96,563	23,769	$ 77,250	103,000	$ 334,750	$ 515,000	**90%**
16	588	$ 2.50	$ 5.00	$ 2.50	31,465	$ 78,663	23,308	$ 58,269	101,000	$ 252,500	$ 505,000	**91%**
17	612	$ 6.00	$ 10.00	$ 4.00	20,219	$ 121,313	11,423	$ 68,538	49,500	$ 297,000	$ 495,000	**92%**
18	622	$ 5.50	$ 10.00	$ 4.50	20,693	$ 113,812	11,308	$ 62,192	49,000	$ 269,500	$ 490,000	**93%**
19	658	$ 3.25	$ 5.00	$ 1.75	38,804	$ 126,113	21,923	$ 71,250	95,000	$ 308,750	$ 475,000	**94%**
20	664	$ 4.50	$ 10.00	$ 5.50	19,990	$ 89,957	11,423	$ 51,404	49,500	$ 222,750	$ 495,000	**95%**
21	667	$ 10.00	$ 20.00	$ 10.00	6,946	$ 69,462	4,038	$ 40,385	15,000	$ 150,000	$ 300,000	**96%**
22	668	$ 3.00	$ 5.00	$ 2.00	17,021	$ 51,062	15,615	$ 46,846	58,000	$ 174,000	$ 290,000	**96%**
23	669	$ 5.50	$ 10.00	$ 4.50	13,494	$ 74,216	7,538	$ 41,462	28,000	$ 154,000	$ 280,000	**97%**
24	712	$ 4.50	$ 10.00	$ 5.50	10,758	$ 48,413	7,269	$ 32,712	27,000	$ 121,500	$ 270,000	**97%**
25	716	$ 6.50	$ 10.00	$ 3.50	9,100	$ 59,150	7,000	$ 45,500	26,000	$ 169,000	$ 260,000	**98%**
26	723	$ 13.00	$ 20.00	$ 7.00	3,635	$ 47,250	3,365	$ 43,750	12,500	$ 162,500	$ 250,000	**98%**
27	771	$ 2.00	$ 5.00	$ 3.00	17,963	$ 35,926	12,923	$ 25,846	48,000	$ 96,000	$ 240,000	**99%**
28	803	$ 5.50	$ 10.00	$ 4.50	10,589	$ 58,239	6,192	$ 34,058	23,000	$ 126,500	$ 230,000	**99%**
29	883	$ 6.50	$ 10.00	$ 3.50	5,390	$ 35,035	5,923	$ 38,500	22,000	$ 143,000	$ 220,000	**99%**
30	956	$ 2.25	$ 5.00	$ 2.75	12,253	$ 27,569	11,038	$ 24,837	41,000	$ 92,250	$ 205,000	**100%**
Total					2,088,944	$ 8,419,067	1,329,538	$ 5,364,740	6,586,250	$ 26,515,750	$ 50,000,000	

TABLE 5.3 Inventory Data and Calculation Notes

The Firm's Annual Inventory Carrying Cost Interest Rate r =	25%	
Current Inventory Level in $ at Cost at the Three DCs = (recall that there are three DCs in the Base Case)	$ 8,419,067	
Current Inventory at Retail Stores in $ at Cost =	$ 7,000,000	
Use the Square Root of n Rule to Calculate the Projected Inventory Level in $ at Cost at the DCs on a Two-DC Scenario	➔	<u>**Square Root of n Rule**</u> The square root of n rule provides an approximation of how the current inventory level at the stocking locations on a network would change, if in the future there are fewer or more stocking locations than currently exist on a firm's network. Below is the formula for the Square Root of n rule, and it should be used to calculate the projected Inventory Level in $ at Cost if the firm operated a Two-DC Network rather than the current Three-DC Network ⬇ Square Root of n Rule Formula = Square Root [(new # of DCs) / (current # of DCs)] × [the Inventory Investment on the Current Network] = SqRt (2/3) × (Current Inventory Investment at DCs)
Use the Following Logic to Project the Inventory at Retail Stores on a Two-DC Network	➔	To calculate the projected inventory at the Retail Stores in a Two-DC Network Scenario, assume that the total inventory investment at the Retail Stores would increase by 10%. The logic is that with two DCs serving the entire market (i.e., the U.S.) rather than the current three DCs, the average lead time (i.e., order cycle time) on orders from the stores to the DCs would increase because the average travel distance and travel time between the DCs and the stores for the truckload deliveries would increase.

TABLE 5.4 Total Weight and Units Shipped by DCs

Firm / DC	*Total Current Annual Units*	*Percent of Demand Shipped by Each DC*	*Units per Day Shipped by the Location*	*lbs. per Day Shipped by the Location*
Total by Firm	6,586,250	100%	25,332	160,000
DC_A	2,634,500	40%	10,133	64,000
DC_B	2,305,188	35%	8,866	56,000
DC_C	1,646,563	25%	6,333	40,000

TABLE 5.5 DC to Retail Stores Outbound Freight Cost Table

Weight From	*Weight to*	*Freight Cost in $ Per lb.***
-	65,000	0.290
65,001	70,000	0.377
70,001	74,000	0.357
74,001	78,000	0.337
78,001	86,000	0.317
86,001	90,000	0.307
90,001	96,000	0.297

** These costs are based on the lbs. shipped per day by the DCs to the Retail Stores.

Note: All of the rates above 65,000 lbs. per day are higher than the rate for 65,000 lbs. and under for the following reason. All rates assuming over 65,000 lbs. per day are based on a two-DC network serving all the retail stores. The under 65,000 lb. rate is based on a three-DC network serving all the retail stores. So all the rates above 65,000 lbs. reflect that fact that when two DCs serve the entire U.S., the average distance between a DC and a retail store will be higher than when three DCs serve the entire U.S. Therefore the rates based on a longer average distance traveled (i.e., the two-DC scenarios) are higher than the rate based on the current or base case three-DC scenario.

Table 5.2 presents annual sales, current inventory, item unit cost, and other related data for ABC's three-DC network. Note that for this analysis, we consider "sales" and "shipments by the DCs" to be identical.[7] [Additionally, this table contains some data that we will not employ in the analyses presented (e.g., profit margin per unit, target inventory, and cumulative sales revenue analysis). However, to illustrate the range of data that distribution network studies often utilize, we include some extra data fields.]

Table 5.3 details the inventory data, a simplifying assumption, and the methodology we will use to estimate inventory requirements for the three different two-DC scenarios.

Tables 5.4 and 5.5 display the data necessary to calculate the annual freight costs of the base case and the three alternative scenarios. Table 5.4 indicates the total weight per day currently shipped by each of ABC's three DCs, while Table 5.5 displays the freight cost table needed to calculate the outbound freight costs from the DCs to ABC's retail stores. For now, notice that the table shows the average cost per lb. on outbound shipments from a DC to the retail stores – depending upon the total lbs. per day shipped by a DC. We will explain this table further in the next section of this chapter where we discuss the analyses based on this data table.

Table 5.6 supplies data on the annual fixed and shutdown costs of the DCs, as well as other miscellaneous data.

TABLE 5.6 DC Annual Fixed and One-Time Shutdown Costs, and Miscellaneous Data

Overall Average lbs. per Unit of All End Items	*6.31619*
Frt cost per lb.: For All Plant to DC Shipments ... note that for simplicity, the cost per lb. is the same for all shipments from the plant to each DC. In a real-world study the costs per lb. will generally vary for each plant–DC combination	$ 0.15625
DC Operations Annual Fixed Costs – for all three DCs in total – i.e., the Base Case	$ 10,000,000
DC Operations Annual Fixed Costs – for any two-DC network scenario (i.e., DC_A closed, DC_B closed, or DC_C closed)	$ 8,000,000
One-Time Costs to Shut Down a DC	$ 250,000
One-Time Freight Costs to Transfer Inventory From a DC If It Is Shutdown	$ 50,000
Assumed Number of Business Days (i.e., DC working and shipping days per year)	260

TABLE 5.7 Item Master Data

Count	*Item Number*	*Cases per Pallet*	*Cases per Tier*	*Tiers per Pallet*
1	128	60	12	5
2	133	80	20	4
3	139	80	16	5
4	292	80	20	4
5	323	80	20	4
6	336	60	12	5
7	349	80	20	4
8	368	80	16	5
9	381	80	20	4
10	440	80	20	4
11	442	60	12	5
12	469	80	20	4
13	480	80	16	5
14	499	80	20	4
15	571	80	20	4
16	588	60	12	5
17	612	80	20	4
18	622	80	16	5
19	658	80	20	4
20	664	80	20	4
21	667	60	12	5
22	668	80	20	4
23	669	80	16	5
24	712	80	20	4
25	716	80	20	4
26	723	60	12	5
27	771	80	20	4
28	803	80	16	5
29	883	80	20	4
30	956	80	20	4

TABLE 5.8 DC Variable Handling Costs

Unit	*Cost per Unit Handling Rate in $*
Case	$ 2.50
Pallet	$ 20.00

Tables 5.7, 5.8, and 5.9 furnish the data and a blank template to facilitate the calculation of the DC variable handling costs. Table 5.7 indicates the cases per pallet, the cases per tier, and the tiers per pallet for each item. In a typical corporate database, these three data fields would be found in what is usually called the item master data module.[8] Note that a "tier" is a row of cases on a pallet. For example, Table 5.7 shows that a pallet of item (product) 128 has 5 tiers (rows) of cases, with 12 cases per tier; and, therefore, 60 cases per pallet (i.e., 5 × 12).

Table 5.8 displays the variable handling costs for a warehouse worker to pick one individual case and one full pallet of a product.[9] As discussed, it costs significantly more per case to pick single, loose cases compared to full pallets of cases, as Tables 5.7 and 5.8 collectively illustrate. Note in Table 5.7 that the number of individual cases on a full pallet of ABC's products ranges from 60 to 80. So, to pick 60 cases individually (i.e., one by one) represents a cost of $150 (60 cases × $2.50 per case) whereas to pick a full pallet of 60 cases costs only $20. In the next section, we will review how to utilize the data in Tables 5.7 and 5.8 to fill out the Table 5.9 template.

Distribution Network Study Calculations

This section illustrates the calculations employed to determine the solutions for each cost component found in the Table 5.1 solution template. In the next section, we will discuss the overall analytic solution itself.

Table 5.10 illustrates how we obtain plant-to-DC inbound and DC-to-store outbound freight costs, and the following provides additional detail:

Plant-to-DC Freight Costs

- For simplicity, we assume the total units shipped per year from the plant to the DCs equals the total units shipped outbound from the DCs to the stores.
- Total units shipped per year = 6,586,250 (Table 5.4),
- Per Table 5.6, the average lbs. per unit = 6.31619 lbs. and the average freight cost per lb. = $0.15625.
- Total units shipped × average lbs. per unit × average freight cost per lb. = $6,500,000[10]

DC-to-Retail Store Freight Costs (Scenario 2: DC B to Stores Example)

- DC B currently ships 56,000 lbs. per day to the stores it serves (Table 5.4).
- DC A closes, and its 64,000 lbs. per day shipped to stores is split equally between DC B and DC C (32,000 lbs. each).
- DC B would now ship 88,000 lbs. per day to the stores in this scenario (56,000 lbs. + 32,000 lbs.).

TABLE 5.9 Template to Calculate Total Annual Variable Handling Costs

Item	*Total DC Shipments to Retail Stores in Units (i.e., in Total Cases)*	*Total Cases Shipped to Retail Stores as Full Pallet Quantities*	*Total Cases Shipped to Retail Stores as Individual Cases*	*Total Full Pallets Shipped to Retail Stores*	*Total Variable Pallet Handling Costs ($)*	*Total Variable Case Handling Costs ($)*	*Total Variable Handling Costs ($)*	*Percent of Cases Picked as Full Pallets*
128								85%
133								85%
139								85%
292								85%
323								85%
336								85%
349								85%
368								85%
381								85%
440								85%
442								85%
469								85%
480								85%
499								85%
571								85%
588								85%
612								85%
622								85%
658								85%
664								85%
667								85%
668								85%
669								85%
712								85%
716								85%
723								85%
771								85%
803								85%
883								85%
956								85%

Notes

1 Units and Cases are the same thing, i.e., units = cases.

2 For simplicity, we assume that for all 30 items, 85% of the cases shipped by the DCs to the Retail Stores are picked as "full pallets." The remaining cases (i.e., 15% of the total cases of each item) are picked as individual loose cases. Note that in the 5th column, where total full pallets shipped is calculated, the calculation for some items may result in a number that is not an integer. Since this is an annual estimate only, this approximation can be rounded off to the nearest integer and will be good.

TABLE 5.10 Illustrative Calculations of Annual Inbound and Outbound Freight Costs

Inbound Freight Costs Plant to DCs		*Outbound Freight Costs in the Close DC_A Scenario*				
			DC A to Stores	*DC B to Stores**	*DC C to Stores**	*Total*
Total Units Shipped	6,586,250	lbs. per Day Shipped Base Case	64,000	56,000	40,000	160,000
Average lbs. per Unit	6.32	lbs. per Day Shipped If DC_A Closed	0	88,000	72,000	160,000
Frt $ per lb.: Plant to DCs	$ 0.156	Frt $ per lb.: DCs to Stores		$ 0.307	$ 0.357	
Total Inbound Freight Costs	$ 6,500,000	Business Days per Year		260	260	
		Total Outbound Freight Costs		$ 7,024,160	$ 6,683,040	$ 13,707,200

* If DC A is closed, then DCs B and C each pick up 50% of DC A's outbound volume.

- Table 5.5 shows that a DC shipping between 86,001 and 90,000 lbs. per day would have an average freight cost per lb. of $0.307.[11]
- So, in this scenario (where DC A is closed), DC B's annual outbound freight costs = $7,024,160 = 88,000 lbs. per day × $0.307 per lb. × 260 business (i.e., shipping) days per year.[12]

<u>*Annual Inventory Carrying Costs*</u>

Table 5.11 illustrates and explains the assumptions and rationale underlying the calculation of the annual inventory carrying costs at the DCs and at the retail stores, in the base case and the three alternative scenarios. The following also offers a brief summary.

<u>*Inventory Investment at the DCs*</u>

- The inventory at cost on the current network of three DCs totals to $8,419,067 (Table 5.2).
- To project the total inventory at cost which a two-DC network (i.e., scenarios 2, 3, and 4) would require to provide the same customer fill rate, we use the square root of n rule (see Exhibit 3.1 in Chapter 3).
- So, [square root (2) / square root (3)] × $8,419,067 = $ 6,874,139 = the projected inventory investment on a two-DC network

<u>*Inventory Investment at the Retail Stores*</u>

- The inventory at cost at all the retail stores served by the current three-DC network totals to $7,000,000 (Table 5.3).
- In the three alternative scenarios where the retail stores are served by just two DCs, the average distance between the DCs and the retail stores all across the U.S. would increase.
- Because the DCs use truckload service to ship replenishment inventory to the retail stores, the average order cycle time on store orders placed on the DCs would therefore increase.

TABLE 5.11 Illustrative Calculations of Annual Inventory Carrying Costs

Firm's annual inventory carrying cost interest rate (r%) = 25%	
Current inventory level in \$ at cost at the three DCs in the current base case	\$ 8,419,067
Projected inventory level in \$ at cost at the DCs in a two-DC scenario – use Square Root of n rule to calculate this*	\$ 6,874,139
Current inventory at retail stores in \$ at cost	\$ 7,000,000
Projected inventory at retail stores on a two-DC network**	\$ 7,700,000
Total annual inventory carrying costs (Base Case) = .25 × (\$8,419,067 + \$7,000,000) = \$3,854,767	
Total inventory carrying costs (only two DCs open) = .25 × (\$6,874,139 + \$7,700,000) = \$3,643,535	

* \$6,874,139 = [Square Root (2 / 3)] × \$8,419,067

** \$7,000,000 × 1.1 = \$7,700,000 [it is assumed inventory investment increases by 10% at retail stores]

- The longer order cycle time on the stores' orders on a two-DC network would necessitate that the retail stores hold more safety stock inventory in order to maintain the same fill rate that they are providing on the current three-DC network.
- Per Table 5.11, we make the (simplifying) assumption that safety stock inventory would increase by 10% at the retail stores under the three different two-DC scenarios.
- Projected total inventory at cost at the retail stores therefore increases to \$7,700,000 in the two-DC scenarios (\$7,000,000 + 0.1 × \$7,000,000).

Inventory Carrying Costs

- ABC's annual inventory carrying cost interest rate (r%) is 25% (Table 5.3).
- Annual inventory carrying costs = Inventory investment costs × r%,
- Annual inventory carrying costs on the current three-DC network = \$3,854,767 = (\$6,874,139 + \$7,700,000) × .25

Annual DC Variable Handling Costs

Table 5.12 displays a completed version of the variable handling template Table 5.9, and an illustration of the analysis performed on item 128. The following summarizes the calculations to determine the variable handling costs for item 128.[13]

- Per Tables 5.7 and 5.2, item 128 has 60 cases per pallet and annual sales of 2,000,000 cases (units).
- We also make the simplifying assumption that 85% of all cases picked in the DCs on orders from stores are picked as full pallets. (In a real-world study, this percentage usually varies by item, and planners would have to determine this percentage separately for each item.)
- So, 1,700,000 cases of item 128 are picked as full pallets (85% × 2,000,000); and the remaining 300,000 cases are picked as single cases (2,000,000–1,700,000).
- 1,700,000 cases picked in full pallet quantities would require 28,333 pallet picks (1,700,000/60).
- Therefore, variable pallet handling costs = \$566,660 = 28,333 × \$20 per pallet picked (Table 5.8),
- Variable single case pick costs = \$750,000 = 300,000 × \$2.50 per case picked (Table 5.8),
- Total variable handling costs for item 128 = \$1,316,660 = \$566,600 + \$750,000

TABLE 5.12 Annual DC Variable Handling Costs Solution and Illustration of Calculations*

Item	*Total Shipments to Retail Stores in Units (i.e., in Cases)*	*Total Cases Shipped in Full Pallet Quantities*	*Total Cases Shipped as Individual (Loose) Cases*	*Total Full Pallets (of Cases) Shipped*	*Total Variable Pallet Handling Costs ($)*	*Total Variable Case Handling Costs ($)*	*Total Variable Handling Costs ($)*
128	**2,000,000**	**1,700,000**	**300,000**	**28,333**	**$ 566,660**	**$ 750,000**	**$ 1,316,660**
133	900,000	765,000	135,000	9,562	$ 191,240	$ 337,500	$ 528,740
139	500,000	425,000	75,000	5,312	$ 106,240	$ 187,500	$ 293,740
292	1,000,000	850,000	150,000	10,625	$ 212,500	$ 375,000	$ 587,500
323	450,000	382,500	67,500	4,781	$ 95,620	$ 168,750	$ 264,370
336	400,000	340,000	60,000	5,666	$ 113,320	$ 150,000	$ 263,320
349	119,000	101,150	17,850	1,264	$ 25,280	$ 44,625	$ 69,905
368	58,500	49,725	8,775	621	$ 12,420	$ 21,938	$ 34,358
381	28,750	24,438	4,313	305	$ 6,100	$ 10,781	$ 16,881
440	113,000	96,050	16,950	1,200	$ 24,000	$ 42,375	$ 66,375
442	55,500	47,175	8,325	786	$ 15,720	$ 20,813	$ 36,533
469	54,500	46,325	8,175	579	$ 11,580	$ 20,438	$ 32,018
480	107,000	90,950	16,050	1,136	$ 22,720	$ 40,125	$ 62,845
499	52,500	44,625	7,875	557	$ 11,140	$ 19,688	$ 30,828
571	103,000	87,550	15,450	1,094	$ 21,880	$ 38,625	$ 60,505
588	101,000	85,850	15,150	1,430	$ 28,600	$ 37,875	$ 66,475
612	49,500	42,075	7,425	525	$ 10,500	$ 18,563	$ 29,063
622	49,000	41,650	7,350	520	$ 10,400	$ 18,375	$ 28,775
658	95,000	80,750	14,250	1,009	$ 20,180	$ 35,625	$ 55,805
664	49,500	42,075	7,425	525	$ 10,500	$ 18,563	$ 29,063
667	15,000	12,750	2,250	212	$ 4,240	$ 5,625	$ 9,865
668	58,000	49,300	8,700	616	$ 12,320	$ 21,750	$ 34,070
669	28,000	23,800	4,200	297	$ 5,940	$ 10,500	$ 16,440
712	27,000	22,950	4,050	286	$ 5,720	$ 10,125	$ 15,845
716	26,000	22,100	3,900	276	$ 5,520	$ 9,750	$ 15,270
723	12,500	10,625	1,875	177	$ 3,540	$ 4,688	$ 8,228
771	48,000	40,800	7,200	510	$ 10,200	$ 18,000	$ 28,200
803	23,000	19,550	3,450	244	$ 4,880	$ 8,625	$ 13,505
883	22,000	18,700	3,300	233	$ 4,660	$ 8,250	$ 12,910
956	41,000	34,850	6,150	435	$ 8,700	$ 15,375	$ 24,075
Total	6,586,250	5,598,313	987,938	79,116	$ 1,582,320	$ 2,469,844	$ 4,052,164

(Continued)

TABLE 5.12 (Continued)

Illustration of Calculations for Item 128

Item	1. Cases per Pallet	2. Total Cases Shipped	3. Percent of Cases Picked as Full Pallets	4. Total Cases Picked as Full Pallets	5. Total Individual Loose Cases Picked
128	60	2,000,000	85%	1,700,000	300,000
128	6. Full Pallets Picked	7. Variable Handling Cost per Pallet	8. Variable Pallet Handling Costs	9. Variable Handling Cost per Case	10. Variable Case Handling Costs
	28,333	$ 20.00	$ 566,660	$ 2.50	$ 750,000
128	11. Total Variable Handling Costs				
	$ 1,316,660				

* While reviewing this table, also read the explanation in the textbook in the subsection titled "Annual DC Variable Handling Costs." The text explains, step-by-step, the calculations that yield the results for Item 128, illustrated directly above. The boxes in the illustration are labelled "1" to "11" to show how to do the analysis, and match the order of the calculations explained in the text.

Annual DC Fixed Costs

Table 5.6 simplifies the process of determining the annual fixed DC operations costs. It indicates that the current three-DC network has annual fixed costs of $10 million, while a two-DC network would have $8 million in annual fixed costs. Directionally, we know that a network with fewer DCs will usually have lower total annual fixed costs than a network with more DCs. Again, however, in a real-world study, significant effort would be required to develop these costs.

Distribution Network Study Solution

Table 5.13 presents the solution to ABC's distribution network analysis. Based upon the three major costs evaluated, it reveals that from a quantitative perspective, closing DC C, and operating a two-DC network from DCs A and B, represents the cost minimizing network design. This network study has illustrated the types of analyses frequently undertaken in distribution network studies. To conclude this section, we now review several general quantitative and qualitative points to keep in mind about distribution network design analyses, using the solution in Table 5.13 to assist this discussion.

Quantitative Notes

As noted, closing DC C (scenario 4), represents the lowest cost solution, followed by scenarios 2 (close DC A) and 3 (close DC B). Each of these two-DC scenarios projects lower annual

TABLE 5.13 Solution to ABC's Distribution Network Study

ANNUAL COSTS		*ALTERNATIVE SCENARIOS*				*ANNUAL SAVINGS OF ALTERNATIVE SCENARIOS THAT CLOSE ONE OF THREE DCs: (Base Case Costs – Scenario Costs)*			*One-Time DC Shutdown Costs*	
Category	*Component*	*Base Case*	*Close DC A*	*Close DC B*	*Close DC C*	*Close DC A*	*Close DC B*	*Close DC C*	*Cost Category*	*Cost*
FREIGHT	Plant to DCs	$ 6,500,000	$ 6,500,000	$ 6,500,000	$ 6,500,000	$ -	$ -	$ -	Costs to Shutdown DC	$ 250,000
	DCs to Stores	$ 12,064,000	$ 13,707,200	$ 13,769,600	$ 13,582,400	$ (1,643,200)	$ (1,705,600)	$ (1,518,400)	Costs to Transfer Inventory	$ 50,000
	TOTAL FREIGHT	$ 18,564,000	$ 20,207,200	$ 20,269,600	$ 20,082,400	$ (1,643,200)	$ (1,705,600)	$ (1,518,400)	Total One-Time Shutdown Costs	$ 300,000
DC OPERATIONS	Variable	$ 4,052,164	$ 4,052,164	$ 4,052,164	$ 4,052,164	$ -	$ -	$ -		
	Fixed	$ 10,000,000	$ 8,000,000	$ 8,000,000	$ 8,000,000	$ 2,000,000	$ 2,000,000	$ 2,000,000		
	TOTAL DC OPS	$ 14,052,164	$ 12,052,164	$ 12,052,164	$ 12,052,164	$ 2,000,000	$ 2,000,000	$ 2,000,000		
INVENTORY	Inv CC at DCs	$ 2,104,767	$ 1,718,535	$ 1,718,535	$ 1,718,535	$ 386,232	$ 386,232	$ 386,232		
	Inv CC at Retail Stores	$ 1,750,000	$ 1,925,000	$ 1,925,000	$ 1,925,000	$ (175,000)	$ (175,000)	$ (175,000)		
	TOTAL INV CC	$ 3,854,767	$ 3,643,535	$ 3,643,535	$ 3,643,535	$ 211,232	$ 211,232	$ 211,232		
TOTAL ANNUAL FRT, DC, & INV CC COSTS		$ 36,470,930	$ 35,902,899	$ 35,965,299	$ 35,778,099	$ 568,032	$ 505,632	$ 692,832		

operating costs than does the current three-DC network. One of the first "quantitative" questions a planner evaluating these results would ask is: how do the one-time costs of shutting down a DC (e.g., DC C) compare to the annual operating savings that would result from a facility closure? Specifically, if we think of these shutdown costs as essentially a one-time investment to generate future annual operating savings, the following questions require examination:

- What is the return on this investment?
- Do the future operating savings projected on a two-DC network guarantee a sufficient return to justify the one-time costs?
- How many years of the projected annual operating savings will it take to pay for these one-time costs?
- What are the risks that the projected savings will either not materialize, or be lower than forecast?
    - It is important to recognize that there always exist risks that the projected annual savings will not fully accrue. Similarly, there is always a risk that planners have underestimated the one-time shutdown and transfer costs.
- In other words, what is the confidence level that the quantitative analysis will prove accurate?

Analysts and management must always assess these and related questions in their evaluation of the quantitative results of a network design study, or any other major analytic exercise, upon its completion.

In the completed case study, Table 5.13 forecasts that the one-time shutdown and transfer costs amount to $300,000. This represents less than 50% of the projected annual savings that would result from closing DC C; and, therefore, projects a return of about 230% on the one-time shutdown costs, and a payback period of less than 6 months.[14] Quantitatively, these results would suggest that ABC may want to consider very seriously the option of switching to a two-DC network to serve its U.S. retail stores.

Qualitative Notes

A good network study must complement a rigorous quantitative analysis with an extensive qualitative evaluation to determine a final decision and course of action. A study that does not balance a quantitative assessment with qualitative considerations and prescient management judgment has much greater risk of resulting in conclusions that lead to faulty decisions than does a well-balanced study. The following represent a sample of the types of qualitative factors that a network design study such as ABC's should consider:

- What are the customer service implications of implementing the quantitative cost-minimizing solution?
- In this case study, would ABC's customers in the service region currently served by DC C react negatively if ABC closed the distribution center?
    - The two-DC scenarios assumed that ABC's retail stores would maintain higher levels of safety stock inventory to ensure that the stores could provide the same current fill rates to their customers – despite the longer average order cycle times between DCs and stores that would occur on a two-DC network.

- However, does the closer proximity of DC C to ABC's stores in DC C's current service region promote a loyalty to ABC by its customers? A loyalty that could wane if DC C was closed, and could this lead to decreased sales and dissatisfied customers in the long run?[15]

- What are the risks to ABC, if any, of having only two DCs instead of the current three?
- Does a third DC give ABC extra distribution capacity as backup in case a fire or other disaster shuts down one of ABC's current DCs for a prolonged period?
- Does operating three DCs instead of two DCs enhance ABC's capabilities to expand its business further in the future?
- Specifically, is there a significant chance that ABC might close one of its three DCs today, only to find that it needs to open a third DC in several years to support a business expansion strategy?

This discussion has highlighted just a few of the qualitative factors a firm must evaluate in any major network design study. Strong qualitative analysis, coupled with rigorous quantitative analysis, facilitates balanced and effective decision-making.

This completes our Excel-based network design study of ABC Inc. Note that we only used straightforward, algebraic formulas to complete this analysis. In the next section, we review how techniques such as mathematical optimization models can also provide powerful, quantitative decision support to supply chain network design and operations planning decisions.

5.3 Using Mathematical Optimization Models for Strategic and Tactical Network Planning

For decades, companies have used mathematical optimization models to provide decision support for supply chain planning activities ranging from long-run strategic network design and facility location to short-run operations scheduling. As early as the 1950s and 1960s, firms in the airline and oil industries had already embraced the use of mathematical optimization models. By the last two decades of the 20th century, industry utilization of optimization models had become widespread, and this expansion has further accelerated in the 21st century. A proliferation of user-friendly, commercially available optimization software products, coupled with the practice of major ERP vendors to increasingly imbed optimization techniques into their software, has jointly contributed to this rapid growth of optimization-based planning.

Linear programming and mixed-integer programming are the mathematical techniques which we broadly categorize as optimization models.[16] Companies that utilized these techniques prior to the 1980s usually hired Ph.D.s in operations research to develop and operate their optimization-based planning models. However, in the 1980s and 1990s, as user-friendly commercial optimization software became more readily available, firms no longer had to hire experts in mathematical optimization to build and run these planning tools, and optimization-based planning flourished in the corporate world.

To demonstrate the analytic power of optimization-based planning tools, we will review several strategic and tactical planning applications frequently found in industry today. In this section, we describe these optimization models in words, rather than through their mathematical formulations. We take this approach because mathematical formulations themselves do not clearly convey to a reader not well-versed in optimization modeling mathematical notation how these models work, nor their immense analytic value. For interested readers, Appendix 5B at the end of this chapter offers examples of optimization models with mathematical formulations.

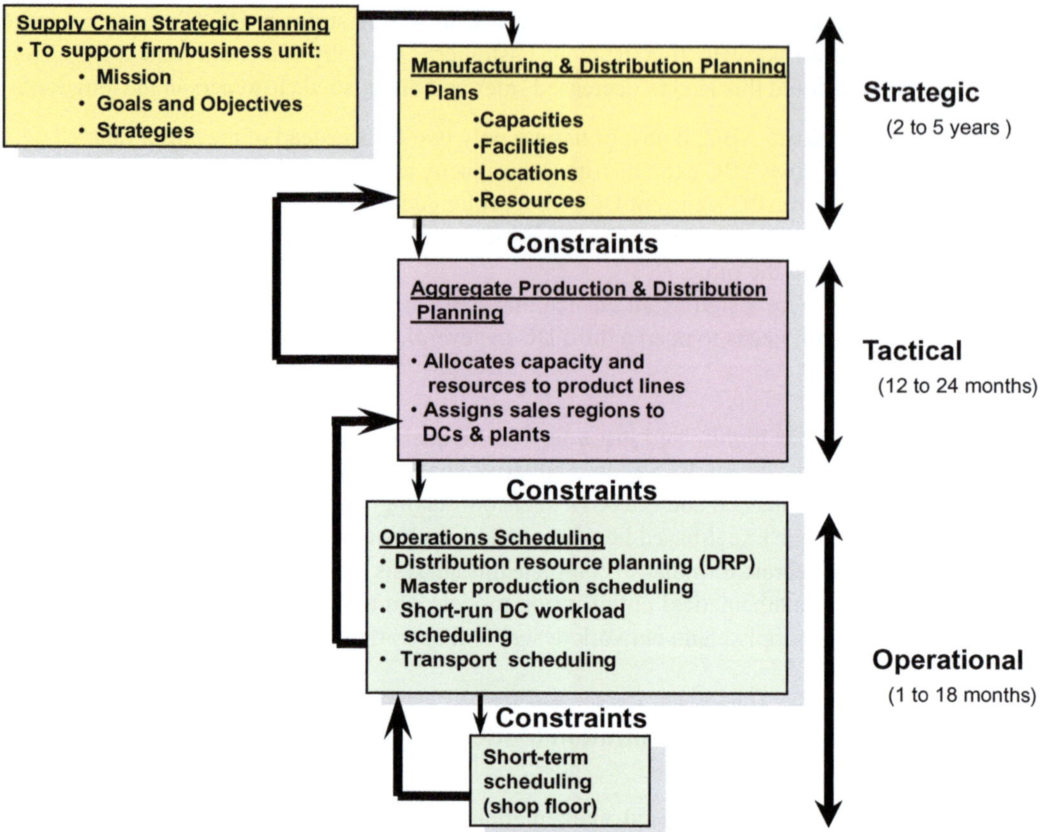

FIGURE 5.4 Hierarchical Manufacturing and Distribution Planning Framework.

The Planning Horizons

Figure 5.4, originally presented in Chapter 4, clarifies the planning horizons that the optimization models presented in this section address. The tactical models typically develop plans for the next 12–18 months, while the strategic models focus on plans for 2–5 or more years in the future. One distinction to keep in mind about these two planning horizons is that:

- tactical models generate plans to optimally utilize a firm's existing infrastructure (e.g., its current plants and DCs), while
- strategic models determine optimal plans for a firm's future infrastructure.

Note also that actions to implement strategic plans may start in the near term (e.g., the planning and the initial construction of a new plant). However, the actual use of the infrastructure built based upon a newly approved strategic plan will not occur for several years until construction is completed (e.g., 2 or more years in the future).

Tactical Planning Optimization Model Examples[17]

We begin by reviewing a tactical production and distribution planning (P&DP) model.[18] To put this model in perspective, the following describes a firm that would use such a model, as well as the typical inputs to this type of model.

Firm Description

1 The firm has a network consisting of several plants and several DCs that serve the U.S. market.[19]
2 The firm's plants ship products to its DCs, and its DCs ship its products to the firm's customer network of several hundred retailer DC locations. (Note that the firm's actual sales to retailers occur when a DC makes a shipment to a retail customer. Thus, DC shipments and company sales are equivalent in this example.)
3 The firm has an existing P&DP optimization model that it developed to generate its annual production and distribution plans.
4 A key input to the model is a demand forecast that projects annual sales by product family, by sales distribution region (SDR).
5 There are over 100 defined SDRs (i.e., geographic regions) that comprise the entire U.S. market in the P&DP model. The forecast for each SDR in the model represents the sum of the forecast total demand of all of the retailer receiving locations in that geographic region (e.g., there would be a SDR to represent demand in the greater Philadelphia, PA region).
6 The demand forecast for each SDR is based upon the approximate portion of total U.S. demand that each SDR has historically comprised, by product family.[20]
7 The P&DP model has the production output rates, the costs per unit, and the capacities by production line, by plant, by product family.
8 Similarly, the model contains the freight costs per unit to ship a product family between all possible origin–destination pairs (i.e., plants–DCs and DCs–SDRs).
9 Finally, the model also has the DC handling (i.e., throughput) rates, costs per unit, and capacities, by DC, by product family.

Description of the P&DP Model Formulation[21]

An optimization model consists of an objective function (i.e., an equation) that one seeks to either minimize or maximize the value of, subject to adhering to a series of constraints. The constraints are a series of equations specifying restrictions or conditions that the model solution must satisfy. Thus, the optimal solution determined by the model is the cost-minimizing, or the profit-maximizing solution that does not violate any of the defined constraints.[22] The objective function and the key constraints of the P&DP model are as follows.

P&DP Model Formulation

1 *Minimize total*: variable plant production costs + variable DC throughput handling costs + plant-to-DC freight costs + DC-to-retailer freight costs,[23]
Subject to:

2 total units of production at all plants ≥ total units of demand by all retailers (i.e., by all SDRs), for each product family,
3 total units of production on each production line of each plant ≤ total units of production capacity on each production line of each plant, in total, and for each product family the production line is capable of producing,
4 total units of throughput at each DC ≤ total units of throughput capacity at each DC, in total, and for each product family,[24]
5 total units shipped from the DCs to the retailers = total units of demand by the retailers, in total and by product family,[25] and
6 total units shipped from the plants to the DCs = total units shipped by the DCs to the retailers, in total and by product family

Based upon the demand forecasts, the costs, and the capacities just described, the P&DP model generates the solution outputs depicted in Exhibit 5.1.

EXHIBIT 5.1 OUTPUTS FROM THE P&DP OPTIMIZATION MODEL

- Distribution plan
  - assigns sales regions (SDRs) to DCs
  - establishes plant-to-DC shipping (supply) plans, and DC-to-retail store (SDR) shipping plans
- Annual production plan, for each plant, by production line, by product family
  - establishes planned operating rates for each plant (i.e., plant capacity utilization rates)
  - assigns production product mixes for each plant (by product family)

Thus, a solution to the P&DP model generates an integrated plan for a manufacturer that will minimize its production and distribution costs over its tactical planning horizon (i.e., the next 12–18 months).[26] The actual solution to a P&DP model for a firm with several plants, several DCs, hundreds of SDRs, and even just 10–20 product families is extremely detailed. Therefore, it is important to create reporting tools (analyses) that automatically summarize model solutions so that planners can analyze the results efficiently. Appendix 5C provides illustrative solution reporting examples.

Interpreting the P&DP Model Formulation

The objective function (1) includes all of the production, distribution, and freight costs that the firm seeks to minimize in its tactical (12-month annual) plan. Importantly, notice that there are no plant or DC fixed costs in the objective function. Our model assumes that the firm developing its tactical production and distribution plan for the following year expects to utilize all its current facilities, and does not have plans to sell any of its facilities in the next year.[27] As previously discussed, a firm will incur the fixed costs (e.g., depreciation) of a plant or DC as long as it owns the facility, regardless of the production and distribution output level of the facility. Therefore, we do not need to include fixed costs in the objective function of the P&DP model, as these costs will not have any impact on the optimal solution obtained.

Constraints (2) assure that the model's production plan for its plants satisfies the firm's forecast of total demand over the planning horizon. The P&DP model has a separate forecast for each product family in each of the model's defined geographic regions (SDRs). To illustrate how large a P&DP model can become, consider a firm which has a model that divides the U.S. into 100 SDRs and uses 30 product families to represent its product line of several thousand unique end items.[28] In this example, constraints (2) would actually consist of about 3,000 individual equations in the P&DP model – i.e., one constraint equation for each unique product family and SDR combination (30 × 100).

Constraints (3) guarantee that the planned production quantities of each product family on each production line do not exceed a production line's capacity to produce that family. Additionally, the constraints restrict the planned total production output on each production line from surpassing the line's overall total annual capacity.

Constraints (4) provide a similar check on the unit throughput at each DC – assuring that a model solution does not plan for more annual volume to move through a DC than the facility can handle.[29] Constraints (5) are often referred to as "balance equations". Namely, these equations guarantee that in a feasible model solution, the total units shipped from the DCs to the retail stores (SDRs) match the total forecast of the retailer (SDR) unit demand specified in the model. These balance equations must be constructed by product family, by SDR in the model.[30] Finally, constraints (6) perform a similar balancing role. These constraints require that each DC receives inbound from the plants the identical number of units which the DC ships outbound to the SDRs assigned by a model solution to be served by that DC. These restrictions hold for both the total units that flow of each product family, and total units overall.

In summary, a manufacturing firm can employ a P&DP optimization model to develop an integrated tactical production and distribution plan. This powerful decision support tool generates a cost-minimizing production and distribution plan that efficiently utilizes a company's existing infrastructure.

A Multi-Period P&DP Model Formulation

The P&DP model is a single-period tactical planning model that does not explicitly include inventory. While this model meets the annual production and distribution planning needs of many firms, some companies prefer or require a 12- or 18-month model which can plan production by the periods within the planning horizon (e.g., by quarterly time buckets).[31] Additionally, these firms often want to explicitly plan for inventory flows and levels by period, and wish to capture inventory carrying costs.

In this section, for illustration, we present a multi-period version of the P&DP model, and denote it as the MP-P&DP model. The example firm we used for the P&DP model remains the same, except now the firm also includes inventory carrying costs in its model, and will plan production and distribution for the next 12 months in quarterly time buckets. This means that the model solution will capture the planned inventory flows from one quarter to the next quarter. We also assume that finished goods inventory is stocked only at the DCs, and that the plants immediately ship the FGI they produce to the DCs (i.e., no FGI is stocked at the plants).

MP-P&DP Model Formulation

1 *Minimize total*: variable plant production costs + variable DC throughput handling costs + plant-to-DC freight costs + DC-to-retailer freight costs + inventory carrying costs, over all periods (i.e., over the annual planning horizon),
Subject to:
2 total units of production at all plants + total units of inventory at the beginning of each period at all DCs ≥ total units of demand by all retailers (i.e., all SDRs), for each product family, for each period in the model,
3 total units of production on each production line of each plant ≤ total units of production capacity on each production line of each plant, in total, and for each product family the production line is capable of producing, for each period,
4 total units of throughput at each DC ≤ total units of throughput capacity at each DC, for each period,[32]
5 total units shipped from the DCs to the retailers = total units of demand by the retailers, in total and by product family, for each period,
6 total units shipped from the plants to the DCs + total units of inventory at the beginning of each period at all DCs ≥ total units shipped by the DCs to the retailers, in total and by product family, for each period, and
7 total inventory at the beginning of each period + total units produced by all plants – total units shipped by the DCs to the retailers (SDRs) ≥ the end of period minimum inventory target, by product family, by DC[33]

The MP-P&DP model generates an integrated production and distribution plan for the tactical planning horizon of a firm (e.g., a 12-month annual plan by quarters) similar to the output of the P&DP model described in Exhibit 5.1. However, as noted, this model's solution output differs from the P&DP model because it also:

- evaluates the costs of carrying inventory in its solution algorithm and yields a plan to minimize the total of variable production, variable distribution, freight, and inventory carrying costs,
- develops a plan for each quarter in the planning horizon (e.g., four periods in an annual model) rather than a single time bucket plan for the entire planning horizon,
- explicitly develops a solution that provides an inventory plan to meet ending inventory targets by product family, by period, and
- plans the flow of inventory from one quarter to the next

A multi-period model can provide a manufacturer with better insights into how it should meet demand over its entire planning horizon, if the firm must plan for seasonal ebbs and flows in demand. For example, suppose a firm has a business where the first half of each year represents well under 50% of the firm's annual demand, and the second half of the year accounts for well over 50% of annual demand. A multi-period model with inventory flows between periods will identify that the manufacturer may need to produce more than actual demand in the first 6 months of the year to build up inventory to help meet demand in the second half of the year.

This completes our discussion of tactical production and distribution planning optimization models. There are numerous variations on the basic single- and multi-period models just reviewed. However, the P&DP and MP-P&DP models are representative of the myriad types of tactical optimization models regularly used in industry today. In the next section, we review strategic planning optimization models.[34]

Strategic Planning Optimization Models

Network facility location decisions are generally classified as strategic planning because the time required to open a major new plant or DC usually spans multiple years. The initial planning process typically takes many months, and once a decision is made to proceed on a new facility, the actual location selection, permitting, and construction processes can last several years.

Mathematical optimization models represent a preeminent quantitative analytic tool to facilitate network location decision-making. To clarify how these models work, we present an illustrative formulation of a plant location optimization model – again described in words rather than in mathematical notation. Appendix 5B, however, offers a mathematical formulation of a strategic planning location model.

A Strategic Plant Location Model

For this illustration, we assume that the same manufacturing and distribution firm which used the P&DP model for tactical planning now has decided to build a new plant on its U.S. network. Demand from the company's retailer customer base has significantly increased, and the firm needs to expand its total manufacturing capacity. The firm has identified six potential locations ranging from California to Vermont to build a new plant. The company's planners have determined that they can modify their existing P&DP tactical model to create a new strategic plant location model.

This new model contains the same basic set of equations (i.e., constraints) that the firm's annual planning P&DP model employs to mathematically describe the company's entire U.S. network. Additionally, however, this strategic version of the P&DP model includes the six locations the firm has identified as potential sites for a new plant. This strategic location model will calculate the firm's total manufacturing and distribution costs with each of the six potential locations added to the network one at a time, and determine the cost-minimizing location of these potential sites for building a new plant. This cost analysis will include the total one-time fixed costs associated with acquiring the land on which to build the plant, as well as all the construction and other related costs associated with preparing to open the facility. Figure 5.5 illustrates the network problem the strategic plant location model will solve.

Strategic Plant Location (SPL) Model Formulation

A facility location problem where an optimization model must determine whether or not to open one or more facilities on a network is usually solved by a mixed-integer programming (MIP) model. MIP models contain binary (or 0-1) variables where a solution value of 0 for a variable representing a potential new location means that the facility is not opened, and a value of 1 indicates that a facility is opened in the optimal cost-minimizing (or profit-maximizing) solution.[35]

In the formulation that follows, we will illustrate how these 0-1, binary variables work. First, however, let's review all of the costs that the SPL model will evaluate to determine which new

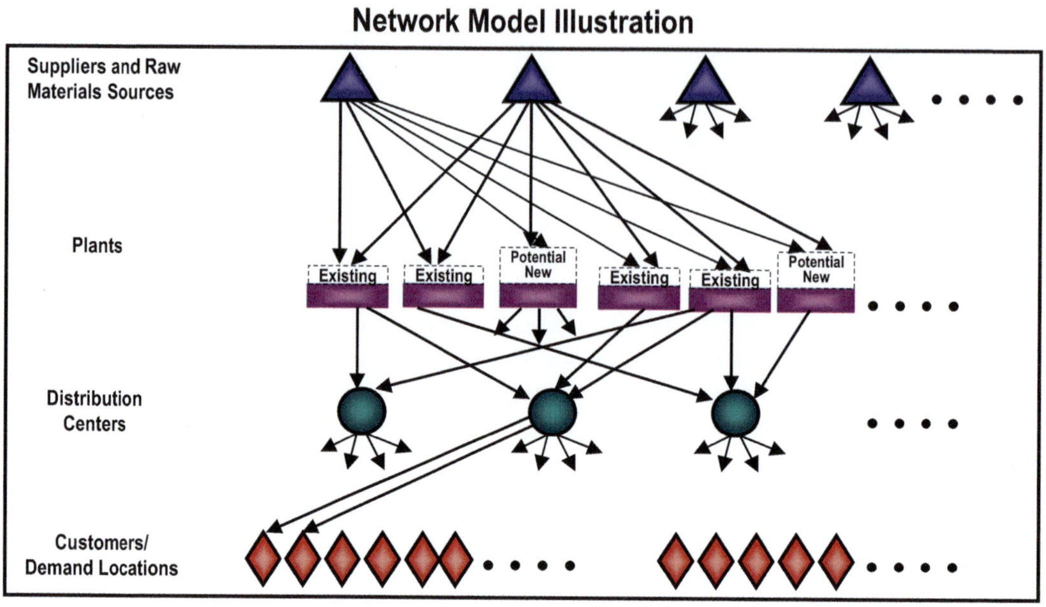

FIGURE 5.5 A Facility Location Optimization Model to Determine the Best Location for a New Plant.

plant location to select from the firm's six candidate sites. The SPL model will find the solution which minimizes the total of the following costs:

- the one-time costs to build a new plant,[36]
- the annual fixed costs of the new plant,
- the annual variable costs of the new plant,
- the annual fixed costs of all the existing plants on the current network,
- the annual variable costs of all the existing plants,
- the annual fixed costs of all the DCs on the current network,
- the annual variable costs of all the DCs on the current network,
- the plant-to-DC annual freight costs (including the freight costs from the new plant), and
- the DC-to-retailer (SDR) annual freight costs

The SPL model is a single-period model that minimizes total costs to obtain the optimal solution. To develop the cost inputs to this model correctly, it is important to recognize the difference between the two types of costs in the model. All costs except for the "one-time costs to build the plant" are annual recurring costs. For example, every year, the company will incur the annual fixed costs and variable costs at each of the current plants on the network. Similarly, operating the current DCs each year will generate annual fixed and variable costs at each facility, and the firm will pay the freight costs to move FGI across the network annually.

The costs to build a plant, however, clearly do not recur annually. Further, these one-time costs generally represent a major investment, and in many cases they will comparatively dwarf the annual costs in the model such as freight costs, and variable and fixed facility costs. For this reason, to include the costs of building a plant in an annual cost model, we must "amortize" this large one-time investment cost into an equivalent "annual cost." This facilitates a model solution that:

1 incorporates the one-time investment costs of building a plant in its cost-minimizing algorithm, and
2 creates a fair and appropriate "apples-to-apples" weighting of both the annual and one-time costs in the model's solution algorithm, and the results obtained.

The process of amortizing a one-time investment cost consists of: (1) determining the time period over which to amortize the cost and (2) deciding upon the appropriate amortization method.[37] For illustration, assume that a firm invests $100 million to build a new plant and it defines the amortization period as 20 years. The amortized annual value in this example would be $5 million (i.e., $100 million/20 years). So, in the SPL model formulation that follows shortly, if the one-time investment cost and amortization period for the new plant were $100 million and 20 years, respectively, $5 million would be the cost assigned in the model for building a new plant. This would place this one-time investment cost and the other annual recurring costs in the model on a comparatively equal-weighted basis.

SPL Model Formulation

- Recall that the firm has identified six potential new locations at which it may build a new plant to expand the capacity of its existing network, and that the optimal solution of the SPL model's MIP algorithm will choose to open only one of these six locations.
- As constraints (7) and (8) in the formulation describe, the one plant (of the six candidate locations) to be opened in the optimal solution will have a value of "1" in the model's solution result, and the other five rejected plant locations will have a value of "0."
- In the objective function of the formulation, we use the notation **"(0 or 1) x"**. Any cost in the objective function with a *"(0 or 1) x"* in front of it indicates that particular cost will have a value (i.e., cost) of "0" for each of the five candidate plant locations not opened by the model solution, while for the plant location to be opened, the cost following the "(0 or 1) x" will be incurred.

1 *Minimize total*: *(0 or 1)* × (amortized one-time cost to build a new plant) + *(0 or 1)* × (annual fixed costs at the new plant) + *(0 or 1)* × (annual variable production costs at the new plant) + annual fixed costs at all current plants + annual variable production costs at all current plants + annual variable DC throughput handling costs + *(0 or 1)* × (annual plant-to-DC freight costs from the new plant) + annual plant-to-DC freight costs from all the current plants + DC-to-retailer freight costs,[38]
Subject to:
2 total units of production at all plants ≥ total units of demand by all retailers (i.e., all SDRs), for each product family,[39]

3 total units of production on each production line of each plant ≤ total units of production capacity on each production line of each plant, in total, and for each product family the production line is capable of producing,[40]
4 total units of throughput at each DC ≤ total units of throughput capacity at each DC, in total and for each product family,
5 total units shipped from the DCs to the retailers = total units of demand by the retailers, in total and by product family,
6 total units shipped from the plants to the DCs = total units shipped by the DCs to the retailers, in total and by product family,[41]
7 Each of the six variables which represents each potential new plant = 0 or 1, and
8 the sum of the six variables which represent each potential new plant = 1

The outputs from the strategic plant location optimization model mirror those of the tactical P&DP model previously described in Exhibit 5.1. The optimal solution to the SPL model produces an integrated production and distribution plan for the example firm's U.S. network. Additionally, the cost-minimizing model solution identifies which one of the six candidate new plant locations the firm should open. Further, the model's detailed production and distribution output shows exactly how the new plant will fit into the existing network. Specifically, the solution output will reveal:

- What product families will be assigned to the new plant?
- How will the production plans for the current plants change, if at all, as a result of opening a new plant?
  - For example, do the product family mixes assigned to the current plants vary from previous assignments with the addition of the new plant?
- Which DCs will the new plant serve?
- What will be the utilization rates of the new plant and the current plants after the introduction of the new plant's additional capacity?[42]
- How much spare production capacity, if any, will exist on the network after the new plant opens?[43]
- Can the current DCs on the network accommodate the additional throughput units that they will have to handle after the new plant begins production?
- What level of capacity utilization will the DCs be operating at given the expanded production volume that will flow through them on the future network?[44]

Interpreting the SPL Model Formulation

The objective function includes all of the production, distribution, and freight costs found in the P&DP model. Additionally, however, the SPL model contains all of the amortized one-time costs associated with building a new plant, as well as the ongoing annual fixed and variable costs that would occur at a new plant. Notice that the SPL model also includes the annual fixed costs at the current plants and DCs, whereas the tactical P&DP model did not. We could have actually excluded the fixed costs at the current plants and DCs because the firm plans to use all of these facilities, and excluding these costs will not change the SPL's optimal solution.

However, by including the fixed costs of the current plants and DCs, the model solution projects the total production, distribution, and freight annual operating costs for the future network with the addition of the new plant.

Constraints (2) through (6) play the same role as constraints (2) through (6) in the P&DP model with one minor difference. Constraints (2) and (3) in the SPL model also include the new plant's planned production output and manufacturing capacity data, along with that of the current plants on the network. The additional constraints, (7) and (8), appended to the tactical P&DP model combine to assure that the optimal model solution opens one, and only one, new plant. Constraints (7) force the six individual variables representing the six potential new plant locations to each have a numerical value of 0 or 1 in the optimal solution.[45] Constraints (8) assure that the model solution does open a new plant, but not more than one.[46]

We close the discussion on strategic and tactical network planning and facility location models with the following comments:

- Mathematical optimization models are extremely powerful analytic tools that provide important quantitative decision support for strategic and tactical production and distribution planning.
- Tactical optimization models often can readily be converted into strategic planning models. For example, we observed that by appending integrality constraints to the tactical P&DP model, we could easily formulate the strategic SPL model.
- Firms with medium- to large-scale manufacturing and distribution networks should use optimization models as a standard business practice to assist in annual (tactical) network planning as well as strategic planning.
- Tactical network planning models frequently contain many of the same variables and constraints as strategic network planning models, and therefore, the data requirements for these two model types often overlap. Thus, a firm that implements tactical optimization-based network modeling as a regularly scheduled, standard business practice positions itself to develop strategic network planning models rapidly – whenever the need to do strategic network planning arises. This is because the firm will always have current data for its existing network, and it will only have to develop a relatively small amount of new data to convert its tactical model to a strategic planning optimization model.[47]

5.4 The Factor Rating Method

The *factor rating method* is another analytic tool frequently used to provide location decision-making support. This method requires planners to first develop a series of factors which they will use to compare the attractiveness of several potential sites under consideration for locating a new facility. Next, planners use a numerical scale to rate each of the potential new locations for each factor. Finally, using all the factors and their ratings of each location for each factor, planners utilize simple multiplication and addition to determine an overall weighted total score for each potential location. The site with the highest score represents the best alternative at which to locate a new facility.

In this section, we present an example of a firm employing the factor rating method to choose the location where it will build a new facility.[48] This example serves to illustrate the method itself, and to demonstrate the mathematical simplicity of this methodology.[49] The basic steps of the factor rating method for any location decision consist of the following:

1. Determine the key *factors* to evaluate in the location selection.
2. For each of the factors identified in step 1, on a scale of 1 to 5, with 5 being the most important, and 1 being the least important, assign a numerical rating for each factor. (That is, assess the importance of each factor.)
3. For each factor, rate each potential location with respect to that factor on a scale of 1 to 10; where 1 is the lowest rating and 10 is the highest rating a location can receive. (That is, assess the relative strength of a potential location in terms of each factor.)
4. For each factor and each potential location (i.e., each unique combination of a factor and a potential location), multiply the factor's rating (from step 2) × the location's rating for that factor (from step 3). These calculations create individual scores for each location/factor combination.
5. For each location, now sum up the individual scores obtained in step 4 to determine a total score for each location.
6. The location that has the highest total score calculated in step 5 is the best location to select for the new facility.

Planners can use the factor rating method to provide quantitative analysis for a broad range of location analyses ranging from international to local site decisions for any type of facility (e.g., a plant or a DC). The following illustrative scenario presents a common application of the factor rating method.

A Plant Location Scenario

The SPL model that our example firm utilized to help select a new U.S. plant location has identified the Lehigh Valley region of Pennsylvania as the optimal cost-minimizing choice. This region is approximately a 40 mile by 20 mile area that includes numerous townships and cities, including Allentown, PA, the largest city in the region.[50] In its SPL model, the firm's planners used a zip code in the centroid of the region to represent the Lehigh Valley as one of the six candidate plant location sites in the U.S.[51] Now the company must select an actual available land site in the Lehigh Valley where it will construct its new plant. To facilitate this selection process, the firm's planners visited the Lehigh Valley region, inspected a number of available sites, and met with the local governmental authorities who have jurisdiction over the available locations. They concluded that two sites in particular represent strong options.

The firm has chosen ten factors that it will consider in choosing between these two locations known as Site A and Site B. To assess the two candidate sites with respect to these ten key location factors, and to weigh their relative importance, the firm will now use the factor rating method.

Column (1) of Table 5.14 displays the ten factors cited as key to the location decision, and column (2) reveals the relative importance of these factors. For example, availability of local labor, with a weight of 5, represents the most important factor; while distance from the nearest rail freight yard, with a weight of 1, holds the least importance in terms of the location decision. Columns 3 and 4 show how the firm rates each site with respect to these ten factors, and the totals at the bottom of columns 5 and 6 provide the overall score for each location. Based on this

TABLE 5.14 Example: Using the Factor Rating Method to Select the Local Site in the Lehigh Valley Area Where the Plant Will Be Built

Location Factors	*Factor Rating*[1]	*Ratings for Each Factor for the Two Potential Sites at Which to Build a Plant*[2]		*Scores for Each Factor for the Two Potential Sites at Which to Build a Plant*[3]	
		Site A	*Site B*	*Site A*	*Site B*
Availability of Local Labor	5	8	9	40	45
Availability of Site for Immediate Use*	4	10	7	40	28
Availability of Additional Land on the Site for Future Expansion	3	4	8	12	24
Business Attitude of Local Community**	3	7	6	21	18
Distance (miles) From Nearest Interstate Highway	3	5	6	15	18
Distance (miles) From Nearest Rail Freight Yard	1	4	8	4	8
Local Land Costs***	4	6	8	24	32
Local Property Taxes	3	7	9	21	27
Proximity to Key Local Suppliers, If Any	2	3	3	6	6
Tax Incentives Offered by Local Government, If Any	4	4	2	16	8
TOTAL				**199**	**214**

Notes

1 The factor ratings scale is 1–5, where 1 means the factor is of relatively low importance and 5 means the factor is of high importance in determining the best location.

2 The scale to rate each site for a factor is 1–10; where 1 means the site rates relatively poorly for a particular factor and 10 indicates the site rates very highly for a particular factor.

3 The formula to compute the score for each factor and location combination is: (Factor Rating) × (Individual Site's Rating for That Factor). For example, the score for Site A's Availability of Local Labor is 5 × 8 = 40. The Total for each site is the sum of the individual factor scores for that site.

* Is the land clear and ready to build on, or is there major demolition and/or clean-up required at the site?

** Is the local township perceived as business-friendly in terms of their local policies and regulations? For example, does the local township exhibit flexibility on zoning questions, etc.?

*** Costs per square foot or total land acquisition cost

analysis, the firm would choose Site B in the Lehigh Valley region to build its new plant – given B's total score of 214 compared to A's 199.

Application of the Factor Rating Method

The scenario just reviewed represents the type of application for which the factor rating method can provide valuable analytic insight. Specifically, the example firm had first utilized a mathematical optimization model to identify the general geographic region in the U.S. where it could locate a new plant most efficiently – based on the six options under consideration. The model had revealed the Lehigh Valley as the optimal area to locate, and now the firm needed to determine an exact site in this region. The selection of an actual physical site requires evaluation of very detailed factors such as the availability of land for future expansion on the site, how business-friendly the local community might be in terms of offering zoning variances, etc. The factor rating method can easily accommodate this level of analytic specificity, as illustrated in Table 5.14. In contrast, a large-scale optimization model such as the SPL model is better suited to analyze the major costs such as freight, distribution, and manufacturing that drive the initial, macro decision regarding what geographic region should the firm locate its plant in. Thus, a two-stage location modeling approach as illustrated in this section represents an effective analytic facility location methodology. Namely, first the SPL model determines the general geographic area where to locate, and second, the factor rating method pinpoints the exact site on which to build a new facility.

Final Notes on the Factor Rating Method

We close the discussion of the factor rating method with several general points about the use of this methodology in location decision-making.

- As just noted, a good use of the factor rating method for location planning is in combination with a strategic optimization model. The optimization model determines a general region where to locate a new plant or DC, and the factor rating method selects the best site within a general region identified by the optimization model.
- Major location decisions, similar to most significant supply chain decisions, require both quantitative and qualitative input. Although the factor rating method is a quantitative methodology, it also has a qualitative dimension. Specifically, decision-makers judge the strength or weakness of potential location sites with respect to individual factors on a scale of 1 to 10. Therefore, one can argue that this represents a "qualitative" assessment by a human being rather than a pure mathematical calculation. In this sense, the factor rating method facilitates qualitative assessments imbedded within a quantitative methodology.
- In summary, the factor rating method offers an easily understood, mathematically simple methodology to provide input to location decisions that require evaluations of numerous complex factors. Further, it facilitates the quantification of sometimes "difficult to quantify" factors such as the business attitude of a local community. In doing so, it incorporates qualitative assessments into a quantitative approach.

Addendum: Using Both a Strategic Facility Location Optimization Model and the Factor Rating Method to Analyze the Same Geographic Region Location Decision

It is important to note that the factor ratings method can be applied to location decisions involving broad geographic regions. For example, consider the SPL model example presented in this section. The SPL model generated a solution that minimized the annual manufacturing, distribution, and freight costs on a network, as well as the amortized one-time investment costs to build a new plant on that network.

The example firm's planners could have also developed a factor rating model to evaluate the types of factors shown in Table 5.14 for the six candidate plant locations. This would provide a more qualitative, judgment-based comparison of the six candidate plant locations to complement the cost-minimizing perspective offered by the SPL model.

Finally, we should note that although an optimization model generates a single, "lowest-cost solution," it is not unusual to obtain solutions where there are several other alternatives whose total costs are just slightly higher than that of the optimal location solution. The model will of course choose the one "optimal" solution. However, particularly in situations where the costs of several alternatives are very close, qualitative considerations become even more important in influencing the final location decision. Thus, a complementary factor rating model that evaluates the same broad geographic region as the SPL model can be extremely valuable when the cost differentials between alternatives are minimal.

5.5 Summary

This chapter began with a background discussion on the types of location decisions that occur at the strategic planning level, and the issues and questions these decisions must address. Next, we considered the topic of distribution network design and stepped through an Excel-based distribution network study problem. This study illustrated the type of data, costs, and analyses needed to develop a distribution center network design plan.

We then explored the role that mathematical optimization planning models can play in providing manufacturing and distribution planning decision support at both the strategic and the tactical levels. The discussion highlighted that significant overlaps often exist between the data required for tactical production and distribution planning models, and for strategic plant and/or DC location planning models. Therefore, firms that have a regularly scheduled tactical optimization model-based planning process position themselves to rapidly develop customized strategic location planning optimization models as the need arises.

Finally, we studied the factor rating method and how this methodology offers an easily implemented and understood quantitative approach to support location decision-making. We noted also that this method incorporates qualitative judgments into a quantitative process. These qualitative assessments provide important complementary outputs to combine with quantitative optimization modeling location results.

Notes

1 In other words, we will not present the mathematical formulations of optimization models, but rather verbally describe what they do, and how they work.
2 A number of global consumer products companies operate networks with multiple manufacturing plants and distribution centers similar to that displayed in Figure 5.1. As stated, this figure is based upon a large consumer products firm's network, although it is not named for confidentiality reasons.
3 So, the DCs operate in a make-to-stock environment.
4 For illustrative purposes, we will not include any other costs, nor delve in depth into the service considerations that would also be studied in real-world practice.
5 The time (and therefore the cost) to travel 200 feet is the same regardless of whether the worker picks one case or one pallet.
6 So, even if a firm owns a DC that for some reason it does not use during a year, the firm still will incur the facility's fixed costs.
7 In a real-world situation where a firm's DCs make shipments to retail stores, and actual sales to customers occur at the retail stores, additional analysis is generally required. For illustrative purposes, we consider DC shipments and company sales to be identical for this case study.
8 The item master data module is one of the foundational components of major ERP systems such as those of SAP, Oracle, Microsoft, and many others.
9 Single cases are often also called "loose" cases.
10 In a real-world study, particularly with multiple plants shipping to DCs, and a diverse product line, more complex calculations would typically be required.
11 See Appendix 5A for an explanation of why Table 5.5 shows average freight cost per lb. decreasing as the daily tonnage shipped by a DC increases.

12 The same approach would be used to calculate the DC–Retail Store costs for scenarios 3 and 4. For the current three-DC network, because each DC ships < 65,000 lbs. per day, a freight cost per lb. of $0.29 is multiplied by the total lbs. shipped to all stores to obtain the outbound freight costs.
13 This same analysis would be carried out for each item.
14 $692,832/$300,000 = 2.309 × 100 = 231%; and $300,000/$692,832 = 0.433, or just over 5 months (0.433 × 12 months = 5.2 months).
15 In a different situation where a firm such as ABC did not own retail stores but rather shipped (and sold) its products to independent retailers from its DCs, the customer service risks described here would become greater.
16 Linear programming is a mathematical technique that either maximizes or minimizes a linear function (an objective function) subject to satisfying defined linear constraints. For example, a production scheduling problem to be solved by a linear programming model would typically have an objective function "to create a production schedule that minimizes production costs" subject to satisfying the forecast "demand" constraints and "production capacity" constraints defined for the problem. Mixed-integer programming is a related mathematical technique that can solve more complicated problems such as whether or not to open or close facilities on a network (i.e., what are termed 0—1 type decisions). Additionally, there are several other mathematical variations on these two techniques.
17 These tactical models are manufacturing and distribution planning tools, and therefore, we could also have discussed them previously in Chapters 4 and 2.
18 See Miller and Liberatore (2021) for a detailed discussion of the actual implementation of a P&DP model at a firm by the author.
19 For simplicity, our example is based on a U.S. market; however, this example would apply to whatever market (global or domestic) that a firm served.
20 The model forecasts are created by allocating to each SDR, the portion of forecast total national demand each SDR historically has accounted for by product family. For example, if a product family in a SDR historically accounted for 1% of the total national demand of that product family, then 1% of the future forecast for that product family in the P&DP model would be assigned to that SDR.
21 The formulations presented here in "words" (rather than mathematical notation), as well as those that follow, are not technically precise. However, each formulation illustrates the basic objective function of the particular model, as well as the major constraint equations that a cost-minimizing or profit-maximizing solution must satisfy. For example, the optimal solution to the P&DP model will minimize the costs described in the objective function, and at the same time will not violate any of the defined constraints.
22 In formulating an optimization model, a user must explicitly define the model as either a cost minimization, or a profit maximization model.
23 DC to SDR freight costs.
24 If the throughput capacity for each product family is identical then capacities by product family are not required.
25 Recall that retailers are grouped into SDRs (geographic sales regions).
26 The annual planning process that most firms carry out represents the most common tactical planning horizon (i.e., a 12-month plan for the following year).
27 If a firm plans to shut down and sell a plant or a DC in the next 12 months, this becomes a longer-term strategic decision, and as reviewed shortly, a different model is required.
28 This is a moderate number of SDRs and product families to represent the geographically distributed demand and the entire product line of a large manufacturer. For many firms, these types of models can require significantly more than 100 SDRs and 30 product families.
29 Constraints (4) assure that the throughput capacity constraints are maintained by product family. The actual number of equations necessary to specify this restriction in the P&DP model can vary depending upon whether or not the throughput constraints at a DC are the same for each product family, or if some or all families have different throughput capacity limits.
30 That is, thousands of individual equations would be required to implement constraints (5) in a medium-sized P&DP model such as one with 30 product families, and 100 SDRs.
31 There exist numerous factors that influence whether a firm will want to use a single-period or multi-period tactical planning model, and we refer the interested reader to Miller and Liberatore (2020) for a detailed discussion of this topic.

32 Note that in some situations, another set of constraints related to the storage capacity of the DCs to hold inventory could be added to this model, if appropriate. For simplicity, these constraints were not added to the MP-P&DP model and the model contains only throughput capacity constraints.
33 Each DC has a minimum end of period inventory target, for each period, by product family. Note this means that planners can set different ending inventory targets by period, for each product family if needed.
34 For the reader interested in reviewing a mathematical formulation of a MP-P&DP model, Appendix 5B displays in mathematical notation, and then explains an actual MP-P&DP model successfully implemented by a major ceramic tile manufacturing and distribution company.
35 MIP models differ from linear programming (LP) models because MIP models have a combination of discrete (binary, 0-1) variables and continuous variables. In contrast, all variables in an LP model are continuous. The previous P&DP models can be solved as LP models because no variables in those two models are restricted to have an integer (0-1) solution value. In a facility location model, however, where the model solution must either "open" or "not open" a new facility, we use a MIP model which allows the location variables to have discrete solutions of 0 (i.e., do not open) or 1 (i.e., open). In the tactical P&DP model, we know in advance that the firm plans to use all of its plants and DCs over the planning horizon of the next 12 months. Therefore, we do not need to use 0-1 variables, and can utilize a LP model rather than a MIP model.
36 For the candidate plant location that the optimal model solution identifies as the best alternative.
37 The reader is referred to any introductory accounting or finance textbook for additional background on amortization. A basic formula for amortization is: [(Initial Cost – Residual Value, if any) / (Useful Life of Asset)]. Amortization is usually done on a straight-line, linear basis, although there are alternative bases than can be used in some cases.
38 DC to SDR freight costs
39 At all the current plants + whichever of the six candidate plant locations is opened.
40 At all the current plants + whichever of the six candidate plant locations is opened.
41 At all the current plants + whichever of the six candidate plant locations is opened.
42 This can be derived from the solution output.
43 This can be derived from the solution output.
44 This can be derived from the solution output.
45 Recall that a value of 1 indicates that a particular location should be opened, while a value of 0 means the firm should not open a plant at a particular location.
46 Since the sum of the six individual variables representing each individual potential plant location must = 1 based on constraint (8), this means five of the six variables must = 0, and one must = 1.
47 For example, assume that a firm conducts a tactical manufacturing and distribution planning review every 6 months to update its current 12- or 18-month rolling network plan. Also, assume that the firm updates all of the data in its tactical optimization model as part of its 6-month standard tactical planning process. Now assume that the firm decides it needs to evaluate its manufacturing capacity requirements for the next 5 years – given a recent long-run forecast that demand will significantly increase from current levels beginning next year. The firm can relatively quickly convert its tactical model into a strategic planning decision support model. From its standardized tactical business planning process, the firm will have current freight, production, and distribution data, and it will have a well-established optimization modeling process. The company will have to enhance its current tactical optimization model with 0-1 (integrality constraints), and it will have to develop data on potential new plant location sites, building costs, etc. However, if the firm did not have a tactical optimization modeling process in place, it would have to spend months developing the data, creating, and then testing an optimization model, etc. to create a strategic optimization model. A firm that has a well-established tactical modeling business process in place can dramatically shorten the time required to create the quantitative decision support required to facilitate a strategic network planning project.
48 This could be the potential location for a new plant, DC, company headquarters, or any other facility.
49 One can argue that the mathematical ease of using the factor rating method enhances its appeal because its simplicity makes it very easy for all users to understand how the solution was obtained, and to discern how much each factor contributed to the final result.
50 Wikipedia contributors. (n.d.). *Lehigh Valley.* In *Wikipedia, The Free Encyclopedia.* Retrieved October 30, 2024, from https://en.wikipedia.org/wiki/Lehigh_Valley
51 It is quite common to use a centralized zip code to represent a geographic region in a large-scale optimization model.

52 The federal legal limit on a truckload shipment in the U.S. is 80,000 lbs. gross vehicle weight. This includes the weight of the trailer and its load, and the tractor. Truckload trailers that are 53 feet can generally accommodate a weight of up to 42,000–45,000 lbs. of freight itself, although this maximum weight can be significantly lower depending on the product or materials being shipped. (https://otfs.net/ftl-max-weight/, accessed 12/3/24; "On Track Freight Systems.")

53 The firm's products still exist; however, the company itself has been acquired and merged into several different companies since it was a stand-alone firm.

54 Portions of this and the previous paragraph were excerpted from Miller and Liberatore (2020).

55 This mathematical formulation previously was published by INFORMS (the Institute for Operations Research and Management Sciences) in its *Interfaces* journal. See De Matta and Miller (1993, volume 23, no. 4) for the complete article.

56 As an example, this notational convention is used to facilitate writing an equation where the notation is meant to show one plant p shipping to another plant p in an equation. In such situations, one does not use p twice as a subscript in a single expression, but rather, for clarity, uses p and p′ as subscripts to show that the equation refers to two different plants in the overall set of plants on the firm's network.

57 This equation is called the "objective function."

58 Keep in mind that Y_{pijt} actually represents many different individual decision variables, all of which must be ≥ 0. There is one decision variable for each product family that is produced on each production line at each plant during each time period. S_{pikt}, $T_{pip't}$, and I_{pit} similarly represent many different decision variables.

59 The model formulation and problem presented in this section was originally published in 2024 in Volume 16, No. 2 of the *International Journal of Data Analysis Techniques and Strategies*. Inderscience, the publisher of this journal, granted permission for this mathematical formulation and model description to be reprinted, and Inderscience retains the copyright of the article.

60 See the discussion earlier in Chapter 5 regarding whether to use geographic regions or specific sites as potential locations for facilities in plant and DC location optimization models.

61 While the model presented here is for a fictitious MDM company, it is patterned after actual models used in practice by firms in this industry.

62 Sales representatives could also pick up product from a FSL located in their local market areas on an occasional, one-off basis. This again represents a standard practice in this industry.

63 The ASCM defines deterministic models as "models in which no uncertainty is included" (ASCM Dictionary, 17th edition). In other words, deterministic models are those where there are no random variables or probabilistic outcomes. Deterministic models obtain a solution based upon a set of defined parameters such as costs per unit and forecasts that are fixed, and not subject to variation.

64 In the cases of building or buying a RDC, and building or buying a FSL, there are one-time construction or purchase costs. These one-time costs are amortized to facilitate a single-period model as is often done in traditional plant and DC location models. These amortized one-time costs are combined with all the other annual fixed costs of operating a facility to generate the total fixed cost charge for each location in the single-period model.

65 Note that third-party distributors incur the freight costs of delivering products to the hospitals. The variable fee per unit charged to the MDM by the third-party distributors reflects their freight, handling, and inventory carrying costs associated with the MDM's products, as well as a planned profit margin. Also note that the third-party distributors own the inventory (i.e., they purchase the product) once the MDM delivers it to them.

66 This is a simple mathematical technique that is used in this model formulation to prevent hubs (RDCs) from shipping to other hubs (RDCs), to prevent field stock locations (FSLs) from shipping to other FSLs, and to prevent shipments from one sales representative's storage locker to another sales representative's locker. Because the transportation cost per unit is set to an extremely high number (or infinity) for these specific potential transport moves, shipments between locations of the "same type" (e.g., FSLs) will not occur in a model solution.

67 The annual interest rate (i.e., percentage) is typically provided by a firm's finance department, or based on an agreement between a firm's logistics and finance organizations. It is usually applied to a firm's standard cost to produce a product, or some similar internal firm standard cost measure.

68 That is, all other operating fixed costs other than amortized fixed costs such as depreciation.

69 That is, the sum of these two expressions represents the total annual inventory carrying costs of the MDM.

70 Integer constraints specify that a location must either be open (i.e., have a value of 1), or be closed (i.e., have a value of 0), in the model's optimal solution.

71 For a full discussion of this facility distribution network design model and the modeling system developed by a MDM firm, see De Matta, Miller, and Peters (2024).

72 A P&DP model would not generate an inventory plan as displayed in the fourth figure because these single-period models generally do not include inventory.

73 Product family forecasts "by customer" would mean the product family forecasts for each customer region defined in the model. Recall that the product family forecast for each customer region would represent the forecast total demand for a product family of all the individual customers in a defined customer region of the model.

74 In this example, the customer is the destination country DC.

Appendix 5A: Truckload Freight Costs per lb. Decrease as the Shipment Weight Increases

Figure 5A.1 graphically portrays the costs per lb. of a U.S. Fortune 500 company's freight expenses on truck shipments throughout the U.S. As the figure illustrates, the cost per lb. decreases as the total weight[52] on a truckload shipment increases. The reason that the freight costs per lb. decrease as shipment weight increases can be explained by the following illustration.

Assume that a freight carrier charges a shipper $2,000 to make a truckload shipment from Philadelphia to Chicago. Freight carriers generally charge a shipper a basic fixed fee for a truckload shipment between a particular origin and destination. (The shipper is basically hiring a driver and a tractor trailer, and the shipper determines how much weight, within legal limits, it will put on the truck.) Clearly, in this example, the shipper's cost per lb. will be lower if it ships more weight (e.g., 40,000 lbs.) rather than less weight (e.g., 20,000 lbs.) – given that the $2,000 shipment cost is fixed (i.e., not dependent on the weight of the load being shipped). Thus, to minimize their truckload freight costs per lb., shippers try to maximize the weight that they load on each shipment.

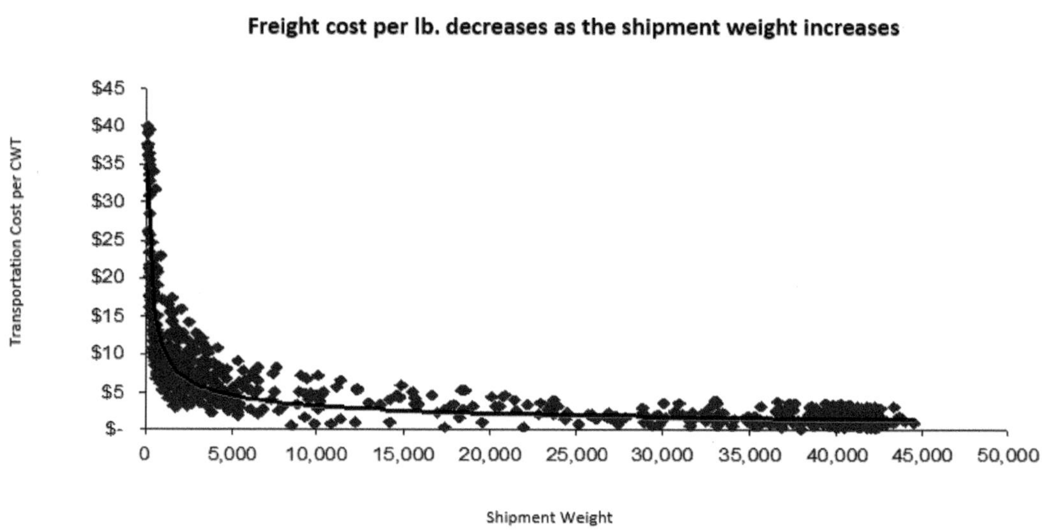

- Per CWT means per hundred lbs. Freight rates and costs are often quoted on a per cwt basis.
- The shipment weight is in lbs.

FIGURE 5A.1 Truckload Freight Costs.

Appendix 5B: Two Illustrative Mathematical Formulations of Optimization Models

This appendix presents two formulations of mathematical optimization models:

1 a tactical, multi-period production and distribution planning (MP-P&DP) model, and
2 a strategic planning facility location model

A Tactical MP-P&DP Model Formulation

The mathematical formulation in this section depicts an actual optimization model developed and implemented by the American Olean Tile Company (AO), a one-time large U.S. ceramic tile manufacturer and distributor.[53] AO manufactured a wide variety of ceramic wall and floor tile products, as well as elaborate mural designs, and the firm sold all of its products nationally. At the time it implemented its MP-P&DP model, AO operated eight factories located across the U.S. from New York to California that supplied approximately 120 sales distribution points (SDPs) which consisted of a combination of third-party tile distributor locations and company-owned stores. Each manufacturing facility had a finished goods warehouse located adjacent to the plant. These factories utilized several different production processes, all of which began with a crushing and milling procedure, and which eventually led to the firing of tile in large kilns. AO produced three basic lines of tile products: (1) glazed tile, (2) ceramic mosaics, and (3) quarry tile.

As the firm's network grew, the lack of coordination which existed between manufacturing planning and distribution planning had become an increasingly significant problem for the firm. For example, AO frequently found itself unnecessarily shipping finished goods inventory back and forth between distribution centers because manufacturing and distribution planned their operations independently. This situation eventually prompted AO's management to sponsor a project to develop and implement a MP-P&DP model to address this planning problem. The objective of implementing this model was to improve the coordination between production, distribution, and inventory planning, and to lower the total annual costs of these functions.[54]

Background Notes

The following notes provide background for the notation and mathematical formulation that follow. The reader interested in a detailed description of this model is referred to Miller and Liberatore (2020) and De Matta and Miller (1993).

- As noted, each plant on this U.S. network had a large DC located adjacent to it. Finished goods were produced in a plant and palletized, and then pallets of the FGI were immediately transported via conveyer or forklift to the adjacent DC.
- Also as noted, SDPs consisted of a combination of third-party and company-owned tile stores that served both contractors and retail customers. SDPs were defined in the model as a specific point (i.e., zip code) located in the center of the actual entire geographic region that each SDP represented. The demand forecast for an SDP represented the projected total demand of all stores served by the tile manufacturer within the SDP.

- The standard unit of measure for ceramic tile is a square foot. Thus, units of forecast demand, production output and capacity, inventory, and shipment quantities are all expressed in square feet.
- This model formulation does not contain any fixed plant or DC costs. As explained earlier in Chapter 5, tactical (e.g., 12- to 18-month) production and distribution planning models generally assume that the firm plans to utilize all of its facilities over the model planning horizon. Therefore, fixed costs will not affect the optimal solution, and they (the fixed costs) can be excluded. If the firm plans to add or sell any facilities over the planning horizon, fixed costs should be included, and a strategic planning facility location model should be used. An example of such a model is provided later in this appendix.

A Multi-Period Production and Distribution Planning Model[55]

Let:

p = index on the plants
i = index on the product families
j = index on the production lines
k = index on the sales distribution points (SDPs)
t = index on the production periods (where each period is 1 quarter, i.e., 3 months in duration)
c_{pijt} = the variable cost per square foot (i.e., per unit) of producing family i at plant p on production line j during period t
v_{pikt} = the cost per square foot to ship family i from plant p to sales distribution point k during period t
p′ = a second index on the plants where $p' \neq p$, for a particular plant p (i.e., p′ includes all the firm's plants except a particular plant p)[56]
$w_{pip't}$ = the cost per square foot to ship family i from plant p to plant p′ (where $p \neq p'$) during period t
h_{pit} = the cost of carrying 1 square foot of family i in inventory at plant p from period t to period t+1
d_{ikt} = square feet of family i demanded at sales distribution point k during period t
o_{pit} = the end of period inventory objective or target (in square feet) for family i at plant p in period t
z_{pijt} = total potential production capacity (in square feet) to produce family i at plant p on production line j during period t

Define the decision variables as follows:

Y_{pijt} = square feet of product family i produced at plant p on production line j during period t
S_{pikt} = square feet of family i shipped from plant p to sales distribution point k during period t
$T_{pip't}$ = square feet of family i shipped from plant p to plant p′ during period t (where $p \neq p'$)
I_{pit} = square feet of family i in inventory at plant p at the end of period t

With all the parameters and decision variables now defined, we formulate this MP-P&DP model as follows:

Minimize:

$$\sum_p \sum_i \sum_j \sum_t Y_{\text{pijt}}\ c_{\text{pijt}} + \sum_p \sum_i \sum_k \sum_t S_{\text{pikt}}\ c_{\text{pijt}} + \sum_p \sum_i \sum_{p'} \sum_t T_{\text{pip't}}\ w_{\text{pip't}} + \sum_p \sum_i \sum_t I_{\text{pit}}\ h_{\text{pit}} \tag{1}$$

Subject to:

$$\sum_p S_{\text{pikt}} = d_{\text{ikt}} \quad \text{for all i, k, t} \tag{2}$$

$$I_{\text{pi(t-1)}} + \sum_j Y_{\text{pijt}} + \sum_{p'} T_{\text{p'ipt}} - \sum_{p'} T_{\text{pip't}} - \sum_k S_{\text{pikt}} - I_{\text{pit}} \geq o_{\text{pit}} \quad \text{for all p, i, t} \tag{3}$$

$$\sum_i (1/z_{\text{pijt}})\ Y_{\text{pijt}} \leq 1 \quad \text{for all p, j, t} \tag{4}$$

$$Y_{\text{pijt}} \geq 0 \quad \text{for all p, i, j, t} \tag{5}$$

$$S_{\text{pikt}} \geq 0 \quad \text{for all p, i, k, t} \tag{6}$$

$$T_{\text{pip't}} \geq 0 \quad \text{for all p, i, p', t} \tag{7}$$

$$I_{\text{pit}} \geq 0 \quad \text{for all p, i, t} \tag{8}$$

Explanation of the Equations

Equation (1) establishes the objective[57] of the model, namely, to minimize total variable production, transportation, and inventory carrying costs, subject to obtaining a solution that satisfies (i.e., does not violate) any of the model's constraints. Each of the constraints (i.e., equations 2 through 8) represents a series of individual equations that specify the conditions which an optimal model solution must satisfy. The conditions that these individual constraints specify are:

- Equation (2) assures that the total square feet (i.e., units) of tile shipped from all plants to each sales distribution point equals the total forecast demand (in square feet) of each SDP, for each product family, in each time period.
- Equation (3) specifies that the end-of-period inventory in square feet is greater than or equal to the minimum inventory target for each product family, at each plant, at the end of each time period.
- Equation (4) assures that in the optimal solution the model obtains, each production line, at each plant, in each period is not scheduled to produce more square feet than the production line's actual production capacity.

- Equations (5) through (8) are "non-negativity" constraints. These simple equations specify that none of the model's decision variables (i.e., Y_{pijt},[58] S_{pikt}, $T_{pip't}$, and I_{pit}) can have a negative value (i.e., a value of less than 0) in the optimal solution. Non-negativity constraints on decision variables are always required in linear programming models. In plain English, these constraints prevent an optimization model from obtaining unrealistic solutions. For example, a production line at a plant clearly cannot produce "negative" quantities of output. A production line will either be utilized – in which case it will produce "positive" quantities of product; or a production line can be idle – in which case it will produce nothing (i.e., a quantity of 0).

The multi-period production and distribution planning optimization model in this appendix is very similar to the MP-P&DP model previously reviewed in Chapter 5. The model in Chapter 5 included explicit DC variable handling costs and DC throughput capacity constraints – which the model in this appendix does not. However, given the similarity of these two models, the reader with questions about the mathematical formulation in this appendix should review again the MP-P&DP model in Chapter 5 to glean additional insights and understanding. Further, the reader interested in a detailed discussion about the optimization model implementation at American Olean Tile Company is referred to Miller and Liberatore (2020) and De Matta and Miller (1993).

A Strategic Planning Facility Location Model[59]

There exist numerous varieties of strategic facility location planning optimization models. These include both plant and DC location models where a firm can use an optimization model to provide quantitative decision support on the selection of a geographic region or a specific site for a new facility.[60] In this section, we review a mathematical formulation for a fictitious medical device manufacturer (MDM) using an optimization model to design a new distribution network to serve hospitals (i.e., its customers) in the U.S.[61]

Background and Problem Description

The medical device industry is a major player in the field of healthcare. Medical devices range from inexpensive products such as syringes and rubber gloves to extremely expensive machines such as MRI (magnetic resonance imaging) devices. In the modeling illustration that follows, a MDM plans to establish a multi-echelon distribution network to serve all hospitals in the U.S. To construct this network, the MDM plans to locate and open several large regional distribution centers, and also to open a series of smaller distribution facilities in local market areas. These local market facilities will be either built and owned by the MDM, or will be owned and operated by third-party distributors with whom the MDM will contract for distribution services.

The MDM has decided that its plants will ship all finished goods directly to regional distribution centers (RDCs), as is the normal practice in the medical device industry. These regional DCs will inventory the entire finished good product line of the MDM. From the RDCs, the MDM will consider all combinations of the following options to deliver products to its customers, namely, hospitals, throughout the U.S.:

1 Ship products directly to hospitals from its RDCs.
2 Open small field stocking locations (FSLs) in local market areas. These FSLs (small depots) would receive shipments from the RDCs, store inventory, and then ship products to the hospitals.

3 Allow MDM sales representatives (i.e., company sales personnel) in local market areas to maintain their own small storage lockers where inventory can be stocked. Sales representatives would personally deliver products to hospitals and medical facilities after receiving orders. Sales representatives would receive shipments directly from the RDCs.[62]
4 Establish contractual agreements with third-party medical device distributors who serve local market areas. Under this option, the MDM would sell its products directly to a distributor in a local market. This distributor would inventory the MDM's products after receiving them from the MDM's RDCs, and then sell and deliver these products to local hospitals.

Model Assumptions and Notation

We formulate this distribution facility location problem as a single-period deterministic model.[63] The fixed costs in the model include:[64]

- the annual fixed costs of building and operating each potential RDC,
- the annual fixed costs of building and operating each potential FSL,
- the annual fee of a storage locker location for each sales representative, and
- the annual fee charged by each third-party distributor to inventory, sell, and deliver the MDM's product line

The variable costs in the model include all transportation costs, distribution handling costs, annual inventory carrying costs, and the per unit fees charged by third-party distributors for handling and shipping services provided.[65] The model employs the following notation:

j = index on plant locations, $j \in J$.
w = index on the hub locations (i.e., regional distribution centers), $w \in W$.
f = index on the field stock locations, $f \in F$.
l = index on third-party logistics (3PL) distributor locations, $l \in L$.
s = index on sales representatives' storage locker locations, $s \in S$.
c = index on hospital locations (i.e., the end customers), $c \in C$.
o= index on distribution facility locations that can ship products outbound: for hubs (i.e., RDCs), $o \in W$; field stock locations, $o \in F$; third-party logistics distributors, $o \in L$; and sales representatives' storage locker locations, $o \in S$.
u= index on distribution facility locations that can receive products inbound from regional distribution centers (i.e., from hubs).
i = index on finished goods product families, $i \in I$.
d_{ci} = annual demand for product family i by hospital c (i.e., the end customer c).
t_{oui} = transport cost per unit to ship a product family i from an outbound origin facility location o to a receiving destination facility location u. Note that $t_{oui} = \infty$ for all shipments between locations of the same type.[66]
u_o = the annual amortized fixed cost of building and of operating a facility location o. Note that for field representatives' storage locations s, u_s is the annual fixed cost lease of storage space.
v_{oi} = the variable handling cost per unit of product family i at a facility location o.
p_{ci} = the price per unit for product family i charged by the MDM to hospital c, when the MDM delivers product directly to hospital c from one of its hubs (RDCs), field stock locations, or sales representatives' storage locker locations.

p_{li} = the price per unit for product family i charged by the MDM to distributor l, when the MDM delivers and sells product directly to a third-party distributor l. Note that distributor l then sells and delivers product family i to hospital c. Also note that p_{ci} and p_{li} can be (and frequently are) different.

q_i = the MDM's standard cost to produce one completed finished good unit of product family i at its plant(s).

τ_{oi} = the target quantity (expressed in weeks of supply) of inventory units of product i at facility location o (i.e., the target number of weeks of inventory to be held at a facility, for example, 4 weeks' supply of inventory).

h = the MDM's annual corporate inventory carrying cost interest rate. Note this is a percentage.[67]

M = a very large number.

The decision variables are:

X_{oui} = the quantity of finished product family i shipped by distribution facility o to distribution facility u.

Z_{oci} = the quantity of finished product family i shipped by a facility location o to fulfill all orders by hospital c.

Y_o = 1, if the facility location o is opened, 0 otherwise.

A Profit-Maximizing Mathematical Optimization Model Formulation

Before reviewing our model formulation, recall that one can construct optimization problems as either cost minimization or profit maximization models. The MP-P&DP model previously presented in this appendix is a cost minimization model. Conversely, in the model that follows, we have formulated a facility location profit maximization problem. Therefore, as the objective function indicates, this model will obtain an optimal solution which maximizes the MDM's profits. Specifically, in this problem, the optimal solution for the MDM will determine which distribution facilities (i.e., RDCs, FSLs, sales representatives' storage locker locations, and third-party distribution locations) the firm should open to maximize its profits (i.e., revenues – costs).

The profit-maximizing problem formulation is as follows:

$$\underset{X,Y,Z}{Maximize} \sum_{i\in I}\left[\sum_{o\in\{W\cup F\cup S\}}\sum_{c\in C}(p_{ci}-q_i)X_{oci}+\sum_{l\in L}\sum_{c\in C}(p_{li}-q_i)X_{lci}\right]-\sum_{o\in\{W\cup F\cup S\cup L\}}u_oY_o-$$
$$\sum_{i\in I}\left[\sum_{j\in J}\sum_{w\in W}\left(t_{jwi}+v_{wi}\right)X_{jwi}+\sum_{u\in\{F\cup S\cup L\}}\left(\sum_{w\in W}t_{wui}+v_{ui}\right)X_{wui}+\sum_{o\in\{W\cup F\cup S\}}\sum_{c\in C}t_{oci}X_{oci}\right]-$$
$$\sum_{i\in I}\sum_{o\in\{W\cup F\cup S\}}\sum_{c\in C}hq_i(\tau_{oi}/52)Z_{oci}-\sum_{i\in I}\sum_{w\in W}\sum_{l\in L}hq_i(\tau_{wi}/52)X_{wli} \qquad (1)$$

Subject to:

$$\sum_{o\in\{W\cup F\cup S\cup L\}}\sum_{c\in C}Z_{oci}=d_{ic},\quad \forall c\in C,\ \forall i\in I \qquad (2)$$

$$\sum_{w \in W} X_{wui} = \sum_{c \in C} Z_{uci}, \ \forall u \in F \cup S \cup L, i \in I \tag{3}$$

$$\sum_{j \in J} X_{jwi} = \sum_{u \in F \cup S \cup L} X_{wui} + \sum_{c \in C} Z_{wci}, \ \forall \ w \in W, \forall i \in I \tag{4}$$

$$X_{oui} \leq MY_o, \ \forall o \in \{W \cup F \cup S \cup L\}, \ \forall u \in \{W \cup F \cup S \cup L\} \setminus o, \ \ \forall i \in I \tag{5}$$

$$X_{oui} \leq MY_u, \ \forall o \in \{W \cup F \cup S \cup L\}, \ \forall u \in \{W \cup F \cup S \cup L\} \setminus o, \ \ \forall i \in I \tag{6}$$

$$Z_{oci} \leq MY_o, \ \forall o \in \{W \cup F \cup S \cup L\}, \ \forall c \in C, \ \ \forall i \in I \tag{7}$$

$$\begin{aligned} Z_{oci} \geq 0, \ X_{oui} \geq 0, \ Y_o \in \{0,1\}, \ \forall o \in \{W \cup F \cup S \cup L\}, \\ \forall u \in \{W \cup F \cup S \cup L\} \setminus o, \ \forall c \in C, \ \ \forall i \in I \end{aligned} \tag{8}$$

We now describe this problem. As noted, the objective is to determine the optimal set of distribution locations, as well as the transportation links that will maximize the MDM firm's "annual profit contribution after logistics costs." Briefly, we define profit contribution after logistics costs as annual total revenue minus cost of goods sold minus all other total logistics costs. As previously outlined, logistics costs include:

- all the annual amortized fixed costs of opening distribution locations,
- the annual fixed costs to operate all opened facilities,[68]
- all variable handling, inventory carrying, and transportation costs, and
- all fixed and variable fees charged by third-party distributors for distribution services that are provided to the MDM

In the objective function (1), the MDM's total gross profit (i.e., revenue minus COGS) is $\sum_{i \in I} \left[\sum_{o \in \{W \cup F \cup S\}} \sum_{c \in C} (p_{ci} - q_i) X_{oci} + \sum_{l \in L} \sum_{c \in C} (p_{li} - q_i) X_{lci} \right]$, while the total annual amortized fixed charges of opening MDM distribution facilities and all other annual fixed operating costs at these facilities, plus the annual fixed third-party distributor's fees charged to the MDM are $\sum_{o \in \{W \cup F \cup S \cup L\}} u_o Y_o$. The total annual freight costs of the MDM, plus the annual variable handling costs at all MDM distribution facilities, plus the annual variable distributor fees charged to the MDM are $\sum_{i \in I} \left[\sum_{j \in J} \sum_{w \in W} \left(t_{jwi} + v_{wi} \right) X_{jwi} + \sum_{u \in \{F \cup S \cup L\}} \left(\sum_{w \in W} t_{wui} + v_{ui} \right) X_{wui} + \sum_{o \in \{W \cup F \cup S\}} \sum_{c \in C} t_{oci} X_{oci} \right]$. Finally, $\sum_{i \in I} \sum_{o \in \{W \cup F \cup S\}} \sum_{c \in C} hq_i (\tau_{oi} / 52) Z_{oci}$ is the total annual carrying cost of those inventories held at the MDM's distribution facilities that are shipped directly to the hospitals, while

$\sum_{i \in I} \sum_{w \in W} \sum_{l \in L} hq_i(\tau_{wi} / 52)X_{wli}$ is the total annual holding cost of inventories held at the MDM's hubs that are shipped to the third-party distributors.[69]

Constraints (2) ensure that demand at each hospital is satisfied. Constraints (3) are "conservation flow equations." Briefly, these equations require that the total quantity of finished goods shipped to hospitals from distributors, field stock locations, or sales representatives' storage locker locations equals the total quantity of these same finished goods shipped from the RDCs to these three facility types. Thus, constraints (3) serve a balancing role in determining the optimal solution. Namely, these equations assure that the third-party distributors, FSLs, and sales representatives' storage locations cannot ship more (or less) to the hospitals than these three facility types receive from the RDCs.

Constraints (4) are conservation flow constraints on finished products supplied by plants that are shipped from RDCs to distributors, field stock locations, or sales representatives' storage locker locations, as well as to hospitals directly from RDCs. Constraints (5) and (6) ensure that finished product can flow between origin distribution facility o and destination distribution facility u only if facilities at both locations o and u are open. Similarly, Constraints (7) ensure that a hospital can be supplied from location o only if o is open. Finally, Constraints (8) are nonnegativity and integer constraints[70] on decision variables.[71]

Summary

In this appendix, we have reviewed a tactical production and distribution planning model, and a strategic facility location model. These two formulations have offered a brief sample of the type of mathematical notation that optimization model developers employ to specify their models on paper. For the reader interested in exploring the mathematics underlying optimization models, we recommend reviewing one of the many introductory textbooks available on linear and mathematical programming.

Appendix 5C: Illustrative Solution Outputs from P&DP and MP-P&DP Mathematical Optimization Models

For this illustration, we assume that a large multi-national firm has numerous plants that manufacture and ship finished goods to the company's DCs located around the world. Each DC then ships these products, upon demand, to the customers in the respective individual country that the DC serves. This global manufacturer utilizes a multi-period production and distribution planning (MP-P&DP) tactical optimization model to determine the following plans for the next 12–18 months:

- a global production plan for each production line of each plant, by product family, and
- a global sourcing plan which indicates the plant to country DC sourcing assignments, and quantity flows by product family

The four figures in this appendix illustrate several of the major outputs of a global MP-P&DP tactical model. Additionally, the first three of these figures depict the solution outputs that a P&DP model, such as the domestic U.S. model described in Section 5.3, would produce.[72] (For a domestic P&DP model, the plants would be represented by plant names

Projected Shipments Over Planning Horizon (000 cases)
(for Product Family #1**)

Final Country DC	Originating Country Plant					
	Colombia	Brazil	Spain	China	United Kingdom	Canada
Argentina	1000					
Brazil	1000	500				
Colombia			500			
Canada		1000				
⋮	⋮	⋮	⋮	⋮	⋮	⋮
France						
⋮	⋮	⋮	⋮	⋮	⋮	⋮
Mexico						1000
⋮	⋮	⋮	⋮	⋮	⋮	⋮
U.S.						1000

**** A table like this would be generated for each product family in the model.**

FIGURE 5C.1 The Model Will Produce a Global Sourcing Plan by Product Family.

** *A table like this would be generated for each product family in the model.*

Production Plan for United Kingdom Plant
(recommended weeks of production over planning horizon)

Product Family	Line 1	Line 2	Line 3
Product Family #1	30	52	0
Product Family #2	15	0	18
Product Family #3	7	0	34
TOTAL	52	52	52

FIGURE 5C.2 The Model Will Also Create a Production Plan by Production Line for Each Plant.

or numbers, rather than countries, and the receiving locations would be various U.S. DC facilities, rather than a DC in a country.)

Figure 5C.1 shows the finished goods shipment quantities planned between each plant and destination country DC by product family. The actual model would produce a plan for each product family and in total. Figure 5C.2 provides an example for one of the firm's plants of the production plan generated for each plant, by production line and by product family. Figure 5C.3 illustrates how the individual production and shipping plans for each plant and product family aggregate to global production and distribution plans. The two tables in Figure 5C.3 highlight the powerful insights that an integrated manufacturing and distribution optimization model generates. The solution algorithm of the model simultaneously evaluates all of the individual costs, capacities, and other constraints such as product family forecasts by customer,[73] to create

Global Production Plan
(cases produced - 000)

	Producing Plant				
Product Family	Barcelona	Cali	....	Toronto	Total
Prod Fam #1					
Prod Fam #2					
Prod Fam #3					
⋮					
Prod Fam #14					
⋮					
Prod Fam #25					
⋮					
TOTAL					

Global Distribution Plan
(cases shipped - 000)

	Originating Country Plant				
Final Country DC	Barcelona	Cali	....	Toronto	Total
Argentina					
Brazil					
Canada					
Chile					
⋮					
Mexico					
⋮					
Turkey					
TOTAL					

FIGURE 5C.3 The Model's Individual Production Line and Product Family Production and Distribution Plans for Each Plant Will Aggregate to a Recommended Global Production and Distribution Plan.

Illustrative Inventory Plan
(FGI in 000 cases at end of 1st period [e.g., quarter])

	Final Country DC						
Product Family	Brazil	U.S.	Italy	Mexico	UK	...	Total
Prod Fam #1							
Prod Fam #2							
Prod Fam #3							
⋮							
Total							

Illustrative Inventory Plan
(FGI in 000 cases at end of 2nd period)

⋮

Illustrative Inventory Plan
(FGI in 000 cases at end of planning horizon)

FIGURE 5C.4 The Model Will Also Produce a Finished Goods Inventory Plan by Location for Each Sub-Period in the Planning Horizon.

the "cost minimizing" integrated production and distribution plan for the entire global network.[74] These algorithms frequently contain tens of thousands of variables, and without the use of a mathematical optimization tool, a planning team cannot develop a truly cost-minimizing plan. It is simply too complex an undertaking without an optimization model. Figure 5C.4 provides a template example of the finished goods inventory plan that a MP-P&DP modeling scenario would produce. For tactical planning purposes, projected inventory flows between periods can represent a valuable planning output.

6

CUSTOMER LOGISTICS

Customer service and the logistics of serving customers represents one of the most critical activities that a supplier must perform. Functions, processes, and strategies designed to satisfy customers by delivering needed or desired goods and services abound. In the last 60 years, numerous initiatives focused on enhancing both the efficiency and the effectiveness of relationships between suppliers and customers have developed and grown. These efforts range from those focused on a specific industry such as Efficient Consumer Response (ECR)[1] to broader initiatives such as Collaborative Planning, Forecasting, and Replenishment (CPFR).[2] In recent decades, Customer Relationship Management (CRM) has become one of the broader, umbrella processes that houses many different supplier–customer activities. Numerous descriptions and definitions of CRM exist including that of Coyle et al. (2017). These authors describe CRM as "the art and science of strategically positioning customers to improve the profitability of the organization and enhance its relationships with its customer base." Coyle et al. further remark that "The concept behind customer relationship management is simple: Align the supplier's resources with its customers in a manner that increases both customer satisfaction and supplier profits."

In this chapter, we will explore several examples of how suppliers quantitatively analyze their relationships with their customers to facilitate the development of *customer logistics* initiatives that will benefit both themselves and their customers. We include an example of a supplier analyzing a collaborative logistics initiative proposed by a customer.

In the next section of this chapter (Section 6.1), we review a simple income statement of a firm. This brief review will illustrate the financial areas of the income statement (and of their operations) that suppliers target when devising collaborative logistics programs to offer to their customers.

When a supplier develops a major logistics program that targets its entire customer base, typically the firm must group its customers into several different segments[3]. Therefore, in Section 6.2, we present two illustrations of customer segmentation schemes, and we outline the criteria suppliers employ to group their customers. In this section, we also highlight several preliminary

DOI: 10.4324/9781003585442-6

steps that firms must take before embarking on the formal development and implementation of a customer logistics program.

Next, in Section 6.3, we present an example of the type of customer bracket pricing program that suppliers frequently offer in an effort to influence their customers' ordering behavior. We will observe the financial efficiencies that these types of customer logistics programs can generate, and we will explore the quantitative analyses that suppliers must perform to develop these programs. In section 6.4, we offer an example of the broader Customer Logistics Order Management (CLOM) programs that suppliers can layer on top of their bracket pricing initiatives in order to create additional shared financial and service benefits with their customers. Finally, in Section 6.5, we consider a situation in which an individual customer approaches a supplier with a collaborative logistics proposal, and we illustrate how the supplier should analyze such a proposal. The chapter then closes with a brief summary section.

To conclude this current introductory section, Exhibit 6.1 presents a series of brief descriptions of customer-centric processes and initiatives commonly found in industry. A review of this exhibit will familiarize the reader with these frequently referenced activities and customer interfacing approaches found in industry today.

EXHIBIT 6.1 CUSTOMER LOGISTICS AND SERVICE ACTIVITIES

- *Collaborative Planning, Forecasting, and Replenishment (CPFR):* 1) A collaboration process whereby supply chain trading partners can jointly plan key supply chain activities from production and delivery of raw materials to production and delivery of final products to end customers. Collaboration encompasses business planning, sales forecasting, and all operations required to replenish raw materials and finished goods. 2) A process philosophy for facilitating collaborative communications. CPFR is considered a standard and is endorsed by the Voluntary Interindustry Commerce Standards Association.*
- *Core customer segmentation:* Every firm that sells to a variety of customers confronts uneven demand. Some customers are highly profitable or have outstanding demand growth potential, others do not.... The key to an effective (customer logistics) system rests in the discipline to realize all customers are "not created equal" and to prioritize and support core customers.**
- *Customer accommodation:* It requires performing order receipt and processing, deploying inventories, storage and handling, and outbound transportation within a supply chain. It includes the responsibility to coordinate with marketing planning in such areas as pricing, promotional support, customer service levels, credit delivery standards, reverse logistics, and life cycle support. The primary market distribution objective is to assist in revenue generation by providing strategically desired customer service levels at the lowest total cost.**
- *Customer relationship collaboration:* The development and administration of relationships with customers to facilitate strategic information-sharing, joint planning, and integrated operations.**
- *Customer Relationship Management (CRM):* The art and science of strategically positioning customers to improve the profitability of the organization and enhance its relationships with its customer base.***

- *Customer Relationship Management (CRM)*: This is a marketing philosophy based on putting the customer first. It involves the collection and analysis of information designed for sales and marketing decision support ... to understand and support existing and potential customer needs. CRM also includes account management, catalog and order entry, payment processing, credits and adjustments, and other functions.*
- *Customer satisfaction:* The results of delivering a good or service that meets customer requirements.*
- *Customer segmentation:* The practice of dividing a customer base into groups of individuals who are similar in specific ways.*
- *Customer service:* 1) The ability of a company to address the needs, inquiries, and requests of customers. 2) A measure of the delivery of a product to the customer at the time the customer specified.*
- *Customer–supplier partnership:* A long-term relationship between a buyer and a supplier characterized by teamwork and mutual confidence. The supplier is considered an extension of the buyer's organization. The partnership is based on several commitments. The buyer provides long-term contracts and uses fewer suppliers. The supplier implements quality assurance processes so that incoming inspection can be minimized. The supplier also helps the buyer reduce costs and improve product and process designs.*
- *Order management:* The planning, directing, monitoring, and controlling of the processes related to customer orders, manufacturing orders, and purchase orders. Regarding customer orders, order management includes order promising; order entry; order pick, pack, and ship; billing; and reconciliation of the customer account.*

Sources:
* ASCM Dictionary, 17th edition (2022).
** Bowersox et al. (2024).
*** Coyle et al. (2017).

6.1 The Financial Components of Their Income Statements That Suppliers Target to Improve with Customer Logistics Programs

Table 6.1 displays the annual income statement of a fictitious manufacturer.[4] This firm produces products in its plants, then ships the FGI to its distribution centers (warehouses), and finally generates revenue (i.e., sales) when it ships FGI from its DCs to its retail customers. In this example, Table 6.1 indicates that transportation and warehousing (i.e., DC operations) cost the firm $15 million annually, or about 15% of total annual revenue.[5]

We can clearly observe from Table 6.1 that any savings in annual freight or warehousing costs that the firm achieves will directly increase the company's earnings before interest, taxes, depreciation, and amortization, and will also raise its overall net income.[6] Therefore, all firms, including our example firm, have a strong incentive to develop and implement customer logistics programs that will increase the efficiency of their warehousing and transportation operations.[7]

TABLE 6.1 An Illustrative Annual Income Statement of a Supplier Firm*

Component	*Symbol*	*Formula*	*$ (millions)*
Revenue (i.e., Sales)	R		$ 100
Costs of Goods Sold	COGS		$ 55
Gross Margin	GM	GM = R – COGS	$ 45
Selling, General, & Administrative (SG&A) Expenses	SG&A		
Research and Development	R&D		$ 2
Marketing	M		$ 4
Transportation (Freight)	F		$ 7
Warehousing**	W		$ 8
Other Operating	OO		$ 2
Total Selling, General, & Administrative (SG&A) Expenses	TSG&A	= Sum of Individual Expenses	$ 23
Earnings Before Interest, Taxes, Depreciation, and Amortization	EBITDA	EBITDA = GM – TSG&A	$ 22
Interest	I		$ 1
Depreciation and Amortization	D&A		$ 2
Taxes***	TX	TX = (tax rate) × (EBITDA – I – D&A)	$ 4
Net Income	NI	NI = EBITDA – (I + D&A + TX)	$ 15

Notes

* Actual income statement formats used in industry vary somewhat by firm, and vary from the example presented here. For instance, there is generally not a sub-total line for "Earnings Before Interest, Taxes, and Amortization." However, for clarity we include this sub-total in this illustration.

** Warehousing is DC Operations.

*** The tax rate shown in the formula on this line would be the firm's corporate tax rate (e.g., 21%).

In the next section, we will review the preliminary steps required to facilitate the development of a customer logistics program.

6.2 Segmenting the Customer Base and Other Preliminary Steps Required to Develop a Customer Logistics Program

Customer logistics programs encompass a wide variety of supplier initiatives ranging from relatively simple bracket pricing plans to expansive strategies covering a broad set of customer service offerings. In this section, we discuss several key analytic steps that suppliers usually undertake in preparation for the development and implementation of a customer logistics program.

Any customer logistics program invariably requires that a supplier segment its customers into multiple groupings or categories. The best number of segments to divide the customer base into will vary by firm, and also often depends on the type of program the supplier plans to develop. In practice, firms generally establish at least three customer segments for broad-based customer logistics initiatives, and sometimes have five or more groupings. For offerings such as a simple quantity-based pricing program, two or three groups (i.e., price brackets) are oftentimes sufficient. One factor that firms must consider in determining the appropriate number of customer segments to establish is the administrative cost and effort that will be required. Complex segmentation schemes with five or more groupings can become difficult to administer.

TABLE 6.2 Bracket Pricing Customer Segmentation Examples

Example 1: A Simple Pricing Structure

Total Order Quantity (Q)	**Q < $10,000**	**Q ≥ $10,000**
Price per Unit ($)	**$10.00**	**$9.00**

Example 2: A Complex Pricing Structure

Total Order Quantity (Q)	**Q < $3,000**	**$3,000 ≤ Q < $6,500**	**$6,500 ≤ Q < $10,000**	**$10,000 ≤ Q < $15,000**	**$15,000 ≤ Q**
Price per Unit ($)	**$11.00**	**$10.50**	**$10.00**	**$9.00**	**$8.50**

TABLE 6.3 Customer Service Inventory Item Fill Rate Segmentation Examples

Example 1: A Simple Service Level Structure

Customer Segment	A	B
Target Item Fill Rate (%)	98%	94%

Example 2: A Complex Service Level Structure

Customer Segment	A	B	C	D	E
Target Item Fill Rate (%)	99%	98%	95%	94%	92%

The A customer segment comprises the firm's top customers and the firm targets to provide the highest annual fill rate to this segment by prioritizing the A customers' orders whenever there are any inventory shortages on weekly orders. In many weeks when inventory is sufficient, all customer orders will be filled completely (i.e., 100%). However, over the course of a year, the A's priority will result in their customer segment receiving a higher overall service fill rate than will any other customer segment in either of the two- or five-bracket systems.

Conversely, structures with fewer categories are less costly and less resource-consuming to administer. Thus, suppliers must compare the additional costs of instituting a complex customer segmentation scheme to the additional benefits expected to accrue from having tightly defined customer segments with differentiated prices and/or services for each grouping.[8]

The following examples illustrate the difference between simple and complex customer segmentation structures.

Pricing Segmentation

Firms in industries such as consumer products frequently offer quantity-based discount pricing in an effort to induce customers to purchase products in larger, more efficient quantities. For example, assume that a supplier has a pricing system based on the total dollar amount of a customer's order. Table 6.2 offers examples of simple and more complex bracket pricing structures.

Service Segmentation

Firms also segment their customer base by offering different service levels to different customer groupings. For illustrative purposes, assume that a supplier targets to service its best customers with a higher inventory item fill rate on their orders than the supplier provides to other groups of its customers. Table 6.3 displays two different item fill rate service segmentation examples.[9]

With these brief introductory examples of customer bracket pricing and customer service segments completed, we now consider several key criteria and then analyses (in section 6.3) that suppliers employ to develop a customer logistics program.

Approaches for Developing a Customer Logistics Program

A firm that is evaluating whether to develop a new customer logistics program (or to enhance an existing program) should at the minimum undertake the following preliminary steps outlined in Exhibit 6.2.

EXHIBIT 6.2 PRELIMINARY STEPS REQUIRED TO EVALUATE AND DEVELOP A CUSTOMER LOGISTICS PROGRAM

1 *Create a Base Case:* The supplier must evaluate the current situation and create a base case that details the current costs to serve its customers and the services offered to customers. The base case should be both quantitative (to calibrate the firm's current costs, and to measure the current service levels provided) and qualitative (to describe the actual services themselves).
2 *Identify the Primary Objectives of the Future Customer Logistics Program:* The supplier must specify the key outcomes that the program seeks to produce.
3 *Outline the Potential Components of the Program:* The supplier should develop a potential list of possible components of the program – with a statement or hypothesis on how each component would help to meet the proposed program objectives.
4 *Evaluate the Scale of the Opportunity to Improve Costs and/or Services:* The supplier should prepare a quick, high-level analysis of the potential opportunity to improve costs and/or services. To be clear, the supplier does not need to perform an extremely detailed, accurate analysis at this point. Rather, utilizing preliminary analyses, and, if appropriate, simplifying assumptions that can later be explored in more detail, the supplier should make an initial projection of the possible range of cost savings and/or service improvements.
5 *Determine If the Potential Opportunity (i.e., the Potential Benefit) Merits the Required Investment:* Customer logistics projects require a significant commitment of time, resources, and money on the part of the supplier. Based on the initial high-level assessment, the potential gains must justify the investment required to develop and implement the customer logistics program. Thus, should the initial analysis in step 4 suggest that the project will generate minimal potential savings, the firm should either abandon or revise the program.

After completing the first four broad steps that Exhibit 6.2 outlines, in step 5, the supplier can then make a final decision as to whether to proceed with the formal development and implementation of the proposed customer logistics program. For perspective, these initiatives often take at least 6 to 18 months to develop and implement, so the opportunity must be significant or the supplier should not pursue the project.[10] However, once a supplier determines in step 5 that the financial and/or service opportunity justifies developing the customer logistics program, more detailed analyses and work can commence.

In the actual development phase, one important step that a supplier should consider is to review its plan with several key customers. Customer feedback at the start of a project is extremely valuable. It can provide guidance and help to fine-tune general ideas into precisely targeted initiatives that customers will embrace. It can also identify components of a supplier's proposed plan that are not viable from the customers' perspective.

A final valuable step that suppliers should consider is to offer a few key customers the opportunity to test collaboratively in advance one or all of the elements of a proposed customer logistics program. This proof-of-concept piloting approach in which a supplier partners with one or a couple customers can reveal what program elements work well, and which elements require modification and/or abandonment.

Criteria Used to Segment the Customer Base

The criteria used by different firms to segment their customer bases varies; however, the *profitability of serving a customer*, and the *total annual supplier sales to a customer* represent two commonly utilized criteria. *Long-term growth prospects* are another criterion frequently considered by suppliers when assigning customers to particular segments. For example, as the growth of the low-cost "dollar store channel" accelerated in the late 1990s and early 2000s, a number of large consumer products manufacturers placed various dollar store competitors in their higher-ranked customer segments. Although the total purchases of these dollar channel stores did not place these firms among the manufacturers' top customers based on sales revenue, the potential for the future growth of this channel was clear. Recognizing this, some manufacturers assigned firms in the dollar store channel to higher customer segments though their sales were lower than other customers in these segments.

A Final Note on the Preliminary Steps to Develop a Customer Logistics Program

We have outlined key preliminary steps required to facilitate the successful development of a customer logistics program. We have also briefly illustrated what customer segmentation schemes are and will explore this in detail in Sections 6.3 and 6.4 which follow. We now close this section by briefly introducing a costing methodology titled *Activity-Based Costing*.

A fundamental requirement for a supplier to create an effective and efficient customer logistics program consists of the ability to accurately understand their firm's true costs to serve each individual customer, and to determine the profitability of serving each customer. Briefly, this means that a supplier must understand its costs to perform individual activities on behalf of a customer such as picking a case in its warehouse that a customer orders or delivering an order to a customer's warehouse. This also means that the firm must accurately capture data on the number of times per year[11] that it performs each activity to serve each customer. Activity-based costing (ABC) models provide exactly this capability. The Association for Supply Chain Management defines ABC as "a model … of resource costs created as a result of activities related to products or services or other items causing the activity to be carried out."[12] Chapter 7 will offer detailed explanations and illustrations of activity-based costing and the vital decision support that ABC models provide for creating customer logistics programs. For now, we simply note the paramount importance for suppliers of maintaining good ABC supply chain models to facilitate an understanding of the profitability and true costs to serve each customer.

6.3 Customer Logistics Bracket Pricing Programs

Suppliers use quantity-based pricing strategies to incentivize their customers to order products in larger, more efficient to serve increments. These strategies involve creating two or more prices for the same item, and applying discounts and/or upcharges (i.e., higher prices) to the standard per unit price for an item. The term "list price" is commonly used to describe the standard, regular unit price for an item.

The term "bracket pricing" is generally used to describe pricing strategies that have multiple levels of prices for a single item depending upon the quantity ordered by the customer. Different firms employ alternative measures to define "quantity levels" including total pounds, dollars, and units ordered. Further, firms vary in how they determine what price bracket a customer is qualified to receive. Some firms base a customer's price on the quantity of each individual order, while other firms measure the customer's average order quantity over a defined time period (e.g., 6 months or 1 year). In the latter approach, a supplier allows a customer to place individual orders that don't meet the "quantity threshold" for the price that the customer pays; however, over the defined time period, the customer's average order quantity must meet the minimum threshold required for their price bracket. In the bracket pricing case that follows shortly, we will assume that our example firm adopts an "average order" over a defined time period approach.

Table 6.2 displayed two bracket pricing examples: one with two price levels for a single item, and one with five price levels. To explore the customer logistics strategy of bracket pricing, in this section we present a case study of a fictitious consumer products firm evaluating whether it should implement a bracket pricing strategy, and, if so, how many price brackets it should establish. This case will illustrate the analytics that the company performs in its evaluative study, as well as the potential logistics efficiencies that a bracket pricing strategy can effectuate. The case is based upon actual bracket pricing studies and implementations in the U.S. conducted by several Fortune 500 companies.

A Bracket Pricing Case Study – GSC Inc

GSC Inc manufactures and delivers consumer products to a wide variety of customers (retailers and wholesalers) in the U.S. GSC serves all its U.S. customers from a single warehouse located in central Pennsylvania. The firm produces five different products, and their customers can order any combination of products on an individual order (i.e., customers can order all five products, just one product, or any other combination). Currently, the firm's pricing policy is as follows:

1 GSC has one *list* price for each product (i.e., it does not currently use a bracket pricing approach).
2 GSC offers "uniform delivered" pricing – this means that GSC pays the freight costs of delivery to all its customers. Further, the price charged to each customer for a product is identical regardless of where the customer receiving location (i.e., the customer "ship to" location) is. Thus, a customer whose warehouse is located 2 miles from the GSC shipping point pays the same price as a customer whose warehouse is located 2,000 miles from the GSC shipping point (i.e., the GSC warehouse).
3 GSC currently has no minimum order quantity. A customer can order just one case of one product, and GSC will deliver the order.

GSC's management recently conducted an internal study of its logistics operations and made the following observations:

1 GSC is shipping numerous small orders per week to customers. The freight and handling costs of these small orders are relatively quite expensive.

2 A number of GSC's competitors have different pricing policies than GSC. Specifically, these competitors use "bracket pricing" structures in which they charge different prices for an item depending upon the quantity that the customer orders.
3 Some competitors have two different prices per item (two price brackets), while others have three different prices per item (three price brackets).

GSC's management has commissioned an internal team to evaluate if GSC should implement a bracket pricing structure whereby GSC would charge different prices for the same item depending upon the quantity ordered by the customer. The team must now perform the analysis and develop recommendations on what new pricing policy, if any, GSC should implement. Management provided a set of directives to guide the project team's work, and Exhibit 6.3 details these directions.

EXHIBIT 6.3 MANAGEMENT DIRECTIONS FOR THE GSC BRACKET PRICING PROJECT TEAM

1 **Evaluate the current pricing and logistics situation at GSC (i.e., create the base case).** Specifically, perform the following analyses:

a Determine the current total revenue of GSC.
b Determine the total freight costs of delivering to all customers.
c Determine the total warehouse handling costs of picking all orders.
d Perform any other pertinent analyses that are appropriate.

2 **Evaluate several alternative bracket pricing scenarios** to determine if by using a bracket pricing structure, GSC may be able to incent its customers to place orders that GSC can handle and deliver more efficiently. Specifically, evaluate if a bracket pricing approach may facilitate potential freight and/or warehouse handling savings for GSC. To do this, perform the following analyses and make the following assumptions:

a Evaluate at least one two-bracket pricing scenario and one three-bracket pricing scenario.
b Use "weight" (i.e., lbs.) as the threshold for establishing brackets.
c Assume that customers will want to order either once per week, or at the individual customer's current order frequency – which is several times per week.
d Assume that customers will not be willing to order once every other week (or less frequently) in order to obtain a lower cost price bracket. (That is, because customers do not want to have relatively high inventory levels – assume that all customers will insist on ordering at least once per week.)

3 **Assess the Bracket Pricing Scenarios**

a Determine the potential freight savings for GSC from each scenario.
b Determine the potential warehouse handling savings for GSC from each scenario.
c Determine the freight and warehouse handling savings associated with each individual discount bracket.

d Calculate the freight and handling savings of each bracket as a percent of the total list price revenue for that bracket.
e Create the "discount price" for each item, for each bracket, by reducing the list price for each item by the percent calculated in step 3d.

The objective is to determine the price bracket structure that will maximize the annual freight and warehouse handling cost savings that GSC Inc can achieve. GSC's rationale is that by maximizing their potential freight and handling savings, and then passing these savings onto its customers, GSC will enhance the competitiveness of their products. In the long run, this is expected to translate into increased total sales revenue and profits. Also, under the U.S. law of the Robinson-Patman Act, it is a legal requirement that the discounts which GSC offers to its higher-volume customers must be justified by the cost savings that GSC achieves in handling and delivering larger orders (in comparison to its smaller orders). In other words, the price discounts offered by GSC on larger orders must be about equal to the relative savings GSC realizes on these orders. Therefore, the process of creating discount prices in a bracket pricing system requires rigorous analysis for both legal and financial reasons.

Bracket Pricing Analysis – Introduction

We now describe and illustrate the analyses the GSC project team will undertake to develop a bracket pricing recommendation. This type of project represents a substantial investment by an organization both in data development and analysis, and in people resources. Further, there exist numerous methodologies and software tools that one can employ to conduct the required analyses. For example, depending upon the size and complexity of the data to be analyzed, software options for this project range from using spreadsheets (e.g., Excel or Google sheets) to various programming languages. Similarly, the actual analytics required can range from relatively straightforward spreadsheet analyses to complex simulation models developed with programming logic.

Given the variety of methodologies and software tools that can be utilized to conduct this type of project, we will focus on presenting the basic steps and logic required to carry out the analysis. The reader who understands the basic steps and logic of the analyses can determine themselves the best software and analytic tools for their particular situation. For ease of presentation, we utilize Excel to facilitate the illustrations that follow.

Beginning the Analysis

A first step for the project team consists of identifying and obtaining the necessary raw data, and then developing the database(s) which will support the analyses. Acquiring the data frequently necessitates pulling data from multiple sources as a firm may not have all the required data on one corporate database. Further, even if one large corporate database houses all the data needed for the project, typically the team will find it efficient to create its own smaller database just for the bracket pricing project.

Tables 6.4 and 6.5 illustrate examples of the different data sets generally utilized in a bracket pricing study.[13] The tables display the following data sets:

1 **Customer Master Data:** This data set provides the customer hierarchy. GSC Inc ships its products to a number of customer DCs around the country. Each of the customer DCs is a

TABLE 6.4 Examples of Data Sets Required for the Bracket Pricing Study

Customer Master Data

Customer	*Customer Number*	*Ship To Location*	*Ship To Location Number*
Save-A-Bunch	100	Save-A-Bunch Boonton	101
Save-A-Bunch	100	Save-A-Bunch Virginia Beach	102
Save-A-Bunch	100	Save-A-Bunch Albany	103
Save-A-Bunch	100	Save-A-Bunch Harrisburg	104
Friendly Shop	200	Friendly Shop Denville	201
Friendly Shop	200	Friendly Shop Hartford	202
Friendly Shop	200	Friendly Shop Lancaster	203
Corner Mart	300	Corner Mart Lewisburg	301
Corner Mart	300	Corner Mart Washington	302
Corner Mart	300	Corner Mart Hackettstown	303
Corner Mart	300	Corner Mart Binghamton	304

Item Master Data

Item	*Case Weight in lbs.*	*Case Cube Cubic Feet*	*Cases per Pallet*	*Cases per Tier*	*Case List Price ($ per Unit)*
1001	30	1.85	24	8	$ 50.00
1002	12	0.62	75	15	$ 65.00
1003	20	1.04	45	15	$ 80.00
1004	15	0.83	60	12	$ 20.00
1005	12	0.68	72	12	$ 45.00

Freight Rate Table

Weight From	*Weight to*	*Freight Cost in $ per lb.*
-	2,000	$ 0.30
2,001	5,000	$ 0.25
5,001	10,000	$ 0.20
10,001	20,000	$ 0.14
20,001	30,000	$ 0.09
30,001		$ 0.04

DC Warehouse Handling Costs

Unit	*Handling Rate per Unit in $*
Case	$ 0.25
Pallet	$ 2.00

TABLE 6.5 Example of Customer Order and Shipment History Data Required for the Bracket Pricing Study

Two Sample Orders From 1 Week of Sales History for Each of the Three Customers

Customer	*Customer Number*	*Ship To Location*	*Ship To Location Number*	*Order Week*	*Day of the Week**	*Order Date*	*Order Number*	*Item*	*Number of Cases of the Item on Order*
Save-A-Bunch	100	Save-A-Bunch Boonton	101	1	2	7/14/20XX	12101	1001	48
Save-A-Bunch	100	Save-A-Bunch Boonton	101	1	2	7/14/20XX	12101	1002	194
Save-A-Bunch	100	Save-A-Bunch Boonton	101	1	2	7/14/20XX	12101	1003	22
Save-A-Bunch	100	Save-A-Bunch Boonton	101	1	2	7/14/20XX	12101	1004	77
Save-A-Bunch	100	Save-A-Bunch Boonton	101	1	2	7/14/20XX	12101	1005	93
Save-A-Bunch	100	Save-A-Bunch Boonton	101	1	3	7/15/20XX	13101	1001	48
Save-A-Bunch	100	Save-A-Bunch Boonton	101	1	3	7/15/20XX	13101	1002	190
Save-A-Bunch	100	Save-A-Bunch Boonton	101	1	3	7/15/20XX	13101	1003	24
Save-A-Bunch	100	Save-A-Bunch Boonton	101	1	3	7/15/20XX	13101	1004	80
Save-A-Bunch	100	Save-A-Bunch Boonton	101	1	3	7/15/20XX	13101	1005	92
………	………	………	………	………	………	………	………	………	………
Friendly Shop	200	Friendly Shop Denville	201	1	1	7/13/20XX	11201	1001	194
Friendly Shop	200	Friendly Shop Denville	201	1	1	7/13/20XX	11201	1002	742
Friendly Shop	200	Friendly Shop Denville	201	1	1	7/13/20XX	11201	1003	69
Friendly Shop	200	Friendly Shop Denville	201	1	1	7/13/20XX	11201	1004	288
Friendly Shop	200	Friendly Shop Denville	201	1	1	7/13/20XX	11201	1005	358
Friendly Shop	200	Friendly Shop Denville	201	1	4	7/16/20XX	14201	1001	180
Friendly Shop	200	Friendly Shop Denville	201	1	4	7/16/20XX	14201	1002	766
Friendly Shop	200	Friendly Shop Denville	201	1	4	7/16/20XX	14201	1003	70
Friendly Shop	200	Friendly Shop Denville	201	1	4	7/16/20XX	14201	1004	306
Friendly Shop	200	Friendly Shop Denville	201	1	4	7/16/20XX	14201	1005	334
………	………	………	………	………	………	………	………	………	………

TABLE 6.5 (Continued)

Two Sample Orders From 1 Week of Sales History for Each of the Three Customers

Customer	*Customer Number*	*Ship To Location*	*Ship To Location Number*	*Order Week*	*Day of the Week**	*Order Date*	*Order Number*	*Item*	*Number of Cases of the Item on Order*
Corner Mart	300	Corner Mart Lewisburg	301	1	2	7/14/20XX	12301	1001	16
Corner Mart	300	Corner Mart Lewisburg	301	1	2	7/14/20XX	12301	1002	60
Corner Mart	300	Corner Mart Lewisburg	301	1	2	7/14/20XX	12301	1003	8
Corner Mart	300	Corner Mart Lewisburg	301	1	2	7/14/20XX	12301	1004	24
Corner Mart	300	Corner Mart Lewisburg	301	1	2	7/14/20XX	12301	1005	29
Corner Mart	300	Corner Mart Lewisburg	301	1	5	7/17/20XX	15301	1001	14
Corner Mart	300	Corner Mart Lewisburg	301	1	5	7/17/20XX	15301	1002	60
Corner Mart	300	Corner Mart Lewisburg	301	1	5	7/17/20XX	15301	1003	8
Corner Mart	300	Corner Mart Lewisburg	301	1	5	7/17/20XX	15301	1004	24
Corner Mart	300	Corner Mart Lewisburg	301	1	5	7/17/20XX	15301	1005	30

* 1 = Monday, 2 = Tuesday, 3 = Wednesday, 4 = Thursday, 5 = Friday.

"Ship To Location" and each customer DC is one of several DCs that the parent customer owns. For illustrative purposes, this example data set includes only three parent customers in total. In a real-world study, a large firm in the U.S. will have many hundreds or thousands of customers and customer ship to locations.

2 **Item Master Data**: This data set provides the individual product characteristics and dimensions such as case weight and cases per pallet. This data is used to calculate the weight of each order line as well as the number of pallets and cases picked for each line. (Case cube and cases per tier – i.e., cases per row of a pallet – are shown to illustrate other item data characteristics frequently utilized in more complex, industry analyses. Note that case cube and cases per tier are not used in this analysis).

3 **Freight Rate Table**: Freight rates are based on the weight of the entire order (i.e., the entire shipment). These rates facilitate the calculation of GSC's freight costs for each individual shipment and for total freight costs. The freight costs per lb. depend upon the shipment weight interval each order falls into. These cost weight intervals are developed by analyzing GSC's recent historical freight costs on truck deliveries.

4 **DC Warehouse Handling Rates**: This provides the cost of handling (i.e., picking and loading onto a truck) a case or a pallet. These rates facilitate the calculation of GSC's total DC handling costs.

5 **Customer Order and Shipment History Data**: This data set provides historical order details on GSC's shipments to its customers' ship to locations (i.e., to its customers' DCs). This data is at the line item level (i.e., at the individual product level). For a bracket pricing study, it is generally recommended to use the most recent 12 months of order history, although different time spans (e.g., 6 months) can be used if the analysts believe that a different time span will provide a more representative picture of the current and future ordering patterns of a firm's customers.

Once the project team collects all the required data from their multiple sources, its next step consists of creating a complete project database to facilitate its analyses. This project database

TABLE 6.6 Examples From Line Item Data Base

Two Sample Orders From 1 Week of the Line Item Database for Each of the Three Customers

Customer	*Customer Number*	*Ship To Location*	*Ship To Location Number*	*Order Week*	*Day of the Week**	*Order Date*
Save-A-Bunch	100	Save-A-Bunch Boonton	101	1	2	7/14/20XX
Save-A-Bunch	100	Save-A-Bunch Boonton	101	1	2	7/14/20XX
Save-A-Bunch	100	Save-A-Bunch Boonton	101	1	2	7/14/20XX
Save-A-Bunch	100	Save-A-Bunch Boonton	101	1	2	7/14/20XX
Save-A-Bunch	100	Save-A-Bunch Boonton	101	1	2	7/14/20XX
Save-A-Bunch	100	Save-A-Bunch Boonton	101	1	3	7/15/20XX
Save-A-Bunch	100	Save-A-Bunch Boonton	101	1	3	7/15/20XX
Save-A-Bunch	100	Save-A-Bunch Boonton	101	1	3	7/15/20XX
Save-A-Bunch	100	Save-A-Bunch Boonton	101	1	3	7/15/20XX
Save-A-Bunch	100	Save-A-Bunch Boonton	101	1	3	7/15/20XX
....	....	....	....	....	....	....
Friendly Shop	200	Friendly Shop Denville	201	1	1	7/13/20XX
Friendly Shop	200	Friendly Shop Denville	201	1	1	7/13/20XX
Friendly Shop	200	Friendly Shop Denville	201	1	1	7/13/20XX
Friendly Shop	200	Friendly Shop Denville	201	1	1	7/13/20XX
Friendly Shop	200	Friendly Shop Denville	201	1	1	7/13/20XX
Friendly Shop	200	Friendly Shop Denville	201	1	4	7/16/20XX
Friendly Shop	200	Friendly Shop Denville	201	1	4	7/16/20XX
Friendly Shop	200	Friendly Shop Denville	201	1	4	7/16/20XX
Friendly Shop	200	Friendly Shop Denville	201	1	4	7/16/20XX
Friendly Shop	200	Friendly Shop Denville	201	1	4	7/16/20XX
....	....	....	....	....	....	....
Corner Mart	300	Corner Mart Lewisburg	301	1	2	7/14/20XX
Corner Mart	300	Corner Mart Lewisburg	301	1	2	7/14/20XX
Corner Mart	300	Corner Mart Lewisburg	301	1	2	7/14/20XX
Corner Mart	300	Corner Mart Lewisburg	301	1	2	7/14/20XX
Corner Mart	300	Corner Mart Lewisburg	301	1	2	7/14/20XX
Corner Mart	300	Corner Mart Lewisburg	301	1	5	7/17/20XX
Corner Mart	300	Corner Mart Lewisburg	301	1	5	7/17/20XX
Corner Mart	300	Corner Mart Lewisburg	301	1	5	7/17/20XX
Corner Mart	300	Corner Mart Lewisburg	301	1	5	7/17/20XX
Corner Mart	300	Corner Mart Lewisburg	301	1	5	7/17/20XX

* 1 = Monday, 2 = Tuesday, 3 = Wednesday, 4 = Thursday, 5 = Friday.

can take many forms and can reside on different platforms (e.g., a local corporate server, a high-powered employee desktop, in the cloud, etc.) For this illustration, we will create a line item database[14] that consolidates the data sets in Tables 6.4 and 6.5 into a single database.[15] To create this single database, the team must envision:

1 which data fields from the data sets in Tables 6.4 and 6.5 it will utilize and
2 what "new calculated fields" it must develop

To build the base case scenario of its bracket pricing study, the team knows that it must determine GSC's current handling costs and also the firm's order shipment freight costs.[16]

Order Number	*Item*	*Number of Cases of the Item on Order*	*Case Weight*	*Cases Per Pallet*	*Case List Price*	*Pallets Picked*	*Cases Picked*	*Weight (lbs.)*	*Revenue ($)*
12101	1001	48	30	24	$ 50	2	0	1440	$ 2,400
12101	1002	194	12	75	$ 65	2	44	2328	$ 12,610
12101	1003	22	20	45	$ 80	0	22	440	$ 1,760
12101	1004	77	15	60	$ 20	1	17	1155	$ 1,540
12101	1005	93	12	72	$ 45	1	21	1116	$ 4,185
13101	1001	48	30	24	$ 50	2	0	1440	$ 2,400
13101	1002	190	12	75	$ 65	2	40	2280	$ 12,350
13101	1003	24	20	45	$ 80	0	24	480	$ 1,920
13101	1004	80	15	60	$ 20	1	20	1200	$ 1,600
13101	1005	92	12	72	$ 45	1	20	1104	$ 4,140
...	...	...	...	...	...	...	...	...	...
11201	1001	194	30	24	$ 50	8	2	5820	$ 9,700
11201	1002	742	12	75	$ 65	9	67	8904	$ 48,230
11201	1003	69	20	45	$ 80	1	24	1380	$ 5,520
11201	1004	288	15	60	$ 20	4	48	4320	$ 5,760
11201	1005	358	12	72	$ 45	4	70	4296	$ 16,110
14201	1001	180	30	24	$ 50	7	12	5400	$ 9,000
14201	1002	766	12	75	$ 65	10	16	9192	$ 49,790
14201	1003	70	20	45	$ 80	1	25	1400	$ 5,600
14201	1004	306	15	60	$ 20	5	6	4590	$ 6,120
14201	1005	334	12	72	$ 45	4	46	4008	$ 15,030
...	...	...	...	...	...	...	...	...	...
12301	1001	16	30	24	$ 50	0	16	480	$ 800
12301	1002	60	12	75	$ 65	0	60	720	$ 3,900
12301	1003	8	20	45	$ 80	0	8	160	$ 640
12301	1004	24	15	60	$ 20	0	24	360	$ 480
12301	1005	29	12	72	$ 45	0	29	348	$ 1,305
15301	1001	14	30	24	$ 50	0	14	420	$ 700
15301	1002	60	12	75	$ 65	0	60	720	$ 3,900
15301	1003	8	20	45	$ 80	0	8	160	$ 640
15301	1004	24	15	60	$ 20	0	24	360	$ 480
15301	1005	30	12	72	$ 45	0	30	360	$ 1,350

Additionally, the total revenue generated by GSC's orders must be calculated. This means that each line item (i.e., row) in the project team's database must include:

- the total pallets picked in the warehouse, if any, to service a line item,
- the total individual loose cases picked in the warehouse, if any, to service a line item,
- the total weight of each line item on an order (because freight costs are based on total weight shipped), and
- the total revenue of each line item on an order

Now that the team has identified the "calculated fields" that it requires, the project team can create the fully populated line item database. Table 6.6 displays sample rows of this database for each of GSC's customers.

As noted, there are numerous software tools ranging from Excel equations and functions to database programming languages that one can employ to fill (i.e., create) the line item database.[17] We now describe the logic and formulas underlying the four "calculated fields" in the far-right columns of Table 6.6. This will allow an interested reader to incorporate the necessary analytic logic into their particular software application.

- **Pallets picked per line item:** The "integral value" of the number calculated by the following formula → *(The number of cases of the item on an order) / (the number of cases per pallet of the item)* = the number of full pallets of an item on an order picked, if any. [Note that if the integral value (i.e., the integer portion) of the result is 0, for example, if a calculation yields a result of 0.28 pallets or some other value < 1, it means that the line item quantity is too small to be picked as a full pallet.][18]
- **Cases picked per line item:** *(The number of cases of the item on the order) – [(the number of cases per pallet of the item) × (the number of full pallets picked of the item on an order)].* → Note that if the line item case quantity on an order is less than the number of cases on a full pallet of the item, then all the cases of the line item will be picked as individual, loose cases.
- **Weight per line item:** *(the lbs. per case of an item) × (the number of cases of the item on the order)*
- **Revenue per line item:** *(the list price of a case) × (the number of cases of the item on the order)*

By appending the new calculated data fields to the data fields obtained from the databases and data sets illustrated in Tables 6.1–6.5, the GSC team completes the development of the line item database for the bracket pricing project. Before moving on to the detailed analytic process of constructing the base case, the GSC project team quickly studies the initial project database for preliminary insights.

As the customer master data in Table 6.4 displays, GSC Inc has three customers and these three customers have a total of 11 DCs (ship to locations) which receive deliveries from GSC. Table 6.7 offers descriptive summary data, generated from the line item database, on the historical orders and shipments to these three customers.

Briefly, the average revenue and average lbs. metrics clearly evidence that Friendly Shop is GSC's largest customer, followed by Save-A-Bunch, and then Corner Mart. In a real-world case where a supplier has hundreds or thousands of customers, this initial view of the customer base can reveal important information. For example, does the summary analysis suggest that

TABLE 6.7 Average Revenue, Weight, and Pallets and Individual Cases Picked per Order, by Customer

	Average Revenue per Line Item	*Average lbs. per Line Item*	*Average Pallets Picked per Line Item*	*Average Cases Picked per Line Item*
ALL ORDERS	$ 3,271	946	0.7	22
Save-A-Bunch	$ 2,365	684	0.4	25
Friendly Shop	$ 10,705	3,096	3.2	28
Corner Mart	$ 761	220	-	15

there exist natural clusters of customers who exhibit similar ordering quantity patterns, or is the customer base very diffused with no obvious groupings? Insights such as these can help analysts formulate their preliminary hypotheses on how to best segment their customer base. Notice also that Table 6.7 demonstrates the efficiency that larger customer orders facilitate for GSC's warehouse operations. The average Friendly Shop order enables the warehouse to pick over three full pallets of product per line item – a very low cost type of pick as shown in Table 6.4. In contrast, GSC's warehouse must pick the average Corner Mart order entirely as individual loose cases – a relatively expensive type of picking operation.

Completing the Base Case

Once the project team finishes its initial review of the line item database, the work to create the current base case scenario commences. The first step consists of designing a template that outlines what the base case analytic results should produce.

Table 6.8, which displays this template, indicates that the analyses must provide results at both the individual customer ship to level, and at the aggregate customer level. Briefly, GSC's bracket pricing options potentially include offering discount prices to its customers based upon:

1 the average order quantities placed by each individual ship to location of a customer or
2 the average order quantities of the "parent" customer evaluated as one entity[19]

The Table 6.8 template reflects the customer logistics cost focus of GSC; namely, to evaluate its current freight and warehouse handling costs incurred to serve its customers.[20] It also clarifies that the project team must transform its line item database (Table 6.6) into an order database.

Why Is It Necessary to Create an Order Database?

The freight cost per lb. of GSC's customer shipments are based upon the total weight on a truckload delivery.[21] GSC delivers orders composed of multiple individual line items to its customers. Therefore, to calculate the freight costs of shipments to customers, the project team must aggregate the total weight of each individual line item on an order into the total weight of the order.[22] This order database will facilitate the calculation of GSC's total freight and handling costs over the historical time period that the project database covers.

Table 6.9 displays two sample orders from the database of all orders placed by GSC's three customers.

The sample orders shown in Table 6.9 represent aggregations of the sample line items depicted in Table 6.6. For example, the first order in Table 6.9 (order 12101) represents the sum

TABLE 6.8 Template for the Analytic Output Results Needed in the Base Case Scenario

Customer Level Summary

Customer	*Total Cases Shipped*	*Total Weight Shipped*	*Total Revenue*	*Average Weight (lbs.) per Order*	*Average Revenue per Order*
Corner Mart					
Friendly Shop					
Save-A-Bunch					
Grand Total or Overall Average					

Ship To Level Summary

Customer	*Ship To*	*Total Cases Shipped*	*Total Weight Shipped*	*Total Revenue*	*Average Weight (lbs.) per Order*	*Average Revenue per Order*
Corner Mart	Corner Mart Binghamton					
Corner Mart	Corner Mart Hackettstown					
Corner Mart	Corner Mart Lewisburg					
Corner Mart	Corner Mart Washington					
Friendly Shop	Friendly Shop Denville					
Friendly Shop	Friendly Shop Hartford					
Friendly Shop	Friendly Shop Lancaster					
Save-A-Bunch	Save-A-Bunch Albany					
Save-A-Bunch	Save-A-Bunch Boonton					
Save-A-Bunch	Save-A-Bunch Harrisburg					
Save-A-Bunch	Save-A-Bunch Virginia Beach					
	Grand Total or Overall Average					

TABLE 6.9 Examples from Order Data Base

Two Sample Orders From 1 Week of the Order Database for Each of the Three Customers

Customer	*Customer Number*	*Ship To Location*	*Ship To Location Number*	*Order Week*	*Day of the Week**	*Order Date*	*Order Number*	*Number of Cases*	*Total Weight*
Save-A-Bunch	100	Save-A-Bunch Boonton	101	1	2	7/14/20XX	12101	434	6479
Save-A-Bunch	100	Save-A-Bunch Boonton	101	1	3	7/15/20XX	13101	434	6504
....	....	....	....	....	....	....	....	....	....
Friendly Shop	200	Friendly Shop Denville	201	1	1	7/13/20XX	11201	1651	24720
Friendly Shop	200	Friendly Shop Denville	201	1	4	7/16/20XX	14201	1656	24590
....	....	....	....	....	....	....	....	....	....
Corner Mart	300	Corner Mart Lewisburg	301	1	2	7/14/20XX	12301	137	2068
Corner Mart	300	Corner Mart Lewisburg	301	1	5	7/17/20XX	15301	136	2020

* 1 = Monday, 2 = Tuesday, 3 = Wednesday, 4 = Thursday, 5 = Friday.

Total Freight Cost	*Average Freight Cost Per Lb.*	*Full Pallets Picked*	*Loose Cases Picked*	*Total Pallet Handling Cost*	*Total Case Handling Cost*	*Total Handling Cost*	*Total Freight and Handling Cost*

Total Freight Cost	*Average Freight Cost per lb.*	*Full Pallets Picked*	*Loose Cases Picked*	*Total Pallet Handling Cost*	*Total Case Handling Cost*	*Total Handling Cost*	*Total Freight and Handling Cost*

Total Revenue	*Total Pallets Picked*	*Total Cases Picked*	*Freight Cost Per Lb of the Order*	*Total Freight Costs*	*Total Case Handling Costs*	*Total Pallet Handling Costs*	*Total DC Handling Costs*	*Total Freight and Handling Costs*
$ 22,495	6	104	$ 0.20	$ 1,296	$ 26	$ 12	$ 38	$ 1,334
$ 22,410	6	104	$ 0.20	$ 1,301	$ 26	$ 12	$ 38	$ 1,339
…………	…………	…………	…………	…………	…………	…………	…………	…………
$ 85,320	26	211	$ 0.09	$ 2,225	$ 53	$ 52	$ 105	$ 2,330
$ 85,540	27	105	$ 0.09	$ 2,213	$ 26	$ 54	$ 80	$ 2,293
…………	…………	…………	…………	…………	…………	…………	…………	…………
$ 7,125	-	137	$ 0.25	$ 517	$ 34	$ -	$ 34	$ 551
$ 7,070	-	136	$ 0.25	$ 505	$ 34	$ -	$ 34	$ 539

of the first five line items in Table 6.6 (e.g., the 434 cases on order 12101 equals the total cases of the line items 1001–1005 for order 12101).

For illustrative purposes, we now describe an approach that involves creating an order database from the line item database (i.e., from Table 6.6). We assume in the following example that the GSC project team has built a line item database in Excel that it will now transform into an order database using Excel functions and logic. This will illuminate the type of logic that private industry practitioners often incorporate into database programming languages (rather than using Excel) to create an order database.[23] Exhibit 6.4 provides an example of the steps and functions that one could use in Excel.[24]

EXHIBIT 6.4 CREATING AN ORDER DATABASE FROM A LINE ITEM DATABASE

1 *Apply the Pivot Table Function to the Line Item Database:* In the Excel sheet that contains the line item database, use the Pivot Table function (i.e., Insert, Pivot Table) and create a new pivot table in a separate sheet of the Excel Workbook.
2 *Choose the Data Fields From the Line Item Database That Are Needed in the Order Database:* Using the Pivot Table function, select all of the data fields from the line item database that are also needed in the order database. For example, fields such as customer, customer number, and order number should be selected. *IMPORTANTLY, do not select the "Item" field for inclusion in the order database (i.e., do not select "Item" as one of the Pivot Table Fields).* By skipping (i.e., not including) the item field in the selected Pivot Table Fields, the user indicates to Excel that the data values in the line item database for all the individual line items on one unique order should be summed to create an aggregated total for that individual order. [For example, as previously noted, Order 12101 in Table 6.9 has 434 cases, the sum of the cases on the five line items (in Table 6.6) that comprise Order 12101.]
3 *Copy and Paste the Values from the Pivot Table Order Database Into a Separate Excel Sheet:* To create an order database that is easy to work with, copy and paste the values from the initial order database created by the pivot table into a second sheet, and format the new sheet (database) as appropriate.
4 *Identify Any Additional Data Fields or Calculated Fields to Append to the Order Database Created in Step 3:* Using the Pivot Table function in step 2, and copying and pasting it into a new sheet in step 3, will create the initial order database based on whatever fields the user selects from the fields in the line item database. However, the order database required to facilitate the analyses that will create the base case may require some additional fields. If so, the user must append to the order database created in step 3 whatever additional order-related data fields are required, and use Excel formulas and/or functions to generate any additional calculated order data fields. For example, the six far-right columns of Table 6.9 (from "Freight Cost per lb. of the Order" to "Total Freight and Handling Costs") represent a combination of newly accessed data and newly calculated data fields.
5 *Add and/or Create Any Additional Data Fields Identified in Step 4:* The following are examples (shown in Table 6.9) of adding new data fields to the initial order database created in

step 3. Once the additional fields identified in step 4 are added and/or created, the order database needed to facilitate the analyses which will create the base case is complete.

a Freight Cost Per lb. of the Order → from the initial pivot table order database, we now know the total weight (lbs.) of each order. For example, Order 12101 weighs 6,479 lbs. To determine the freight cost per lb. of shipping this order, we could use the Vlookup function in Excel to obtain the freight cost per lb. from the Freight Rate Table (see Table 6.4).[25]
b Total Freight Costs → (total weight of an order) × (freight cost per lb. of the order)
c Total Case Handling Costs → (total cases picked) × (handling cost per case)
d Total Pallet Handling Costs → (total pallets picked) × (handling cost per pallet)
e Total DC Handling Costs → (total case handling costs) + (total pallet handling costs)
f Total Freight and Handling Costs → (total DC handling costs) + (total freight costs)

The completion of the order database facilitates the next two major steps of the bracket pricing analysis:

1 populating the base case analytic template displayed in Table 6.8 and
2 evaluating the freight and warehouse handling cost savings opportunity which a bracket pricing program potentially could generate for GSC.

Populating the Base Case Template
The input of the base case scenario results into the Customer Level and Ship To Level templates (Table 6.8) represents a straightforward task. As always, numerous analytic options exist to perform this work, and for illustrative purposes, Exhibit 6.5 summarizes how one can do this in Excel.[26] (The user employing a programming language to perform this task would construct logic to aggregate values for selected data fields just as an Excel Pivot Table does.)

EXHIBIT 6.5 POPULATING THE BASE CASE SCENARIO TEMPLATE

The Customer Level Summary

1 *Apply the Pivot Table Function to the Order Database:* In the Excel sheet that contains the order database, use the Pivot Table function (i.e., Insert, Pivot Table) and create a new pivot table in a separate sheet of the Excel Workbook.
2 *Choose the Data Fields From the Order Database That Are Needed in the Base Case Template:* Using the Pivot Table function, select all of the data fields from the order database that are also needed in the base case scenario template. For example, fields such as customer, total cases shipped, and total weight shipped should be selected. *IMPORTANTLY, do not select the following data fields from the order database (Table 6.9) for the base case template pivot table: ship to location, ship to location number, order week, day of the week, order date, order number.* By skipping (i.e., not including) these fields in the selected Pivot Table Fields,

the user indicates to Excel that the base case template pivot table should "aggregate" the data values in the rows of the order database for each of these fields. For example, the number of cases ordered should not be shown by order week or ship to location, but rather should be aggregated to the total cases ordered by a customer.

3 *Copy and Paste the Values from the Pivot Table Base Case Scenario Template into a Separate Excel Sheet:* To create a base case scenario template that is easy to work with, copy and paste the values from the initial base case template created by the pivot table into a second sheet, and format the new sheet (database) as appropriate.

4 *Note on Fields Such as Average Weight, Average Revenue, and Average Cost per lb.:* When using the Pivot Table function, to obtain an "average" rather than a "total" (e.g., average weight per order vs. total weight shipped), it is necessary to choose the option to have Excel calculate an "average" for a Pivot Table Field. The default in an Excel Pivot Table Field is to sum the values of all the fields (rows) that the pivot table is aggregating. So, the user must specify the option that tells Excel to calculate the average for a Pivot Field. (Use the Excel "Help" function or another help source for specific details.)

The Ship To Level Summary

- The process of populating the Ship To Level template with data results is identical to that used to populate the Customer Level template with the following exception. The Ship To location field should be selected as a Pivot Table Field because we want to obtain summary results at the Ship To Level rather than at the Customer Level. All other fields "not selected" in step 2 of the Customer Level Pivot Table are similarly not selected for the Ship To Level Pivot Table.

Table 6.10 displays summary results of the base case analysis at both the ship to and customer levels. Before discussing the results we note that these represent "annualized" results. The actual database which generated these results contained only 8 weeks of order and shipment historical data.[27] Therefore, in Table 6.10, while the average values (e.g., the average order and shipment weight) are exactly what the analysis of the 8 weeks of data history produced, the totals such as total cases represent 8-week values extrapolated to a projected annual value.

Why Annualize Results Based on Smaller Historical Data Sets, and How Is This Done?

Regardless of the time duration of the historical data set utilized, stating analytic results on an annual basis provides corporate managers and their organizations with a better perspective than do partial year results.[28] As a standard business practice, virtually all firms devote significant time and effort to annual planning and budgeting processes. Managers of corporate functions such as marketing, finance, research and development, and of course logistics and supply chain management all know the annual budgets and costs of their respective operations. Therefore, managers can understand the relative magnitude (small or large) when presented with analytic results stating that a proposed project or program will "save X dollars per year" or "increase or decrease revenue by X dollars per year." In contrast, results stated in terms of savings or revenue changes over a fraction of a year (e.g., 8 weeks or 3 months) force managers themselves to translate a projected change in costs or revenues to an annual basis.

Multiple methodologies abound to annualize results from a study based on less than one full year of data. Briefly, the simplest approach is to multiply the initial study results by a multiplier that converts all values such as total costs, total revenues, and total cases to their annual equivalents. For example, in a study based on 6 months of historical data, we would multiply all "total" values by 2 to annualize the results.[29] While this simple approach is used quite frequently, keep in mind that it will not account for factors such as seasonality, recent trends (either positive or negative), and future factors which may be known but which are not represented in historical data (e.g., upcoming new product introductions). For these reasons and others, it is sometimes appropriate to employ more sophisticated methods to annualize historical results.

Results from the Base Case

Table 6.10 reveals that GSC's annual freight and handling costs total just over $1.5 million per year. Because reducing the firm's annual logistics (i.e., freight and handling) expenses represents a principal objective of the bracket pricing project, this cost represents a key benchmark figure that GSC will compare against the bracket pricing scenarios it will model shortly.

The results in Table 6.10 also allow the GSC project team to extract additional insights for its plans to develop and analyze potential bracket pricing scenarios. Table 6.11 illustrates one example of the information that the GSC team can deduce from Table 6.10.

A key objective of the bracket pricing project is to incentivize customers to order GSC's products in larger, more efficient quantities than their current purchases. Utilizing the base case results in Table 6.10 which are displayed again in the two far-right columns in Table 6.11, one can calculate:

1 the average number of orders each customer location places per week and
2 what the average order weight of each customer location would be if the customer only ordered from GSC once per week

This data provides initial insights to the GSC team on possible weight (i.e., lb.) thresholds that the firm could establish for customers to qualify for discount prices. Briefly, GSC believes that its customers wish to order products at least once per week. Based on previous customer feedback, GSC understands that most customers would not consider ordering once every two weeks (in larger quantities) because the customers' inventory carrying costs would increase. However, GSC believes that customers would consider ordering once per week rather than multiple times per week, if that allowed them to purchase products at a lower discount price than the current single list price that GSC offers.

The far-right column in Table 6.11 reveals the weight thresholds which GSC's customers and customer locations could meet ordering once per week based upon their historical purchase

TABLE 6.10 Base Case Summary: Annualized Version of Customer Order and Shipment History

Ship To Level Summary

Customer	*Ship To*	*Total Cases*	*Total Weight*	*Total Revenue (at List Price)*[a]	*Average*[b] *Order and Shipment Weight*	*Average*[c] *Order Value (at List Price)*[d]
Corner Mart	Corner Mart Binghamton	5,876	88,478	$ 304,330	567	$ 1,951
Corner Mart	Corner Mart Hackettstown	7,501	113,276	$ 389,350	726	$ 2,496
Corner Mart	Corner Mart Lewisburg	21,411	320,509	$ 1,107,210	2,055	$ 7,098
Corner Mart	Corner Mart Washington	11,057	165,653	$ 572,358	1,062	$ 3,669
Friendly Shop	Friendly Shop Denville	174,974	2,608,574	$ 9,023,528	25,082	$ 86,765
Friendly Shop	Friendly Shop Hartford	89,252	1,333,176	$ 4,610,483	12,819	$ 44,332
Friendly Shop	Friendly Shop Lancaster	59,391	888,537	$ 3,065,758	8,544	$ 29,478
Save-A-Bunch	Save-A-Bunch Albany	30,992	463,762	$ 1,597,635	2,230	$ 7,681
Save-A-Bunch	Save-A-Bunch Boonton	90,136	1,341,139	$ 4,658,518	6,448	$ 22,397
Save-A-Bunch	Save-A-Bunch Harrisburg	23,608	354,283	$ 1,219,140	1,703	$ 5,861
Save-A-Bunch	Save-A-Bunch Virginia Beach	45,819	684,834	$ 2,363,790	3,292	$ 11,364
Total		**560,014**	**8,362,218**	**$ 28,912,098**	**4,730**	**$ 16,353**

Customer Level Summary

Customer	*Total Cases*	*Total Weight*	*Total Revenue (at List Price)*[f]	*Average*[g] *Order and Shipment Weight*	*Average*[h] *Order Value (at List Price)*[i]
Corner Mart	45,845	687,915	$ 2,373,248	1,102	$ 3,803
Friendly Shop	323,616	4,830,287	$ 16,699,768	15,482	$ 53,525
Save-A-Bunch	190,554	2,844,017	$ 9,839,083	3,418	$ 11,826
Total	**560,014**	**8,362,218**	**$ 28,912,098**	**4,730**	**$ 16,353**

Notes

[a] Each of GSC's products currently has a single price that customers pay regardless of the quantity ordered. This is called the "list" price and that is standard terminology for the normal (or catalog) price of an item.

[b] Note that in the "total" row of the Customer Level and Ship To Level tables, the average shown is the weighted average. It is not the simple average of the respective 11 and 3 rows in each of the two tables.

[c] See note b.

[d] See note a.

[e] See note b.

[f] See note a.

[g] See note b.

[h] See note b.

[i] See note a.

[j] See note b.

Total Freight Cost	*Average[e] Freight Cost per lb.*	*Total Pallets Picked*	*Total Individual Cases Picked*	*Total Pallet Handling Costs*	*Total Case Handling Costs*	*Total Handling Costs*	*Total Freight and Handling Costs*
$ 26,543	$ 0.30	0	5,876	$ -	$ 1,469	$ 1,469	$ 28,012
$ 33,983	$ 0.30	0	7,501	$ -	$ 1,875	$ 1,875	$ 35,858
$ 81,415	$ 0.25	0	21,411	$ -	$ 5,353	$ 5,353	$ 86,768
$ 49,696	$ 0.30	0	11,057	$ -	$ 2,764	$ 2,764	$ 52,460
$ 234,772	$ 0.09	2,867	12,285	$ 5,733	$ 3,071	$ 8,804	$ 243,576
$ 186,645	$ 0.14	1,320	13,494	$ 2,639	$ 3,374	$ 6,013	$ 192,657
$ 177,707	$ 0.20	728	17,271	$ 1,456	$ 4,318	$ 5,774	$ 183,481
$ 115,941	$ 0.25	0	30,992	$ -	$ 7,748	$ 7,748	$ 123,689
$ 268,228	$ 0.20	1,138	24,148	$ 2,275	$ 6,037	$ 8,312	$ 276,540
$ 106,285	$ 0.30	0	23,608	$ -	$ 5,902	$ 5,902	$ 112,187
$ 171,208	$ 0.25	377	26,163	$ 754	$ 6,541	$ 7,295	$ 178,503
$ 1,452,422	**$ 0.17**	**6,429**	**193,804**	**$ 12,857**	**$ 48,451**	**$ 61,308**	**$ 1,513,730**

Total Freight Cost	*Average[j] Freight Cost per lb.*	*Total Pallets Picked*	*Total Individual Cases Picked*	*Total Pallet Handling Costs*	*Total Case Handling Costs*	*Total Handling Costs*	*Total Freight and Handling Costs*
$ 191,637	$ 0.28	0	45,845	$ -	$ 11,461	$ 11,461	$ 203,098
$ 599,124	$ 0.12	4,914	43,050	$ 9,828	$ 10,762	$ 20,590	$ 619,714
$ 661,661	$ 0.23	1,515	104,910	$ 3,029	$ 26,228	$ 29,257	$ 690,918
$ 1,452,422	**$ 0.17**	**6,429**	**193,804**	**$ 12,857**	**$ 48,451**	**$ 61,308**	**$ 1,513,730**

TABLE 6.11 Illustrative Potential Customer "Ordering" Insights From the Base Case Scenario

Ship To Level Summary

Customer	*Ship To*	*Total Weight*	*Current Average Order and Shipment Weight*	*Current Average[a] Number of Orders and Shipments per Week*	*Average Shipment[b] Weight If Customers Would Only Order Once per Week*
Corner Mart	Corner Mart Binghamton	88,478	567	3.0	1,702
Corner Mart	Corner Mart Hackettstown	113,276	726	3.0	2,178
Corner Mart	Corner Mart Lewisburg	320,509	2,055	3.0	6,164
Corner Mart	Corner Mart Washington	165,653	1,062	3.0	3,186
Friendly Shop	Friendly Shop Denville	2,608,574	25,082	2.0	50,165
Friendly Shop	Friendly Shop Hartford	1,333,176	12,819	2.0	25,638
Friendly Shop	Friendly Shop Lancaster	888,537	8,544	2.0	17,087
Save-A-Bunch	Save-A-Bunch Albany	463,762	2,230	4.0	8,919
Save-A-Bunch	Save-A-Bunch Boonton	1,341,139	6,448	4.0	25,791
Save-A-Bunch	Save-A-Bunch Harrisburg	354,283	1,703	4.0	6,813
Save-A-Bunch	Save-A-Bunch Virginia Beach	684,834	3,292	4.0	13,170

Customer Level Summary

Customer	*Total Weight*	*Current Average Order and Shipment Weight*	*Current Average[c] Number of Orders and Shipments per Week*	*Average Shipment[d] Weight If Customers Would Only Order Once per Week*
Corner Mart	687,915	1,102	3.0	3,307
Friendly Shop	4,830,287	15,482	2.0	30,963
Save-A-Bunch	2,844,017	3,418	4.0	13,673

[a] Formula for this column = [(total weight) / (average order and shipment weight)] / 52.

[b] Formula for this column = (current average order and shipment weight) × (current average number of orders and shipments per week).

[c] Formula for this column = {[(total weight) / (average order and shipment weight)] / 52} / (number of ship to locations of the customer).

[d] See note b.

rates.[30] GSC can use these insights as it now progresses to the next steps of its analysis, which include:

1 evaluating the potential savings opportunity that once per week customer purchases could produce and
2 simulating the potential customer responses and logistics savings that alternative bracket pricing scenarios might generate

Evaluating the Potential Freight and Handling Costs Savings

To estimate accurately the potential logistics cost savings that a bracket pricing initiative could produce, GSC must evaluate how it expects each customer would respond to this program. We explore shortly how GSC can develop these projections; however, before doing this, GSC can (and should) quickly determine the maximum potential savings that a bracket pricing program could create. GSC can accomplish this easily by simply calculating the savings that would result if all customers ordered just once per week.[31] GSC understands that it is not realistic to expect all customers to order just once per week, but evaluating once per week ordering by all customers will establish the maximum potential benefit for the firm of offering a bracket pricing program.

The GSC project team employs a two-step process to analyze the impact of weekly customer ordering. First the team must aggregate its current historical line item database into a weekly line item database. Then, analysts must convert the weekly line item database into an order database, just as previously done to perform the base case analysis.[32] Exhibit 6.6 summarizes how to perform this process using an Excel database.[33]

EXHIBIT 6.6 CREATING A WEEKLY ORDER DATABASE FROM THE BASE CASE LINE ITEM DATABASE

1 *Apply the Pivot Table Function to the Base Case Historical Line Item Database:* In the Excel sheet that contains the line item database, use the Pivot Table function (i.e., Insert, Pivot Table) and create a new pivot table in a separate sheet of the Excel Workbook.
2 *Choose the Data Fields from the Base Case Line Item Database That Are Needed in the Weekly Line Item Database:* Using the Pivot Table function, select all of the data fields from the base case line item database that are also needed in the weekly line item database. For example, fields such as customer, customer number, and order number should be selected. *IMPORTANTLY, do not select the "Day of the Week," "Order Date," and "Order Number" fields for inclusion in the weekly line item database.* By skipping (i.e., not including) these fields in the selected Pivot Table Fields, the user indicates to Excel that the data values in the base case line item database for each individual line item ordered by a customer in a particular week should be summed to a total for that line item for that week. This will create a weekly line item database for each ship to location of each customer.
3 *Copy and Paste the Values from the Pivot Table Weekly Line Item Database into a Separate Excel Sheet:* To create a weekly line item database that is easy to work with, copy and paste the values from the initial weekly line item database created by the pivot table into a second sheet, and format the new sheet (database) as appropriate.

4 *Append the Additional Required Data Fields and Calculated Fields to the Weekly Line Item Database Created in Step 3:* Add case weight, cases per pallet, case list price, pallets picked, cases picked, weight (lbs.), and revenue ($) to the initial weekly line item database – just as was done to convert Table 6.5 into Table 6.6 previously. Note that the first two appended fields are data fields while the last four fields must be calculated.
5 *Choose the Data Fields from the Weekly Line Item Database That Are Needed in the Weekly Order Database:* Use the same processes (including the use of a pivot table) and logic as previously described in Exhibit 6.4 for this step.
6 *Add and/or Create Any Additional Data Fields Identified in Step 5:* Use the same process and logic as previously described in Exhibit 6.4 for this step. Once the additional fields identified in step 4 are added and/or created, this will complete the weekly order database needed to analyze the potential savings opportunity that weekly ordering by customers could generate.

TABLE 6.12 What Is the Maximum Logistics Cost Savings Opportunity if GSC's Customers All Order Just Once per Week Instead of the Current Multiple Times per Week?

All Totals Shown Are Annualized

Scenario	*Total Freight Costs*	*Total Handling Costs*	*Total Freight and Handling Costs*	*Total List Revenue*	*Freight Costs as a Percentage of List Revenue*	*Freight and Handling Costs as a Percentage of List Revenue*
Base Case	$ 1,452,222	$ 61,308	$ 1,513,730	$ 28,912,098	5.0%	5.2%
Once per Week Orders and Shipments	$ 889,289	$ 35,150	$ 924,439	$ 28,912,098	3.1%	3.2%
(Base Case) – (Once per Week Orders and Shipments)	**$ 562,933**	**$ 26,158**	**$ 589,291**	**$ -**	**1.9%**	**2.0%**

Once the GSC project team has converted its historical line item base case database into a weekly customer order database, it can then estimate the approximate maximum cost savings a bracket pricing program could potentially yield. Specifically, analysts can simply sum the freight costs, and the case and pallet handling costs of all the orders in the weekly order database. Table 6.12 compares GSC's annualized freight and handling costs in a scenario where all its customers ordered just once a week to the current (i.e., base case) costs that GSC currently incurs.

Table 6.12 reveals that GSC's freight and handling costs would decrease by approximately $589,000 per year if every customer location consolidated their current multiple orders per week into one larger, single weekly order. As previously noted, while GSC understands that not all customers would agree to place orders just once a week, this estimate identifies the maximum potential savings for the firm of a bracket pricing program. The far-right column of Table 6.12

shows that an annual savings of $589,000 would translate into a 2% reduction in current annual logistics costs. For GSC, and for most firms, a 2% decrease in annual costs represents a very substantial potential savings. With this understanding, the GSC team can develop a bracket pricing program – confident that the additional investment in time and resources necessary to complete this initiative has a possible return that justifies the effort.[34]

Finally, note that total revenue in Table 6.12 remains identical both under once per week customer ordering, and in the base case. This results because GSC currently has just a single "list" price per unit for each of its products. Therefore, the quantity ordered of a product by a customer does not affect the unit price, regardless of how small or large the customer's order quantity.

Clarifying the Potential Logistics Savings – An Example

To enhance one's understanding of an analytic result based on a large data set, it is often helpful to examine a small example or subset of the problem. Table 6.13 illustrates the impact of consolidating to once per week ordering and shipping for a single customer location (the Save-A-Bunch Boonton DC), for one week of the GSC project team's historical database.

This table shows that the Boonton DC of Save-A-Bunch placed four individual orders during the first week of the historical study period of the base case. GSC received and processed each of these orders on separate days, and then made four separate shipments to the Boonton DC during this week. Table 6.13 also displays how one consolidated order during this week for the same quantity of the same products would have appeared. Note that while the total number of cases, the total weight, and the total revenue would have been the same, the total full pallets and individual cases picked by the warehouse differ. Specifically, the GSC warehouse would have picked 29 full pallets and just 96 individual cases to fulfill one consolidated order. In contrast, the warehouse actually picked 24 full pallets and 423 individual cases to fulfill the four actual orders received during the week.[35]

Clearly, GSC could have handled and delivered one large order much more efficiently than the four separate small orders that it actually received from the Boonton DC in week #1 of the historical data set. The following summarizes the weekly savings in GSC's logistics costs that a single, consolidated weekly order from the Boonton DC would have facilitated.

Scenario	*Freight Cost per lb.*	*Freight Costs*	*Case Handling Costs*	*Pallet Handling Costs*	*Total Handling Costs*	*Freight and Handling Costs*
Base Case	**$.20**	**$5,207**	**$106**	**$48**	**$154**	**$5,361**
Weekly	**$.09**	**$2,343**	**$24**	**$58**	**$82**	**$2,425**
BC – Weekly	**$.11**	**$2,864**	**$82**	**($10)**	**$72**	**$2,936**

Briefly, these costs show that:

- The freight cost per lb. and total freight costs decrease as a result of GSC making just one larger shipment per week.
- The total handling costs drop significantly because the order for each line item is approximately four times larger than in the base case – thereby facilitating more full pallet picks and fewer individual case picks. (This is why pallet handling costs actually increase

TABLE 6.13 Current Base Case Customer Ordering vs. Simulated Once per Week Customer Ordering: An Example

Customer	*Customer Number*	*Ship To Location*	*Ship To Location Number*	*Order Week*	*Day of the Week**	*Order Date*	*Order Number*	*Number of Cases*	*Total Weight*	*Total Revenue*	*Total Pallets Picked*	*Total Cases Picked*
The Four Orders From Week #1 of the Historical Base Case Order Database for the Save-A-Bunch Boonton Customer DC												
Save-A-Bunch	100	Save-A-Bunch Boonton	101	1	2	7/14/20XX	12101	434	6479	$ 22,495	6	104
Save-A-Bunch	100	Save-A-Bunch Boonton	101	1	3	7/15/20XX	13101	434	6504	$ 22,410	6	104
Save-A-Bunch	100	Save-A-Bunch Boonton	101	1	4	7/16/20XX	14101	437	6513	$ 22,545	6	107
Save-A-Bunch	100	Save-A-Bunch Boonton	101	1	5	7/17/20XX	15101	438	6539	$ 22,615	6	108
………	………	………	………	……	………	………	………	………	………	………	………	………
The One Consolidated Order for Week #1 From the Once-per-Week Customer Ordering Database for the Save-A-Bunch Boonton Customer DC												
Save-A-Bunch	100	Save-A-Bunch Boonton	101	1			1_101	1743	26035	$ 90,065	29	96

* 1 = Monday, 2 = Tuesday, 3 = Wednesday, 4 = Thursday, 5 = Friday.

with weekly ordering. However, the decrease in the case handling costs of weekly ordering significantly outweighs the increase in pallet handling costs.)

- The total freight and handling costs to serve the Boonton DC diminish substantially.

Finally, note that we did not calculate the percent savings that weekly ordering would create for this single-customer example. The actual and potential savings of a large customer logistics program such as this bracket pricing program will vary dramatically by customer. Further, the costs of serving some portion of the customer base usually does not change.[36] Therefore, it is generally not accurate or appropriate to extrapolate the percentage change in service costs with respect to one customer to the larger population of all customers. Instead, the appropriate approach is to develop potential "percentage change" estimates based on the entire customer base, as shown in Table 6.12.[37] However, it can be quite insightful to examine individual customers to gain a better understanding of how a customer logistics program will influence and/or motivate both individual, as well as all customers.

Developing Bracket Pricing Thresholds and Simulating the Expected Customer Response

GSC believes that customers will consolidate their orders to a once per week frequency, if GSC offers sufficiently large discounts off its list prices for larger-quantity orders. GSC's previous discussions with customers have revealed that if a customer believes that the discount savings will exceed the higher inventory carrying costs that result from purchasing larger quantities less frequently, then the customer will switch to larger, less frequent purchases. However, as previously discussed, customers in general are *not* willing to consolidate their purchase orders to less frequently than once per week. Given this input, the GSC project team must now determine the following:

1. the minimum customer purchase quantity thresholds required for a customer to obtain a discount bracket price,
2. how many discount brackets GSC will offer to customers,
3. the percentage discount off a product's list price that will be given to discount customers, and
4. the actual per unit discount prices for each of its products

The first step to establish the minimum purchase quantity threshold(s) consists of evaluating the quantities of products that GSC customers currently purchase per week.[38] GSC has decided that it will use the total weight (i.e., the total lbs.) of an order to determine whether a customer will pay the list price or a discounted price. Additionally, the project team plans to measure each customer's average order quantity over a defined historical time period (e.g., 6 months) to assign each customer as either a "list" or a "discount" bracket price customer.[39]

The far-right two columns of Table 6.14 display the *average order weight of each ship to customer location of GSC:*

1. *currently* – i.e., the base case, and
2. *per week* – based on the sum of each location's actual individual orders during each week of the order database history. The weekly average order weight column allows the GSC team to evaluate what are the average weekly lbs. thresholds its different customers could exceed – based on their recent historical purchase levels. This data provides valuable insights in the weight threshold selection process.

TABLE 6.14 Average Customer "Ship To" Order Weights: Based on Current and Weekly Ordering[a]

Customer	*Ship To*	*Annual Total Cases Purchased*	*Annual Total Weight (lbs.)*	*Annual Total Revenue at List Price*	*Base Case Average Order and Shipment Weight (lbs.)*	*Weekly Average Order and Shipment Weight (lbs.)*
Corner Mart	Corner Mart Binghamton	5,876	88,478	$ 304,330	567	1,702
Corner Mart	Corner Mart Hackettstown	7,501	113,276	$ 389,350	726	2,178
Corner Mart	Corner Mart Washington	11,057	165,653	$ 572,358	1,062	3,186
Save-A-Bunch	Save-A-Bunch Harrisburg	23,608	354,283	$ 1,219,140	1,703	6,813
Corner Mart	Corner Mart Lewisburg	21,411	320,509	$ 1,107,210	2,055	6,164
Save-A-Bunch	Save-A-Bunch Albany	30,992	463,762	$ 1,597,635	2,230	8,919
Save-A-Bunch	Save-A-Bunch Virginia Beach	45,819	684,834	$ 2,363,790	3,292	13,170
Save-A-Bunch	Save-A-Bunch Boonton	90,136	1,341,139	$ 4,658,518	6,448	25,791
Friendly Shop	Friendly Shop Lancaster	59,391	888,537	$ 3,065,758	8,544	17,087
Friendly Shop	Friendly Shop Hartford	89,252	1,333,176	$ 4,610,483	12,819	25,638
Friendly Shop	Friendly Shop Denville	174,974	2,608,574	$ 9,023,528	25,082	50,165

[a] Ranked in Ascending Order Based on Current (i.e., Base Case) Average Order Weight.

The GSC project team has decided that its customers can qualify as a "discount bracket" customer: (1) on an individual ship to location basis or (2) based upon the average order weight of all of a customer's ship to locations collectively. Table 6.15 presents data in the same format as Table 6.14, but based upon the average order weight of all the orders of the overall "parent" customer (i.e., Corner Mart, Save-A-Bunch, and Friendly Shop).

This table reveals that the three Friendly Shop ship to DCs' total purchases average over 30,000 lbs. per location each week, while the four Save-A-Bunch and four Corner Mart ship to DCs average 13,673 lbs. and 3,307 lbs., respectively.

Now that the GSC project team understands the product quantities in lbs. that its customers purchase per week, its next step consists of constructing simulation models to analyze predicted customer ordering behavior under alternative bracket pricing structures. To build these simulation models requires that GSC analysts develop programming logic that will evaluate how each customer ship to location will react to different potential weight thresholds. Specifically, GSC must predict whether a customer ship to location will continue to place multiple orders per week on GSC (i.e., the current base case), or alternatively consolidate their purchases to once per week.

Table 6.16 details the logic that GSC must program into its simulation models. For illustrative purposes, the example in this table assumes that GSC establishes a two-bracket pricing system where:

1. orders < 10,000 lbs. receive the current GSC list price and
2. orders ≥ 10,000 lbs. receive a lower, discount price

Under this bracket pricing scenario, based on the "Weekly Average Order and Shipment Weight" column in Table 6.16, we observe the following:

1. The ship to locations of Corner Mart Binghamton through Save-A-Bunch Albany cannot average ≥ 10,000 lbs. per week based on their current purchasing levels. Thus, these locations would have no financial incentive to consolidate to weekly ordering, and therefore, GSC should assume these ship to locations would continue to order multiple times per week, in this bracket pricing scenario.

TABLE 6.15 Average "Customer" Order Weights: Based on Current and Weekly Ordering[a]

Customer	*Annual Total Cases Purchased*	*Annual Total Weight (lbs.)*	*Annual Total Revenue at List Price*	*Base Case Average Order and Shipment Weight (lbs.)*[b]	*Weekly Average Order and Shipment Weight (lbs.)*[c]
Corner Mart	45,845	687,915	$ 2,373,248	1,102	3,307
Save-A-Bunch	190,554	2,844,017	$ 9,839,083	3,418	13,673
Friendly Shop	323,616	4,830,287	$ 16,699,768	15,482	30,963

[a] Ranked in Ascending Order Based on Current (i.e., Base Case) Average Order Weight.

[b] The average order weight columns are based on the average order weight of all of a customer's individual ship to locations.

[c] See note b.

TABLE 6.16 Illustration of "Expected" Customer Behavior – Ship to Level Analysis (Assuming Two Price Brackets – List and Discount – and Assuming the Threshold for a Ship To Location to Obtain the Discount Price Is an Average Order ≥ 10,000 lbs.)

Customer	*Ship To*	*Annual Total Cases Purchased*	*Annual Total Weight (lbs.)*	*Annual Total Revenue at List Price*	*Base Case Average Order and Shipment Weight (lbs.)*	*Weekly Average Order and Shipment Weight (lbs.)*	
Corner Mart	Corner Mart Binghamton	5,876	88,478	$ 304,330	567	1,702	***No Incentive for These Ship To Locations to Order Weekly Because the Threshold is Too High for Them to Reach***
Corner Mart	Corner Mart Hackettstown	7,501	113,276	$ 389,350	726	2,178	
Corner Mart	Corner Mart Washington	11,057	165,653	$ 572,358	1,062	3,186	
Corner Mart	Corner Mart Lewisburg	21,411	320,509	$ 1,107,210	2,055	6,164	
Save-A-Bunch	Save-A-Bunch Harrisburg	23,608	354,283	$ 1,219,140	1,703	6,813	
Save-A-Bunch	Save-A-Bunch Albany	30,992	463,762	$ 1,597,635	2,230	8,919	
Save-A-Bunch	Save-A-Bunch Virginia Beach	45,819	684,834	$ 2,363,790	3,292	13,170	***These Ship To Locations Will Switch to Weekly Ordering Because They Can Obtain the Lower Discount Price By Ordering Weekly***
Save-A-Bunch	Save-A-Bunch Boonton	90,136	1,341,139	$ 4,658,518	6,448	25,791	
Friendly Shop	Friendly Shop Lancaster	59,391	888,537	$ 3,065,758	8,544	17,087	
Friendly Shop	Friendly Shop Hartford	89,252	1,333,176	$ 4,610,483	12,819	25,638	***No Incentive for These Ship To Locations to Order Weekly Because They Already Average ≥ 10,000 lbs. per Order***
Friendly Shop	Friendly Shop Denville	174,974	2,608,574	$ 9,023,528	25,082	50,165	

2 The ship to locations of Save-A-Bunch Virginia Beach, Save-A-Bunch Boonton, and Friendly Shop Lancaster will switch to once-per-week ordering from their current multiple orders per week. By changing their order behavior, these locations will qualify for the lower, discount price.
3 Friendly Shop Hartford and Friendly Shop Denville will continue to order multiple times per week.[40] Based on their current respective average order weights, if GSC offered a discount price for orders ≥ 10,000 lbs., these two locations would each obtain the discount price without changing their current order patterns.

Briefly, Table 6.16 suggests that a two-price bracket system would not be optimal for GSC. The results shown in this table project that only 3 of GSC's 11 customer ship to locations would change to weekly ordering.

As noted, Table 6.16 illustrates the logic that a simulation model designed to predict "customer behavior" must contain. Table 6.17 illustrates this same concept for a three-price bracket structure.

This pricing scenario assumes the following:

1 orders < 10,000 lbs. receive the current GSC list price,
2 orders ≥ 10,000 lbs. and < 25,000 lbs. receive the first discount price, and
3 orders ≥ 25,000 lbs. obtain the second discount price – which offers a larger discount off the list price than does the first discount price

This table illustrates that a three-bracket pricing structure (compared to a two-price bracket structure) offers more flexibility for a supplier to incent customers to change their behavior. For example, while Friendly Shop Hartford had no incentive to order weekly under the two-bracket scenario in Table 6.16,[41] in the three-bracket scenario of Table 6.17, the 25,000 lb. threshold for the lower second discount price would motivate Hartford to order weekly.

A simulation model that incorporates the customer ordering prediction logic illustrated in Tables 6.16 and 6.17 facilitates the creation of a new order database for analysis. Previously, we observed that GSC evaluated the potential maximum savings benefit possible (i.e., the maximum potential opportunity) if all customers switched to weekly ordering. The output of GSC's simulation model(s) based on predictive customer ordering logic is an order database that contains a "mix" of customer orders. Those ship to locations that can obtain lower, discount prices will have "weekly" orders in the order database created by the simulation model. Conversely, the orders of those ship to locations that cannot qualify for a lower discount price by ordering once per week will remain as they exist in the base case order database (i.e., multiple individual orders per week).

Determining the Weight Thresholds to Simulate

GSC's project team must now determine the actual weight thresholds to test in its simulation models. It also has to decide how many price bracket options to evaluate. For illustrative simplicity, we assume that GSC will consider either a two- or three-bracket pricing structure.[42]

The most common and simplest method used to develop potential thresholds is to review visually (i.e., manually) the average purchase quantities of a firm's customers. A visual review, coupled with a firm's internal understanding of its customers developed through long-term relationships, generally leads to logical thresholds to test via simulation.[43] Table 6.18 illustrates

TABLE 6.17 Illustration of "Expected" Customer Behavior – Ship to Level Analysis (Assuming Three Price Brackets – List, Discount 1, Discount 2 – and Assuming the Thresholds for a Ship To Location to Obtain the Discount 1 and Discount 2 Prices Are Average Orders ≥ 10,000 lbs. and < 25,000 lbs. (for D1), and ≥ 25,000 lbs. (for D2), respectively)

Customer	*Ship To*	*Annual Total Cases Purchased*	*Annual Total Weight (lbs.)*	*Annual Total Revenue at List Price*	*Base Case Average Order and Shipment Weight (lbs.)*	*Weekly Average Order and Shipment Weight (lbs.)*	
Corner Mart	Corner Mart Binghamton	5,876	88,478	$ 304,330	567	1,702	***No Incentive for These Ship To Locations to Order Weekly Because the Threshold is too High for them to Reach***
Corner Mart	Corner Mart Hackettstown	7,501	113,276	$ 389,350	726	2,178	
Corner Mart	Corner Mart Washington	11,057	165,653	$ 572,358	1,062	3,186	
Corner Mart	Corner Mart Lewisburg	21,411	320,509	$ 1,107,210	2,055	6,164	
Save-A-Bunch	Save-A-Bunch Harrisburg	23,608	354,283	$ 1,219,140	1,703	6,813	
Save-A-Bunch	Save-A-Bunch Albany	30,992	463,762	$ 1,597,635	2,230	8,919	
Save-A-Bunch	Save-A-Bunch Virginia Beach	45,819	684,834	$ 2,363,790	3,292	13,170	***These Ship To Locations Will Switch to Weekly Ordering to Obtain Discount Price 1***
Friendly Shop	Friendly Shop Lancaster	59,391	888,537	$ 3,065,758	8,544	17,087	
Friendly Shop	Friendly Shop Hartford	89,252	1,333,176	$ 4,610,483	12,819	25,638	***These Ship To Locations Will Switch to Weekly Ordering to Obtain Discount Price 2***
Save-A-Bunch	Save-A-Bunch Boonton	90,136	1,341,139	$ 4,658,518	6,448	25,791	
Friendly Shop	Friendly Shop Denville	174,974	2,608,574	$ 9,023,528	25,082	50,165	***Will Not Order Weekly. Already Average ≥ 25,000 lbs.***

TABLE 6.18 Average Order Weights: Based on Weekly and Base Case Current Ordering[a]

Customer	*Ship To*	*Base Case Average Order and Shipment Weight (lbs.)*	*Weekly Average Order and Shipment Weight (lbs.)*	*Customer*	*Base Case Average Order and Shipment Weight (lbs.)*[b]	*Weekly Average Order and Shipment Weight (lbs.)*[c]
Corner Mart	Corner Mart Binghamton	567	1,702	Corner Mart	1,102	3,307
Corner Mart	Corner Mart Hackettstown	726	2,178	Save-A-Bunch	3,418	13,673
Corner Mart	Corner Mart Washington	1,062	3,186	Friendly Shop	15,482	30,963
Corner Mart	Corner Mart Lewisburg	2,055	6,164			
Save-A-Bunch	Save-A-Bunch Harrisburg	1,703	6,813			
Save-A-Bunch	Save-A-Bunch Albany	2,230	8,919			
Save-A-Bunch	Save-A-Bunch Virginia Beach	3,292	13,170			
Friendly Shop	Friendly Shop Lancaster	8,544	17,087			
Friendly Shop	Friendly Shop Hartford	12,819	25,638			
Save-A-Bunch	Save-A-Bunch Boonton	6,448	25,791			
Friendly Shop	Friendly Shop Denville	25,082	50,165			

[a] Ranked in Ascending Order Based on Average "Weekly" Order Weight.
[b] The average order weight columns are based on the average order weight of all of a customer's individual ship to locations.
[c] See note b.

how a visual inspection by GSC of its customers' average order quantities yields logical weight thresholds to test.

Based upon the data in Table 6.18, the GSC team decided that it would evaluate the following two "ship to level" and two "customer level" bracket pricing alternatives:

Ship to Level Bracket Pricing Options

A **two brackets: (1) List < 13,000 lbs. and (2) Discount ≥ 13,000 lbs.**
B **three brackets: (1) List < 13,000 lbs., (2) 13,000 lbs. ≤ 1st Discount < 30,000 lbs., and (3) 2nd Discount ≥ 30,000 lbs.**

Customer Level Bracket Pricing Options

C **two brackets: (1) List < 13,000 lbs. and (2) Discount ≥ 13,000 lbs.**
D **three brackets: (1) List < 13,000 lbs., (2) 13,000 lbs. ≤ 1st Discount < 30,000 lbs., and (3) 2nd Discount ≥ 30,000 lbs.**

Thus, GSC selected 13,000 lbs. as the average order weight threshold required to obtain the discount price in the two-bracket system; and 13,000 lbs. and 30,000 lbs. as the first and second discount price thresholds, respectively, in the three-bracket system. This is a judgment call and there is no right or wrong answer here. However, the following points describe the thought process that GSC (and suppliers in general) employs to arrive at these decisions.

1 *There is a logical break at 13,000 lbs.*

   - At the ship to level, this will incent Virginia Beach, Lancaster, Hartford, and Boonton to consolidate to weekly ordering – based upon their weekly average order weights.
   - Additionally, at the customer level, this will incent Save-A-Bunch to have all three of its locations each order once per week. If the Save-A-Bunch Harrisburg and Albany DCs order once per week, as well as the Save-A-Bunch Virginia Beach DC, then at the customer level, Save-A-Bunch averages over 13,000 lbs. per order. So even though Harrisburg and Albany cannot average over 13,000 lbs. per week individually, they can receive the discount price by consolidating their ordering to facilitate a customer level average order weight exceeding 13,000 lbs.

2 *30,000 lbs. is a better threshold than 25,000 lbs. for the second discount bracket in a three-bracket pricing structure.*

   - 25,000 lbs. would incent Hartford and Boonton to consolidate to weekly ordering at the ship to level.
   - However, Denville already averages over 25,000 lbs. per order and would continue to order twice per week rather than switching to once per week.
   - Friendly Shop can average over 30,000 lbs. at the customer level if its Denville location, along with Lancaster and Hartford, each order once per week.
   - Thus, a 30,000 lb. threshold incentivizes GSC's largest single ship to location, Friendly Shop Denville, to consolidate its orders to once per week.

3 *In summary, a three-bracket pricing system, with average order weight thresholds of 13,000 lbs. and 30,000 lbs. respectively, will motivate all of GSC's seven largest ship to customer locations to order weekly.*

   - This is a key consideration. GSC primarily bases its threshold decisions on what weight breaks will incent its larger customers and customer locations to consolidate their ordering. If these larger customers change their ordering behavior, it will have a significant impact on GSC's overall logistics costs and potential savings.
   - If GSC's smaller customer locations change to weekly ordering, while this would be helpful, it will not have a major impact on GSC's overall logistics costs.
   - GSC's four smallest customer locations – the Corner Mart ship to DCs – will be list price customers, and GSC does not expect these locations will consolidate their orders to once per week.

Logistics Cost Analysis of Four Potential Bracket Pricing Scenarios

GSC next analyzes the projected logistics costs and savings that each of the four bracket pricing scenarios would produce. The GSC project team builds four separate simulation models that incorporate the respective pricing logic of each scenario. As previously illustrated, the first output of each model consists of a revised (i.e., simulated) order database that reflects how GSC would expect each customer ship to location to order in each pricing scenario. Recall also that GSC has already developed a base case order database and a weekly order database. Therefore, the simulation models, for each scenario, will:

1 Determine how each customer ship to location would be expected to order in that scenario (i.e., will the ship to change to ordering once per week or will it continue to order multiple times per week, as it currently does).
2 Based on step 1, the simulation model will copy the order data from either the base case or the weekly order database into a new order database for each scenario – depending upon the determination made in step 1.

Once a simulation model develops an order database for one of the new bracket pricing scenarios, the program would then calculate the projected annual logistics costs of a bracket pricing scenario – based upon the order database of that particular scenario.

Simulation Model Output and Results

Every firm will customize the outputs of their simulation models to meet their needs. In this section, we briefly illustrate examples of typical outputs of these models. However, as one would expect, in practice, firms generally develop much more extensive analyses and reporting outputs than shown here.

Table 6.19 displays one of the outputs that GSC's simulation models generate for each of the four bracket pricing scenarios under consideration. The table shows analytic results for Scenario B, under which GSC would offer three price brackets at the customer ship to level.[44] This reporting includes:

- a projection of freight and handling costs in total, and by customer ship to, for the scenario,
- the projected annual cost savings for GSC that this scenario would generate,
- the projected annual savings stated in purchase costs and as a percentage that each discount customer ship to location would gain, and
- the recommended price per unit for the discount bracket (or brackets) for each of GSC's products[45]

Table 6.20 compares the projected total freight and handling costs of each scenario to GSC's current operation (i.e., to the base case).

Based upon these simulation results, the GSC team decided to implement a three-price bracket system at the customer level. Table 6.20 shows that this scenario projects the largest annual logistics cost savings ($553,520) of the four alternative scenarios. This is not a surprising result because as previously discussed, having three price brackets rather than two affords GSC a greater opportunity to incent more customers to order weekly. Further, as also discussed, offering this pricing at the "customer level" may incentivize some ship to locations that would not consolidate on their own to order weekly in order to facilitate a "customer" average order weight that qualifies for a discount bracket.[46]

Finally, a supplier does not have to choose between either a ship to level or a customer level bracket pricing approach. GSC (or any firm in a situation such as described here) could elect to implement a bracket pricing system where each parent customer has the option to choose to participate either at the customer level or at the ship to level. Offering customers this option

TABLE 6.19 Scenario: Three Price Brackets with Weight Thresholds at 13,000 lbs. and 30,000 lbs. to Qualify for Discounts at the Customer Ship to Level

Bracket	*Customer Ship To Location*	*Total Freight & Handling Costs (i.e., Logistics Costs)*	*Total Weight Ordered & Received (lbs.)*	*Average Logistics Costs per lb.*	*Average Logistics Savings per lb. of Discount Brackets vs. Current Base Case*	*Total Revenue at List Price (i.e., Gross Revenue)*	*Final Projected Disc If Pass 100% of Logistics Savings to Customers*	*Final Projected Net Revenue If Pass 100% of Logistics Savings to Customers*	*Final Proj'd Disc % If Pass 100% Of Logistics Savings To Customers*
(1)	*(2)*	*(3)*	*(4)*	*(5)*	*(6)*	*(7)*	*(11)*	*(12)*	*(13)*
List Price Bracket	Corner Mart Binghamton	$ 28,012	88,478	$ 0.32		$ 304,330		$ 304,330	
	Corner Mart Hackettstown	$ 35,858	113,276	$ 0.32		$ 389,350		$ 389,350	
	Corner Mart Lewisburg	$ 86,768	320,509	$ 0.27		$ 1,107,210		$ 1,107,210	
	Corner Mart Washington	$ 52,460	165,653	$ 0.32		$ 572,358		$ 572,358	
	Save-A-Bunch Albany	$ 123,689	463,762	$ 0.27		$ 1,597,635		$ 1,597,635	
	Save-A-Bunch Harrisburg	$ 112,187	354,283	$ 0.32		$ 1,219,140		$ 1,219,140	
	TOTAL OR AVERAGE	**$ 438,974**	**1,505,959**	**$ 0.29**	—	**$ 5,190,023**		**$ 5,190,023**	
First Discount Price Bracket	Friendly Shop Hartford	$ 124,316	1,333,176	$ 0.09		$ 4,610,483	$ 68,462	$ 4,542,020	1.48%
	Friendly Shop Lancaster	$ 128,032	888,537	$ 0.14		$ 3,065,758	$ 45,629	$ 3,020,129	1.48%
	Save-A-Bunch Boonton	$ 124,937	1,341,139	$ 0.09		$ 4,658,518	$ 68,871	$ 4,589,646	1.48%

	Save-A-Bunch Virginia Beach	$ 98,940	684,834	$ 0.14		$ 2,363,790	$ 35,168	$ 2,328,622	1.48%
	TOTAL OR AVERAGE	**$ 476,225**	**4,247,685**	**$ 0.11**	**$ 0.069**	**$ 14,698,548**	**$ 218,130**	**$ 14,480,418**	**1.48%**
Second Discount Price Bracket	Friendly Shop Denville	$ 111,831	2,608,574	$ 0.04		$ 9,023,528	$ 268,570	$ 8,754,957	2.98%
	TOTAL OR AVERAGE	**$ 111,831**	**2,608,574**	**$ 0.04**	**$ 0.138**	**$ 9,023,528**	**$ 268,570**	**$ 8,754,957**	**2.98%**
TOTAL OR AVERAGE FOR ALL CUSTOMERS		$ 1,027,030	8,362,218	$ 0.12		$ 28,912,098	**$ 486,700**	$ 28,425,397	1.68%
	Base Case Frt & Hnd	**$ 1,513,730**	**Projected Scenario Savings in Frt & Hnd**			**$ 486,700**			

Item	*Current List Price*	*Recommended First Discount Bracket Price*	*Recommended Second Discount Bracket Price*	*Percent Discount 1st Disc vs. List Price*	*Percent Discount 2nd Disc vs. List Price*
1001	$ 50.00	$ 48.46	$ 46.91	3.08%	6.2%
1002	$ 65.00	$ 64.38	$ 63.76	0.95%	1.9%
1003	$ 80.00	$ 78.97	$ 77.94	1.28%	2.6%
1004	$ 20.00	$ 19.23	$ 18.46	3.85%	7.7%
1005	$ 45.00	$ 44.38	$ 43.76	1.37%	2.7%

TABLE 6.20 Logistics Costs under Alternative Bracket Pricing Scenarios

All Totals Shown Are Annualized

Scenario	*Total Freight Costs*	*Total Handling Costs*	*Total Freight and Handling Costs*	*Total Freight and Handling Costs vs. Base Case Costs*
Base Case	$ 1,452,222	$ 61,308	$ 1,513,730	
Scenario A: Two Price Brackets at Ship To Level	$ 1,109,594	$ 49,181	$ 1,158,775	$ 354,955
Scenario B: Three Price Brackets at Ship To Level	$ 979,166	$ 47,864	$ 1,027,030	$ 486,700
Scenario C: Two Price Brackets at Customer Level	$ 1,170,949	$ 44,796	$ 1,215,745	$ 297,985
Scenario D: Three Price Brackets at Customer Level	$ 920,549	$ 39,661	$ 960,210	$ 553,520

provides the customer base greater overall flexibility to qualify as a discount bracket customer, and can also facilitate even greater logistics efficiencies and savings for the supplier.

Bracket Pricing Summary

A bracket pricing program can play a foundational role for a supplier in establishing an efficient customer logistics network. In this section, we have reviewed key analytic steps that a fictitious consumer products supplier, GSC, undertook to evaluate the potential logistics savings that a bracket pricing program could create for its network. These steps included:

1 utilizing a variety of separate data sets to create an historical order and shipment database,
2 creating historical line item and order databases,
3 performing analyses to create a base case that revealed the logistics costs, and other key metrics which described GSC's current customer logistics operations,
4 evaluating the maximum potential logistics savings (i.e., potential opportunity) that once per week ordering by all customers could stimulate (this step confirmed that the potential savings were sufficient to justify GSC further pursuing a bracket pricing program),
5 determining the bracket pricing weight thresholds and scenarios to evaluate,
6 creating and utilizing simulation models to analyze the potential savings of each scenario – based on programming logic that projected how each customer would react to each scenario (i.e., would the customer change to weekly ordering, or continue to order multiple times per week), and
7 selecting for implementation purposes the bracket pricing scenario that would yield the largest annual logistics savings for GSC

To conclude, it is important to recognize that there are many facets to the development and implementation of a bracket pricing program by a supplier. We have focused on the analytical dimension of this process. However, to ensure the successful implementation of a bracket pricing program after its analytic development, firms must address several other major components of the process. Internally, a firm must educate its own employees on its new pricing approach. If a firm's own employees are not well-versed on their pricing policies, they certainly will not be able to explain it to their customers. Additionally, the supplier will have to revise all of its internal software and management systems that pricing policy changes will affect. Equally important, the supplier must communicate clearly with all of its customers what the new bracket pricing program entails, how it will affect customers individually, when the program will take effect, etc.

In summary, the analytic dimension of developing a customer logistics bracket pricing program represents just one significant component of the many which a firm must address to assure a successful bracket pricing implementation.

6.4 Customer Logistics Order Management and Service Programs

The customer logistics initiatives of suppliers in industries such as consumer products often include both service and pricing programs. Previously, in Section 6.3, we explored the quantity-based bracket pricing program of a supplier, GSC Inc. In this section we review examples of customer logistics service programs. Larger suppliers in particular often offer their customers a range of different service options, in addition to quantity-based price discount options. Similar to bracket pricing programs, these service programs seek to influence the ordering behavior and purchase patterns of customers such that both the supplier and the customer enjoy operating efficiencies and improved service levels.

Before reviewing an illustrative supplier's customer logistics program, it is important to note that these programs and the customer segmentation schemes that frequently accompany these programs are also developed for competitive reasons. Supplier firms seek to distinguish themselves from their competitors by promoting their service programs as superior to the programs offered by their competitors. Thus, the supplier strategy of offering customer logistics service programs has a marketing and long-run demand creation component, as well as a supply chain operations efficiency component. We focus on the efficiency component of service programs in this section.

An Illustrative Customer Logistics Service Program

Figure 6.1 depicts a typical customer logistics order management service program of a supplier. Note that this fictitious supplier segments its customer base into four groups, and that the targeted service levels vary by group. This program has six service attributes, the first five of which are:

- item fill rate,
- order cycle time,
- delivery window time,
- payment terms, and
- customer service support personnel

While there are many other service components that suppliers may offer, these five rank among the most frequently provided. (The notes at the bottom of Figure 6.1 further describe delivery window time, payment terms, and support personnel.)

Hypothetical Service Offering

SERVICE OFFERING	*CUSTOMER SEGMENT A*	*CUSTOMER SEGMENT B*	*CUSTOMER SEGMENT C*	*CUSTOMER SEGMENT D*
Item fill rate	99%	98%	97%	95%
Order cycle time	2 to 3 days	2 to 4 days	2 to 5 days	2 to 5 days
Delivery window time[1]	Within 1 hour of request	Within 1 hour of request	Within 2 hours of request	Within 2 hours of request
Payment terms[2]	2/10 net 30	2/10 net 30	2/10 net 30	Cash on delivery
Customer service support personnel	Dedicated supplier team[3] at customer's headquarters	Dedicated supplier team[3] at supplier's headquarters	Dedicated supplier customer service representative at supplier's headquarters	General customer service group at supplier's headquarters
Joint supplier/customer collaborative tactical and strategic planning meetings	Monthly meetings plus once-a-year meeting of the firms' presidents	Quarterly meetings	--------------------	--------------------

FIGURE 6.1 Illustrative Service Offerings by Customer Segment.

[1] The window of time during which the supplier's delivery will be made based upon the appointment time at the customer's receiving location (e.g., at the customer's receiving DC). So, for example, if the receiving DC of an "A Customer" gives a delivery appointment of 11 am next Tuesday to the supplier, this means the supplier's delivery truck must arrive between 10am and 12 noon next Tuesday at the customer's DC.

[2] Payment terms of 2/10 net 30 mean that the supplier will give the customer a 2% discount if the customer pays their invoice in full within 10 days after receiving the invoice. Otherwise, the customer must pay the supplier in full within 30 days, and there is no discount.

[3] Dedicated supplier teams are a small group of supplier employees who devote 100% of their time to a specific customer. A team of employees provides a higher level of customer support and collaboration compared to just one or two customer service representatives dedicated to a customer.

The sixth attribute shown in Figure 6.1, joint supplier/customer collaborative planning meetings, represents a service that suppliers generally reserve for a limited set of key customers. In particular, large suppliers commonly have regularly scheduled monthly, quarterly, and annual meetings (at the president of company level), where personnel ranging from junior levels to extremely senior levels collaborate on initiatives that vary from tactics to improve short-term operations to long-run product development and joint operations strategies. Notice this fictitious supplier does not offer this service to its C and D customers.

Section 6.2 previously discussed customer segmentation approaches, and we noted that the criteria utilized by suppliers to group their customers varies – with total annual customer purchases and the profitability of serving an individual customer among the more frequently used measures. In addition to being sales volume- and profitability-based, suppliers sometimes link their segmentation designations, or some of their service offerings, to whether a customer will agree to engage in selected operations efficiency initiatives. For example, a supplier may choose to locate a dedicated team of its own employees at a customer's headquarters, only if the customer agrees to a partnership agreement where the supplier and customer engage in several service efficiency initiatives. Exhibit 6.7 presents an illustrative list of customer logistics initiatives designed to create improved operational efficiencies for both the supplier and the customer.

EXHIBIT 6.7 ILLUSTRATIVE CUSTOMER LOGISTICS ORDER MANAGEMENT AND OPERATIONS EFFICIENCY INITIATIVES

1 *Single Super Purchase Order/Single Invoice Customer Orders:*

  a Any customer location such as a receiving DC consolidates all of its individual orders for a supplier into one single (super) PO per week, which it submits to the supplier.
  b Larger customers often have multiple buying groups within their Purchasing department. Frequently each group creates their own purchase orders just for the items that their group buys from a supplier.
  c If each customer buying group places their POs independently on a supplier, the supplier can either process and ship the orders separately, or the supplier must spend time each week consolidating all the different orders from the different customer buying groups – so that the supplier can make one efficient consolidated delivery to the customer.
  d Under the Super PO initiative, the customer agrees to consolidate all their orders for a particular week, for a particular receiving location, before the customer submits the PO to the supplier.
  e The supplier then agrees to send the customer a single invoice in response to the single PO.

2 *Efficient Payment Process*

  a All customer payments to the supplier must be electronic.
  b All payments must be made in an agreed upon standard format and process.

3 *No Touch Orders*

a A mutually agreed upon percentage (e.g., 85%) of the customer's annual purchase orders to the supplier must be perfect in terms of format, quantity, pricing, etc. so that the supplier's order management system can process the customer order without any supplier personnel having to correct, edit, or in any way modify the purchase order.
b All purchase orders must be submitted electronically.

4 *Efficient Pricing and Promotion Process*

a The customer must agree that the supplier can transmit all pricing updates electronically (e.g., changes in per unit prices of individual products), and that the customer will electronically confirm that all pricing updates were received and input into the customer's systems accurately.
b The customer must agree that the supplier can utilize a similar electronic process to communicate and receive customer confirmation of the prices and terms for all promotions and promotional items.
c All transactions must be done electronically and in a standardized, agreed upon format.

5 *Efficient Receiving*

a The supplier must guarantee an agreed upon level of picking and delivery accuracy on items ordered by the customer (e.g., a warehouse pick accuracy of 99.99% or greater). Additionally, the supplier must document the accuracy of its pick process to the agreed upon satisfaction of the customer.
b Based upon this promised level of item and quantity delivery accuracy, the customer receiving location must agree to facilitate a fast unload at their warehouse receiving docks of truckload deliveries from the supplier. Specifically, the customer must agree that their receiving location will not physically (i.e., manually) count the cases as they are being unloaded at the receiving dock.
c A reconciliation process after the speedy unloading process at the receiving dock must be agreed to by the customer and the supplier (i.e., a process to reconcile the extremely occasional situation where the case count, or the item itself, is discovered to be wrong, after the initial unload process at the receiving dock).

Firms that have already segmented their customers' service levels as illustrated in Figure 6.1 based on the sales revenue or profitability of individual customers on an ongoing basis frequently continue to develop additional customer logistics efficiency initiatives such as described in Exhibit 6.7. These firms employ varied approaches with respect to whether to link the existing and the newer initiatives. Some firms will link the assignment of an individual customer to a service segment based upon whether or not the customer agrees to participate in new collaborative efficiency initiatives. Other firms separate the assignment of a customer to a service segment from the customer's willingness to engage in collaborative supply chain efficiency initiatives. In some cases, a supplier may informally link its customer segmentation and operations efficiency strategies, and the following example illustrates how a supplier might do this.

Assume a supplier has an established segmentation strategy, and all of its customers already have a designation (e.g., all customers are defined as A, B, C, or D customers). The supplier may select a couple of its key "A" customers and ask them to participate in collaboratively testing an initiative with the supplier (e.g., the efficient receiving initiative). If the prototype test proves successful, then the supplier may expand this initiative to other customers. Further, the supplier might eventually link participation in this initiative by a customer with the service segment classification that a customer is assigned.

The Analytics and Challenges of Implementing Customer Logistics Efficiency Initiatives

The development of a bracket pricing program requires rigorous analytic evaluation, and similarly, to develop a program of customer logistics efficiency initiatives, a supplier must also carefully analyze all of the current costs, and potential future savings and benefits an efficiency program will generate. Further, to implement a collaborative efficiency initiative with a customer can be very challenging and requires strong relationship management skills on the part of the supplier. To illustrate the point, we consider an example that contrasts the greater challenge for a supplier of convincing a customer to participate in a single super purchase order (PO)/single customer invoice efficiency initiative than to participate in a bracket pricing program.

Bracket pricing example:

- A customer begins placing one 34,000 lb. order per week instead of two 17,000 lb. orders per week because a supplier implements a bracket pricing program with a discount price for orders > 30,000 lbs.
- The first week of the program, the supplier's freight costs decrease because it ships one 34,000 lb. truck to the customer, rather than two 17,000 lb. trucks.
- The first week of the program, the customer's purchase costs decrease because its purchase cost per unit drops since it is now purchasing products from the supplier at a lower, discount price.

Single super purchase order/single customer invoice example:

- A customer begins placing one super PO per week instead of its prior process of placing 20 small, individual POs per week scattered over 5 business days.
- The supplier begins processing the one super PO per week and issuing one single consolidated invoice per week to the customer.
- The supplier's customer service group begins to spend less time per week on the customer's purchase orders because the customer service group no longer has to manually consolidate 20 individual POs into one group of "linked orders" to be shipped together on one truck.
- The customer's "buyer group" begins to spend less time per week reviewing the supplier's invoice because the customer receives one single, consolidated invoice rather than 20 individual invoices.
- In the short run the customer's costs do not decrease. The purchasing group still maintains the same number of people and devotes the same level of other resources to support its buying group's activities.

- Similarly, in the short run, the supplier still maintains the same number of people and devotes the same level of other resources to support its order management/customer service group.
- In the long run (i.e., over many months and years), savings will accrue to the customer and the supplier because both will eventually be able to reduce or re-allocate the total resources devoted to their respective PO and invoicing processes.

The challenging issue the supplier must negotiate:

The supplier offers its customer a financial incentive to consolidate the customer's ordering process (i.e., to participate in the bracket pricing quantity discount program).[47] Specifically, the supplier essentially says "aggregate your orders to once per week, and your unit and total purchase costs will decrease."

However, the supplier cannot offer its customer a financial incentive to consolidate the customer's purchase orders into one super PO per week.[48] Instead, the supplier must convince the customer that their collaborative single super PO and single invoice processes will create operating efficiencies and savings that each organization will accrue in the long run.

As the preceding example illustrates, in general, customer logistics order management and operations efficiency programs do not yield immediate, tangible financial savings for customers (or for suppliers). However, innovative customers that choose to engage in collaborative efficiency initiatives with suppliers can achieve long-run operating improvements that enhance the customer's competitiveness among its peers. Similarly, innovative suppliers that identify potential operating efficiencies for themselves and their customers, and who invest in strong relationships with their customers, can reap long-term operational improvements and savings.

6.5 A "Supplier–Customer" Logistics Collaboration Initiated by a Customer

Sections 6.3 and 6.4 illustrated customer logistics initiatives developed by suppliers. Now we consider the reverse situation when a customer approaches a supplier with a proposal designed to enhance overall supply chain operation efficiencies. Although supplier-initiated programs are more common, customers themselves also approach suppliers with logistics proposals. While this most frequently occurs in the case of large customers who represent a significant portion of a supplier's total sales, innovative smaller and moderate-sized customers similarly may develop logistics efficiency proposals.[49]

In this section, we review a case where a large retail customer approaches a manufacturer with a customer logistics proposal that will facilitate more efficient handling operations in the customer's DCs. The proposal would also benefit the customer by reducing the inventory levels of the supplier's products at the customer's DCs.

In the case that follows, we discuss how the supplier should evaluate the customer's proposal to determine whether or not to accept it. We focus on how the supplier identifies the potential changes in its operations and warehouse costs that the proposal would require, as well as any other benefits the supplier might accrue from collaborating with its customer on this proposal.

Additionally, we briefly examine the general conditions on a joint supplier–customer logistics network under which a customer-initiated proposal:

1 will benefit both parties or
2 will not benefit both parties

Background

Customer: The customer is a large, big-box mass merchandise retailer. This customer's purchases account for over 25% of the supplier's total annual sales in the U.S.

Supplier: The supplier is a large manufacturer that produces a wide variety of consumer and over-the-counter healthcare products. It primarily distributes (i.e., sells) its products through the standard and secondary distribution/marketing channels for consumer products (e.g., mass merchandisers, grocery stores, pharmacies, convenience stores, clubs, etc.).

Network: The logistics network echelons that the proposal would impact consist of the supplier's DCs, the customer's DCs, and the customer's retail stores in the U.S. Figure 6.2 illustrates this network.

Current Inventory Replenishment Operations on the Network

Retailer DC to Retailer Store Inventory Replenishment:

- At present, the customer maintains several weeks of inventory of all of the supplier's products in its DCs (i.e., in the customer's DCs).
- Each customer DC provides daily inventory replenishments (i.e., shipments) to the customer's large retail stores that serve consumers. Each customer DC supplies about 100–150 of the customer's retail stores.

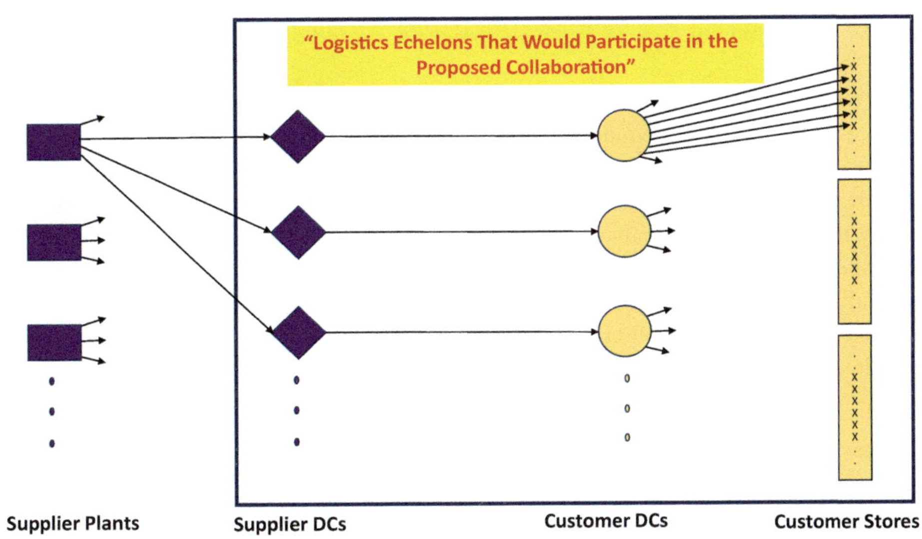

FIGURE 6.2 Supplier–Customer Supply Chain Network.

- Each store of the retailer places inventory replenishment orders daily on the retailer DC assigned to serve them.
- Retailer stores can order any quantity of cases and/or pallets of any product from their supplying DC. Therefore, stores can order just a single case or multiple pallets of a single product depending upon their inventory replenishment needs.
- The majority of items ordered by the stores from the DCs are in less than full pallet quantities (i.e., the item quantities are generally several cases rather than a full pallet of cases).

Supplier DC to Customer DC Inventory Replenishment:

- Each customer DC places multiple orders per week on the supplier DC that serves them.
- The inventory management systems of the customer DCs generate orders for the supplier DC's items based upon established reorder points and safety stock targets for each item.
- A very high percentage of the individual items and the total case quantities ordered by the customer DCs are in full pallet quantities.
- This results because each customer DC supplies inventory to between 100 and 150 individual retailer stores. Therefore, even for the slower-selling items of the supplier, the collective inventory replenishment requirements of 100–150 stores usually amount to one or more full pallets.[50]

Customer Proposal

The retailer has requested that the supplier DC begin to pick and ship *Store Pallets* to their DCs (i.e., to the retailer's DCs). Store pallets would be individual pallets picked by the supplier's DC warehouse personnel that only contain cases of inventory that an individual retailer's store required. Every pallet of product shipped by the supplier's DC to the customer's DC would hold replenishment inventory ordered just by an individual retailer store.[51]

Under the customer's proposal, when a customer DC received a truckload delivery from the supplier DC, the following process at the customer DC would occur:

1. A store pallet would be unloaded at the inbound receiving dock.
2. The store pallet would immediately be transported across the DC to the outbound DC loading dock area.
3. The store pallet would then immediately be loaded onto a truck scheduled to make the next delivery to the retailer store for which the store pallet was ordered. (This is called a "cross-dock" operation or cross-docking.)
4. Once fully loaded with all of the supplier's pallets for a particular store, plus all other inventory quantities from other suppliers required by that same store, the outbound truck would leave the customer DC and make its delivery to the retailer's store.

Customer Benefits

- Reduced customer DC warehouse handling costs:[52]
  - The customer warehouse no longer has to put away full pallets of inventory from the supplier into its inventory storage area, and then later pick and load the case quantities that a store orders.

  - Instead, the customer DC would simply cross-dock the store pallet from its inbound receiving docks to its outbound shipping docks.
- Reduced inventory investment levels at the customer DCs:
  - The DC no longer stores inventory of the suppliers' products. It simply receives, cross-docks, and ships out the supplier's inventory.[53]
- Reduced warehouse storage space for inventory at the customer DCs:
  - This results because the DCs no longer hold the supplier's products in inventory at their facilities.

Supplier's Evaluation of the Customer Proposal

The supplier immediately recognizes that the customer's proposal would create some additional operating costs at its own DCs. Further, there are no intuitively obvious other savings for the supplier that might offset the higher DC operating cost that the supplier expects it would incur by picking store pallets. Nevertheless, in the spirit of fostering strong supplier–customer relationships, the supplier decides to evaluate the potential impact of this proposal on its operations and costs. This will facilitate the supplier's response to the customer, including a thorough discussion and negotiation of possible options even if ultimately the supplier turns down the proposal.[54]

The supplier identifies the following expected operational changes this proposal would necessitate:

- Increased DC warehouse handling costs:
  - Currently, the supplier's DCs receive almost exclusively full pallet orders for its items from the customer's DCs. This allows supplier warehouse personnel to efficiently pick and load full pallets directly onto trucks destined for customer DCs.
  - In contrast, purchase orders from individual stores will contain a much higher percentage of total cases that the supplier DC will have to pick as individual loose cases. Because the retailer's DCs each serve between 100 and 150 of the retailers' stores, clearly the average case quantity per item on a store PO will be only about 1% or so of the average quantity per item ordered currently by the retailer's DCs.[55]
  - A store pallet will consist of a mix of cases of different items (e.g., a pallet with 80 total cases that has 2 cases of item A, 3 cases of item B, 1 case of item C, etc.). Once a worker completes the picking of all the cases for a store pallet and then stacks the cases in rows on the pallet, the worker will usually secure the pallet by wrapping plastic shrink wrap around the entire pallet. (Figure 6.3 displays a shrink-wrapped pallet.) This represents another required operational step that the warehouse worker does not currently perform.
- Increased number of purchase orders processed by the supplier:
  - Currently each of the retailer DCs sends a large, single PO to the supplier's DC that serves them. Under the proposal, 100–150 individual store POs would be sent to the supplier's DC rather than the current single PO. This would increase the supplier's PO processing costs as the annual number of POs processed would increase by 100–150 times.[56]

FIGURE 6.3 A Store Pallet of Different Items After It Is Assembled and Shrink-Wrapped.

In summary, the supplier's preliminary evaluation of the retailer's proposal identifies that accepting the customer's proposal would create significant additional operational costs for the supplier. The next step for the supplier would consist of carefully quantifying what this cost would amount to annually. Once the supplier quantifies these costs, the firm then can discuss the proposal with the retailer.

Our focus in this section is on identifying the analyses the supplier must address. Therefore, rather than review the detailed steps of the required analyses just identified that the supplier would have to perform, we now consider some general conditions and opportunities that can lead to successful collaborations and negotiations between suppliers and customers.

Supply Chain Conditions and Opportunities That Can Facilitate Successful Negotiations

In an ideal supplier–customer relationship, the optimal perspective for both parties to evaluate logistics proposals should center on the following question:

- *Does the collaborative logistics proposal under consideration potentially reduce their collective total supply chain operations costs or generate other mutually beneficial outcomes?*

If the proposal would reduce the total annual *combined* logistics operations costs of the two firms, then an opportunity exists to implement the proposal successfully – assuming that the two firms can agree on a mutually acceptable distribution of the savings between them. On the other hand, if the proposal will increase the total annual combined logistics operations costs of the two parties, or if it will not facilitate an outcome under which both parties perceive that they benefit – it will be much more difficult to implement successfully.

Opportunity for Negotiation and Win-Win from Supplier's Perspective

The supplier has identified that their logistics costs will rise under the customer's proposal, and their analysis has projected the actual expected annual cost increase. From the supplier's perspective, the question now becomes:

- *Can the retailer, whose logistics operating costs will decrease under this proposal, compensate the supplier sufficiently to offset these higher supplier operating costs?*

Compensation for the supplier can take several forms, and may or may not be immediately accrued. Examples of the retailer's potential compensation to the supplier include the following:

- The direct monetary payment by the retailer to the supplier to offset the supplier's higher operating costs, and
- The granting of special marketing or other non-monetary promotional considerations to the supplier by the retailer. For example, the retailer might:
  - offer highly desired shelf space and shelf locations to the manufacturer in the retailer's stores or other similar perks designed to boost sales,[57]
  - agree to stock more of the supplier's product line in addition to those products already carried by the retailer, and
  - allow the supplier special end-cap locations in their stores to place promotional items

In addition to receiving tangible compensation from the retailer, the supplier may take other factors into consideration in assessing the proposal. For example, the supplier may think that agreeing to the retailer's proposal will facilitate greater purchases by the retailer in the long run, or will make the retailer more amenable to future operational changes that the supplier plans to initiate with the retailer.

Opportunity for Negotiation and Win-Win from a Retailer's Perspective

The customer understands that their proposal will increase logistics operating costs for the supplier. Additionally, the retailer has analyzed and knows the expected warehouse operating and inventory carrying costs savings that their proposal will generate for themselves annually. Further, the retailer's supply chain professionals should be able to develop an estimate of the approximate annual increase in costs that the supplier will incur if it implements the proposal. Finally, the retailer's store management, marketing, and finance groups should be able to develop an estimate of the potential revenue and profit gains the supplier might experience from potential marketing promotions and store placement options that the retailer could choose to offer.

Summary: The Opportunity for Negotiation of a Win for Both Parties

Both the retailer and the supplier can evaluate the potential joint supply chain costs, revenues, and/or additional benefits that the retailer's proposal will create. On this basis, they can enter a negotiation to determine if both can agree to implement the retailer's proposal, or some variation on the original proposal. As noted, both parties should approach the discussions collaboratively and with initial estimates of the potential costs, revenues, and/or other benefits the proposal could generate. This means that the retailer understands the implications for both themselves and the supplier, and that similarly the supplier has evaluated the proposal's impact on both parties. Under these conditions, both parties can begin the negotiations with an understanding of whether the proposal may lead to an overall positive impact on their joint (i.e., supplier–customer) supply chain. If both parties perceive that there may be an overall positive outcome on their joint supply chain from a collaboration on the proposed initiative, this will increase their willingness to negotiate options. However, if one or both parties' pre-negotiation analysis suggests an overall negative impact on their joint supply chain, the probability of a successful agreement on the proposal will decrease significantly.[58]

6.6 Summary

This chapter began with a general review of customer logistics and service activities. Next, we examined an illustrative income statement of a supplier to identify those logistics costs such as freight and warehouse operations that a supplier's customer logistics and order management initiatives can target for efficiency improvements. In Section 6.2, we then discussed the frequent need for a supplier to segment their customer base, as well as other steps often undertaken to facilitate the development of a customer logistics program.

In Section 6.3, we reviewed how a fictitious consumer products manufacturer, GSC Inc, analyzed how the implementation of a bracket pricing program could incentivize their customers to place larger, more efficient order quantities. This review highlighted the importance for a supplier of first evaluating the potential opportunity for savings improvements before embarking on the substantial analytic and organizational management effort required to develop and implement such a program.

We followed up the bracket pricing review by illustrating in Section 6.4 the type of service offerings that suppliers sometimes provide to different segments of their customer base. We observed that while the implementation of a bracket pricing program yields immediate logistics cost savings for suppliers and purchase cost savings for discount bracket customers, customer logistics service programs facilitate mutual supplier–customer efficiencies that can take many months and often years to take full effect. Finally, in Section 6.5, we considered the reverse situation in which a customer proposes a joint logistics program with a supplier. We reviewed how a supplier can evaluate such a proposal, and the supply chain conditions that may facilitate mutual agreement on a proposal by a supplier and a customer.

To conclude, well-constructed bracket pricing and customer logistics/order management programs can generate mutual gains for both the supplier and the customer. Success occurs when both parties enjoy cost savings and/or service benefits. Initiatives where one party gains and one party loses rarely succeed in the long run.

Notes

1 ECR is a joint trade and industry body working toward making the grocery industry as a whole more responsive to consumer demand and promote the removal of unnecessary costs from the supply chain. (Efficient Consumer Response." *Wikipedia: The Free Encyclopedia*, Wikimedia Foundation, https://en.wikipedia.org/wiki/Efficient_Consumer_Response. Accessed October 12, 2024).

2 See Exhibit 6.1 for a description of CPFR.

3 The reasons why suppliers often segment their customer bases will be explained as the chapter progresses.

4 The reader interested in fully understanding an income statement is referred to any standard introductory accounting or finance textbook.

5 Transportation and warehousing are major areas of expense for most firms. To be clear, however, Table 6.1 is illustrative and not meant to suggest that these two costs usually represent the equivalent of about 15% of annual revenue for most firms. These expenses will of course vary from firm to firm.
6 The impact on EBITDA is one-for-one (e.g., $1 million in freight and warehouse savings increases EBITDA by $1 million). The impact on net income is slightly less than one-for-one because of the impact of taxes on EBITDA.
7 Keep in mind that any customer logistics programs designed to improve the efficiency of operations must also maintain the existing service levels necessary to satisfy customers.
8 Briefly, the more narrowly defined (i.e., tightly defined) a customer segment is, the more precisely a supplier can align their costs to serve a customer segment with the costs of the services offered to a particular segment. On the other hand, the more broadly defined (i.e., wide) a customer segment is, the less precisely can a supplier match their costs to serve a particular segment with the costs of the services provided to that segment. Ideally, a supplier wants to align their costs to serve each customer with the costs (and levels) of the service provided to each customer. By having many customer segments rather than just a few, a supplier can more tightly define what it charges or what services it offers to each segment. The more similar all customers are in a segment in terms of their purchase levels and services required, the more closely a supplier can match its costs to serve a customer with the costs of its services to that segment.
9 Section 6.4 will provide more details and examples.
10 To successfully implement a major customer logistics program, a supplier must invest substantial money and people resources in preparing its customer base for all the changes the program will require of the supplier's customers. This is generally a major process in itself, in addition to all the internal work a supplier must do to develop and launch a program. Further, this external phase typically cannot start until the supplier's internal development process is completed or near completion. And this external phase of the project often includes a lengthy "selling" component in which the supplier's representatives meet with many customers to encourage them to participate in the program.
11 Or whatever time period over which the firm is measuring its costs (e.g., per month).
12 ASCM Dictionary, 17th edition, 2022.
13 Different firms will require different data fields. The examples presented here represent the standard, basic data fields generally utilized.
14 Recall that a line item is a single item on an order. An order can contain just one item or many items (e.g., one order placed by a large consumer products retailer on a large manufacturer and/or distributor frequently contains several hundred line items.)
15 There are many alternative ways to perform this data consolidation process depending upon the data processing tools and computing environment used by a particular firm. It is beyond the scope of this textbook to delve into these myriad options. We will therefore focus on the logic that analysts must utilize to create a single consolidated database. A user interested in following the methodology outlined here can incorporate this logic into the tools that are available in their particular computing environment.
16 In industry, a firm often may extend its focus beyond just warehousing and freight costs, although these are almost always a principal area of investigation.
17 The reader can determine what tools best suit their application.
18 This analysis assumes that GSC warehouse operations fulfill their customer orders by picking individual orders (i.e., an order pick operation). Picking by "customer orders" is a commonly used approach in warehouse operations.
19 As described earlier in this chapter, firms can implement bracket pricing policies where the customer's price is determined on the basis of: (1) each individual order quantity, or (2) the average order quantity of the customer over a defined time period. In this case, we assume that GSC will use an average order over a defined time period policy. For example, GSC could base the price per case (i.e., per unit) that a customer is charged on the customer's average order quantity over a 6-month duration. This would mean that to qualify for a defined discount price per case, a customer's average order over each 6-month historical period would have to exceed a defined quantity in order for the customer to receive a discount price.
20 Table 6.8 offers a sample of many, but not all, of the analytic results required.
21 See Appendix 5A.
22 As noted previously, multiple programming approaches can accomplish this task. Further, although we create an order database for illustrative purposes, via programming languages one could calculate

freight costs without formerly creating an order database. For example, a program could be written that adds the weight of each line item on an order to obtain the total order weight, and then the program could next reference the freight rate table in Table 6.4 to determine the appropriate cost per lb. to calculate the total freight cost of each order.

23 Further, as previously referenced, some practitioners will simply construct programming logic that completes the base case analysis without formally creating an order database.

24 As usual, there are multiple ways to do this in Excel (i.e., other ways to do this besides what we present here).

25 It is not necessary to include freight cost per lb. as a field in the order database. Alternatively, the total freight cost data field could be calculated directly in a more complicated formula. Because the freight costs per lb. do vary by order, it was included for illustration. In contrast the handling costs per case and per pallet do not vary and it would be more repetitive to include these fields in the order database. Therefore, total case handling and total pallet handling costs were calculated directly in a more complex formula.

26 See an Excel help manual or query Google for specific details.

27 As previously noted, it is generally recommended to use an historical data set spanning at least 6 months, and ideally 1 year. For this illustrative case, we employed a smaller data set.

28 This is also true if historical data sets greater than 1 year are used (e.g., 18 months of data).

29 Recall that all average values remain unchanged.

30 That is, the average shipment weight if customers would only order once per week.

31 Note that by assuming all customers would order once per week, GSC does not have to develop analytic simulation models that contain the complicated programming logic necessary to predict which customers will order once per week, and which customers will continue to order in their current patterns of multiple times per week.

32 Recall that the line item database must be converted into an order database to calculate freight costs – which are based on the total order and shipment weight. Exhibit 6.4 previously described this process.

33 As usual, we note that this process can also be performed using database programming software. For larger databases, this is the approach most frequently used in practice rather than an Excel-based approach.

34 Note that if the weekly order database analysis had suggested a much smaller maximum potential return (e.g., 0.5% or less), GSC likely would have decided not to move forward with the development of a bracket pricing program.

35 24 full pallets = 6 × 4, and 423 individual cases = 104 + 104 + 107 + 108.

36 That is, the costs to serve that portion of the customer base who continue to order multiple times per week will remain unchanged.

37 In some cases, it may also be possible to estimate percent savings changes based upon a well-known, established subset of the customer base. For example, a firm may have done previous studies and determined that a particular subset of 200 of the firm's 2,000 total customers provide representative analytical results that the firm can confidently extrapolate to its entire customer base.

38 That is, for each customer, the sum of the customer's current multiple purchases per week.

39 Firms that use this average order approach usually establish 6- or 12-month "monitoring" periods. Discount customers receive their assigned discount prices on all orders during this monitoring period. However, to maintain their "discount status," customers must meet or exceed a defined threshold on their average order during a monitoring period in order to retain their "discount customer" status for the following monitoring period.

40 We can deduce that these two ship to locations are currently ordering twice per week because multiplying their respective current base case average order weights by 2 yields the average weekly order weights shown for these locations.

41 Because the location was averaging over 10,000 lbs. per order in the current base case.

42 While some firms employ more than three price brackets (e.g., four or five), two or three brackets represent the most commonly used bracket pricing approaches.

43 It is important to note that a firm can conduct more complex analyses to determine weight-based (or other) thresholds. For example, another approach consists of defining some target percentage of total annual sales that a firm wants to fall into each price bracket. Then, the thresholds required to facilitate that the targeted percent of annual sales for each price bracket materializes can be determined. Once these alternative thresholds are determined, then the simulation model to create a projected order database can be constructed, and the subsequent cost savings analyses of this database would be developed.

44 Recall this means that the price each of a customer's ship to locations (i.e., receiving DCs) would pay is based on the average order weight of the particular ship to location.
45 To determine the recommended price per unit for each discount bracket, GSC must calculate the decrease in individual product prices that will result in a reduction in the total purchase costs of the entire customer base equal to GSC's annual logistics costs savings. In other words, GSC must determine for the discount bracket(s) the unit price decreases it can offer to discount customers that will reduce GSC's annual net revenue by the same amount that GSC will save in annual freight and handling costs. These calculations must factor in the different weights per case of each product, and the expected sales distribution mix for each product. Sales distribution mix refers to how much of a product's annual sales is projected to sell at list price, and how much is expected to sell at a discount price.
46 It is important to note that it is also possible for a ship to level scenario to project greater savings than a customer level scenario under some circumstances.
47 For those customers that can meet the discount quantity thresholds.
48 Because the supplier does not gain any financial savings immediately.
49 Larger customers in general have more influence with suppliers than do smaller customers because of the financial leverage their higher purchase levels afford them with a supplier.
50 The inventory management system of the customer DCs generally will round orders of an item to an even pallet quantity. For example, if a customer DC requires one full pallet (with 50 cases per pallet) plus 30 additional loose cases of a supplier item, the system will order two full pallets. So, in this example, the customer's need is for 80 cases, but its system rounds the order to 100 cases.
51 Note that a truckload delivery from a supplier DC to a customer DC would contain store pallets for multiple stores.
52 For completeness, we note that the retailer may require a slightly higher level of inventory investment at its stores in order to maintain its current fill rate (i.e., inventory availability) for its store customers (i.e., for consumers). Currently, a retailer's store places its orders on the retailer's DC assigned to serve the particular store. If the supplier accepts the retailer's proposal, then as discussed, a store's purchase order would be picked by the supplier. Under the retailer's proposal the store pallet would flow from the supplier DC to the retailer DC (where it is cross-docked), and then moved from the retailer DC to the store. It is likely that the order cycle time on a store pallet order placed by a retailer store would be longer than the order cycle time on an order from a retailer store to a retailer DC. This is because there are two transport moves required to fulfill the proposed store pallet ordering process, compared to just one transport move when a retailer store orders the supplier's products directly from a retailer's DC. The retailer would and should factor this marginal impact on retail store inventory levels into their inventory analysis of their proposal.
53 In practice, a customer DC may decide to still maintain a very limited quantity of emergency or back-up inventory for certain key supplier items. However, even in this situation, the level of supplier inventory at the customer DC would significantly decrease.
54 A key to good customer relationships for a supplier is an ability and willingness to discuss options with its customers. Simply turning down proposals without any discussion does not foster collaborative relationships.
55 The retailer's total annual demands placed on the supplier remain identical under the retailer's proposal. Thus, if each current retailer DC PO is replaced by 100–150 individual retail store POs, the average case quantity per item on PO would decrease by a ratio of approximately (1/100) to (1/150).
56 As the number of annual POs processed increases, the likelihood of errors or other issues that would require manual intervention by supplier personnel would also increase. Increased manual interventions would result in increased labor processing costs.
57 For example, the retailer could offer to inventory more of the supplier's products on the most heavily traveled aisles in the retailer's stores. (Retailers and suppliers both know which aisles in a retailer's stores consumers most frequently pass through.) Additionally, as noted, the retailer could offer to stock more of the supplier's products on the middle and eye-level shelves of its stores. Suppliers highly value the placement of their products on these shelves rather than on the bottom or lower shelves, or on very high shelves. Placement of products on heavily traveled aisles and on eye-level shelves generally leads to higher sales.
58 Because in this case, there are not positive benefits and/or savings to split between the two parties. (That is, if the collective impact of the proposal on the combined supply chain of the two parties is negative, then only one party will be better off if the proposal is implemented.)

7

END-TO-END SUPPLY CHAIN ANALYSIS

In this chapter, we examine selected analytic techniques and methods that facilitate logistics management and decision-making across the supply chain. While the analytic methods may focus on one area of the supply chain (e.g., a manufacturer evaluating the profitability of its sales to a customer), the techniques themselves can generally be employed end-to-end across a supply chain.

We begin in Section 7.1 by reviewing a framework that a firm can employ to organize all of the performance metrics which it maintains to monitor and manage its supply chain. Next, Section 7.2 illustrates several measures used to evaluate the cash flow of a firm from the beginning to the end of its own supply chain. We then review in Section 7.3 the powerful analytic tool called activity-based costing (ABC). This methodology allows firms to understand accurately their true costs to serve their customers, to produce individual products, and to deliver products to customers. This section includes an illustration of how the ABC models of a firm's supply chain operations facilitate the development by a supplier of individual income statements (i.e., profit and loss statements) for each of its customers. In section 7.4 we then explore several additional key concepts and techniques that play an important role in logistics management and decision-making including:

1 economies of scale,
2 per unit and percentage of sales cost measures,
3 measures such as total annual cases shipped which are often used as "proxies" for total warehouse activity and output per year, and
4 risk management

Finally, the chapter concludes with a short summary.

7.1 Organizing Performance Metrics to Monitor a Firm's Activities across Its Entire Supply Chain

Selecting and monitoring key performance measurements is an important component of analytics-based decision-making and logistics management. A well-designed performance management system facilitates: 1) monitoring how well the current logistics system is operating

DOI: 10.4324/9781003585442-7

as compared to targeted goals and 2) if performance is not meeting the targets, then it provides the impetus to exercise control, and, if necessary, implement adjustments to obtain alignment between actual performance and targeted goals.[1]

As a result, the logistics organizations of most firms employ an array of dashboards, scorecards, key performance indicators (KPIs), and/or other measurement indices to monitor their performance.[2] The development and availability of insightful measurements and metrics such as KPIs is a prerequisite for an effective performance management system. However, how a firm organizes its KPIs, and how these KPIs align with its logistic management decision framework and strategy, represents an equally important issue. Thus, firms must not only have strong KPIs, but these KPIs must align seamlessly with the firm's logistics management framework, activities, and strategy.

In this section, we present a hierarchical logistics performance framework that enables a firm to synchronize its logistics management plans and decisions with performance measures that monitor the impact of actions taken. This framework provides a vehicle to house all of a firm's logistics performance measures that monitor activities ranging from daily operations (e.g., delivering an order to a customer) to major long-run functional performance (e.g., the overall customer on-time delivery rate of a logistics organization for an entire year). These measures or KPIs can be monitored using a scorecard or dashboard, as shown in Table 7.1 and Figure 7.1, respectively. We will illustrate how this performance framework aligns with a firm's logistics management activities and can be applied to specific logistics functions.

TABLE 7.1 Example of a Logistics Scorecard[a]

KPI (Key Performance Indicator)	*2024 Actual*	*2025 Goal*	*Month Actual*	*YTD (Year to Date) Actual*
On Time Delivery	86.7%	88.0%	89.9% ▲	79.2% ▼
Retail in Stock	97.4%	97.5%	96.9% ▼	97.2% ▲
Distribution-to-Store Fill Rate	95.1%	95.5%	94.5% ▼	94.2% ●
Case Fill Rate	96.2%	97.6%	94.4% ▼	95.3% ▼
Display Case Fill Rate	98.0%	98.0%	98.3% ▲	97.3% ▼
Over, Short, & Damaged	0.29%	0.35%	0.21% ▼	0.21% ▲

Notes

[a] A triangle facing upwards means the metric is improved compared to last month (for Month Actual metrics) or compared to last year to date (for YTD Actual metrics), a triangle facing down means the metric is worse than last month or last year to date, and a circle means the metric is the same as last month or last year to date.

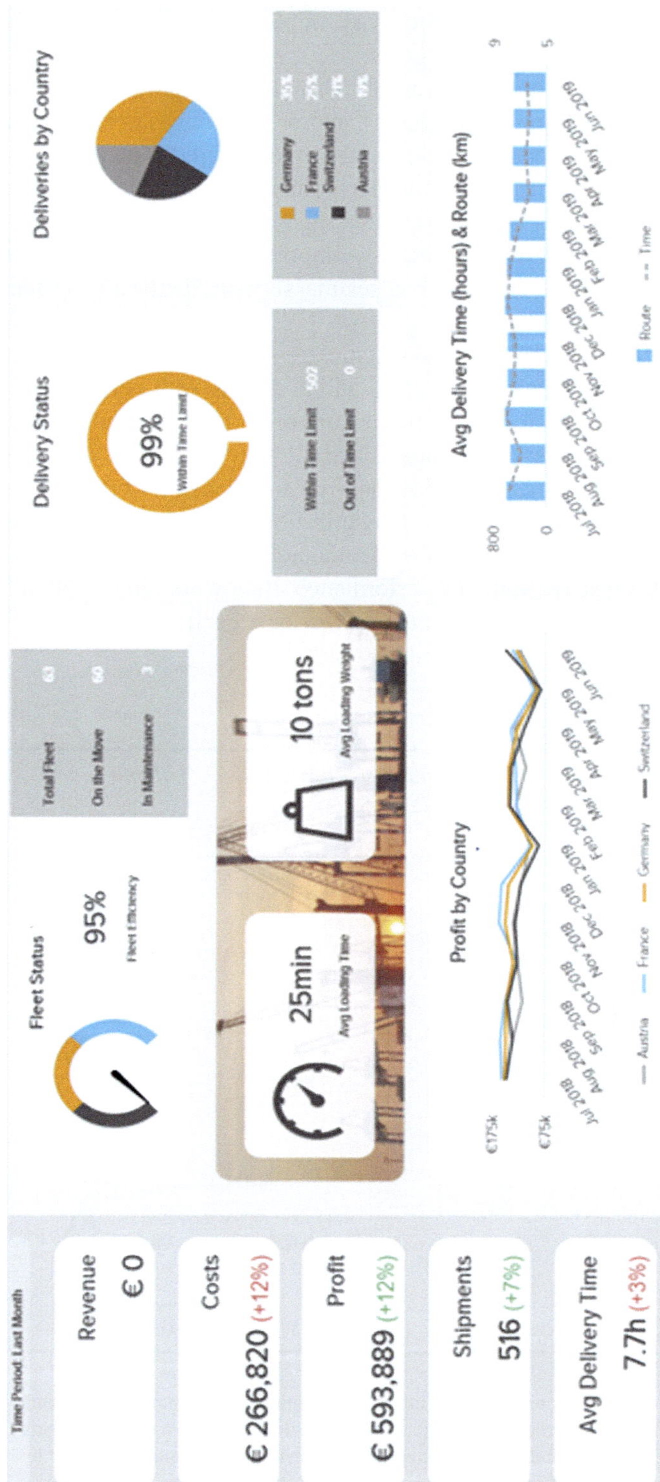

FIGURE 7.1 Example of a Logistics Dashboard.

Measures, Metrics, and Indices

Before presenting our logistics performance management framework, we first distinguish the difference between measures, metrics, and indices. A *measure* requires no calculations and has simple dimensions. Some logistics examples include units of inventory and backorder dollars. A *metric* requires a calculation or a combination of measures, often in the form of a ratio. Logistics examples include inventory future days of supply, inventory turns, and sales dollars per stockkeeping unit (SKU). An *index* combines two or more metrics into a single indicator, usually used to track trends in the outputs of a process. Two logistics examples are a perfect order fulfillment index and a facility utilization index for a network of plants. A performance management system typically comprises a set of measures, metrics, and indices. Since metrics and indices utilize measures, we will frequently use the term *measure* when either a measure, metric, or index might be appropriate. A KPI is a metric that an organization has identified as one that is closely aligned with its objectives, and that closely tracks or predicts performance.

A Hierarchical Logistics Performance Framework

To construct a framework that includes performance measures ranging from those which monitor daily operations, to those which evaluate long-run initiatives and activities, we employ a "hierarchical" approach. Specifically, we utilize a hierarchical logistics performance framework (HLP) where the scale or relative magnitude of an operation or activity that a performance measure monitors determines where it fits in the hierarchy.

The HLP has three levels: the strategic, the tactical, and the operational. Within each of these three levels of the HLP framework, we further differentiate performance measures as either external or internal. *External measures* focus upon the effectiveness of a firm's shipments or flows across its network and to customers, while *internal measures* evaluate a firm's efficiency in producing or delivering its outputs and services. Typical external performance metrics are order and line item fill rates on customer orders. For example, when a mass merchandiser places an order to a product supplier, these metrics track whether the supplier delivers the total order and the individual items, respectively, on time and complete as ordered. However, these external metrics do not evaluate the supplier's order delivery cost, such as whether the order was delivered on time but by expensive air freight rather than the originally planned surface transportation because of a production delay. In this instance, while the order delivery was effective (i.e., it met the customer's time requirement), it was not efficient (i.e., it was more costly than a normal surface delivery). Internal performance metrics such as "distribution cost per case" and "freight cost per pound" would be adversely affected by using the more expensive air delivery mode, if surface delivery is the normal mode planned for a lane.

Figure 7.2 displays the HLP framework, showing the three levels (strategic, tactical, and operational), and the two measurement perspectives (external and internal). At the strategic level from an external perspective, this framework spans the firm's facilities network, through plants, distribution centers, customers, and consumers. From the internal perspective at the strategic level, we include the firm's largest top-level functions related to logistics, such as distribution. At the tactical level, performance measures are required for such activities as warehouse operations and transportation, since these are the key functions of distribution. Drilling down into warehouse operations, we see from Figure 7.2 that it has five major sub-functions or

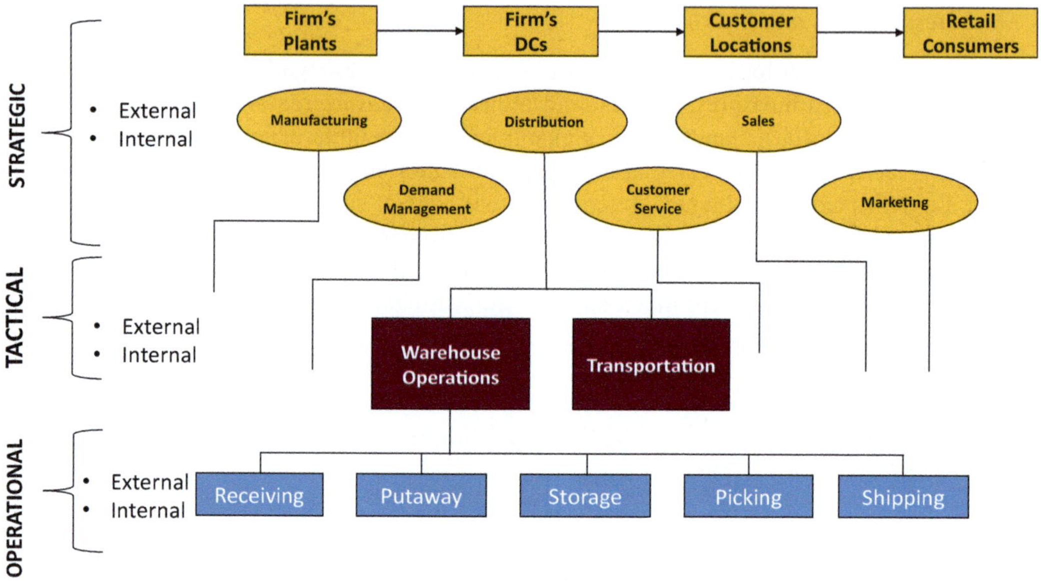

FIGURE 7.2 Hierarchical Logistics Metrics Framework.

processes at the operational level: receiving, putaway, storage, picking, and shipping. Internal and external performance measures are required at each level in this framework.

Applying the Hierarchical Performance Framework to Specific Logistics Functions

Figure 7.3 indicates how internal and external performance measures are set across the three levels of the HLP framework, continuing with distribution as our example. For the distribution organization (strategic level), percent of scheduled customer shipments delivered on time, and the average and variance of order cycle lead time represent external metrics, since they help to measure flows across the supply chain. They are strategic since they address the mission of the distribution function, ensuring delivery of products and services to customers in a timely manner. The total distribution cost per unit delivered is an internal, strategic metric since it measures the efficiency of distribution at the highest organization level.

At the tactical level, the percent of lines or orders picked correctly, and the percent of orders picked on the scheduled day, represent external metrics because they evaluate the impact of warehouse operations across the supply chain. When a warehouse picks an order correctly, it contributes to the ultimate successful delivery of products to a customer who has placed an order. Similarly, when a warehouse picks an order on the scheduled day, this contributes toward a successful on-time delivery of products to a customer. The third tactical metric shown in Figure 7.3, total warehouse costs per unit of throughput, represents an internal metric, since it offers a summary view of the internal cost (and efficiency) of the warehouse operation.

Focusing on the warehouse receiving function at the operational level, the percent of cases (or lines) received correctly (i.e., accurately) is an example of an external performance metric. We categorize this metric as external because the accuracy with which this function receives inbound shipments will impact the next stage of the logistics flow. For example, suppose that

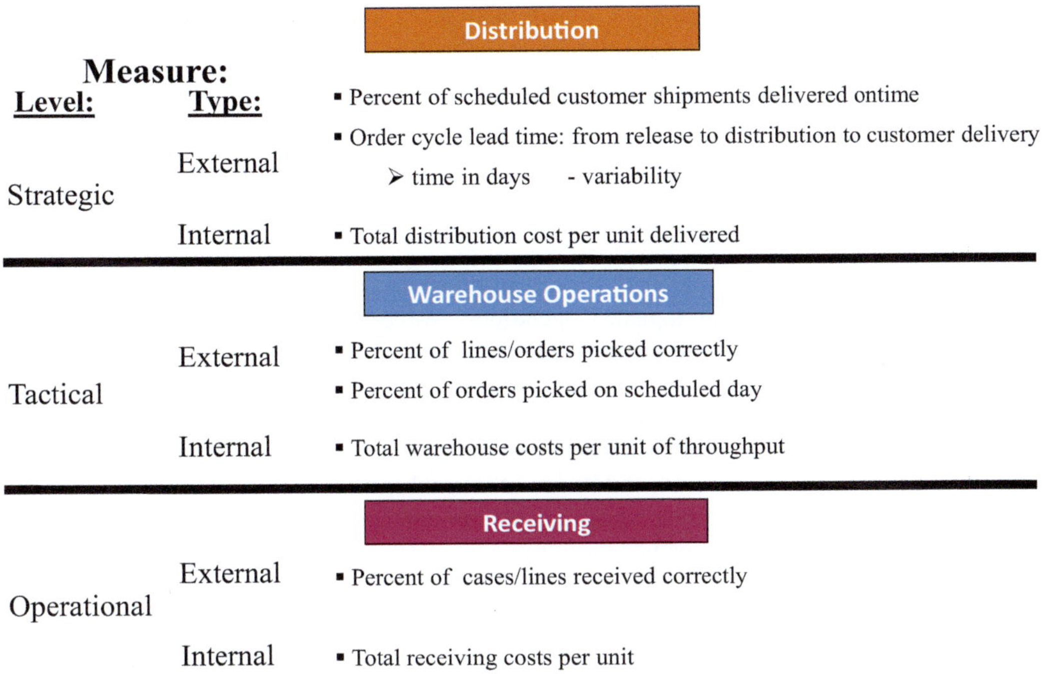

FIGURE 7.3 Illustrative Hierarchical Performance Measures for Distribution Function.

the receiving area miscodes an inbound receipt as product A, when in fact it received a delivery of product B. If this error remains undetected, this inventory of product B will then be put away into inventory classified as product A. Then, at some future point, this product could be picked and delivered to a customer who ordered product A, thereby creating a customer service issue, since the product delivered would really be product B (and not A as ordered). Therefore, the percent of lines or cases received correctly is classified as an external measure. In contrast, total receiving cost per unit has an internal orientation and will be of most immediate concern to receiving and warehouse personnel.

As another brief example consider manufacturing, which is slotted at the strategic level in Figure 7.2. A major manufacturing function such as fabrication would be at the tactical level, with fabrication sub-functions such as machining placed at the operational level (not shown in Figure 7.2). Manufacturing cost per unit would be an example of an internal performance metric at the strategic level, processing cost per unit would be an internal metric at the tactical level, while item defect rate would be an external metric at the operational level.

The HLP framework offers several important benefits. First, it provides a unified framework for aggregating performance measures across an organization. It enables a firm to organize its key performance measurements into a structure that leads to relatively few, high-level, strategic measures (e.g., between 10 and 25) that monitor overall firm performance. These are sometimes referred to as KPIs or key performance indicators. Second, this structure facilitates having additional performance measures that: (1) monitor smaller components of a firm's operation and (2) align with overall firm objectives. In this way all functional areas can develop and maintain their own measures and contribute to an overall measurement system. In addition, each function can then focus on a few key measures to help improve its performance. Finally, the HLP can contribute toward aligning the collective activities of a firm to meet a desired mission and set of objectives. For example, if a firm has a comprehensive measurement system in place that covers its major functional areas, managers can view the system in its entirety to identify any potential misaligned activities or objectives.

Summary

In this section we discussed the need for organizations to use KPIs and other measurements to help monitor and control logistics operations. We presented examples of scorecards, dashboards, and commonly used metrics. A HLP framework for organizing logistics measures was developed that addresses the strategic, tactical, and operational levels. This framework accommodates external metrics, such as order and line fill rate that focus on effectiveness, as well as internal metrics, such as distribution cost per case and freight cost per pound that focus on efficiency. The HLP framework and its use of internal and external measures can be applied to specific logistics functions, with transportation and warehouse operations given as examples. Advantages of the framework include the ability to:

1 aggregate measures across the entire organization,
2 focus on a few key strategic measures, and
3 establish a set of measures targeted for specific logistics functions, in such a way that all measures are aligned with the achievement of the company's mission and objectives

Addendum

In addition to creating a hierarchical framework to organize its KPIs, a firm can also formulate a *logistics performance index* (LPI) to assess the overall performance of its logistics activities. Miller and Liberatore (2021) proposed and illustrated how a company can develop a customized index to monitor its own logistics operations, and Appendix 7A describes this index and how to construct it.

7.2 Monitoring Cash Flow across the Supply Chain

Cash flow represents a key measure of a firm's financial strength. Strong annual cash flow generally indicates that a company is on sound financial footing, while weak cash flow may portend that a firm faces serious financial challenges. Supply chain operations significantly impact a firm's cash flow. Thus, while managing a firm's cash flow usually falls under the purview of a company's finance organization, supply chain and logistics managers must also monitor cash flow and how their operations impact this important financial variable.

In this section, we review and illustrate the "cash-to-cash" cycle which is also frequently called the "cash conversion cycle".[3] Briefly, the cash-to-cash or cash-conversion cycle (CCC) measures the time duration in days between when a company pays its suppliers for inventory and when the firm receives cash from its customer for selling that inventory or the goods produced from that inventory. For a retailer the CCC metric measures the time between when finished goods are bought from a supplier and when those same finished goals are sold to a customer, and the retailer has received the cash for the sale. For a manufacturer, the CCC measures the time between when inventories of raw materials and work-in-process (WIP) received from suppliers are paid for and when these inventories are converted into finished inventory and sold to a customer, and the manufacturer has received the cash for the sale. In this section, we will illustrate the cash-to-cash cycle of a manufacturer that purchases raw materials and WIP inventory, and then uses these inventories to produce finished good inventory to sell to customers.

Cash Flow Example: The Consumer Products Manufacturing Corporation

The Consumer Products Manufacturing Corporation (CPMC) produces and sells a wide variety of consumer products. This manufacturer supplies both small and large retailers who stock CPMC's products in their stores, and sell these products to consumers. CPMC has just completed its fiscal year and wishes to compare its cash flow performance for the just-ended year to the previous year using the CCC metric.

Calculating the Cash Conversion Cycle

To calculate its cash conversion cycle, CPMC must first calculate three key cash flow metrics which provide insights on the efficiency of the firm's operations. These include:

1 Days Inventory Outstanding (DIO),
2 Days Sales Outstanding (DSO), and
3 Days Payables Outstanding (DPO)

These three metrics measure the impact of different components of the firm's operations on the company's cash flow. Briefly, for a defined time period (e.g., 1 year), these three metrics are calculated as follows:[4]

1 *Days Inventory Outstanding* = (Average Inventory) / (Average Sales per day at cost)
Where:
   - Average Inventory = (beginning of period inventory + end of period inventory) / 2 and
   - Average Sales per day at cost = (Annual Cost of Goods Sold) / 365

2 *Days Sales Outstanding* = (Average Accounts Receivable) / (Average Revenue per day)
Where:
   - Average Accounts Receivable = (beginning of period accounts receivable + end of period accounts receivable) / 2 and
   - Average Revenue per day = (Annual Revenue) / 365

3 *Days Payable Outstanding* = (Average Accounts Payable) / (Average Sales per day at cost)
Where:
   - Average Accounts Payable = (beginning of period accounts payable + end of period accounts payable) / 2

These three metrics facilitate the following calculation of the cash cycle conversion:

- $CCC = DIO + DSO - DPO$

Per this formula, we can observe that low values of DIO and DSO facilitate a shorter CCC and good cash flow, while higher values of DPO similarly have a positive effect on a firm's cash flow. It is beyond the scope of this text to discuss DIO, DSO, and DPO strategies. However, we should note that firms generally do not blindly just strive to maintain very low DIOs and DSOs, and very high DPOs. Rather, companies must seek the optimal mix of DIO, DSO, DPO, and CCC days that balance their needs for good cash flow with the similar cash flow needs of their customers and suppliers. A balanced approach leads to strong, stable manufacturer–customer and manufacturer–supplier relationships from which all parties can collectively benefit in the long run.

Two-Year Analysis of CPMC's Cash Flows

Table 7.2 presents selected data for the last 3 years from CPMC's annual income and balance sheet statements. These data points facilitate an analysis of the firm's annual cash flows for 2024 and 2025.

Table 7.3 illustrates the calculations required to determine CPMC's cash flow for these 2 years. In the top portion of the table, note that we first calculate average accounts receivable, average inventory, and average accounts payable based on their end of year values found in Table 7.2. As shown under the "Calculations" portion of Table 7.3, we then utilize the previously defined formulas for DIO, DSO, and DPO to derive the cash flow associated with each of these individual operations. Finally, we compute CPMC's cash conversion cycle for both 2024 and 2025 by subtracting DPO from the sum of DIO and DSO. Note that the CCC is calculated first in days, and then in weeks simply by dividing the total days of the CCC by 7.

The last two rows of Table 7.3 indicate that compared to 2024, CPMC did improve their annual cash flow in 2025 by about 7 days or 1 week.[5] Briefly, we observe that a significant decrease in DIO and a slight increase in DPO both contributed to improvements in CPMC's cash flow, and these two positive factors outweighed the negative impact of a slight increase in DSO.

TABLE 7.2 Selected Data from CPMC's 2023–2025 Financial Statements ($ 000)

	2023	*2024*	*2025*
Revenue[a]	$ 12,000	$ 13,000	$ 14,000
Cost of Goods Sold[b]	$ 7,400	$ 7,900	$ 8,400
Accounts Receivable (at close of 12/31)[c]	$ 1,400	$ 1,600	$ 1,800
Inventory (at close of 12/31)[d]	$ 2,400	$ 2,600	$ 2,200
Accounts Payable (at close of 12/31)[e]	$ 2,300	$ 2,500	$ 2,500

Notes

[a] From Income Statement.

[b] See note a.

[c] From Balance Sheet.

[d] See note c.

[e] See note c.

TABLE 7.3 Data and Calculations to Determine CPMC's Cash Conversion Cycle (CCC) in 2024 and 2025

Required Data	*2024*	*2025*
Revenue	$ 13,000	$ 14,000
Cost of Goods Sold	$ 7,900	$ 8,400
Average Accounts Receivable[a]	$ 1,500	$ 1,700
Average Inventory[b]	$ 2,500	$ 2,400
Average Accounts Payable[c]	$ 2,400	$ 2,500
Calculations		
Average Sales Revenue per Day = **(Revenue / 365)**	$ 35.62	$ 38.36
Average Sales per Day at Cost = **(Cost of Goods Sold / 365)**	$ 21.64	$ 23.01
Average Inventory in Days (DIO) = **(Avg Inventory / Avg Sales per Day at Cost)**	115.5	104.3
Average Receivables in Days (DSO) = **(Avg Accounts Receivable / Avg Sales Revenue per Day)**	42.1	44.3
Average Accounts Payable in Days (DPO) = **(Avg Accounts Payable / Avg Sales per Day at Cost)**	110.9	108.6
Cash-to-Cash Conversion Cycle in Days = **(Avg Inventory in Days + Avg Accounts Receivable in Days – Avg Accounts Payable in Days)**	46.7	40.0
Cash-to-Cash Conversion Cycle in Weeks = **(Avg Inventory in Days + Avg Accounts Receivable in Days – Avg Accounts Payable in Days) / 7**	6.7	5.7

Notes

[a] These data points are obtained for each year by taking the average of their respective values on 12/31 of the prior year and 12/31 of the current year. For example, the average inventory for 2024 = (inventory on 12/31/23 + inventory on 12/31/24) / 2. Similar calculations are performed for accounts receivable and accounts payable.

[b] See note a.

[c] See note a.

In this section, we have reviewed how to determine the cash-to-cash or cash conversion cycle of a firm. The CCC of companies can vary substantially depending upon the type of firm (e.g., materials supplier, distributor, manufacturer, or retailer), the industry (e.g., pharmaceuticals vs. consumer products), or the type of operation (e.g., ecommerce, brick-and-mortar, service). The efficiency and effectiveness of supply chain and logistics operations can significantly affect a firm's cash flow both positively and negatively. Thus, supply chain managers should monitor and carefully manage the impact of their operations on cash flow. We close this section with a few general comments.

- Logistics operations often most directly impact DIO or average inventory in days at cost.
- Further, DIO represents a metric and cash flow determinant that firms can sometimes improve without having any impact, positive or negative, on their suppliers' or customers' respective cash flows.
- For example, a firm's forecast accuracy does impact the total level of safety stock inventory that a company must maintain in order to provide a targeted fill rate to its customers.[6] The better the forecast accuracy, the lower the total safety stock required, while the worse the forecast accuracy, the more safety stock required to facilitate achieving the fill rate target.
- Therefore, if a firm can improve the accuracy of its forecasts over time,[7] eventually the firm should be able to reduce its average inventory investment while still maintaining the same customer fill rate. This would improve the company's cash flow while having no impact on its customers or suppliers.

- In contrast, to reduce average accounts receivable days, or to increase average accounts payable days, requires that a firm interact with its customers or suppliers, and in some way impact these other firms' cash flows.

7.3 The Role of Activity-Based Costing in Logistics and Supply Chain Analytics

Activity-based costing (ABC) has helped many companies for decades gain a true understanding of their costs to produce and distribute products to customers. ABC provides a precise, accurate view of costs at very granular levels, namely, at the individual product, service, and customer level. As illustrated in this section, this differs from traditional accounting systems that are best suited to generate cost analyses at the overall firm, function, and facility level; but which distort costs at more granular levels such as the individual product or customer level.[8]

ABC first gained prominence in the corporate world during the 1980s as a new methodology that allowed manufacturers to accurately capture their true costs to produce individual products. Two of the original developers of this approach, Robert Cooper and Robert Kaplan, described this methodology in a seminal 1988 article titled "Measure Costs Right: Make the Right Decisions."[9] These authors argued that because traditional accounting systems *proportionately* allocate a manufacturer's indirect overhead costs based upon gross measures such as the total dollar sales of each product produced, this results in distorted individual product cost calculations.[10] Further, when firms use aggregate measures to proportionately allocate costs such as marketing and distribution to individual products, the potential for major distortions in product costing dramatically increases.

Successes during the 1980s in applying ABC methods to manufacturing prompted an eventual expansion of this methodology to other key components of logistics (e.g., distribution). Firms such as Proctor & Gamble and Warner-Lambert began using ABC models to determine their overall costs to serve individual customers (e.g., Walmart), and to evaluate the costs of offering different individual services to customers (e.g., services such as vendor-managed inventory and advanced shipment notices – ASNs).[11] To illustrate how ABC decision support contributes to a firm's understanding of distribution and other related costs, let's consider the following example where a company is evaluating the profitability of its three major distribution channels.

A Distribution Channels Profitability Example

Assume company XYZ is a manufacturer and distributor of pharmaceutical and consumer products, and it sells its products through three primary distribution channels: mass merchandisers, wholesalers, and small retailers. Now let's evaluate the overall profitability of each channel based upon: (1) a traditional accounting system and (2) an ABC system. Assume that XYZ's traditional cost accounting system allocates its distribution center's (DC's) costs based upon either the total dollars or weight shipped to each customer and channel. Typically, customers, channels, and products do not consume DC resources (such as labor and machine time) proportionately to their dollar or weight volume, so a traditional cost accounting system will distort the true costs. Suppose the XYZ DC distributes a mix of low-valued to high-valued products with a wide range in the dollar value per pound, and it receives, stores, and ships products in everything from individual eaches (e.g., pharmaceutical products) to pallet quantities (e.g., bulk consumer products). In addition, assume there are small pick lines (for eaches), automated conveyor lines (for cases), and forklifts (for bulk pallets) to move product from inventory storage to the shipping dock. Finally, there is a separate pick area to serve the special requirements of the three largest customers, and all modes of transport are used, from truckload to ground parcel to next-day air. An ABC view of costs at this facility would differ substantially from that of a traditional aggregate volume-based perspective.

Figure 7.4 shows the difference in the net profit generated by the three different distribution channels as calculated by traditional volume-based accounting and then by an ABC approach. In contrast to the "volume-driver"-based accounting system that uses only sales dollars to allocate costs, XYZ's ABC system employs many more drivers. For example, the DC may use a case pick operation to serve small retailers and a bulk pick operation to serve wholesalers and mass merchandisers. The ABC system would accurately calibrate the different costs of serving customers using the two different operations. It also would evaluate the costs of all other major components involved in serving customers such as order management, transportation, and sales force activities. In this fictitious case, one can observe that based on the ABC costing system, the small retailer channel provides the smallest profit margin (4%), while the mass merchandise (11%) and wholesale (9%) channels yield a higher return. Conversely, the traditional costing system incorrectly indicates that the small retailer channel generates the highest profit margin (16%), followed by the mass merchandise (9%) and wholesale (7%) channels, respectively.

Note that in the traditional system, XYZ's $84 million total annual operating expenses are allocated to each channel based upon that channel's proportion of total gross revenue (e.g., the small retailer channel's operating expense equals 100/700 × $84 million). This top-down, gross allocation of operating expenses distorts XYZ's cost to serve each channel. In contrast, the ABC methodology calculates the cost to serve each channel in a bottom-up approach. Specifically, the cost of services performed by the manufacturer for individual customers is tabulated based

TRADITIONAL ACCOUNTING				
	Mass Merchandisers	Wholesalers	Small Retailers	Total
	$(MM)	$(MM)	$(MM)	$(MM)
Gross Revenue	400	200	100	700
Cost Of Goods	300	160	70	530
Gross Margin	100	40	30	170
Trade Promotions	16	2	2	20
Total Operating Expenses	48	24	12	84
Net Profit	36	14	16	66
Net Profit (%)	9.0%	7.0%	16.0%	9.4%

ABC COST-TO-SERVE				
	Mass Merchandisers	Wholesalers	Small Retailers	Total
	$(MM)	$(MM)	$(MM)	$(MM)
Gross Revenue	400	200	100	700
Cost Of Goods	300	160	70	530
Gross Margin	100	40	30	170
Trade Promotions	16	2	2	20
ABC Assignments:				
♦ Logistics Mgmt	8	4	5	17
♦ Order Mgmt	10	5	6	21
♦ Customer Mgmt	10	6	5	21
♦ Sales Force Activities	12	5	8	25
Total Operating Expenses	40	20	24	84
Net Profit	44	18	4	66
Net Profit (%)	11.0%	9.0%	4.0%	9.4%

FIGURE 7.4 Illustration of Activity-Based Costing (Channel Profitability as Measured by Traditional Accounting vs. ABC).

on the cost to perform the particular activity, and the number of times each activity is performed for a customer. In the simple example presented in Figure 7.4, these services performed (i.e., activities) include logistics management, order management, customer management, and sales force activities. This example illustrates the alternative, more accurate cost and profitability insights that an ABC system can generate, and the dangers of making decisions using the volume-driver approach rather than an ABC system.

The ABC Models Underpinning ABC Systems

To develop an accurate ABC system, a firm must first develop a good process model of each activity or operation of interest. XYZ requires that its ABC system capture how its costs to deliver products to each customer differ. At the minimum, therefore, XYZ must create ABC models of its DC operations and transportation delivery processes. Further, as Figure 7.4 illustrates, XYZ is evaluating its costs by customer (and distribution channel) in terms of sales force activities and customer service. In practice, this would necessitate that XYZ construct and maintain process models of each of these major components of the order-to-delivery process. For illustrative purposes, we briefly consider DC operations, which represents one of the key activities of this overall process.

Figure 7.5 illustrates the process and cost model that XYZ would maintain for this operation. A team of DC operations and accounting/finance personnel would develop the process flows and cost analyses necessary to generate this model. A review of Figure 7.5 shows that the cost per unit (i.e., per pallet, case, or each) of every activity is calibrated. XYZ can combine this DC ABC model with its databases that provide data on how many cases, pallets, and eaches its DC picks and ships to each customer, in order to assess the costs XYZ incurs in serving each of its customers from the DC. XYZ would need similar models of the other major activities (e.g.,

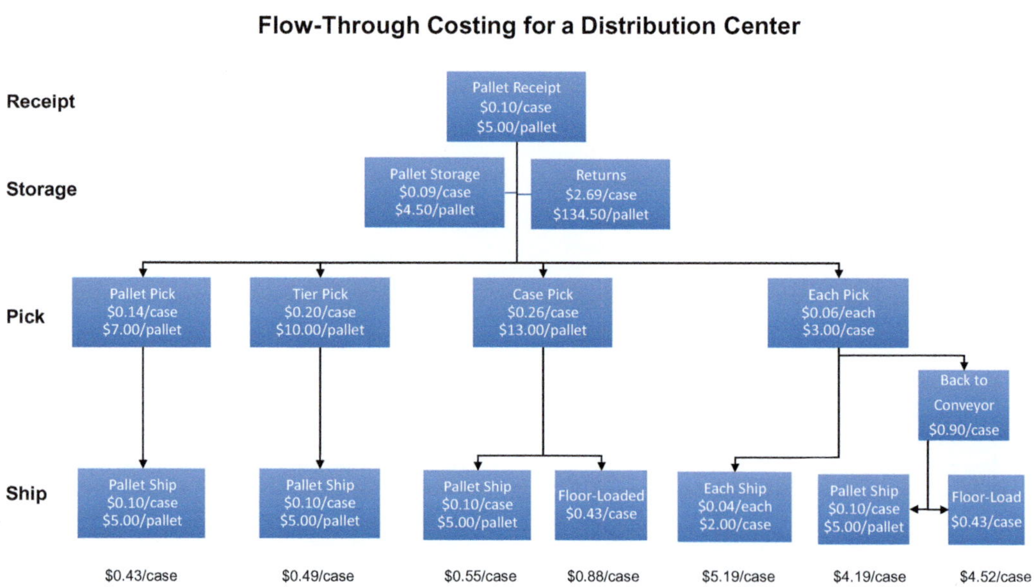

FIGURE 7.5 An ABC Model of a DC Operation.

transportation) utilized in serving its customers. Collectively, these ABC process models would facilitate XYZ's evaluation of the true cost to serve each customer.

Why ABC Is More Critical Than Ever in Logistics Operations and Strategy

Omni-channel and the business-to-consumer (B2C) delivery process represents one of the most dynamic, rapidly evolving areas of logistics operations. Further, the escalating competition that B2C suppliers face to provide same- or near-same-day deliveries to consumers (often with no delivery fee) places many suppliers under severe cost pressures. Business-to-business (B2B) suppliers similarly face ever-increasing service demands and cost pressures, and many suppliers now compete in both the B2B and B2C worlds. To compete today, and to design efficient, profitable delivery strategies for tomorrow, demands that suppliers accurately know their costs to deliver *every product to every customer*. Suppliers managing without this essential information have little hope of designing and executing efficient and effective delivery network strategies and operations. Only suppliers armed with an accurate, ABC-based view of their delivery costs at the individual product and customer levels can successfully compete in the long run. We conclude this discussion of the use of the ABC methodology in supply chain analytics with an illustration of how ABC models facilitate a supplier's development of individual customer cost and profit analyses. This represents just one illustration of the myriad analyses enabled by good ABC supply chain models.

Using Activity-Based Costing Models to Develop Individual Customer and Supplier Income Statements

ABC models allow a manufacturer (supplier) to generate individual income statements (i.e., profit and loss analyses) for each of their customers. Conversely, the development of ABC models by a customer (e.g., a retailer) facilitates the creation of individual profit and loss (i.e., P&L) statements for each of the customer's suppliers. Further, these individual P&Ls then can become key inputs to a supplier's initiative to establish customer segmentation plans and ultimately the customer logistics programs previously studied in Chapter 6. In this section, we briefly outline this process.

Figure 7.6 displays an annual P&L generated by a manufacturer for a fictitious customer. A firm heavily committed to ABC will have individual models of some or all of the following logistics functions: warehousing, transportation, order management/customer service, and manufacturing. Additionally, it might also have ABC models of non-logistics functions such as sales. All of these models can provide results at the individual customer and product level.[12] The annual costs to serve an individual customer or produce an individual product for a customer then become inputs to the customer's P&L.

A glance at Figure 7.6 shows the following:

1 The transportation costs to serve a customer, developed by an ABC model, would be input into line 7 (Other Variable Expenses).
2 The warehousing and order management/customer service costs, developed by other ABC models, would be input into line 10 (Operations).
3 The costs to produce the products purchased by a customer, developed by another ABC model, enter line 4 (Cost of Goods Sold) of the P&L.

A Customer Profitability Analysis – 12 Month P&L					
Item	**$**	**% to Sales**	**Item**	**$**	**% to Sales**
1. Gross Sales	$66,942,069	102.6%	8. Direct Profit Contribution	$40,456,238	62.0%
2. Returns & Cash Discounts	$1,687,428	2.6%	9. Selling Expenses	$1,263,569	1.9%
3. Net Sales	$65,254,641	100.0%	10. Operations (including warehouse & order management)	$998,447	1.5%
4. Cost of Goods Sold	$16,208,665	24.8%	11. Operating Profit	$38,194,223	58.5%
5. Gross Margin	$49,045,976	75.2%	12. Write-Offs	$38,105	0.1%
6. Promotional Costs	$6,677,284	10.2%	13. Adjusted Operating Profit	$38,156,118	58.5%
7. Other Variable Expenses (including freight)	$1,912,454	2.9%			

FIGURE 7.6 An Illustrative Manufacturer's P&L for an Individual Customer.

Additionally, the sales force-related cost to serve a customer, also developed by an ABC model, would appear on line 9 (Selling Expenses).[13]

ABC Takeaways

There are several key takeaways we will briefly address in closing, and we offer additional references on ABC for the interested reader.

1 First, it is important to note that ABC costing systems are intended to *complement* traditional accounting and financial systems, and should not be viewed as replacements or threats to a firm's existing systems. Rather, ABC systems facilitate detailed insights on a firm's true cost to serve individual customers, to offer specific customized services to customers, and so on.

2 It is imperative that an ABC system utilize the same underlying data and database sources as the other accounting systems of a firm. ABC systems will employ the data differently and may have additional input sources than do the traditional accounting systems; however, the "total costs" of the two systems must be identical. In other words, any cost analysis generated by an ABC system must align with a firm's financial reporting system at an "aggregate level." As illustrated in Figure 7.4, individual cost analyses (such as the cost to serve different distribution channels) will differ between the ABC and traditional accounting systems. However, at the aggregate operating cost level, the systems must agree.

3 To develop ABC models of its operations, a firm should utilize operational colleagues working with accounting/finance colleagues in a team-based approach. For example, to construct an ABC model of a distribution center, the project team should include several DC managers, as well as other logistics and accounting personnel.
4 Commercial software is available to facilitate the development and deployment of ABC systems, or alternatively a firm can develop its own ABC models to complement its existing accounting systems.

Summary[14]

One cannot overemphasize the fundamental role that ABC should play in a firm's logistics planning and strategy. ABC models provide illuminating insights for a firm on the true costs of customer service, production, and acquisition activities. Unlike high-level cost accounting systems, ABC models evaluate costs at the lowest, most granular activity level (e.g., picking a case in a warehouse). These models accurately differentiate costs by customer, product, supplier, and many other dimensions, thereby facilitating better decision-making, resource allocation, and strategy development. Finally, as noted, ABC models represent complementary decision support tools and must align with a firm's higher-level financial and cost accounting systems.

7.4 Economies of Scale and Consolidation in Supply Chain Management

The desire to improve the efficiency of a firm's operations through economies of scale and the consolidation of quantities produced, shipped, and processed represents a strong driving force in supply chain and business decision-making. This effort to achieve efficiencies through the consolidation of activities manifests itself in numerous supply chain functions. In this section we review and illustrate several simple examples in different functional areas. The following represents just a few illustrative cases of these consolidation efforts:

- *Manufacturing*: Producers seek to maximize a plant's output, thereby allowing the firm to allocate its annual fixed costs such as plant depreciation over more units – which lowers the plant's average cost per unit produced. Manufacturers utilize strategies such as planning long production runs of products, and minimizing the number of changeovers and setups on a production line to effectuate these efficiencies.
- *Transportation*: A plane, a railcar, a truck trailer, or a cargo container has a fixed cubic capacity. Additionally, transport vehicles and containers have a maximum physical weight that they can safely carry, usually specified by a safety-related legal maximum allowable weight. As a general rule, to minimize their freight costs per lb. or per cubic foot, shippers try to maximize the total weight and/or cube per shipment.
- *Customer Service and Order Management*: Basic activities such as a supplier processing purchase orders (POs) from a customer can often be made more efficient by consolidating multiple POs into one or fewer larger POs. In general, suppliers often find it efficient to minimize repetitive transactions – such as processing POs or generating invoices – by consolidating these transactions when possible.[15]

We close this discussion of economies of scale and consolidation with two simple analytic examples. Table 7.4 illustrates how a manufacturing plant with annual fixed costs of $1,000,000 and variable costs per unit of $20 achieves lower average costs per unit produced as output ramps up from 100,000 to 200,000 units produced per year. As previously discussed, as annual output increases, the plant can allocate its $1 million in fixed costs over more units, leading to a lower average unit manufacturing cost. The last row in Table 7.4 shows that in this example, average production costs per unit drop from $30 to $25, as annual output increases from 100,000 to 200,000 units.

Table 7.5 offers an illustration of how freight costs per lb. decrease, as the total weight shipped on a truck increases. In this fictitious example, a shipper must pay $6,000 for a truckload shipment from Portland, Maine to Los Angeles, California. Note that as the total weight shipped doubles from 20,000 lbs. to 40,000 lbs., the freight cost per lb. halves from $0.30 to $0.15.

The brief examples offered in this section represent just a small sample of the myriad opportunities found across supply chains to achieve efficiencies through economies of scale and consolidation. Thus, achieving efficiencies through consolidating activities represents a driving theme in the logistics planning and strategic efforts of many firms.

7.5 Minimizing Total Logistics Costs and Total Landed Costs[16]

The concept of minimizing total logistics costs rather than minimizing individual functional costs (e.g., transportation costs) represents a foundational theme of sound supply chain management. The evolution to the current state of supply chain management from its predecessors of "physical distribution" in the 1960s and 1970s, and "logistics management" in the 1980s and early 1990s, has centered on a management approach of increasingly integrated cross-functional decision-making.[17] This contrasts with the more isolated, individual function-based decision-making characteristic of the early physical distribution era in particular. The current emphasis on minimizing total logistics costs as a key driver in guiding efficient decision-making exemplifies this evolution which occurred over many decades to the integrated, holistic philosophy that permeates supply chain management today. In this section we offer a description of total logistics costs, and also discuss "landed costs," a term often used synonymously or interchangeably with total logistics costs. Figure 7.7 illustrates the typical logistics cost components of a multi-national manufacturing and distribution firm.

Different companies have varied definitions of what they include in their calculations of total costs. However, a firm's internal definition of total logistics costs should include all the costs of producing or purchasing a product, and then shipping that product to the final receiving point (i.e., destination) to which the firm delivers the product. Bowersox et al. (2024) summarize these costs as follows:

> Integrated logistics (incorporates) five interrelated areas: Order processing, inventory, transportation, warehousing and materials handling, and facility network. Total logistics cost, sometimes referred to as landed cost, is the sum of costs related to performance and administration of each of these areas of work.

To be clear, in our definition, we have explicitly added manufacturing costs to Bowersox et al.'s description of integrated logistics. Note also that Bowersox et al. describe that total logistics cost is sometimes alternatively referred to as "landed cost." We will discuss this further shortly.

As noted in the bullet at the bottom of Figure 7.7, firms should develop supply chain plans that minimize their total logistics costs, *while importantly also meeting customer service*

TABLE 7.4 Illustration of Economies of Scale at a Manufacturing Plant

Data	*Annual Fixed Costs[a] =*	*$1,000,000*	*Variable Cost per Unit Produced[b] =*		*$20*	
Annual Units Produced by Plant	100,000	120,000	140,000	160,000	180,000	200,000
Annual Fixed Costs	$ 1,000,000	$ 1,000,000	$ 1,000,000	$ 1,000,000	$ 1,000,000	$ 1,000,000
Annual Variable Costs = **(Units Produced) × (Variable Cost per Unit)**	$ 2,000,000	$ 2,400,000	$ 2,800,000	$ 3,200,000	$ 3,600,000	$ 4,000,000
Annual Total Costs = **(Annual Fixed Costs) + (Annual Variable Costs)**	$ 3,000,000	$ 3,400,000	$ 3,800,000	$ 4,200,000	$ 4,600,000	$ 5,000,000
Average Cost per Unit Produced **= (Total Costs) / (Units)**	***$ 30.00***	***$ 28.33***	***$ 27.14***	***$ 26.25***	***$ 25.56***	***$ 25.00***

Notes

[a] Fixed costs do not vary with the level of output produced by the plant. In contrast, variable costs consist of direct labor, materials, and other cost components that vary with the level of output produced.

[b] See note a.

TABLE 7.5 Truckload Freight Cost per lb. Illustration

Data	*Truckload Freight Rate per Mile[a] =*	*$ 2.00*	*Total Travel Miles From Portland, ME to Los Angeles, CA =*	*3,000*	*Cost of a Truckload Shipment =*	*$ 6,000*
	Cost per lb. Analysis					
Total lbs. Shipped	20,000	25,000	30,000	35,000	40,000	
Freight Cost per lb. = (total miles × cost per mile) / (total lbs. shipped)	**$ 0.30**	**$ 0.24**	**$ 0.20**	**$ 0.17**	**$ 0.15**	

Note

[a] The rate per mile, distance, and cost per lb. shown are illustrative and not actual.

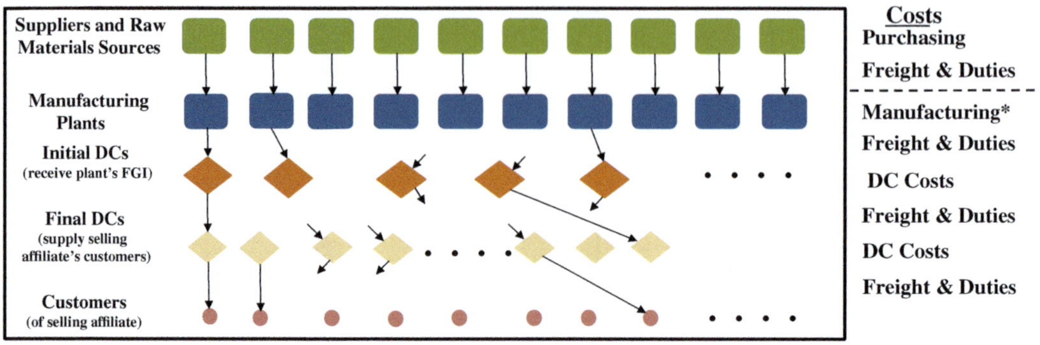

- *Lowest total logistics costs are achieved by an integrated manufacturing and distribution plan (for a network) that minimizes the sum of all costs, including in ventory costs, subject to meeting customer demands and service requirements*

* Manufacturing costs usually include all costs incurred prior to manufacturing, as well as the manufacturing costs themselves. In other words, the costs to purchase materials which become inputs to the plants' production process, as well as any logistics costs incurred to bring the materials to the plants, are reflected in the plants' cost of production.

FIGURE 7.7 Illustrative Logistics Costs of a Multi-National Manufacturer and Distributor.

and demand requirements. A supply chain plan that focuses solely on minimizing costs (and maximizing profits), to the detriment of customer service and demand fulfillment requirements, will not succeed in the long run. When formulating their supply chain and logistics strategies, companies must first determine the customer service and demand fulfillment rates that will allow them to compete successfully. Once a firm ascertains these requirements, then it can plan and execute a strategy to minimize total logistics costs subject to meeting these defined requirements.

Landed Costs

The terms total landed costs and total logistics costs are sometimes used synonymously, as previously noted. In the context of "supply chain decision-making," both terms convey (or should be interpreted as meaning) that for any decision, all pertinent costs should be considered in order to ensure that the best or optimal decision is made.[18] This tenet applies to all decisions ranging from the long-run strategic to the short-run operational.

Previous chapters in this book have highlighted several examples of decision-making based upon minimizing total logistics or total landed costs. For example, Chapter 2 illustrated the importance of simultaneously evaluating both freight and inventory costs in making transportation mode choice decisions (e.g., air vs. ocean). Chapter 5 discussed the importance of utilizing mathematical optimization models[19] that incorporate a comprehensive set of manufacturing and distribution costs to facilitate network design and facility location decisions. To close this section, we review another landed cost example, namely, minimizing costs in cross-border, product sourcing decisions.

We preface this example by first observing that there exist numerous, often complex cost components and regulations in international trade, and the reader is referred to Reid (2025), Gopalan (2025), and Kim (2021) for detailed discussions of these costs and regulations. To

TABLE 7.6 Cost Comparison of Three Alternative Suppliers for Imports Galore[a]

Cost Component	*Total Annual Costs ($ 000)*		
	Supplier 1 (in Country A)	*Supplier 2 (in Country B)*	*Supplier 3 (in Country C)*
Purchase Costs[b]	$ 204.0	$ 210.0	$ 205.0
International Freight Costs to U.S. Port of Entry	$ 6.0	$ 3.0	$ 3.5
Import Duties (5%)	$ 10.2	$ 10.5	$ 10.3
Customs Clearance Fees	$ 1.0	$ 1.0	$ 1.0
Inland Freight Costs: U.S. Port of Entry to the Imports Galore Warehouse	$ 1.5	$ 1.5	$ 1.5
Insurance Costs on Product While In-Transit (2%)	$ 4.1	$ 4.2	$ 4.1
Total Landed Costs[c]	$ 226.8	$ 230.2	$ 225.4

Notes

[a] This analysis assumes that Imports Galore makes a one-time annual purchase of 1,000 units for the entire year at the beginning of the year. The purchase terms are FOB Origin which means that Imports Galore takes ownership of the product as soon as it exits from the supplier's inventory storage and shipping location (e.g., its warehouse). Therefore, Imports Galore is responsible for all the freight costs, insurance, etc. related to the transportation of the product from the supplier's location to Imports Galore.

[b] Based on the current exchange rates between the U.S. dollar and the individual currencies of Country A, Country B, and Country C, respectively. Thus, these annual purchase costs can change as the currency exchange rates fluctuate.

[c] Inventory costs are not included in this analysis because in this scenario Imports Galore makes a one-time purchase of product from the supplier for the entire year at the beginning of each year. Additionally, the total landed costs of the purchase are quite close for each of the three potential suppliers. Therefore, for simplicity, we can exclude inventory costs from this analysis. In a different scenario where Imports Galore would be regularly ordering replenishment inventory from the supplier throughout the year, and where Imports Galore planned to maintain safety stock of the product, it would be appropriate to include inventory costs in this analysis. Including inventory costs in the analysis would become particularly important if there was a significant difference in the inventory replenishment lead times each of the three potential suppliers provided, and if there was a significant difference in the total landed costs (excluding inventory costs) of each potential supplier.

illustrate a general method to calculate landed costs on imported products, we consider the following fictitious scenario.

Imported Product Scenario

Imports Galore Inc. is an American distributor that specializes in selling imported products to its U.S. customer base. The firm is planning to add a new product to its current product portfolio, and is choosing between three alternative suppliers located in three different countries for its single supplier for this new product. Imports Galore plans to import 1,000 units per year of this product which it will sell to its U.S. customer base over the course of the year. Table 7.6 details the cost analysis that the company has performed for each of these three potential suppliers.

Table 7.6 illustrates the typical cost components, in addition to product cost, that comprise total landed costs for a firm importing finished products or materials. As footnote c in Table 7.6 explains, inventory costs were excluded in this analysis because the scenario assumes that Imports Galore is making a single, one-time purchase of its total product requirements for the year. However, in other scenarios, inventory costs often need to be included.

The analysis indicates that Supplier 3 in country C offers the lowest total landed cost alternative. Imports Galore will now couple this cost analysis with other qualitative factors to determine its supplier selection.

Summary

Supply chain management in the 2020s has evolved into a holistic, highly integrated process. The understanding by the supply chain profession of the importance of minimizing total logistics costs, rather than individual functional costs, represents a key element of this evolution. Finally, we note again that when minimizing total logistics costs, firms should minimize total costs subject to meeting customer service and demand fulfillment requirements.

7.6 Risk Management[20]

In recent decades, and especially since the Covid-19 pandemic exposed the vulnerabilities of supply chains in virtually all industries, risk management has taken on a significantly heightened importance in supply chain strategy and decision-making. This section first presents an overview of a general process by which firms can develop a supply chain risk management strategy. Next it offers an illustration of a technique to develop a quantitative perspective on the cost of risk management strategies. This methodology can help to assess the costs of risk mitigation strategies such as utilizing additional suppliers in disparate geographies, maintaining backup plants and/or extra capacity, and other similar strategies. This quantitative approach can be coupled with other more qualitative factors to facilitate the development of a well-informed supply chain risk management decision-making process and strategy.

We begin with a brief review of the types of risk that firms must assess in creating their risk management strategy. This review provides background context for the methodology we will introduce. Further, recognizing that we cannot explore in detail the topic of risk management strategies in this short section, we also provide additional references in Chapter 7 endnote 21 for readers interested in exploring this topic in depth.[21] After our review of risk types and strategies, we then present our risk management quantitative methodology using a manufacturing network design strategy example for illustrative purposes.

Categories of Risk

When constructing a supply chain risk management strategy, a firm can assure that it undertakes a holistic view of all potential threats by first evaluating general categories of risk, and then considering specific individual risks. *Why take this two-step approach?* The danger of immediately focusing on a few known risks to a firm before first performing a broad review across all risk types is that immediately diving into specifics may cause some less obvious but important risks to be overlooked; hence the need for a two-step approach.

Figure 7.8 presents nine broad categories of generic risks (column 1), and offers examples of each category of risk (column 2). Note that these risks range from those over which a firm has direct control (e.g., the operational risk of "inadequate manufacturing" capacity or capability), to risks such as tornadoes and hurricanes (natural risks) which a firm cannot control. There are other important distinguishing attributes of risk types and the reader interested in an extensive discussion of this topic is again referred to the several references given in a previous endnote earlier in this section.

TYPE OF RISK	SOURCE
Supply risks	Disruption of supply, inventory, schedules, and technology access; price escalation; quality issues; technology uncertainty; product complexity; frequency of material design changes
Operational risks	Breakdown of operations; inadequate manufacturing or processing capability; high levels of process variations; changes in technology; changes in operating exposure
Demand risks	New product introductions; variations in demand (fads, seasonality, and new product introductions by competitors); chaos in the system (the bullwhip effect on demand distortion and amplification)
Security risks	Information systems security; infrastructure security; freight breaches from terrorism, vandalism, crime, and sabotage
Macro risks	Economic shifts in wage rates, interest rates, exchange rates, and prices
Policy risks	Actions of national governments such as quota restrictions or sanctions, as well as actions of regional and local government entities
Competitive risks	Lack of history about competitor activities and moves
Resource risk	Unanticipated resource requirements
Natural risks*	Tornadoes, tsunamis, hurricanes, fires, pandemics

*Natural risks have been added to the original eight types of risks noted in Manuj and Mentzer (2008).

Source: Manuj and Mentzer (2008)

FIGURE 7.8 Summary of Risk Types and Sources.

TYPE OF RISK	ILLUSTRATIVE ALTERNATIVE STRATEGIES
Supply risks	Multiple sourcing, operational flexibility, risk sharing
Operational risks	Maintain duplicative or excess capacity, high levels of maintenance
Demand risks	Postponement, risk sharing with customers, high levels of safety stock
Security risks	High investment levels in security technology, minimize sourcing and firm-owned infrastructure in less stable geopolitical environments, high levels of physical security investment
Macro risks	Currency hedging initiatives, diversification of product lines
Policy risks	Avoid significant investments in perceived unfriendly international markets, invest heavily in lobbying practices
Competitive risks	Defensive product line and entire company mergers and acquisitions, acquisition of key competitive personnel, first to market approaches
Resource risk	Conservative balance sheet approach including high cash balances
Natural risks*	Avoid facility location in geographies subject to frequent earthquakes, tornadoes, and hurricanes

*Natural risks have been added to the original eight types of risks noted in Manuj and Mentzer.

Source for column 1: Manuj and Mentzer (2008).

FIGURE 7.9 Commonly Used Risk Management Supply Chain Strategies.

Figure 7.9 closes this brief review of risk types and risk management strategies. For each type of risk identified in Figure 7.8, Figure 7.9 displays common strategies often employed to mitigate the threat of each risk type. For example, a heavily utilized "supply risk strategy" consists of employing multiple sources to procure individual products or materials. While using more sources rather than fewer sources generally reduces the opportunity to minimize acquisition costs, it also lessens a firm's dependence on any single supplier.

This type of risk mitigation trade-off (i.e., cost versus level of vulnerability) leads to the question: *What is a good approach or methodology to quantify the trade-offs inherent to risk management strategies?*

A Quantitative Methodology for Supply Chain Risk Management Assessment

To illustrate our methodology for quantifying the cost of a supply chain risk management strategy, let's assume that a firm is developing its global manufacturing and distribution network strategy for the next 3–5 years. In this example, we will focus on plant locations and capacity plans, and note that a similar process would occur for distribution network locations. For illustrative purposes, we narrow our example to evaluations of supply, operational, and natural risks only. In practice all pertinent risk types displayed in Figure 7.8 would be considered.

The methodology we present consists of a six-step process. We will assume that our firm has a model with which it evaluates the total network manufacturing and distribution costs of all potential network plant locations under consideration. This costing model can be a mathematical optimization model available through commercial software (see Miller and Liberatore, 2020) or any other tool that a firm maintains (e.g., spreadsheet costing analyses). The only requirement is that a firm have some type of model which can evaluate the total costs of any proposed manufacturing network, and can identify the lowest cost network solution among different alternatives. (That is, the firm utilizes a model that can determine which plants to open and operate, what products and quantities should be produced by each plant, which demand points should be served by which plants, and so on).

Figure 7.10 outlines the first three steps of our six-step process to quantify the costs of alternative risk management strategy options. These first three steps consist of selecting all the potential locations to be considered in developing the strategic manufacturing network plan. In practice, all of a firm's existing plants are generally included in this type of analysis, as well as all potential new locations under consideration. Note that this candidate selection process requires the development of all pertinent data necessary to model the costs, capacities, and production capabilities of each location, a process previously described in Chapter 5.

Step 2 plays a critical role in addressing the risk management dimension of this process. In this step, the original set of candidate plants selected in step 1 is reviewed to ascertain if a sufficiently diverse set of potential locations has been selected to mitigate the firm's previously identified risks. For example, is there potential sufficient excess (backup) manufacturing capacity, are there enough potential locations in low "natural risk" geographies, and so on. If step 2 reveals that any risk types have not been sufficiently addressed in step 1, then in step 3, new potential locations that help mitigate against these risk types are added as potential candidate locations. At the conclusion of step 3, the firm has now selected all potential locations to include in its modeling analysis that will plan its future manufacturing network.

In step 4 (see Figure 7.11), the firm runs its network modeling tool to determine the lowest-cost (or most profitable) set of plant locations for its future network. We designate

Step 1: Do an "unconstrained" selection of all potential viable locations

- That is, employ the firm's normal process to identify all potential manufacturing sites
- Similarly employ the firm's normal process to identify all potential capacities (and technologies) for its plants

Step 2: Review the list of potential locations and capacities against the risks previously identified by the firm

- For example, are there enough potential duplicative plant locations and is there sufficient excess capacity?
- Are there enough potential locations in low "natural risk" geographies?

Step 3: Add more potential locations and/or capacity if the review in step 2 reveals insufficient protection against any of the "Risk Types"

FIGURE 7.10 Select the Potential Candidate Locations to Evaluate.

Step 4: Use network modeling analytics to determine the optimal manufacturing network-based on all the candidate locations and capacities identified via steps 1, 2, and 3

- That is, determine the locations that will minimize total network landed costs
- This is the lowest-cost, "unconstrained" solution
- *For illustration, assume the annual cost of this optimal, lowest-cost solution is $200 million*

Step 5: Rerun the network model with constraints to assure risk mitigation strategies are implemented

- Risk mitigation examples include:
  (A) there must be a minimum of "X" sources
  (B) there must be a minimum of "Y" duplicative, excess capacity
  (C) there must be a minimum of "Z" plants in geographies with low risk of natural disasters
- The values of X, Y, and Z are determined internally by the firm

FIGURE 7.11 Perform Modeling Analysis.

this initial optimal plant location plan as the lowest-cost "unconstrained" solution because no risk mitigation requirements (i.e., constraints) are explicitly imposed on this solution. In other words, we allow the network model to choose whatever set of locations will minimize total network manufacturing and distribution costs from those identified as candidates in steps 1 through 3.

For illustrative purposes, let's assume, as shown in Figure 7.11, that the total annual costs of this lowest-cost, optimal network are $200 million. Recall that this solution simply minimizes total annual costs based on all potential plant locations the network model selects, and it does not consider or incorporate any risk mitigation strategies.

Now, as Figure 7.11 describes, in step 5 we rerun our network model, placing specific constraints in the model to assure that individual or groups of risk mitigation strategies are implemented. For example, to reduce "supply risk," the firm may decide it must operate some minimum number of plants. If the optimal lowest-cost solution does not have enough open locations to satisfy this requirement, then the model is rerun with an additional constraint specifying that this minimum number of plants must be opened. This revised network solution plan will have a higher annual total cost, and possible reasons for this could include that for any given level of production, having a higher number of plants on a network often reduces the economies of scale opportunities. The model would similarly be rerun to incorporate other risk management strategies such as having a defined minimum excess level of capacity available,

Step 6: Compare the costs of the optimal, lowest landed cost solution (e.g., $200 million) to the cost of each "constrained" risk mitigation solution

Scenario	Annual Cost ($ Millions)	Annual Risk Mitigation Incremental Costs($ Millions)
Unconstrained, Lowest Landed Cost	$200	—
"Supply Risk" Mitigation Strategy	$240	$40
"Operational Risk" Mitigation Strategy	$220	$20
"Natural Risk" Mitigation Strategy	$250	$50
"Combined Supply, Operational and Natural Risk" Mitigation Strategy	$280	$80

FIGURE 7.12 Evaluate the Costs of Risk Mitigation Strategies.

or a minimum number of locations in low-risk geographies. Again, total annual network costs will increase in these revised scenarios for a variety of potential reasons; for example, the "low risk geographies" locations may be more expensive than some previously selected lower-cost locations. Finally, the model is rerun in a scenario that constrains the solution obtained to include all the individual risk management strategies the firm has developed.

The multiple model runs collectively undertaken in steps 4 and 5 facilitate step 6. Here, as Figure 7.12 details, the firm compares the projected annual costs of the unconstrained lowest-cost network plan to the various risk management scenarios modeled. For example, our illustration shows that the individual "supply," "operational," and "natural" risk mitigation strategies would increase total manufacturing and distribution network annual costs by $40 million, $20 million, and $50 million, respectively. Additionally, a network plan that incorporated all three risk management strategies projects to cost $80 million more annually, than would the unconstrained, lowest-cost network. Results such as those shown in Figure 7.12 provide a firm with a much-needed quantitative estimate of the costs of alternative risk mitigation strategies.

Summary

The relative importance of supply chain risk management was increasing rapidly prior to the coronavirus pandemic, and it has grown exponentially since then. Making well-informed decisions on the appropriate level of risk mitigation actions to invest in represents a difficult challenge for a firm and its supply chain professionals. Good decision-making requires a careful balancing of both qualitative and quantitative factors.

In this section, we have introduced a process that supply chain managers can utilize to enhance the quantitative input side of the risk management decision-making process. We illustrated this quantitative process employing a manufacturing and distribution network example. Importantly, however, the methodology detailed herein can be utilized to address many different types of supply chain analyses and decisions. The basic requirement to employ this methodology for any major decision is simply as follows: one must be able to develop, model, and cost a series of different strategies (scenarios) that address a requirement (e.g., planning a future manufacturing network) with alternative levels of risk mitigation strategies deployed in each scenario.

Addendum: The Demand Side

It is important to recognize that there is another critical element of strategic risk management costing, namely, evaluating the lost revenues and profits associated with a firm's inability to meet customer demand because of supply disruptions. If a firm cannot satisfy demand for any reason (e.g., insufficient production capacity or a plant being temporarily incapacitated by a hurricane), the potential revenue and profit losses must be factored into the risk management strategy decision. This is a challenging, complicated process and beyond the scope of this text. However, this must also be addressed to facilitate a comprehensive risk management strategy decision-making process. Examples of the inputs required for this lost revenue (i.e., demand side) of the analysis include:

- estimated lost revenues and profits per day from all identified potential supply disruptions,
- estimated duration (in days) of each potential supply disruption in the event a specific risk materializes (e.g., a hurricane at a plant), and
- estimated probability per year of each specific risk occurring (e.g., the probability of having a hurricane that damages a particular plant)

This brief list illustrates the types of costs and variables that must also be considered. The potential lost demand side (i.e., the potential lost revenue and profit) analysis can be combined with the supply side methodology described in this section to develop a complete analytic picture.

7.7 Cost per Unit and Ratio Analysis

Two types of measures frequently utilized to monitor and evaluate supply chain performance are cost per unit and ratio analysis metrics. These metrics, which are often very straightforward to calculate, provide logistics professionals with valuable insights on activities across the supply chain. Each of these two categories of measures offer different perspectives. Further, in many cases, accurate assessments of a logistics function require both of these perspectives, and an evaluation based on only one of the two measurements provides an incomplete, or even distorted, view. In this section, we review several examples of these measures and present a simple case that illustrates why developing an accurate analysis generally requires both metric types.

Cost per Unit and Ratio Analysis Metrics[22]

The cost of a functional activity such as distribution, measured as a percent of annual sales revenue, represents an important metric. The calculation of this metric is obtained by dividing the annual cost of a function by the annual sales revenue of a firm. For example, if a company had sales of $100 million during a year, and its distribution costs that year amounted to $3 million; then the firm's distribution costs represent 3% of total revenue, calculated as the ratio of $3 million / $100 million. This metric is important because it reveals how much a particular function consumes of a firm's total annual cash intake from sales. In the long run, a sustainable business requires that its annual revenues cover all of its annual costs plus produce an annual profit.[23] Therefore, it is critical that a company monitor and manage what percent of its annual revenues it expends on each major function or activity. This includes all corporate functions such as marketing, sales, and research and development, in addition to supply chain activities. Briefly, companies employ percent of sales metrics to assist in key efforts such as:

- monitoring and managing overall firm profitability,
- benchmarking individual functions in their organization vs. competitors, and
- assessing the operational efficiency of individual functions

Percent of sales analysis is heavily influenced by the selling price of a firm's goods. Therefore, for many applications, it is very important to evaluate supply chain operations on a "cost per unit" basis, as well as by a percent of sales ratio analysis. There exist numerous different units of measure that firms and industries utilize. Before discussing units of measure further, let's illustrate the varied perspectives that percent of sales and cost per unit analyses provide.

Table 7.7 compares the freight costs of two fictitious firms from the consumer products and pharmaceutical industries. The "calculations" section of this table shows that on shipments delivered via truck, the firms have average freight costs per delivery of $3,000 (consumer) and $1,500 (pharmaceutical), respectively. Additionally, the companies deliver an average of 400 and 200 cases per delivery. While the consumer firm's average freight costs and cases delivered per shipment are double those of the pharmaceutical firm, the differential in their respective average revenue per case sold is dramatically greater. While the pharmaceutical company generates an average of $5,000 per case sold, the consumer products firm receives an average of $200.[24]

The first row of the "analysis" section of Table 7.7 reveals that judged on a percent of sales revenue basis, the pharmaceutical firm has much lower freight costs than does the consumer

TABLE 7.7 Illustration: The Freight Costs of a Consumer Products Firm and a Pharmaceutical Firm

Annual Data	*Consumer Products Company*	*Pharmaceutical Products Company*
Number of Shipments[a]	10,000	1,000
Total Cases Shipped	4,000,000	200,000
Total lbs. Shipped	200,000,000	5,000,000
Total Sales Revenue	$ 800,000,000	$ 1,000,000,000
Total Freight Costs	$ 30,000,000	$ 1,500,000
Calculations		
Average Freight Cost per Shipment = **(Freight Costs / Shipments)**	$ 3,000	$ 1,500
Average Number of Cases Delivered per Shipment = **(Cases / Shipments)**	400	200
Average Revenue per Case = **(Revenue / Cases)**	$ 200	$ 5,000
Average lbs. per Shipment = **(lbs. / Shipments)**	20,000	5,000
Analysis		
Average Freight Cost as a Percent of Sales Revenue = *(Freight Costs / Revenue)*	3.75%	0.15%
Average Freight Cost per Case = *(Freight Costs / Cases)*	$ 7.50	$ 7.50

Note
[a] For all shipments in the U.S. delivered via truck service.

products firm – 0.15% compared to 3.75%. However, based on this percent of sales analysis, *can one draw the conclusion that the pharmaceutical firm has a more efficient freight operation than does the consumer products firm?* The answer is no! The reason the pharmaceutical firm's freight cost as a percent of sales is so low results from the high price per case of its products. Moreover, as Table 7.7 shows, measured by freight cost per case delivered, the two firms have identical average per unit costs of $7.50.

Based on the analysis in Table 7.7, it would be incorrect to assert that the pharmaceutical company operates a more efficient transportation network than does the consumer products company. However, if one only had the freight cost as a percent of sales metric available, one could mistakenly infer that the pharmaceutical firm runs a more efficient transportation network because its freight costs as a percent of sales are so much lower than those of the consumer products firm. The additional perspective afforded by the comparative freight cost per unit of each company ($7.50 per case each) signals that the consumer products firm does not necessarily operate a less efficient transportation network.

How to Compare the Transportation Networks of the Two Firms

In practice, to compare the transportation operations of these two firms would require a much more extensive analysis than simply a comparison based on the freight cost as a percent of sales and the freight cost per case delivered metrics. Also importantly, a comparison between these two firms may not be very helpful in determining the respective efficiencies of their two networks.

First, these two firms operate in very different industries. Therefore, if we wanted to evaluate the efficiency of each firm's transportation network, we should compare each firm to the other firms in their respective industries (i.e., to their competitors). This would provide a much more insightful and accurate basis for an evaluation. For example, it could be that the metrics of $7.50 per case delivered and freight costs equivalent to 3.75% of annual revenue represent very efficient measures in the U.S. consumer products industry. Meanwhile, the metrics of $7.50 per case delivered and freight costs equal to 0.15% of revenue may represent only average or mediocre performance in the pharmaceutical industry.[25] Thus, benchmarking (i.e., comparing) the transportation network of a firm to other firms in its industry represents a better first step, if an analyst wishes to assess the efficiency of a particular firm's operations.

The process of benchmarking one firm's operations against other firms requires careful planning to generate accurate, insightful results.[26] Further, many companies regularly engage in benchmarking both externally (i.e., the evaluation of other firms) and internally (i.e., the comparison of operations within their own firm). A detailed discussion of benchmarking is beyond the scope of this section. However, the reader interested in exploring benchmarking further is referred to Monczka et al. (2011) and Handfield et al. (2025) as good starting references.

In summary, cost per unit and ratio analysis metrics provide valuable, different perspectives. And we will shortly explore these metrics further. However, first we review the different types of units of measure that supply chain professionals utilize in cost and related analyses.

Units of Measure

Analysts employ many different "units of measure" to calculate supply chain performance metrics. The particular activity that is being evaluated determines the appropriate unit of measure

(UOM) to utilize in calculating a metric. A few examples of units of measure commonly used in logistics metrics include the number of cases, pallets, eaches, orders, line items, customer calls, and lbs.

In most cases, one can readily discern what units of measure are appropriate to evaluate a logistics activity. For example, a firm assessing the costs of its trucking will utilize UOMs such as cost per mile, cost per lb., and cost per case shipped.[27] However, sometimes it is necessary to develop a UOM that represents a proxy for a broad set of activities such as all of those that occur in a large warehouse operation.

Suppose we want to develop a UOM for the total work performed by a warehouse over a year. Figure 7.13 presents a simplified depiction of the major operations within a warehouse. At the minimum, these include receiving, putaway, storage, picking, and shipping.[28]

One approach to developing a UOM that collectively represents all of these activities is to ask: *what is the basic mission or role of this warehouse?* Clearly, it has many roles, but ultimately the mission of the warehouse is to ship cases of products to its customer to satisfy their demands. Therefore, we can use the UOM of "total cases shipped" by the warehouse as a proxy or estimate of the total work performed by the facility over a defined time period (e.g., 1 year).

Developing a UOM to represent a broad range of activities such as those of a plant, a warehouse, or an entire distribution organization must be carefully planned. Further, it should be recognized that a UOM used to estimate the output of a very broad activity may not accurately capture all key components of that activity. Thus, managers should take this into consideration when using metrics for assessment purposes. (Exhibit 7.1 at the end of this section offers an example of a warehouse where outbound cases shipped would not represent a good proxy for the total work performed by the warehouse.)

In this section, we have briefly reviewed cost per unit and ratio analysis metrics. We conclude this discussion with an illustrative analysis of the performance of a fictitious firm's logistics network using these metrics, as well as several customer service metrics detailed in previous chapters.

Table 7.8 displays the income statement, and selected annual demand, shipping, and inventory data for Everyday Goods Inc. Table 7.9 then evaluates the cost and service performance of the firm's logistics network based on the data in Table 7.8.

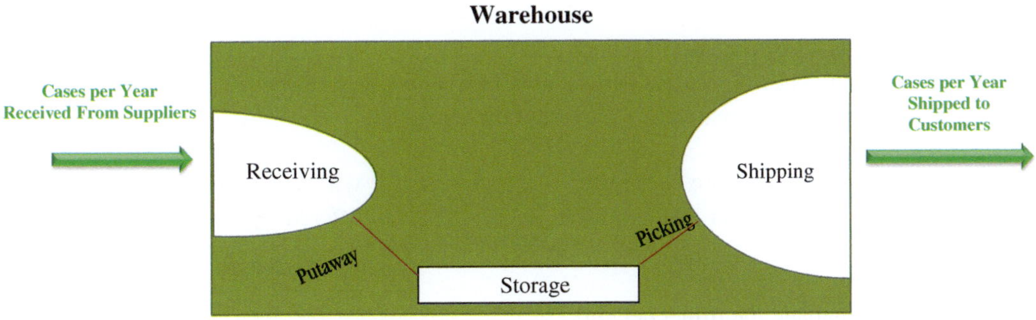

FIGURE 7.13 Using Annual Cases Shipped as an Estimate of the Total Work Performed per Year in a Warehouse.

TABLE 7.8 Income Statement and Selected Annual Performance and Inventory Data for Everyday Goods Inc.

*Annual Income Statement**		*Selected Performance Data*	
		Shipping and Demand Data	
Sales (i.e., Revenue)	**$ 1,017,000**	Annual Shipments	50,000
Costs of Goods Sold	**$ 500,000**	On Time Shipments	47,000
Gross Margin	**$ 517,000**	Annual Cases Ordered	90,000
Selling, General, & Administrative (SG&A) Expenses		Annual Cases Shipped	89,100
Research and Development	$ 20,000		
Marketing	$ 40,000	**Miscellaneous Assets**	
Transportation (Freight)	$ 29,000	Inventory	$ 50,000
Warehousing**	$ 25,000		
Inventory Carrying Costs	$ 10,000		
Other Operating	$ 10,000		
Total Selling, General, & Administrative (SG&A) Expenses	**$ 134,000**		
Earnings Before Interest, Taxes, Depreciation, and Amortization	**$ 383,000**		
Interest	**$ 12,000**		
Depreciation and Amortization	**$ 24,000**		
Taxes***	**$ 124,400**		
Net Income	**$ 222,600**		

Notes

* Actual income statement formats used in industry vary somewhat by firm, and vary from the example presented here. For instance, there is generally not a sub-total line for "Earnings Before Interest, Taxes, and Amortization." However, for clarity we include this sub-total in this illustration. Additionally, the numbers shown are simply for illustration and not necessarily representative of the typical distribution of expenses among different components of an income statement.

** Warehousing is DC Operations.

*** The taxes shown on this line would be based on the firm's corporate tax rate.

Table 7.9 provides an initial, high-level overview of the performance of the logistics network of Everyday Goods Inc.[29] It evaluates the company's network from multiple dimensions including:

- customer service (on-time performance and fill rate),
- operational efficiency (inventory turns and several cost per case analyses), and
- expense and revenue consumption (several ratio analyses)

The results in Table 7.9 are simply for illustration so we will forego discussing them. The important point, however, is that the multiple perspectives offered by these metrics allow a logistics manager to:

- monitor and manage the firm's network,
- externally benchmark his/her network vis-à-vis competitor's networks, and

TABLE 7.9 Ratio, Cost per Unit, and Customer Service Analysis for Everyday Goods Inc.

Ratio Analysis		*Customer Service Analysis*	
Freight Costs as a Percent of Sales = **(Freight Costs / Sales)**	2.9%	On-Time Performance = (Shipments Delivered On-Time / Annual Shipments)	94.0%
Warehouse Costs as a Percent of Sales = **(Warehouse Costs / Sales)**	2.5%	Case Fill Rate = (Annual Cases Shipped / Annual Cases Ordered)	99.0%
Inventory Carrying Costs as a Percent of Sales = **(Inventory Carrying Costs / Sales)**	1.0%		
Logistics Costs as a Percent of Sales[a] = **(Logistics Costs / Sales)**	6.3%		
Annual Inventory Turns[b] = **(Cost of Goods Sold / Inventory)**	10.0		
Cost per Unit Analysis			
Freight Costs per Case[c] = (Freight Costs / Annual Cases Shipped)	$ 0.33		
Warehouse Costs per Case = (Warehouse Costs / Annual Cases Shipped)	$ 0.28		
Inventory Carrying Costs per Case = (Inventory Carrying Costs / Annual Cases Shipped)	$ 0.11		
Logistics Costs per Case = (Logistics Costs / Annual Cases Shipped)	$ 0.72		

Notes

[a] Logistics Costs are defined as the sum of Freight, Warehousing, and Inventory Carrying Costs for this illustration.

[b] While inventory turns is not a ratio calculated as a percent of sale, it is a ratio as its formula illustrates

[c] Cases are defined as the unit of measure in this illustration.

- internally benchmark his/her network by:
  - comparing the operations of different facilities on his/her network and
  - comparing the performance of his/her operation's performance to their performance in previous year(s)

EXHIBIT 7.1 EXAMPLE OF WHY "TOTAL CASES SHIPPED" MIGHT NOT ACCURATELY REPRESENT THE ANNUAL WORK EFFORT OF A WAREHOUSE[30]

- There are numerous potential work activities that a warehouse may perform. Some of these activities may not directly (or indirectly) support the warehouse's mission of shipping goods to customers.
- Examples of such activities include:
  - handling returns goods that are not eventually re-shipped to customers – e.g., returns that have to be disposed of rather than resold,

- disposing of significant quantities of excess, damaged, discontinued, or otherwise obsolete inventories that have accumulated over a period of years,
- repackaging or repairing significant quantities of inventory for which the warehouse normally does not have responsibility,
- performing significant labeling, assembly, or specialized packaging activities beyond the normal defined responsibilities of the warehouse, and
- performing extra normal receiving, inspection, and related activities associated with an unexpected major product recall

7.8 Summary

This chapter explored a number of analytic techniques and methods, and it examined several principles that drive managerial decisions on logistics networks. These methodologies and principles, while diverse, share the common characteristics that supply chain professionals employ these approaches end-to-end, across the supply chain to evaluate decisions ranging from procurement to customer delivery.

We began with an illustration of a hierarchical framework that companies can employ to organize and monitor all of their supply chain metrics from the strategic to the operational levels. Then we discussed how and why firms carefully monitor and manage the impact of their operations on cash flow. This led to a review of the essential role of activity-based costing in logistics and supply chain analytics.

Next, we turned our attention to the concepts of economies of scale, and the consolidation of volumes and activities. We observed that to enhance the efficiency of their operations, firms consolidate their inputs and outputs whenever possible. This pursuit of consolidation manifests itself in procurement, manufacturing, distribution, and transportation strategies, as well as many other activities.

Following the discussion of economies of scale, we then illustrated the importance of making decisions based upon minimizing total logistics and landed costs – rather than minimizing the costs of individual functions. Next, we discussed the growing influence of risk management in overall supply chain decision-making. This review introduced an illustrative methodology that companies can utilize to quantify the costs of strategic network design decisions. Most recently, we considered the need to employ both cost per unit and ratio analysis to generate insightful, balanced cost analyses.

In summary, there are numerous methodologies and principles that enhance decision-making across the supply chain. This chapter has provided a sample of some of the most important and heavily utilized of these.

Notes

1 Portions of this section are excerpted from Miller and Liberatore (2020). Additionally, Liberatore and Miller (2021) and Miller (2024) also present the concept of a hierarchical performance measurement system.

2 The concepts of "control towers" and "digital twins" are increasingly used by firms when describing their supply chain performance measurement activities. The reader is referred to Scriven (2024) for a brief introduction to these concepts.

3 See Thieuleux (2023) or Hayes (2024) for brief explanations of the CCC, or any introductory finance textbook for a more detailed discussion.
4 The calculations shown are for 1 year.
5 40.0-46.7 = a decrease of 6.7 days, and 5.7-6.7 = a decrease of 1 week.
6 See Coyle et al. (2017), Bowersox et al. (2024), or Chopra and Meindl (2016).
7 For example, a firm may launch an initiative to increase forecast accuracy by implementing new forecasting methodologies and algorithms over time.
8 Some of the concepts and text in this section previously appeared in *Materials Handling and Logistics* magazine (July, 2017) and are presented here with the kind permission of *MH&L*. These concepts later appeared in Miller and Liberatore (2020) with the permission of *MH&L*, and portions of this section are excerpted and modified from Miller and Liberatore (2020).
9 Cooper and Kaplan (1988).
10 Indirect overhead costs are expenses such as heating, lighting, and supervisory management. In manufacturing operations, note also that direct labor costs, direct labor hours, and machine hours associated with producing individual products are other common "bases" or "drivers" for proportionately allocating overhead costs.
11 See, e.g., Liberatore and Miller (1998).
12 ABC models are also frequently defined at other levels such as division, location, brand, and others (see, e.g., Liberatore and Miller, 1998).
13 To be clear, in addition to the logistics and sales activities, all the firm's other costs will also be found in this P&L.
14 Readers interested in learning more about ABC systems are referred to the following references as a good starting point: Chea (2011), Cooper and Kaplan (1988), and Liberatore and Miller (1998).
15 It is beyond the scope of this text to explore in detail the costs associated with transactions such as processing POs. Briefly, however, there are often costs associated with performing small, simple transactions. For example, even if a firm has systems that automatically process an electronically received PO, manual intervention is typically required on some subset of these transactions to address errors that may occasionally occur such as an incorrect price, quantity ordered, etc. Similarly, human intervention may be required to address issues such as consolidating two or more POs onto one truckload delivery, and so on.
16 In private industry, some firms will include production costs in their internal definition of total logistics costs, while other firms will separate all manufacturing activities and costs from logistics costs. For discussion in this section, we include production costs in total logistics costs. Further, regardless of whether a firm classifies production costs as a component of logistics costs or alternatively separates production costs from other logistics costs; minimizing total supply chain costs requires that a firm make its decisions based on total manufacturing and acquisitions costs, and all other logistics costs.
17 See Coyle et al. (2017) and Bowersox et al. (2024) for a review of this evolution.
18 By pertinent costs, we mean any costs (e.g., inventory, transportation, production, etc.) which will be affected by a particular decision.
19 Or other models such as simulation or spreadsheet models.
20 Portions of this section are excerpted from Miller (2022) and with the kind permission of *Materials Handling and Logistics* magazine.
21 The reader is referred to the following references for additional discussion and background on supply chain risk management: Chaudhuri et al. (2020), Liberatore and Miller (2021), Lynch (2017), Manuele (2005), Manuj and Mentzer (2008), and Pettit et al. (2010).
22 Braun and Tietz (2024) define *ratio analysis* as a tool utilized for "Evaluating the relationships between two or more key components of financial statements. Financial analysts employ ratio analysis to assess a firm's efficiency, overall performance and financial strength."
23 Note that firms can have other sources of funds besides sales revenues including loans, lines of credits, investor funding (e.g., for start-up ventures), investment income, etc. However, in the very long run, to sustain itself, one generally expects a firm to generate a profit from its annual sales revenues.
24 The average price of a pharmaceutical product on a per unit basis is generally much higher than that of a consumer product. However, the prices shown here are fictitious, and for illustrative purposes only.
25 We note again that the metric values presented are illustrative only and not based on actual industry measures.

26 The Council of Supply Chain Management defines benchmarking as

> the process of comparing performances against the practices of other leading companies for the purpose of improving performance. Companies also benchmark internally by tracking and comparing current performance with past performance. Benchmarking seeks to improve any given business process by exploiting 'best practices' rather than merely measuring best performance .... Studying best practices provides the greatest opportunity for gaining a strategic, operational, and financial advantage.
>
> (CSCMP Glossary, 2013)

27 To be clear, the actual UOMs are miles, lbs., and cases.

28 Warehouse operations typically also include handling returns and other activities not mentioned here.

29 In practice, one would utilize additional customer and operational efficiency metrics in particular. However, the metrics in Table 7.9 represent a good, illustrative starting set of high-level metrics with which to evaluate a logistics network.

30 The example assumes that the warehouse being described normally has responsibility only for receiving inbound finished goods product shipments from suppliers, inventorying these products, and picking and shipping finished goods products to customers.

31 World Bank, Logistics Performance Index, https://worldbank.org/, accessed 6/21/25.

32 "Logistics Managers Index." Council of Supply Chain Management Professionals (CSCMP). The LMI is a collaborative effort issued by researchers at Arizona State University, Colorado State University, Florida Atlantic University, Rutgers University, and the University of Nevada, Reno in conjunction with the CSCMP.

33 Miller and Liberatore (2020).

34 Portions of this section are excerpted from Miller and Liberatore (2021).

35 An alternative approach for developing weights for KPIs is to utilize an operations research technique known as the analytic hierarchy process (AHP). The AHP methodology incorporates qualitative human judgments into a rigorous mathematical structure which can be used to develop relative weights of importance between different variables (e.g., between KPIs). Miller and Liberatore (2021) illustrate how to use the AHP to create relative weights for each KPI.

36 The time period for our example index is quarters of a year (i.e., 3 months). However, an index can be constructed for whatever time duration a firm believes is most appropriate and insightful for their business (e.g., time periods of 1 year, 1 month, etc.).

37 Once a firm builds an LPI and begins to update the index on a regular basis (e.g., after the completion of any future quarter), the index for any quarter is calculated by comparing the "just completed" quarter to the original baseline quarter (i.e., to the first quarter of the index). The example in Table 7A.1 displays the first two quarters of an index. For illustration, however, assume a firm builds a quarterly index and has maintained it for 10 years (40 quarters). At the end of the 41st quarter, the formula to calculate the points for a KPI in the 41st quarter would compare the values of that KPI in the 41st quarter vs. the 1st (baseline) quarter.

38 That is, by summing the values in the (Point × Weights) column of Table 7A.1.

Appendix 7A: Logistics Performance Indices

The concept of a logistics performance index (LPI) to monitor overall logistics performance is not new. In 2007, the World Bank first introduced a LPI which it developed as a tool to evaluate and compare the logistics assets, capabilities, and performances of different countries.[31] More recently in 2016, a collaborative effort between the Council of Supply Chain Management and researchers at several universities produced the Logistics Managers' Index (LMI). CSCMP releases this report monthly, and its authors describe this index as follows.[32] "(Each month) we gather the responses of over 100 professionals on the movement and direction of eight key logistics metrics. These metrics are aggregated into the Logistics Managers' Index." Since its inception, the LMI has become an index that provides supply chain professionals with valuable monthly insights on the general strength and direction of the U.S. logistics industry.

In 2020, Miller and Liberatore[33] proposed a methodology with which companies can combine their most important KPIs in a weighted points system. This technique creates one overall index to monitor the strength or weakness of a firm's individual logistics performance from one time period to the next. The following section describes this index.

Creating Customized Indices to Monitor Logistics Operations[34]

A logistics performance index (LPI) can be used to monitor a firm's progress in managing its logistics activities. It can also be linked to an organization's planning process to determine how well it is achieving its supply chain strategies and objectives. The KPIs that are most closely linked to the organization's strategy and objectives, or management priorities should be included in the index. An advantage of creating a LPI is that overall logistics performance is represented by a single aggregate measure that offers managers an initial, high-level logistics perspective.

The LPI is a weighted average of the points associated with all the KPIs that comprise the index. The individual weights define the relative importance of each KPI in contributing to the LPI. These weights can be developed through discussions with the logistics planning and/or management team, or during the supply chain strategic planning process. One approach for developing the weights is to allocate 100 points across the KPIs, and it is the approach shown here.[35]

For the example that follows, we assume that a fictitious firm has identified a set of ten KPIs which it believes will best monitor and assess its logistics performance. After selecting these KPIs to include in its LPI, a team of supply chain managers assessed the relative importance of each KPI to the firm's overall logistics performance. Based on these discussions and assessments, the team assigned each KPI a weight (or relative value) in the LPI. We now review how the firm developed its LPI.

Constructing the Index

The first step is constructing a baseline value or score for the index in the initial baseline period, such as the first quarter of 2025.[36] The baseline value provides an index score against which we can then measure the value of the index in subsequent time periods. Table 7A.1 illustrates the computation of the baseline index. The value for the baseline quarter represents the actual value of the KPI during the initial time period. For example, 93% is the baseline value for perfect order fulfillment. To initiate the baseline index, each KPI is assigned 100 points. That is, a 93% value of perfect order fulfillment is linked to 100 points. To determine the baseline value of the

LPI we multiply each KPI's baseline points (100 in all cases) by its weight, and then sum the results, as shown in Table 7A.1. Note that by construction the baseline value of the LPI is always 100, since the weights sum to 100%.

We can now compute the LPI for the next quarter. The first step consists of determining the "Points" value in the next quarter for each KPI in the index. To illustrate the calculations, from Table 7A.1 we employ two KPI examples: (1) Perfect Order Fulfillment and (2) Customer Order Cycle Time.

Perfect Order Fulfillment

- An increase in the perfect order fulfillment percentage represents an improvement in performance.
- Table 7A.1 shows that this KPI increased from 93% to 94% from the baseline quarter to the next quarter.
- To determine the percentage change from the baseline to the next quarter, we utilize the following formula:
  - 100 × [(New KPI value – Baseline KPI value) / Baseline KPI value],[37] or 100 × [(94% – 93%) / 93%] = 1.08% improvement.
- Thus, perfect order fulfillment improved by 1.08% from the baseline quarter to the next quarter.
- Therefore, as Table 7A.1 indicates, the perfect order fulfillment points for the next quarter are:
  - 100 + 1.08% × 100 = 101.8.

This same process can be used for all KPIs for which an increase in value represents an improved performance, and a decrease in value indicates a poorer performance. In Table 7A.1, all of these KPIs are shown in a non-bolded, non-italicized font.

However, for the remaining (bolded and italicized) KPIs in Table 7A.1, our calculation process must change because an increase in value represents a diminished (i.e., poorer) performance, while a decrease in value indicates an improved performance. Customer order cycle time falls into this latter category of KPIs, and we use this KPI to illustrate the calculations required to determine the points for the KPIs in this second category.

Customer Order Cycle Time

- A decrease in customer order cycle time represents an improvement in performance.
- Table 7A.1 reveals that this KPI decreased from 5 days to 4 days from the baseline quarter to the next quarter.
- The following formula calculates the percentage change from the baseline quarter to the next quarter:
  - 100 × [(Baseline KPI value – New KPI value) / Baseline KPI value] or 100 × [(5-4) / 5] = 20% improvement.

TABLE 7A.1 Illustrative Logistics Performance Index

KPI Definition	*Baseline Quarter*[1]				*Next Quarter*			
	KPI's Value	*Points*[2]	*Weights*	*(Points × Weights)*	*KPI's Value*	*Points*[3]	*Weights*	*(Points x Weights)*
1. Perfect Order Fulfillment (%)	93.0%	100.00	0.15	15.00	94.0%	101.08	0.155	15.16
2. Customer Order Cycle Time (days)	5.0	100.00	0.10	10.00	4.0	120.00	0.10	12.00
3. Customer Order Fill Rate (%)	95.0%	100.00	0.10	10.00	93.0%	97.89	0.10	9.79
4. Cash-to-Cash Order Cycle Time (days)	30.0	100.00	0.12	12.00	31.0	96.67	0.12	11.60
5. Distribution-to-Store Fill Rate (%)	90.0%	100.00	0.10	10.00	88.0%	97.78	0.10	9.78
6. Inventory Turnover (value)	8.0	100.00	0.11	11.00	7.5	93.75	0.11	10.31
7. Inventory Carrying Cost/Inventory Value (%)	20.0%	100.00	0.07	7.00	19.0%	105.00	0.07	7.35
8. Case Fill Rate (%)	96.0%	100.00	0.10	10.00	95.0%	98.96	0.10	9.90
9. Total Logistics Costs/ Total Sales Revenue (%)	9.00%	100.00	0.08	8.00	8.50%	105.56	0.08	8.44
10. Over, Short, & Damaged (%)	0.30%	100.00	0.07	7.00	0.28%	106.67	0.07	7.47
		Baseline Index[4] =		**100.00**	**Next Quarter's Index[4] =**			**101.80**

Note on KPIs: If a KPI in the KPI Definition column is bolded and italicized, then improved performance from one time period to the next period is shown by a decrease in the value of that KPI from the first period to the second period. For example, a decrease in order cycle time from one period to the next would represent an improved performance. If a KPI is not bolded and italicized, then improved performance is reflected by an increase in the value of that KPI from one period to the next period. For example, an increase in perfect order fulfillment from one period to the next would represent improved performance.

1 That is, the first quarter of the index.

2 Each KPI starts out with a points value of 100 in the first (i.e., the baseline) period of the index. For example, if a firm started to maintain this index beginning in the first quarter of 2025, then all the KPIs would start with 100 points in that first quarter as shown above.

3 How to calculate the "Points" values for the quarter(s) following the baseline quarter is explained in the text.

4 To calculate the index value for a quarter, we do the following calculations: (1) for each KPI, multiply the points for that KPI by the weight of that same KPI, and then (2) sum the ten values obtained in step 1. The total obtained by summing the ten numbers in step 1 yields the index value for that quarter. In other words, the sum of the ten values in the ("Points × Weights") column equals the value of the index for that quarter.

- Thus, customer order cycle time improved by 20% from the baseline quarter to the next quarter.
- Therefore, the customer order cycle time points for the next quarter are:
  - 100 + 20% × 100 = 120.

Once all the KPI points for the next quarter are determined, we can compute the LPI for the next quarter by multiplying each KPI's points in the next quarter by the same weights used to compute the baseline index, and then summing the results.[38] In our example as shown in Table 7A.1, the overall change in performance was good, increasing from the baseline index value of 100 to next quarter's index value of 101.80. This 1.8% increase indicates that the firm has made significant progress in executing its logistics activities. The individual KPIs comprising the LPI can be examined to determine the main drivers to the changes (if any) in its value. For example, the improvement to customer order cycle time led to an increase in the LPI of (120–100) × .10 = 2.00 points, while the reduction in inventory turnover led to a (100–93.75) × .11 = 0.69 drop in the index. Over time, the change and rate of change in such an index provide a quantitative perspective on overall progress. The LPI can be included in a dashboard used to track logistics activities.

Summary

In this appendix we have shown how to create a customized index to monitor a firm's progress in achieving its logistics objectives. An advantage is that overall logistics performance can be monitored by a single aggregate measure that provides a high-level perspective. We close this appendix with the following additional points:

- Creating a customized logistics performance index for an individual firm is a challenging undertaking.
- It is easy to select a set of KPIs and develop an index using the methodology just outlined.
- However, to construct an index where changes from one period (e.g., quarter) to the next represent a good or accurate indicator of changes in overall logistics performance is difficult.
- Briefly, the following are examples of the types of analysis required to evaluate or validate whether an index is an insightful measure.

  1 When determining which KPIs to include in a LPI, test the proposed index against historical company data. For example, evaluate the results the proposed index would have generated over the last 5–10 years. Then, have the supply chain professionals developing the index evaluate questions such as:

     - Do the changes in the index over the last 5–10 years (e.g., 20–40 quarters) correspond with the general perception at the firm of its logistics performance over this time period?
     - Do the changes in the index over time correspond with the perceptions of the firm's customers over time – as measured by customer surveys, etc.?

  2 A more rigorous quantitative approach would consist of using techniques such as multiple regression, analysis of variance, and related statistical techniques, to determine which logistics KPIs correlated most closely with a firm's revenues, profits, and/or other

measures of business success. The rationale for this approach is that the objective of a firm's logistics organization is to help facilitate the success of a business. Therefore, logistics metrics that correlate closely with overall business performance should comprise the KPIs in the firm's LPI.

The reader interested in further exploring the use of quantitative methods to evaluate the correlation of KPIs with overall firm logistics and business performance is referred to Liberatore and Miller (2016) and Miller and Liberatore (2015) as starting references.

8

FINAL THOUGHTS ON SUPPLY CHAIN AND LOGISTICS ANALYTICS

In this book, we have presented numerous analytical techniques and methodologies which provide decision support for planning and operations across all components of a firm's supply chain from materials procurement to finished goods delivery to customers. These tools collectively serve to enhance a supply chain organization's success in meeting its customers' and suppliers' needs, while at the same time they help to minimize costs and maximize profitability (i.e., enable effective and efficient operations).

The topics covered in this book represent just a portion of all the methodologies available today; however, they span a broad swath of the logistics analytics decision support tools that supply chain professionals utilize on a regular basis. Further, the methodologies presented here can be readily adapted to other supply chain activities and decisions not explicitly addressed in this book.

We commenced this book with a discussion of what supply chain and logistics analytics is, and what planning levels and time horizons this discipline supports. We observed that analytics facilitates decision-making across all facets of planning and operations from the very short run to the most distant future time horizon. Further, we noted the simple, but apropos definition of analytics contributed by the Association of Supply Chain Management; namely, "(Analytics is) the review of typically large sets of business data using mathematics, statistics, and computer software to identify meaningful patterns in the data to help in decision-making."[1][

Our first analytics application began with a review of a transportation mode choice decision-making methodology in Chapter 2. This technique explicitly incorporated the impact of transportation mode choice on a firm's inventory investment requirements. Next, we examined the analytic approach employed by a manufacturer to evaluate its U.S. distribution network. In this distribution network design problem, we observed the importance of making decisions based on: (1) total logistics costs and (2) customer service requirements. This tenet pertains to almost all supply chain decisions and strategies. Namely, decisions should be based on total logistics costs rather than the costs of an individual function.[2] Further, the concept of planning "efficient" operations should be thought of as attempting to "minimize costs" subject to meeting "customer service requirements." (That is, minimizing costs blindly without considering customer service requirements is not a viable long-term strategy.)

DOI: 10.4324/9781003585442-8

Chapter 3 started with a review of inventory planning concepts, costs, and metrics. We then examined how to organize the entire product line of a firm to facilitate activities such as production planning and scheduling. Next, we reviewed the key planning technique of establishing an ABC inventory classification scheme for a firm's entire product line. This included a review of how to build databases to support ABC inventory planning. Chapter 3 concluded with several inventory planning and replenishment illustrative analyses.

In Chapters 4 and 5, the discussion turned to the subjects of manufacturing, network design, and facility location. We considered several case studies which illustrated how firms employ optimization models and related analytic tools to guide their strategic, tactical, and operational network planning and scheduling decisions. We discussed methodologies that facilitate balancing manufacturing and inventory carrying costs in production planning and scheduling, and techniques for integrating end item production scheduling and long-run product family production planning. We also studied different strategies which manufacturers facing short-run production capacity shortages can employ to navigate through this issue. Finally, we also reviewed an analytic technique called the *factor rating method* which has many applications, including facility location decision support.

Chapter 6 explored the subject of customer logistics. We began by observing that the costs of transportation and warehouse operations represent key components of income statements that suppliers target to improve through customer logistics programs. We illustrated how firms segment their customer base into distinct subgroups to facilitate the implementation of customer logistics programs. This chapter also detailed the types of analyses that suppliers perform to develop bracket pricing programs to offer to their customers. The chapter then closed with a case study where a customer approaches their supplier with a proposed logistics program designed to improve the efficiency of their joint supply chain operations. We reviewed the analyses that the supplier carried out in order to determine whether to accept the proposal. The case study highlighted an important principle of collaborative supplier–customer logistics efficiency programs. Namely, if a joint program between a supplier and a customer, or a customer and a supplier, has the potential to lower their overall combined supply chain costs, then the initiative can succeed – if both parties can agree on how to share the savings.

Most recently, Chapter 7 presented a broad mix of analytic techniques, frameworks, methods, and supply chain principles that apply end-to-end across a firm's supply chain. Key techniques and frameworks included:

- a hierarchical framework to house all of a firm's supply chain metrics,
- an activity-based costing approach to measure supply chain costs,
- the measurement of how supply chain operations impact a firm's cash flow, and
- a methodology to create a customized supply chain index for an individual firm

Key supply chain tenets and strategies that we highlighted included:

- the role of economies of scale and economies of consolidation in driving supply chain strategies and decisions,
- the importance of considering total logistics costs (rather than individual function costs) in supply chain decision-making, and
- the importance of measuring logistics costs on both a unit and a ratio (or percent of sales) basis

In conclusion, in this book we have attempted to share many of the logistics analytics decision support methods and tools that have ably assisted supply chain and logistics professionals for decades, including this author. Moving forward, these analytics tools and others will continue to provide supply chain professionals with critically needed decision support to facilitate sound management decisions. We encourage logistics practitioners to utilize these and other analytics tools on a regular basis, and we encourage students to learn and embrace analytics-based decision support methods. They lead to better logistics decision-making.

Notes

1 ASCM Dictionary, 17th edition (2022).
2 This tenet does not apply to isolated decisions that affect only a single activity or function, and which do not have any impact on customer service levels.

REFERENCES

Ackoff, R. L. (1970). *A Concept of Corporate Planning.* New York, NY: Wiley Interscience.

Acumen Information Systems. (n.d.). *When not to use the square root law*. Retrieved October 29, 2025, from https://acumenfl.com/blog/when-not-to-use-the-square-root-law

Anthony, R. N. (1965). *Planning and Control Systems: A Framework for Analysis.* Boston, MA: Harvard University Press.

ASCM Dictionary. (2022). (17th ed.). Annandale, VA: ASCM (APICS) Educational and Research Foundation.

Bowersox, D., Closs, D., Cooper, M., and Bowersox, J. (2024). *Supply Chain Logistics Management*, 6th Edition. New York, NY: McGraw Hill.

Braun, K., and Tietz, W. (2024). *Managerial Accounting*, 7th Edition. Hoboken, NJ: Pearson.

Brown, R. G. (1959). *Statistical Forecasting for Inventory Control.* New York: McGraw Hill.

Brown, R. G. (1963). *Smoothing, Forecasting and Prediction of Discrete Time Series.* Englewood Cliffs, NJ: Prentice Hall.

Brown, R. G. (1967). *Decision Rules for Inventory Management.* New York: Holt, Rinehart and Winston.

Chaudhuri, A., Ghadge, A., Gaudenzi, B., and Dani, S. (2020). A Conceptual Framework for Improving Effectiveness of Risk Management in Supply Networks. *The International Journal of Logistics Management*, 31(1), 77–98. www.emeraldgrouppublishing.com/journal/ijlm

Chea, A. (2011). Activity-Based Costing System in the Service Sector: A Strategic Approach for Enhancing Managerial Decision Making and Competitiveness. *International Journal of Business and Management*, 6(11), 3–10.

Chopra, S., and Meindl, P. (2016). *Supply Chain Management: Strategy, Planning and Operation*, 6th Edition. New York, NY: Pearson.

Cooper, R., and Kaplan, R.S. (1988). Measure Costs Right: Make the Right Decisions. *Harvard Business Review*, 66(5), 96–103.

Council of Supply Chain Management Professionals (CSCMP). (2013). *Supply Chain Management Terms and Glossary.* https://cscmp.org/CSCMP/Educate/SCM_Definitions_and_Glossary_of_Terms/CSCMP/Educate/SCM_Definitions_and_Glossary_of_Terms.aspx?hkey=60879588-f65f-4ab5-8c4b-6878815ef921

Council of Supply Chain Management Professionals (CSCMP). (2025). Logistics Managers Index. Available at www.the-lmi.com/ [June 21, 2025].

Coyle, J ., Langley, C. J., Novack, R., and Gibson, B. (2017). *Supply Chain Management: A Logistics Perspective*, 10th Edition. Boston, MA: Cengage Learning.

De Matta, R., and Miller, T. (1993). A Note on the Growth of a Production Planning System: A Case Study in Evolution. *Interfaces*, 23(4), 116–122.

De Matta, R., Miller, T., and Peters, E. (2024). A Medical Device Distribution Network Design Strategic Planning Process and Optimization Model. *International Journal of Data Analysis Techniques and Strategies*, 16(2), 126–161.

Gopalan, R. M. (2025). What Is Landed Cost and Why Does It Matter? Drip Capital Inc. doi: https://dclcorp.com/blog/supply-chain/landed-cost/.

Handfield, R., Giunipero, L., Monczka, R., and Patterson, J. (2025). *Purchasing and Supply Chain Management*, 8th Edition. Boston, MA: Cengage Publishers.

Hax, A., and Meal, H. (1975). Hierarchical Integration of Production Planning and Scheduling. In M. A. Geisler (Ed.), *TIMS Studies in Management Science, Vol. 1, Logistics* (pp. 53–69). Amsterdam: North-Holland.

Hayes, A. (2024). What Is the Cash Conversion Cycle (CCC)? Investopedia. doi: www.investopedia.com/terms/c/cashconversioncycle.asp.

Kim, S. M. (2021). *Payment Methods and Finance for International Trade.* Singapore: Springer Nature Singapore Pie Ltd.

Liberatore, M. J., and Miller, T. (1998). A Framework for Integrating Activity Based Costing and the Balanced Scorecard into the Logistics Strategy Development and Monitoring Process. *Journal of Business Logistics*, 19(2), 131–154.

Liberatore, M. J., and Miller, T. (2016). Outbound Logistics Performance and Profitability: Taxonomy of Manufacturing and Service Organizations. *Business and Economics Journal*, 7(2), 1–9. www.hilarispublisher.com/open-access/outbound-logistics-performance-and-profitability-taxonomy-ofmanufacturing-and-service-organizations-2151-6219-1000221.pdf

Liberatore, M. J., and Miller, T. (2021). *Supply Chain Planning: Practical Frameworks for Superior Performance*, 2nd Edition. New York, NY: Business Expert Press.

Lynch, G. (2017). *Uncertainty Advantage: Leadership Lessons for Turning Risk Inside Out*. Bloomington, IN: Archway Publishing.

Maister, D. H. (1976). Centralization of Inventories and the Square Root Law. *International Journal of Physical Distribution*, 6(3), 124–134.

Manuele, F. (2005). Risk Assessment & Hierarchies of Control. *Professional Safety*, 50(5), 33–39.

Manuj, I., and Mentzer, J. (2008). Global Supply Chain Risk Management. *Journal of Business Logistics*, 29(1), 133–155.

Mayer, A. (2013). Supply Chain Metrics That Matter: A Closer Look at the Cash-to-Cash Cycle (2000–2012). *Supply Chain Insights LLC Report*, November 11.

Miller, T. (1991). A Note on Integrating Current End Item Inventory Conditions into Optimization Based Long Run Aggregate Production and Distribution Planning Activities. *Production and Inventory Management Journal*, 32(4), 74–80.

Miller, T. (2016). Explore All Your Options to Choose the Right Transportation Mode. *Material Handling & Logistics*, July/August, 30–34.

Miller, T. (2022). A Methodology to Quantify the Cost of Supply Chain Risk Management Strategies. *Material Handling & Logistics* (posted on website, September 13). www.mhlnews.com/global-supply-chain/article/21250478/a-methodology-to-quantify-the-cost-of-supply-chain-risk-management-strategies

Miller, T. (2024). Enhancing Supply Chain Performance Measurement Frameworks with External Global Indicators. *Supply Chain Management Review*, January/February, 38–49.

Miller, T., De Matta, R., and Xu, M. (2016). High Level Inventory Network Modeling Approaches. In Bryan Christiansen (Ed.), *The Handbook of Research on Global Supply Chain Management* (pp. 15–44). Harrisburg, PA: IGI Global.

Miller, T., and Liberatore, M. J. (2015). Outbound Logistics: Strategies, Performance, and Profitability. *Material Handling & Logistics*, April 15. 18–23. www.mhlnews.com/transportation-distribution/outbound-logistics-strategies-performance-and-profitability

Miller, T., and Liberatore, M. J. (2020). *Logistics Management: An Analytics Based Approach*. New York, NY: Business Expert Press.

Miller, T., Wise, D., and Clair, L. (1996). Transport Network Design and Mode Choice Modeling for Automobile Distribution: A Case Study. *Location Science*, 4(1/2).

Monczka, R., Handfield, R., Giunipero, L., and Patterson, J. (2011). *Purchasing and Supply Chain Managemen*t, 5th Edition. Boston, MA: South-Western Cengage Learning.

Pettit, T., Fiksel, J., and Croxton, K. (2010). Ensuring Supply Chain Resilience: Development of a Conceptual Framework. *Journal of Business Logistics*, 31(1), 1–21.

Reid, H. (2025). Landed Cost: What It Is and How to Calculate It. *DCL Corporation*. doi: https://dclcorp.com/blog/supply-chain/landed-cost/.

Rens, P. J., and Kleijnen, J. P. C. (1978). IMPACT Revisited: A Critical Analysis of IBM's Inventory Package "IMPACT". *Production and Inventory Management*, 19(1), 71–90.

Scriven, J. (2024). *The Digital Control Tower: Beyond Supply Chain and Manufacturing*. Forbes Technology Council. doi: www.forbes.com/councils/forbestechcouncil/2024/08/07/the-digital-control-tower-beyond-supply-chain-and-manufacturing/.

Stock, J., and Lambert, D. (2001). *Strategic Logistics Management*, 4th Edition. New York, NY: McGraw Hill.

Thieuleux, E. (2023). *Cash to Cash Cycle: How to Calculate and Improve It?* ABC Supply Chain. doi: https://abcsupplychain.com/cash-to-cash-cycle-how-to-calculate/.

Venkataraman, R., and Pinto, J. (2020). *Operations Management: Managing Global Supply Chains*, 2nd Edition. Los Angeles, CA: Sage.

World Bank. (2025). *Logistics Performance Index*. Available at: https://lpi.worldbank.org/.

Zinn, W., Levy, M., and Bowersox, D. J. (1989). Measuring the Effect of Inventory Centralization/Decentralization on Aggregate Safety Stock: The Square Root Law Revisited. *Journal of Business Logistics*, 10(1), 1–14.

INDEX

Note: Page numbers in *italics* and **bold** denote figures and tables, respectively. References to Notes section show both the page number and the note number (224n35).

For Product Safety Concerns and Information please contact our
EU representative GPSR@taylorandfrancis.com Taylor & Francis
Verlag GmbH, Kaufingerstraße 24, 80331 München, Germany